Invisible People and Proc

Invisible People and Processes

Writing Gender and Childhood into European Archaeology

EDITED BY

JENNY MOORE AND ELEANOR SCOTT

LEICESTER UNIVERSITY PRESS
LONDON AND NEW YORK

Leicester University Press
A Cassell imprint
Wellington House, 125 Strand, London WC2R 0BB
127 West 24th Street, New York, NY 10011

First published 1997

British Library Cataloguing in Publication Data
A catalogue record for this book is available from the British Library
ISBN 0 7185 0023 7 Hardback
0 7185 0024 5 Paperback

Library of Congress Cataloging-in-Publication Data

Invisible people and processes: writing gender and childhood into
European archaeology / edited by Jenny Moore and Eleanor Scott.
p. cm.
Includes bibliographical references and index.
ISBN 0–7185–0023–7 (hardcover). ISBN 0–7185–0024–5 (pbk.)
1. Social archaeology – Europe. 2. Women – Europe – History.
3. Children – Europe – History. 4. Sex role – Europe – History.
5. Europe – Antiquities. I. Moore, Jenny, 1950–. II. Scott,
Eleanor, 1960–.
CC72.4.I58 1996
936–dc20   96–14620
                                                                        CIP

Typeset by York House Typographic Ltd, London
Printed and bound in Great Britain by Biddles Ltd, Guildford and King's Lynn

Contents

Part 3: Writing Children and Childhood

Contributors

MARY BAKER is a part-time lecturer in Gender Archaeology at the University of Wales, Lampeter and a Postgraduate in the Department of Archaeology at the University of Southampton.

DR BARBARA BENDER is a Reader in the Department of Anthropology, University College, London.

LYNNE BEVAN is Finds Supervisor for the Birmingham University Field Archaeology Unit.

DR BRIAN BOYD is a Research Fellow, Corpus Christi College, Cambridge.

DR ANDREW T. CHAMBERLAIN is a Senior Lecturer in Archaeology, University of Sheffield.

DR JOHN CHAPMAN is a Reader in Archaeology, University of Durham.

NYREE FINLAY is a Postgraduate in the Department of Archaeology, University of Reading.

DR ROBERTA GILCHRIST is a Reader in Archaeology, University of Reading.

MARY HARLOW is a Postgraduate in the Department of Ancient History and Archaeology, University of Birmingham.

LOUISE A. HITCHCOCK is a Postgraduate in the Department of Art History, University of California, Los Angeles, USA.

DR IAN HODDER is a Reader in Archaeology, University of Cambridge.

DR LINDA HURCOMBE is a Lecturer in Prehistory in the Department of History and Archaeology, University of Exeter.

DR DIMITRA KOKKINIDOU is a specialist in Macedonian prehistory and Greek Language Advisor for the Ministry of Education in Melbourne, Australia.

KURTIS S. LESICK is a Postgraduate in the Department of Archaeology and Prehistory, University of Sheffield.

MALCOLM LILLIE is a Field Officer for the Humber Wetlands Project, University of Hull and a Postgraduate in the Department of Archaeology and Prehistory, University of Sheffield.

Dr S. J. Lucy is a Lecturer in Archaeology in the Department of Archaeology, University of Durham.

Jenny Moore is a Postgraduate in the Department of Archaeology and Prehistory, University of Sheffield.

Dr Marianna Nikolaidou is a Research Associate at the Institute of Archaeology, University of California, Los Angeles, USA.

Dr Marina Picazo is a Lecturer in Ancient History at the Facultat d'Humanitats, Universitat Pompeu Fabra, Barcelona.

Dr Elizabeth Rega is a Lecturer in the Department of Joint Sciences, W. M. Keck Science Center, Claremont, California, USA.

Dr Eleanor Scott is a part-time Lecturer in Archaeology in the Department of Archaeology at King Alfred's College and for the Open University.

Joanna Sofaer Derevenski is a Postgraduate in the Department of Archaeology, University of Cambridge.

Alex Woolf is a Lecturer in Archaeology, in the Department of Archaeology, University of Wales, Lampeter.

List of Illustrations

List of Tables

Preface and acknowledgements

Two meetings in 1993 form the background to this book. The first was a day school organized by Jenny Moore on 'Women and Children in the Neolithic', and the second a session organized by Eleanor Scott on 'Ideologies of gender' at the Theoretical Archaeology Group (TAG) conference in Durham. Linda Hurcombe played a significant part in the production of this volume by introducing Jenny Moore and Eleanor Scott in Durham and suggesting collaboration on a joint publication project; and Graeme Barker was instrumental in helping to shape and focus the resulting volume.

Tim Darvill and Gordon Barclay, co-ordinators of the Neolithic Studies Group, supported Jenny Moore's idea of a Neolithic Studies Group day meeting dedicated to 'Women in the Neolithic', and Gordon suggested the inclusion of children in the proceedings; their confidence and continued support, particularly from Tim Darvill, are much appreciated. Jenny Moore is very grateful for the support and advice given by Barbara Ottaway, Andrew Chamberlain, and Mark Edmonds of the Department of Archaeology and Prehistory at Sheffield. Correspondence with Mary Beaudry of Boston University has proved invaluable. The stimulating postgraduate community in Sheffield also made their contribution, and Jenny Moore acknowledges their vital interest and feedback. A small grant towards the preparation costs of the volume was obtained from the Department of Archaeology and Prehistory at Sheffield by Barbara Ottaway, on behalf of Jenny Moore.

Eleanor Scott would like to thank all the original contributors to the Durham TAG session, especially discussant Roberta Gilchrist. She also thanks her colleagues Tony King, Chris Gerrard and Nick Thorpe who have enthusiastically supported her teaching of new modules on the archaeology of gender. Travel, research and preparation costs for the TAG session and the volume were partly met by a small research grant from King Alfred's College, Winchester.

This book is dedicated to the memory of
Jenny Coombs

Introduction: On the incompleteness of archaeological narratives

ELEANOR SCOTT

Incomplete narratives

Because historical and archaeological interpretations – our narratives about the past – are cultural constructions, they are necessarily incomplete. They comprise and include those facets of human existence deemed important to the author of the narrative at the time of writing. As we have progressed through the twentieth century, trends have arisen in 'the proper study of mankind'. The rise of the New Archaeology or processualism in the 1960s and 1970s concerned itself with 'big issues' such as the importance of ranking and hierarchies in cultural change, particularly the development of complex societies. Robust and fervent criticisms of processualism – that it was inappropriately environmentally determinist, biologically reductionist and lacking in an understanding of the significance of both the symbolic realm and individual action – led to the gradual emergence of other ways of 'reading' the past, and indeed questions were asked about which data were selected to be 'read' in the first place.

Addressing symbolic concerns, the anthropologically-inspired structuralist schools sought to identify order in the seeming chaos of human material culture and ideas, with a particular emphasis on art and ritual. The usefulness of their basic tenet, dualism (seeing human culture in terms of pairs of binary opposites such as male, female; public, private), is still debated. Is the world really organized by people into such sets of categories of opposition (Miller 1982)? And even if such substantive categories do exist, how might we recognize them with any kind of objectivity? Is objectivity about observations ever achievable or even desirable?

The continuing debate has led to the emergence of an ever-widening range of approaches to archaeology. A key component of these 'post-processualist' approaches has been and remains feminist studies, in the forms of critique, remedial research (or historical revision) and theory building (Ovrevik 1991: 738; Wylie 1991: 38–44). Out of, and alongside, feminist approaches grew gender studies in archaeology. Among the significant questions and problems which feminist and gender archaeologies have broached are: why has the past been written as being almost exclusively populated by adult males? And what is the role of gender in cultural change? These questions are fundamental to archaeology as a whole, and do not merely represent the 'fringe' interests of a minority.

Playing the game of invisibility

Imagine you are playing a game with your child. You want the game to be educational – to teach the child something of the world around it. You decide on the card game Happy Families, sets of cards depicting families according to their occupation. But you want this game to be *really* interesting, to reflect the useful, fascinating and important aspects of life; so you customize the cards. First, you remove all the lowly, too-common-even-to-think-about occupations. Bye bye Mr Bun the Baker, hello Mr Alloy the Specialist Craftsman. Next, you remove all cards picturing a Mrs, Miss or Master; after all, their presence is *implied* by the existence of the adult males. The end result is a fine game for a child, represent-ing all that's important in the world: Mr Specialist Craftsman, Mr Paramount Chief, Mr Trade Networker, Mr Ritual Shaman and Mr Military General. Collect the set and win an archaeology degree.

How are the unwanted cards of human existence discarded by archaeologists? Indeed *why* are the unwanted cards discarded? How and why are women and children made invisible in narratives on the past? Why scholars should want to make women invisible is much debated. The fact that most academic archae-ologists have been and are male has led to charges that they are – perhaps unwittingly – misogynists who would very much like women to disappear into an 'ideal' world of domestic and reproductive passivity both in the past and in the present. A less confrontational approach is to examine the western culture in which archaeologists have been socialized, seeking the sources of the social values which they project back onto the past under study. As Gilchrist has observed, 'the discipline . . . increasingly strives to engage with current political issues' (Gilchrist 1994: x).

With regard to women, the 'how' question is fairly straightforward to answer. Feminist social analysts, looking at social history and political theory in partic-ular, have identified three main ways – 'tricks of the trade' – in which woman are made to disappear from analyses (Thiele 1992): exclusion; pseudo-inclusion; and alienation. Recent research on women in Roman archaeology and ancient history shows these processes operating quite clearly (Scott 1995: 176–9). Exclusion is simply where women are excluded from analyses altogether; what is deemed normative is male. No allowance is made for the existence of women and their different lives and experiences. Such an example might be a set of statistics designed to look at 'the nation's health' which are only collected from male patients (as used to happen with the study of heart attack diagnosis and prognosis); another example might be an analysis of the nation's average earnings based entirely on men's salaries. Archaeologically, exclusion is fre-quently practised, from the original exclusionary device of calling humans 'Man' to the textbooks and analyses which are implicit and sometimes explicit in their focus: adult male or male-dominated institutions and activities. Thiele (1992: 27) stresses that the exclusion of women is an active process rather than one of passive neglect:

> It is not a simple case of lapsed memory: these theorists don't just forget to talk about women; rather, women are structurally excluded from the realm of discourse

or, for the sake of theoretical preoccupations and coherency, they are deliberately dropped.

Pseudo-inclusion is now more widely practised than exclusion in political theory, history and archaeology. Pseudo-inclusion is tokenism; women are included briefly for form's sake, but are then marginalized or dismissed without forming an integral part of the analysis. Such works include archaeology textbooks on prehistoric or classical societies which have separate – and short – sections on women, rather than the existence of women being a factor in the overall narrative. Women are seen as a category, rather than gender being seen as an underlying process. Another trick of the trade, often used in conjunction with pseudo-inclusion, is alienation. Women are included in analyses but only in terms of categories which are deemed to be of interest to the investigator; invariably women's experience is interpreted through male categories because the methodologies and values of the theorists remain androcentric. Thus women appear in narratives as mothers, wives and prostitutes. In some texts on pre-history they make their only appearance in lists of exchangeable commodities, where paramount chiefs control the trade of luxury goods 'and women'.

A world of important occupations and heroes, positioned firmly in the sphere of formal adult male authority, is precisely the world which historians and archaeologists have traditionally created for themselves in the nineteenth and twentieth centuries. Although a desire for attitudinal change has been sometimes apparent in recent years, attempts to shift the focus of past narratives from a narrow élite male perspective to a more egalitarian view have been met with a surprisingly fierce reactionary backlash from academic and political pundits. In September 1995, Dr Nicholas Tate, chief adviser to the government on the national curriculum, accused teachers of selling Britain short, arguing that Britain's sense of national identity was being eroded because trendy history teachers were ignoring Britain's great heroes. This, according to Raphael Samuel writing in the *Guardian*, seemed to be a call for the adoption of Thomas Carlyle's 'Great Man' theory of history first propounded in the 1840s, a form of power worship which all but ignored impersonal forces of development. But Gary Bushell, writing in Britain's most widely read newspaper the *Sun*, and quoted by Samuel (1995: 27) supported Dr Tate all the way:

> The notion of great achievers doesn't fit the quasi-Marxist view of today's education 'experts'. Individual achievement has been downgraded in favour of learning about mass movements and the teaching of social history.

Samuel was able to offer a more considered viewpoint:

> Professional historians [and by implication, archaeologists], who deal by prefer-ence with such aggregates as state formation or collective mentality, will hardly be sympathetic to Dr Tate's views ... Leaders – we will point out – drawing perhaps on Max Weber's theory of 'charisma' – are not causes but effects, authority figures on whom we project our fantasies of omnipotence. *(ibid.)*

Although archaeologists differ from historians in that they do not project their fantasies onto 'named' figures, they nevertheless have created their unnamed heroes – the paramount chiefs and the craft specialists. Of course such figures as these presumably existed, but it is the assumption of their maleness coupled with the importance attached to these agents and no others with regard to social reproduction and cultural change which create problems.

Post-modernism: the latest invisibility trick?

A recent development in archaeology, debate about which is confined to the élites who are able to discourse on post-modern theory, but whose effects will trickle down to all in archaeology, is that of deflating entire archaeological paradigms. This might well be deemed to be yet another 'trick of the trade' which this time could be used to make whole feminist and gender archaeologies invisible.

These are certainly interesting times for archaeologists. History is finished and science is corrupt, according to the participants in a major crisis in the intellectual life of the Western world. 'It is a crisis which particularly affects the writing and reception of history. But it is not confined to history, for what is at issue is the possibility of objective knowledge of any kind' writes Professor K. Thomas (1994: 12). The last decade and a half has seen the collapse in academia of claims to certainty. The hitherto value-free objective status of science, for example, has been questioned by social historians who have exposed its ideological underpinnings, masculine bias and socially-constructed agenda. History, which provides countries with their national mythologies, has been rejected by women, blacks and other not-so-minority groups, who see the textbooks about the past as being Eurocentric, racist, sexist and homophobic (Thomas 1994: 12)

But there are real dangers inherent in the post-modernist argument, dangers which lurk in its very strengths. It is the changing nature of modern societies which has bred scepticism about the old certainties, and scepticism about the possibility of any objective historical truth which is not the vehicle of some particular interest group. This tendency has been powerfully reinforced by the theories of Foucault and Derrida, who claim that language itself is the barrier to 'objective truth'. To the post-modernist there can be no such thing as objective knowledge, for texts are subject to multiple and conflicting interpretations; indeed, the meaning of a particular text only comes into existence as it is read – it has no pre-existing autonomous, individual meaning (Thomas 1994: 12) The truth is what you make it. But if nothing is real, then all histories and archaeologies – including androcentric and chauvinistic archaeologies – must all be as valid as each other. Therefore, despite my pleasure at the growth of alternative readings of the evidence, I am suspicious of the post-modernist philosophy, because I feel that the apparent deep disillusionment with 'knowable history' is functioning in an interesting way: it may be a mechanism of male intellectual thought functioning (unconsciously?) as a saboteur of all intellectual endeavour. That is, if intellectual life has to stop being ideologically underpinned by the learnt interests of the great white male, then could it be that they're going to make damn sure that no other 'known' intellectual life survives to be experienced by anyone?

Incidentally, as 'texts' can mean both literal written texts, such as documentary sources or archaeological textbooks, *and* the metaphorical 'text' of material culture, one might begin to feel that historical archaeologists – such as Romanists like myself – ought to be among the deeply disillusioned academics rejecting all hopes of intellectual liberation, seeing in every ideology a desire to control data and theory and so control both 'truth' and, with it, people. For classical archaeologists, however, ignorance has been bliss. For the most part, they remain a stolidly untheoretical lot, and many of them have yet to experience the epistemological doubts which have afflicted their prehistoric colleagues. Neither has the challenge of multiculturalism and the class debate so far provoked much of a response from the writers of the history and archaeology of antiquity.

Changing archaeology: the structuring principles of society

What will probably change the face of archaeology, particularly historical archaeology, in the next 20 years is an awareness of the theoretical debates in other historical, social and literary disciplines, and an incorporation of certain themes into our research programmes and publications. These themes will of course be those chosen and then injected into the discipline by the people with the most clout, but interestingly the nature of the people with clout is changing; so I envisage the themes as being age groups, gender, rank and race. There are a number of near-universal structuring principles in human societies, notably age, gender, class and race. Each person in each society belongs to a social rank or class, a racial or ethnic group, an age group and a gender, and the other members of that society are aware of this and use the information to fix their own and each other's positions within society. Most books on ancient 'societies' actually write about rank/class from an adult male perspective, and while this is perhaps an understandable approach, mimicking as it does the structures given importance in our own society, it excludes more than it includes and can hardly, therefore, be said to construct complete pictures of 'society' in the past. We need to address also the two structuring principles which have been neglected: age and gender.

Universal structuring principles are not, however, universally manifested throughout the world and throughout the past. There is great variability in the construction of gender and childhood, for example, between cultures; and of course it is the study and the interpretation of such variability which is the stuff of archaeological research. How we measure this variability is a moot point. A contention exists that we cannot locate women in the past, because there are methodological problems in actually observing them. But this is not so much a methodological problem as theoretical nonsense. If we cannot locate women in the past, then how can we be sure that we have located men? And children? Logically, *everyone* in the past is therefore invisible – an intolerable proposition.

This is indeed a complex problem of social theory. It is not enough to look for, say, women or infancy or poverty in the past, if the ideologies underpinning the search are critically unexamined and flawed. This is also not a search for *categories* but a search for *processes*. It is not enough to look for categories of evidence in the past called 'women', or 'men', or 'children', or 'the poor'; it is a search for what it was about the particular cultural processes of that time and place which *made* women, men and children.

The agency of women and children

Archaeological debate is increasingly one of structure and agency. But acknowledging the importance and the interdependence of structure and agency, as has begun to happen in archaeology over the past decade, does not necessarily bring egalitarian or complete narratives on the past. Agency can be surprisingly male in its presentation.

Why does agency tend to be male? In the whodunit novels *Why Didn't They Ask Evans?* by Agatha Christie and *From Doon With Death* by Ruth Rendell, Evans and Doon each hold the key to an understanding of the deadly shenanigans in the books. Evans and Doon are shadowy agents, awaiting identification, and the final surprise revelations only succeed because Evans and Doon are found to be *women* – and the gentle reader has up until this point assumed what it is common in our society to assume, that interesting and important action, events and changes must always be instigated by (adult) males. Christie and Rendell play cleverly on our ingrained system of social and ideological values, whereby all significant agency is male. There is a similar process at work in the puzzle about the surgeon: a surgeon announces 'I cannot operate on this patient: he is my son', but then the patient's father walks into the room; how can this be? The surgeon is the patient's mother. It fools a lot of people. Agency is male by default.

One of the significant achievements of feminist and gendered archaeology is not only the recognition of the significance of gender constructions as processes embedded in social structures, but also the recognition of the significance of female agency. This volume also addresses a related theme: the agency of children. As the concept of childhood is bounded by socialization and familism, children are essentially seen as the recipients of social influences, passive in social processes and the object of types of parenting.

> In this frame the children do not have the same ontological status as adults. They are not social actors and are never attributed with powers of social agency, as they are seen to play no part in the construction of their own social world.
>
> (Chandler 1991: 135)

Sociologists have long argued (Chandler 1991; Jenks 1982) that the model of childhood was constituted to support a particular model of social order and adulthood and they argue for a programme to make children conceptually visible and active in social analysis. 'It is only' writes Chandler 'when "normal" families collapse or fail to be formed that there is a significant interest in children' (1991: 135–6). Although feminist studies have initiated strong and successful research and study programmes to make women and their agency more visible, there has been no similar programme for children. Even within much feminist research children retain a residual status, a form of social baggage, confirming the woman's domestic identity through the duties and emotional ties of mother-hood. There is, however great scope to examine the status and identities of children and their relationship to women and men and the power structure of the family. There is also scope to appreciate that children's cultures, transmitted from child to child through social contact, exist to the extent of their being prime movers in intra- and inter-generational linguistic change and cultural prefer-ences. Children do not merely reflect their parents' desires; they signal cultural norms, certainly, but they also strain against them until deemed to be sufficiently socialized. Children also do work. In non-Western industrial societies, children do and did form a significant part of the workforce. Like women, however, in analyses this work has seldom been recognized on its own merits; it has been deemed to be sharing in the male head of household's work, or a way of earning a little pin- or pocket-money. It is as if the laws of thermodynamics do not apply to women and children, and their expended energies are somehow not real.

The treatment of infants seems to raise particular conceptual problems in archaeology. The material remains of infants necessitate discussion of infant death, which many scholars find emotive and which some students greet with voyeuristic fervour. Suffice to say, the question of whether infanticide was practised on any great scale in prehistory and antiquity is still an unresolved question, yet one of fundamental importance in understanding a society's demographics and ideology. There seems to be, admittedly on anecdotal evi-dence alone, a belief among archaeologists 'in the know' that preferential female infanticide was widely practised in the past because females were not as highly valued as males. Both parts of this belief need careful handling. Firstly, although there is widespread evidence in the archaeological record for high rates of infant mortality, there is very little direct evidence for the practice of infanticide. Infant paleopathology is as yet a somewhat imprecise science; it is, for example, impossible to sex infant skeletal remains and difficult to determine cause of death. Secondly, to say that females were not valued as highly as males is to misunderstand the effects of class and to over-simplify and universalize the effects of customs such as dowries and bride price. Further, one must ask whether overall patterns of excess female mortality, particularly mortality result-ing from pregnancy and childbirth, would necessitate a further culling of females through preferential infanticide; and why devalue a rarity? Rather, infanticide may have 'preferred' neither male nor female as a widespread cultural norm, but been a general 'contraceptive' device. A further question remains about the apparently special treatment given to deceased infants in the archaeological record. In many prehistoric and classical contexts, infants – including premature births and neonates – are found buried under floors and walls, near agricultural features, with grave goods, and/or associated with ritual features (Scott 1991, 1993). These are not cases of careless women dumping their unwanted bastards into any handy hole in the ground; if we can get ourselves past the Victorian obsession with baby-dropping, we might be able to detect complex patterns of ritual and ideological treatment of deceased infants, and further be able to contextualize the evidence to understand more of gender relations, power structures within the family and funerary practices in general.

Masculinity and the body

Given that until relatively recently most archaeological narratives about 'people' were in fact implicit discussions about perceived past male experience written in terms of modern male experience, it is perhaps ironic that there is so little explicit literature on the cultural constructions of *masculinity*. This is doubly ironic with regard to historical archaeological periods such as that of classical antiquity where our literary evidence was written by men, for men, and was produced through the particular male structures of that specific place and time: these sources do not 'speak for themselves'. Taken in tandem with other examples of material culture, these texts provide a startling array of data with which to examine the social and political construction of masculinity in the Greek and Roman world. The Medieval period, too, is a rich source of information on ideas of gender and the body.

In our contemporary world, which Giddens (1990) has termed as 'late' or 'high' modern, the body is becoming increasingly central to the modern person's sense of self-identity (Shilling 1993: 1). The effects of this fundamental shift in perception have yet to become fully clear, but it seems fair to say that never before have *men* as well as women been barraged with so many unrealistic images of perfection which 'speak' of the ideal constructions of sexuality. The 'Beauty Myth' for women has been extensively explored (e.g. Wolf 1990), but the phenomenon of 'pressure imagery' for men has been less well explored. Male pressure imagery is characterized by advertisements featuring young men who are usually white and tanned, who have extremely well defined muscular bodies, especially the pectorals, stomach, biceps and glutaeus maximus. Their facial features are symmetrical and well defined and proportioned, and are thus considered attractive, and they sport luxuriant heads of hair although curiously the rest of their bodies appear to be hair-free. These types of images have existed before: they mimic the classical canon of the Polykleitan ideal, the handsome youthful features of Alexander the Great and the strong symmetrical grace of the Emperor Augustus. Such images have also existed before in the late modern era, but in specialist and obvious areas of retail, such as body-building, and the overt sexuality was absent. What differs with this new proliferation of pressure imagery for men is that a vast volume of 'body traffic' is being used to sell a host of quite ordinary products: chocolate, ice-cream, cars, wine, beer, diet cola, aftershave, as well as body-shaping items; and these are adverts which address both men and women as consumers.

Such preoccupation with the body as a defining social force is a peculiarly late modern development. What is particularly interesting is the way in which, as our gender boundaries become blurred with shifts in the sexual divisions of labour, economic categories and dress codes, so the corporeal bodily differences are being invoked and the possibilities of bodily differentiation made to embody sexuality, desire and self identity. Men develop muscles in order to grow in size;

women become thinner, leaner, flatter, smaller. The flirtation in the 1980s and early 1990s with extremely thin fashion models and its relationship with child-hood female anorexia is now well debated. An explanation for very thin models in the fashion industry has been fairly convincingly laid at the door of the powerful and misogynistic homosexual fashion designers who wish women to look like teenage boys; it is interesting that almost immediately after successful deconstructions of the 'superwaif' were published (e.g. Faludi 1991; Wolf 1990) came news that 'the breast is back in'. Ludicrous though such 'debates' might appear, they nevertheless inform more useful debates about structure and agency.

It is possible, therefore, that we, as late modern archaeologists, place undue emphasis on the body as a means of expressing gender differences, of expressing the ideals of femininity and masculinity. As Shilling observes:

> In the affluent West, there is a tendency for the body to be seen as an entity which is in the process of becoming; a *project* which should be worked at and accom-plished as part of an *individual's* self-identity. This differs from how the body was decorated, inscribed and altered in traditional societies as it is a more reflexive process, and is less bound up with inherited models of socially acceptable bodies through rituals in communal ceremonies.
>
> (Shilling 1993: 5)

Would a Bronze Age Briton or a Roman have had self-identity? They would have had an identity, certainly, but for both men and women this was defined not by individual concerns – there was no individual self-identity informed by the body – but rather by the concerns of kinship, gender and class. Seen in this light, the visible material culture of the archaeological record – that is, surviving monuments and texts – can be read as an elaborate narrative of the concerns of particular classes and genders (notably, the 'upper class' male).

In ancient Athens and Rome, for example, this male existence was primarily a political existence, and the mechanism of its social reproduction was oratory and political history. It might therefore be argued that in the Roman world, for example, masculinity was not in fact measured by levels of direct sexual activity or paternity, nor economic success, nor bodily prowess, nor dress; masculinity was conferred by means of public political activity (denied to women). The first emperor Augustus became the embodiment of masculinity, and his building programme and other reforms gave the green light to monumentality and a concern with lineage as being legitimate political and thus masculine concerns. The contradiction of Augustan society was that the required Republican virtues – austerity, self-sufficiency, control – had to be espoused in a conspicuous fashion. Also, at a time of rapid and fundamental social change, he re-introduced the pantheon of gods and goddesses into Roman society – deities whose images were timeless, unchanging, and loaded with the symbolism of gender roles. He further adopted and accepted an assemblage of titles which reinforced each other – *pontifex maximus* (chief priest), *imperator* (general in a state of perpetual triumph) and *princeps* (first citizen) – as well as adopting a recognizable and unchanging physical image; but his masculinity was embodied in the former political presence, not the latter physical image. If, in ancient Rome, masculinity was embodied in the political process, it follows that there would have been differential access to masculinity just as there was differential access to political power. This may also explain the apparent 'apathy' of Roman women to political emancipation remarked upon by modern scholars as some kind of failing on their part (e.g. Dudley 1970: 46).

A further mechanism of differential access to power through gender in the ancient world leads us to return to the question of monumentality. It has been argued of the ancient Greek data by Foxhall that the creation of monuments by men is a deliberate attempt by them to connect with posterity. Through her detailed analysis of perceptions and manifestations of posterity in the ancient Greek world, Foxhall introduces the revolutionary concept that *time itself is gendered* (Lin Foxhall pers. com.); what we know about the classical world is what classical men have left us – often quite consciously in the form of monuments and inscriptions – and is, therefore, what they have let us know. There is scope in this argument for examination of a number of historical contexts.

The archaeology of gender, sociology and popular culture

Gender studies are firmly rooted in the tradition of sociology, and sociology has been a source for archaeology of many important theories concerning aspects of social structure. It is perhaps surprising, then, that when sociology borrows from archaeology in order to provide historical and prehistorical perspectives for works on gender studies, the results are sometimes ludicrous. In Fallon *et al.* (1994), a respected text on the sociology of eating disorders, the 'historical' chapters are full of assertions of the 'ancient wisdom' variety, alluding to an ill-understood past cobbled together by a reading of dubious and dated secondary texts such as Stone's *When God Was a Woman*. The contribution by Wooley reveals a reading of Gimbutas (1989), Eisler (1988), and Stone (1976). His research permits him to make with some confidence the following assertions:

> *Patriarchy.* In the nature-worshipping societies of old Europe the capacity to give birth and to sustain life apparently made women's bodies sacred, and gave rise to the invention of the goddess. These goddess-worshipping cultures are evidenced by thousands of female figurines, such as the Venus of Willendorf (25,000 BC) ... Over a period of about 2500 (*sic*) years, culminating with the fall of Crete 3000 years ago, patriarchal cultures conquered, suppressed, and merged with these goddess-worshipping cultures ... These new power alignments based on gender became the model for slavery.
>
> (Wooley 1994: 21–3).

These sociologists simply do not know what they are reading and what they are writing. Whose fault is this? The sociologists' perhaps, for being too lazy to read reviews and refutations of Gimbutas *et al.* and for not looking at primary sources, or the archaeologists' for not making such materials more accessible?

The problem is also evident in books and articles in the fields of women's studies and popular culture. While there is clearly an interest of some significance in the prehistory and ancient history of gender, there is little evidence of serious academic sources being used to write the narratives. This is possibly a compelling reason in its own right for archaeologists and ancient historians to join in the debate on gender studies. An entire current generation of 'third wave' feminists seem devoid of sound historical and archaeological information to support and *refine* their social studies. This apparent dearth of good, accessible information has resulted in many bizarre, yet high profile, pronouncements on gender roles in the past. For example, the illustrious feminist writer Naomi Wolf in her work *The Beauty Myth* writes with intriguing assertiveness on hitherto debatable roles on women in prehistoric societies (1990: 11 ff.). It is interesting then that her entire source for this passage is cited as 'the historian Ros Miles'. (Ros Miles is in fact a journalist and is also responsible for the bonkbuster *East of Eden*.) If one turns to the relevant book by Miles, *The Women's History of the World* (1988), one may see some awesome 'historical' statements ('The homosexuality of ancient Greece in fact institutionalized the supremacy of the phallus, denying women any social or emotional role other than childbearing', p. 68) which frequently jump unashamedly from mesolithic horticulture to the Roman imperial court and even Moslem Arabia in order to make some spurious point about the 'great goddess' and the 'rise of the phallus', giving the impression that the past resides in some kind of olden days limbo which may be dipped in and out of at will for immutable ancient wisdom. Miles's archaeological sources do not even include Gimbutas; they are, in their entirety, Nigel Calder's *Timescale* (1984) and *The Times Atlas of World History* (1986) *(sic)*. I have located Miles as the main source for other feminist writers' 'historical perspectives on women'. Suffice to say, when one can trace the underpinning of Naomi Wolf's best-selling statements on feminism back to *The Times Atlas of World History*, I believe that we have some legitimate cause for concern. This is not a problem of feminism; it is a problem of scholarship. More, not fewer, books on the archaeology of gender are needed on bookshop shelves.

References

Chandler, J. (1991) *Women Without Husbands: an Exploration of the Margins of Marriage.* London: Macmillan Education Ltd.

Dudley, D. (1970) *Roman Society.* London: Pelican.

Eisler, R. (1988) *The Chalice and the Blade.* San Francisco: Harper and Row.

Fallon, P., Katzman, M.A. and Wooley, S.C. (eds) (1994) *Feminist Perspectives on Eating Disorders.* New York: Guildford Press.

Faludi, S. (1991) *Backlash: the Undeclared War Against Women.* London: Chatto.

Giddens, A. (1990) *The Consequences of Modernity.* Cambridge: Polity Press.

Gilchist, R. (1994) *Gender and Material Culture: the Archaeology of Religious Women.* London: Routledge.

Gimbutas, M. (1989) *The Language of the Goddess.* London: Thames and Hudson.

Jenks, C. (ed.) (1982) *The Sociology of Childhood: Essential Readings.* London: Batsford Academic and Educational.

Miles, R. (1988) *The Women's History of the World.* London: HarperCollins.

Miller, D. (1982) 'Artefacts as products of human categorisation processes' in I. Hodder, (ed.) *Symbolic and Structural Archaeology*. Cambridge: Cambridge University Press.

Ovrevik, S. (1991) 'Engendering archaeology', review article in *Antiquity* 65, 738–41.

Samuel, R. (1995) 'The people with stars in their eyes'. The *Guardian* 23 September, p.27.

Scott, E. (1991) 'Animal and infant burials in Romano-British villas: a revitalisation movement' in P. Garwood, D. Jennings, R. Skeates and J. Toms (eds) *Sacred and Profane*. Oxford: Oxford University Committee for Archaeology, Monograph 32, 115–21.

Scott, E. (1993) 'Images and contexts of infants and infant burials: some thoughts on some cross-cultural evidence'. *Archaeological Review from Cambridge* 11, 1.

Scott E. (1995) 'Women and gender relations in the Roman Empire' in P. Rush (ed.) *Theoretical Roman Archaeology: Second Conference Proceedings* (TRAC 2). Worldwide Archaeological Series 14. Aldershot: Avebury UK.

Shilling, C. (1993) *The Body and Social Theory*. London: Sage.

Stone, M. (1976) *When God was a Woman*. San Diego: Harcourt Brace Jovanovich and Harvest.

Thiele, B. (1992) 'Vanishing acts in social and political thought: tricks of the trade' in L. McDowell and R. Pringle (eds) *Defining Women: Social Institutions and Gender Divisions*. Cambridge: Polity Press.

Thomas, K. (1994) 'The death of certainty'. The *Guardian* 6 September, p.12.

Wolf, N. (1990) *The Beauty Myth*. London: Chatto and Windus.

Wooley, O.W. (1994) 'And Man created "woman": representations of women's bodies in western culture' in P. Fallon, M.A. Katzman and S.C. Wooley (eds) *Feminist Perspectives on Eating Disorders*. New York: Guildford Press, pp.17–52.

Wylie, A. (1991) 'Gender theory and the archaeological record; why is there no archaeology of gender?' in J.M. Gero and M.W. Conkey (eds) *Engendering Archaeology: Women and Prehistory*. Oxford: Blackwell.

Part 1

Theory and Review

1 A viable past in the pictorial present?

LINDA HURCOMBE

Viable human populations necessarily include two biological sexes, sufficient numbers of both, and their interaction. The archaeological literature shows a past peopled mainly by men (e.g. 'Early man', 'craftsmen', 'big men') and with little consideration for the interaction between genders. As it is represented, the human race simply does not have a viable prehistoric population.

(Hurcombe 1995: 87)

Introduction

This research is part of a larger analysis of the BIG problem – Biased Inter-pretations of Gender (Hurcombe 1995). The disease of gender bias has two sets of symptoms: visual and verbal. The focus here will be on the visual images, as they clearly demonstrate the gender roles archaeologists have uncritically as-signed to the past. In general, images of the past do not contain viable popula-tions because they do not have sufficient numbers of women or children; if reconstruction drawings encapsulate our gendered vision of the past, it is a miracle that the human race has survived to the present day!

Individually, almost all of the images present a scene which may well have occurred. Hence, they are not usually challengeable on academic grounds, but they are presenting a *collective* impression which often cannot be justified. The point of this chapter is to show how the images constructed demonstrate a limited and biased understanding of prehistoric society. In other words, these images also show how interpretations of past society are flawed. Other authors draw attention to the problems of obtaining gendered information from images of the past (e.g. see Coles 1990 and Donald and Hurcombe in press a) and of the problems of contemporary reconstructions (e.g. Burtt 1987, Hurcombe in press, Jones and Pay 1990, Molyneux in press, Moser 1992a, 1992b, 1993). All these reconstructions are showing biases that have a much broader base and are currently being researched (Bell *et al.* 1993, Claassen 1992, Conkey and Spector 1984, Donald and Hurcombe in press b and c), Engelstad 1991, Gero 1985, Gero and Conkey 1991, Gilchrist 1991, Jennbert in press, Smith and Du Cros 1993). This chapter focuses on images of Neolithic and Early Bronze Age society and activities, and I intend to examine the gender and age depictions before discussing the way in which gender roles are portrayed in those activities which particularly mark the Neolithic period. Examples, drawn from popular books and museum postcards, are analysed to show how ideas about the social status and setting of a role are a pervasive aspect of these images. Alternative views of some of these same roles drawn from ethnographic contexts, historical art and photographs will be compared to identify elements and ideas missing from the archaeological reconstruction images.

Numbers of women and children

A series of recent postcards depicting Linear Bank Keramik (LBK) scenes, dated 1989, are used as a starting point. They are by Benoît Clarys and are produced by a Belgian museum. Parts of the postcard series have no images of people (e.g. drawings of artefacts), and so these are not included in this discussion. Figure 1.1 shows a schematic representation of the images. This has the advantage of firstly, removing beautiful artwork so that concentration is focused on the composition, secondly, allowing the definite male and female figures to be indicated (via equal shadings), and thirdly, ensuring that the collective impression of the images is appreciated. The originals are eye-catching images, with positive features. In particular, they contain children who are often missing from images of the past. There are, however, problems even with these modern reconstructions. Although there are four identifiable men and three identifiable women, the ratio of adults to children is 9:3 and the activities connected with each gender are stereotyped. This is not as offensive as the postcard captions. Figure 1.1 (a) is labelled 'hunting', (b) 'woodcutter', (c) 'harvesting' and (d) 'flintworking'. By analogy, Figure 1.1 (e) of a woman raising two pots might be labelled 'potter'. In fact, this image is labelled 'a village scene' and the woman is the only image looking directly out of the picture at the viewer. She also has one breast bare. To label this anomalous image 'a village scene' is offensive.

The scenes in this group of very attractive images of LBK life could all have happened, but their *collective* analysis reveals problems; a non-viable population, and limited interpretations of how many women there were and what roles they played in the society, namely, harvester, corngrinder, and 'displayer' of 'pots'!

Staying with the LBK society, a recent colour 'encyclopaedia' magazine in Polish but by a French company (Gallimard Larousse 1991), showed a panoramic scene of LBK life. The figures are mostly of ambiguous gender, but there are 47 adults and 7 children. Yet, it is suggested that in a biologically successful society up to 50% will be children. Hence, this attractive picture of a thriving LBK village has fundamental flaws. This could scarcely be seen as a successful society capable of reproducing itself. Furthermore, in the same publication there is an illustration of tomb-building with no children. By making this an adult activity, the role of children in communal monument building is negated. Where children are excluded, a large number of women will also be excluded. Closer analysis reveals that there are *c.* 160 adults in the tomb-building scene. Allowing for half of these to be female (which they do not seem to be), there is a marked absence of children. Using the contemporary cliché of 2.3 children per couple,

Figure 1.1 Schematic diagrams of postcard images of the LBK by Benoît Clarys. Stippling indicates male figures and diagonal lines female figures.

there should be some 183 children causing havoc somewhere just outside this scene. The missing children are presumably supervised by their missing elderly grandparents, because in this same illustration there are also hardly any grey heads and no bald patches. This is part of a general pattern of few or no elderly people portrayed in reconstruction images.

The so-called 'Bush barrow Warrior' as illustrated by Jane Brayne (in Richards 1991: 80, fig. 13) is a very rare figure, but this is not because he has a lot of gold jewellery including a 'sceptre', was buried under the Bush barrow and has been the subject of numerous papers. He is unique because in her image, he is going bald. Obviously, male hair loss is a very recent phenomenon because I know of very few receding hairlines on male figures in all of the prehistoric images I have looked at so far. Although this point is amusing, it is also significant. The gender portrayals of the past show idealized unrealistic people.

Activities for genders and ages

Obviously, the images we have of prehistoric people contain idiosyncracies other than gender bias. The points raised above show that images are selective in terms of which genders and ages are shown, and may be biased by the activities which are reconstructed. Returning to the issues of labour and gender, other muscular projects are also deemed irrelevant for the realm of women and children. It seems that modern western society cannot conceive of women labouring, and children's labour is discounted also. Recent English Heritage books have some visually striking images of prehistoric activities. It is interesting to see how popular books on two of England's most famous monuments fare in the analysis of gender.

In the *Avebury* volume Judith Dobey (in Malone 1989: 63, fig. 43) portrays two flintknappers, both male, judging by the stubble on their chins. Her black and white house interior scene (p.43 fig. 25), and her colour reconstructions (plates 1, 3, 4, 7, 10 and 11) usually include a range of ages and also a few children: gender is either very obscure or both sexes are represented. Indeed, many scenes have processions leading away. The figures have turned their backs in order to avoid reconstructing the gender. However, for the labour scenes (e.g. plate 7) children are once more absent.

For the *Stonehenge* volume (Richards 1991), Jane Brayne's images also obscure gender whilst portraying imperfect people and some life and activity (e.g. plates 3–5). Her flintknapper (p.45 fig. 34) is not some idealistic perfect figure, but a character which could be either male or female. However, the reconstructions of the stones being transported on rafts (plate 10) seem to show males steering the raft with women and children standing on the banks; on the sidelines of this activity. Her harvest scene (plate 3) includes adults and children and, if you accept that skirts denote women, then it is also a female activity with the male looking after the animals and carrying on the male/animal associations of hunting (plate 5). Her illustrations are certainly less objectionable than those in some previous Stonehenge publications. But the choice of scene or activity raises the issue of what signifies the Neolithic, and what gender roles each sex is assigned within the key activities which are taken to define the period.

The Neolithic is generally characterized by farming (both plants and animals); by technology (e.g. pottery and polished stone tools); by living arrangements (more settled communities set among a farming landscape) and by ritual arrangements (notably, communal monuments involving a great deal of labour). How do the genders and ages fare in these classic roles of the Neolithic? Considering the often quoted generalizations 'woman the gatherer' and 'man the hunter', one might expect farming to involve both sexes with women portrayed as plant cultivators and men as animal farmers, while ideas about 'woman the potter' and 'man the stonetoolmaker' clichés would equalize the gender contributions to new artefact types. If a community is encapsulated in images of lifestyle, then women, men and children should all be present. However, these expectations are often not realized. Women and children are not usually, or obviously, included in monument building activities, so one of these key areas is seen as male dominated, and by implication, any ritual or religious transactions. The artefact and farming associations are examined further.

Artefacts, age and gender

Artefact production is generally perceived as an adult activity, but children are beginning to feature more in recent portrayals. The Benoît Clarys images on the right in Figure 1.1 all show children looking at an adult. Figure 1.1(d) indicates a child watching a male flintknapper, similarly Tracey Croft has an image of a child watching flintknapping (in Dyer 1990: 20, fig. 4).

Starting with images of artefact production and use, most images convey that polished stone axes were made and used by men. This may indeed have been the case and could be supported by general ethnographic surveys (Hayden 1992), but there is no direct evidence for this. However, the polished stone axe associations are merely carrying on a general trend for men to be depicted as the makers of any stone tools. There are very few illustrations in academic books which show a female flint knapper, so perhaps this is scarcely surprising. Moser discusses this issue and reproduces illustrations by Worthington Smith (1894) and Breuil (1949) of women knapping (Moser 1993: 80–1, figs 3, 4a and 4b). The discussion of women as stone toolmakers is not confined to images alone: the academic debates are beginning to question the accepted image of 'man the tool-maker' (Bird 1993; Gero 1991).

Although it would seem likely that similar clichés would lead to images of women making pots, I found this was not so pervasive as the male making stone tool association. At the start of this chapter I showed the image of the woman *holding* pots yet not being depicted as the potter. This 'usage rather than manufacture' choice of scene is often selected. Where manufacture is shown, it is often just a 'hands and materials' view (e.g. Gallimard-Larousse 1991: 114 image). However, many flint-knapping illustrations of the *technique* are similarly a 'hands only' detail (e.g. Clarke *et al.* 1985: 165). Hence, the issue here is not the selection of illustrations to explain the *techniques* of manufacture but images of *scenes* of manufacture which illustrate ideas about a social context. Men are associated with the social context of stone tool production much more strongly than women are associated with the social context of pottery production. Recent research is examining the role of women in pottery production (e.g. Mitchell 1992; Wright 1991). In the book entitled *Symbols of Power at the Time of Stonehenge*, the chapter on craftwork (Clarke *et al.* 1985: Chapter 5) is divided into discussions of different material categories. The flint section by Caroline Wickham Jones is carefully gender neutral, but the discussion of pottery is peppered by the term 'craftsmanship' and the title of the chapter is 'The importance of craftsmen'! Clearly, skilled artefact production is conceived as a male activity and it is this conception that directs the illustrations of scenes of production.

Farming, age and gender

A similar issue arises over illustrations of farming activities. Males are usually depicted as herdsmen, and women are sometimes seen as the harvesters of the crops (e.g. Gallimard Larousse 1991: 114–15). Given the very strong association of the male–animals, female–plants images I had observed from the earlier hunter-gatherer prehistoric scenes (Hurcombe 1995), I was intrigued to find some male depictions of harvesting. Some of these are perfectly acceptable as they show a *community* harvesting a ripe crop. For example, in the images by Benoît Clarys, Figure 1.1(c) shows four people involved in the harvest. This seems a likely scenario for temperate climates. Other images instead give harvesting to a male figure, while the female figure processes the corn (e.g. Souvenir 1990: 23). My questioning of why this should be so eventually led to the examination of farming images from a number of different sources other than the archaeological scenes (see below).

If arable farming is taken as a whole, there are further anomalies in the selection of activities depicted in reconstruction drawings. The crop growing regime does not only include harvesting – activities associated with crop husbandry might include preparing the soil, scattering seed, weeding, threshing, winnowing, storing the grain and grinding the seeds to flour. Of all of these other tasks, the grinding activities are most often portrayed and many images show it as a lone and drudgelike task (e.g. Dyer 1990: 91, fig. 39). At the very least it can be argued that the images of 'farming' focus on a narrow range of plant husbandry tasks.

Moving to the male/animal-husbandry expected tasks, most images are of adult males as shepherds (e.g. Jane Brayne, plate 5 in Richards 1991). There are no scenes of tethered animals waiting to be killed, nor of culling, butchery and selective breeding, and for later periods there are no scenes of castration or milking. It would seem that the activities deemed 'safe subjects' for animal farming are in their own way as restricted as the arable tasks. However, my observations of animal care conflict with these images. In a badlands area of Pakistan where there are both local and long distance transhumance animal herds, the people I observed tending the animals as they graze have usually been children or young adults. It is not a job reserved for adults. Furthermore, conversations over a Sardinian goat herder who lived on the high pastures showed that the goatherder was seen as a rich man in terms of ownership, yet a poor one because he had to live away from the society of the village. Taking a herd of animals out every day is a tiresome occupation. Owning the animals may make someone wealthy, but a wealthy person is unlikely to want the lowly status of a shepherd. There are a number of sources which show that children were often the tenders of animals. Examples are the biblical David the shepherd boy, the fictional Peter the goat boy in the children's classic *Heidi* by Johanna Spyri and in European folk sources there is the goose girl of the fairy tales, and the nursery rhyme about Little Bo Peep! On a more serious note, I have seen several girls tending animal flocks and women with animals in Pakistan. Consequently, the adult male shepherd image is not to my mind essential, nor even likely. Instead, I think archaeologists see domestic animals as important – they are part of what signifies the Neolithic – and hence adult males are portrayed in the scenes showing pastoralism. The ideology seems to be that if animal farming is new and signifies an important change in prehistory, then it cannot be child's play!

Alternative views

I wanted to look for other ways of portraying farming roles and since most of my archaeological images had shown temperate climates, I spent some time researching British rural photographs, and European landscape painters as well as ethnographic images. Paintings by Constable are well-known to be accurate in terms of landscape details. Some of his pictures show children and women. For example 'The Cornfield' (1826) shows a small boy with animals; 'Dedham Vale Morning' has a woman walking and a smaller figure, a child, with animals; 'Summer Morning' (1830) has a woman milking in the fields. Brueghel's paintings show both sexes involved in the harvesting and depict it as a social occasion; however, there are no children. There are women with rakes and both men and women are carrying loads. Medieval images also contain women engaged in farming tasks (e.g. Fox 1985).

A search through some ethnographic images of plant harvesting showed that obtaining plant foods was sometimes more of a challenge than one might expect; plant collecting required a tool to harvest a prickly plant (e.g. early eighteenth century painting, California, reproduced in McClendon 1992 fig. 49), involved innovative time-saving equipment such as a beater and collecting basket (e.g. 1920s photograph by Edward S. Curtis, California, reproduced in McClendon 1992 fig. 53). Other images show that a grinding task could be seen as a social activity carried out in the company of other women (photograph by Dr John W. Hudson c. 1901 of a group of Mono (California) women crushing acorns on a bedrock mortar, in McClendon 1992 fig. 51, and see also Jackson 1991). English historical photographs from 1844–1914 (reproduced in Winter 1966), also show women in harvesting teams and other rural roles.

Conclusion

The images from these disparate sources highlight what is missing from most of the archaeological reconstructions; vigour, social activity, equipment and complexity. These images indicate that the archaeological reconstructions are full of stereotyped, idealized or unrealistic people with unsophisticated views of social contexts. This is true both for the range and style of activities envisaged, and for the genders and ages which might undertake them. Why are women and children invisible in so many reconstruction scenes? – because their activities are not valued or taken into account in archaeological theories. Where activities which could logically be seen as partly female or childrens' tasks are seen as significant, these tasks are then portrayed as adult male activities e.g. tending animals.

Images of the past are important; they make an immediate impact on the viewer, and reach a far larger audience than articles in academic journals. They also indicate the gender and age assumptions of archaeologists. It is time to have a more critical view of reconstruction images and see them for what they are – fundamentally flawed images, demonstrating the unviable past envisaged in the pictorial present; not by the illustrators, but by the archaeologists.

Acknowledgements

I would like to thank Sue Roulliard for preparing the illustration, and Jenny Moore for the invitation to present the paper which gave rise to this chapter.

References

Bell, D., Caplan, P. and Karim, W.J. (eds) (1993) *Gendered Fields: Women, Men and Ethnography*. London: Routledge.

Bird, C.F.M. (1993) 'Woman the toolmaker: evidence for women's use and manufacture of flaked stone tools in Australia and New Guinea' in L. Smith and H. Du Cros *Women in Archaeology: A Feminist Critique*. Canberra: Australian National University Press, pp.22–30.

Burtt, F. (1987) '"Man the Hunter": bias in children's archaeology books'. *Archaeological Review from Cambridge* 6 (2), 157–74.

Claassen, C. (ed.) (1992) *Exploring Gender through Archaeology*. Madison, WI: Prehistory Press.

Clarke, D.V., Cowie, T.G. and Foxon, A. (1985) *Symbols of Power at the Time of Stonehenge*. Edinburgh: HMSO/National Museum of Antiquities of Scotland.

Coles, B. (1990) 'Anthropomorphic wooden figurines from Britain and Ireland'. *Proceedings of the Prehistoric Society* 56, 315–33.

Conkey, M.W. and Spector, J. (1984) 'Archaeology and the study of gender' in M.B. Schiffer, (ed.) *Advances in Archaeological Method and Theory 7*. New York: Academic Press, pp.1–38.

Donald, M. and L. Hurcombe, (eds) (in press a) *Gender and Material Culture: the Representation of Gender, vol. 1*. London: Macmillan.

Donald, M. and Hurcombe, L. (eds) (in press b) *Gender and Material Culture: Archaeological Perspectives, vol. 2*. London: Macmillan.

Donald, M. and Hurcombe, L. (eds) (in press c) *Gender and Material Culture: Historical Perspectives, vol. 3*. London: Macmillan.

Engelstad, E. (1991) 'Images of power and contradiction: feminist theory and post-processual archaeology'. *Antiquity* 65, 502–514.

Gero, J.M. (1985) 'Socio-politics and the woman-at-home ideology'. *American Antiquity* 50, 342–50.

Gero, J.M. (1991) 'Genderlithics: women's roles in stone tool production' in J.M. Gero and M.W. Conkey (eds) *Engendering Archaeology: Women and Prehistory*. Oxford: Blackwell, pp.163–93.

Gero, J.M. and Conkey M.W. (eds) (1991) *Engendering Archaeology: Women and Prehistory*. Oxford: Blackwell.

Gilchrist, R. (1991) 'Women's archaeology? Political feminism, gender theory and historical revision'. *Antiquity* 65, 495–501.

Hayden, B. (1992) 'Observing prehistoric women' in C. Claassen (ed.) *Exploring Gender Through Archaeology*. Madison, WI: Prehistory Press, pp.33–47.

Hurcombe, L.M. (1995) 'Our own engendered species'. *Antiquity* 69, 87–100.

Hurcombe, L.M. (in press) 'Gender representations in prehistory' in B. Molyneux (ed.) *The Cultural Life of Images: Visual Representation in Archaeology*. London: Routledge.

Jennbert, K. (in press) 'From the inside: a contribution to the debate about the introduction of Agriculture' in L. Domanska, R. Dennell and M. Zvelebil (eds) *The Transition to Farming in the Baltic Region*. Sheffield: Sheffield Academic Press.

Jackson, T.L. (1991) 'Pounding acorn: women's production as social and economic factors' in J.M. Gero and M.W. Conkey (eds) *Engendering Archaeology: Women and Prehistory*. Oxford: Blackwell, pp. 301–25.

Jones, S. and Pay, S. (1990) 'The legacy of Eve' in P. Gathercole and D. Lowenthal (eds) *The Politics of the Past*. London: Unwin Hyman, pp. 160–71.

Mitchell, C. (1992) 'Activating women in Arikara ceramic production' in C. Claassen (ed.) *Exploring Gender Through Archaeology*. Madison WI: Prehistory Press, pp. 89–94.

Molyneux, B. (ed.) (in press) *The Cultural Life of Images: Visual Representation in Archaeology*. London: Routledge.

Moser, S. (1992a) 'The visual language of archaeology: a case study of the neanderthals'. *Antiquity* 66, 831–44.

Moser, S. (1992b) 'Visions of the Australian Pleistocene: prehistoric life at Lake Mungo and Kutikina'. *Australian Archaeology* 5, 1–10.

Moser, S. (1993) 'Gender stereotyping in pictorial reconstructions of human origins' in L.J. Smith and H. Du Cros (eds) *Women in Archaeology: A Feminist Critique*. Canberra: Australian National University Press.

Smith, L. and Du Cros, H. (eds) (1993) *Women in Archaeology: A Feminist Critique*. Canberra: Australian National University Press.

Wright, R.P. (1991) 'Women's labour and pottery production in prehistory' in J.M. Gero and M.W. Conkey (eds) *Engendering Archaeology: Women and Prehistory*. Oxford: Blackwell, pp. 194–223.

Image sources

Brayne, Jane in J. Richards (1991) *English Heritage Book of Stonehenge*. London: English Heritage/Batsford.

Clarys, Benoît (1989) Postcard series of LBK scenes Editions du CEDARC. Treignes, Belgium: Musée du Malgré Tout.

Constable in A. Wilton (1979) *Constable's 'English Landscape Scenery'*. London: Collonade at the British Museum; and in A. Smart and A. Brooks (1976) *Constable and his Country*. London: Elek.

Croft, Tracey in J. Dyer (1990) *Ancient Britain*. London: Guild.

Dobie, Judith in C. Malone (1989) *English Heritage Book of Avebury*. London: English Heritage/Batsford.

Gallimard Larousse Encyclopédie Découvertes Junior (1991) (Polish edition) *Nr 8 Neolithic Revolution*.

Fox, S. (ed.) (1985) *The Medieval Woman: an Illuminated Book of Days*. London: Collins.

McClendon, S. (1992) 'Californian baskets and basketmakers' in L. Mowat, H. Morphy and P. Dransart (eds) *Basketmakers*. Oxford: Pitt Rivers Museum, pp. 51–75.

Souvenir, S. (text and images) (1990) *La Prehistoire, 1. Les Ages de la Pierre*. Editions du CEDARC, Treignes, Belgium: Musée du Malgré Tout.

Winter, G. (1966) (1972 edition) *A Country Camera 1844–1914*. Newton Abbot: David and Charles.

2 The power of gender archaeology

BRIAN BOYD

> Revision calls not for alternatives, but a completely new focus of enquiry, and a new set of categories geared to the changed social reality.
>
> (Bauman 1992: 53)

In her 1991 paper, 'Women's archaeology? Political feminism, gender theory and historical revision', Roberta Gilchrist raises a number of important issues which may be summarized by her closing remarks:

> To date, feminism, gender and the study of women have been marginal to mainstream archaeology. In some cases this is partly a product of choice, since women-only groups are thought more supportive, and because integration within the establishment might be thought to compromise feminist aims and theory. But surely we must challenge existing attitudes at their source? The significance of feminism, gender and women in archaeology will be acknowledged only when our future is built through integration with the wider discipline.
>
> (1991: 500)

While agreeing with the overall political premise of this statement, I would like to confront its underlying assumptions in order to address some uncertainties: uncertainties within the disciplinary structure of archaeology, uncertainties about the analytical procedures of an 'engendered' archaeology, and some personal uncertainties on speaking about and writing (pre)histories of gender relations.

Following Gilchrist, the main issues may be identified as follows:

1. Feminism, gender, and the study of women have been marginalized.
2. There are difficulties in accepting, and a reluctance to accept, integration within 'the establishment' of mainstream archaeology.
3. There is a need to expose the inherent biases of the intellectual and historical traditions of the existing dominant structures in order to gain acceptance for the study of gender in archaeology.

The first point is uncontentious. Of all the social sciences, archaeology has been notoriously slow (reluctant) to incorporate perspectives from the vast amount of literature on feminism and gender studies. For instance, it has been frequently pointed out (e.g. Gero and Conkey 1991) that the manuscript for Conkey and Spector's 'Archaeology and the study of gender' had been circulating for several years before it was finally published in 1984, and it was not until 1988 that the first archaeological conference ('The Wedge' conference in Georgetown, South Carolina) specifically on gender and women took place (a small gathering of around 20 people). The current situation may not be quite as bad as when Alison Wylie asked at that conference, 'Why is there no archaeology of gender?' (Wylie 1991), but despite over 200 publications on the subject (e.g. *Archaeological Review from Cambridge* 1988; Claassen 1992, 1994; Ehrenberg 1989; Gero and Conkey 1991; Gilchrist 1994; Seifert 1991; Walde and Willows 1991), real accommodation of gender-informed perspectives in liberal mainstream archaeology is still far from evident.

The second point is discussed in the next section on reworking archaeological categories. Moving on then to the third point, most current archaeological studies of women and gender are characterized by the critique of male bias in accounts of the past. It is often argued that once the inadequacies of such bias are exposed, and the historical and intellectual traditions which informed its construction are subjected to feminist critique, then the way will be open to write histories of women, histories of gender relations, and so on, which can then be integrated into the hopefully-enlightened mainstream. Obviously 'challenging existing attitudes at their source' is an essential step towards the transformation of what we may call the 'dominant discourse', but it is only a first step. It is not enough simply to expose and critique, because the real challenge is to move beyond the feminist perspectives which created the conditions for the critique of androcentrism, and which highlighted the politically all-pervasive nature of gender, towards writing truly 'engendered' histories; histories which analyse the material conditions within which gender relationships between women and men were negotiated. This involves much more than 'integration', or 'getting to grips with the data' or 'bringing together theory and practice', or any other such well-intentioned, but well-worn, sentiment, and this takes us back to the second crucial point raised above, and to the quote from Bauman which opens this article.

Reworking categories

What has gone virtually unnoticed, or at least unwritten, is that the recent introduction of feminist perspectives from the other social sciences into archaeology demands a *complete reworking of existing archaeological categories*; a shift towards a 'new focus of enquiry'. Much of what stands for gender archaeology so far produced has failed to make any real impact since its theoretical orientation conforms to – and, therefore, contributes to the reproduction of – existing academic and disciplinary frameworks, whether traditional, processual or postprocessual. As a result, gender studies in archaeology continue to be regarded as 'fringe', as a subordinate language within the existing dominant structure. That is, the kinds of knowledge produced by gender archaeologies are not deemed relevant within the larger structure. Only that which is considered acceptable by those institutionalized structures – those which legitimate selected knowledge forms – count within the dominant discourse. For example Paul Bahn has written recently:

> The latest outbreak – which bears a great resemblance to the good old days of the new archaeology (primarily a racket for the boys) – is gender archaeology, which is actually feminist archaeology (a new racket for the girls). Yes, folks, sisters are doing it for themselves ... Hardly a month goes by without another conference on 'gender archaeology' being held somewhere by a host of female archaeologists (plus a few brave or trendy males who aspire to political correctness). Some of its aims are laudable, but the bandwagon shouldn't be allowed to roll too far, as the new archaeology did, before the empresses' lack of clothes is pointed out by gleeful cynics.
>
> (1992: 321)

Bahn goes on to say that the 'balloon of pomposity' needs bursting in order to rid archaeology of those whom he sees as 'too serious' and 'self righteous'. The paper from which this quote is taken appeared in a volume of *Archaeological Review from Cambridge* entitled 'Humour and Archaeology'; quite fittingly, since Bahn's misplaced and ill-timed comments are something of a joke in themselves.

To achieve emancipation, and to avoid such vacuous 'criticism', theoretically distinctive archaeologies of gender cannot effectively operate through modified versions of existing categories. Grillo argues:

> Subordinate languages may be powerful in their own domains, and indeed may create 'no-go' areas for the dominant culture. They may even, as with counter-cultures and anti-languages, offer satisfying alternative versions of reality and thus have an appearance of autonomy. But it is an autonomy of a limited kind. Reserved areas of language may be tolerated, not everyone need be incorporated.
>
> (1989: 228)

Taking this position further, David Bloor (1982), in his examination of Durkheim and Mauss' proposition that 'the classification of things reproduces the classification of men' (*sic*), has argued that stability in any system of knowledge comes from the collective decisions of its creators and users. It derives from the *active protection* of parts of the network, and the requirement that certain laws and classifications be kept intact and all adjustments and alterations carried out elsewhere:

> The rest of the network then becomes a field of resources to be exploited to achieve this end – a place where thresholds can be moved with relative ease; where complexity or blame can be conveniently located, or troublesome cases relegated.
>
> (Bloor 1982: 280)

So, certain laws are protected and rendered stable because of their assumed utility for purposes of justification, legitimation and social persuasion. It is these social interests that ultimately sanction the form of the knowledge system, so that social categories are ultimately reflected in and responsible for knowledge categories.

'Seeing' gender

To avoid what Gilchrist terms the compromising of feminist aims and theories through their 'integration with the establishment', it is time to structure our work through a different set of assumptions, involving primarily a rejection of the protracted epistemological debate. That is, the search for a *methodology* with which to 'find women in the material remains of the past'. However, this implies that once we have a methodology (or methodologies) we can somehow 'do' gender archaeology. Cheryl Claassen observes that, 'In spite of 20 years of the new archaeology, a decade of post-processualism and a furious 5 years of feminist archaeology/archaeology of gender, we still approach artifacts, ecofacts, features and their matrix in essentially the same ways we have for 100 years. For positivists, or feminist empiricists, theoretical discussions beg the issue of field methods. How can we see gender in the archaeological record?' (1992: 6). I wish to argue here that we will never 'see' gender in the material remains of the past. We will never 'see' social relations of any sort. As Gilchrist is so far alone in pointing out, 'gender is no longer considered a problem of methodology, but rather one of social theory' (1991: 498). But has the concern with social theory in recent years altered the ways in which archaeologists perceive gender relations (in the past and in the present)? The lack of critical approaches to gender in some of the major post-processual writings (e.g. Shanks and Tilley 1987a, 1987b) has already been noted (e.g. Engelstad 1991), but even those which do address gender issues, such as Hodder's *The Domestication of Europe* (1990), tend to fall back on structural dichotomies which simply reproduce the traditional analytical categories man/woman, wild/domestic, and thus implicitly rely on notions of universal femininity or masculinity. This is disappointing, since so-called contextual approaches have otherwise facilitated a move away from such cross-cultural universals. How can we discuss the specific social or cultural contexts of, say, the practices of prehistoric gatherer-hunters at the inception of agriculture, if we fail to similarly theorize and contextualize the gender relations which may have informed the ways in which such practices were executed?

Similarly, the very ways in which archaeologists have struggled to define 'gender' are loaded with such generalization. It is often said that 'gender is a primary structuring principle of societies' but, again, this statement is so vague as to be meaningless. Outside western intellectual analytical constructs, 'gender' is not a principle, a concept, a 'useful category of analysis'. If anything definable, gender partly constitutes the processes whereby people perceive, define and negotiate their relationships with each other (Gay Y. Blasco 1995; Strathern 1980). Such processes will be culturally, socially and historically specific, and it is the (pre)histories of these processes that we should endeavour to write if we wish to produce pasts which are truly 'engendered'.

On speaking and writing

How then may we produce such accounts? A crucial feature in our reworking is for us to expand the scope of the current debate to write histories which are the results of dialogue between men and women of all genders. As I argued earlier, we must now go beyond the feminist critique and address a number of hitherto 'difficult' areas, although always bearing in mind why histories have been written in particular ways. For example, although it is essential to have solidarity on feminist and gender issues, as with 'women-only' groups, a new solidarity should now be an incorporating rather than an excluding practice. That is, in what ways can feminist perspectives draw in male feminists, and how may they contribute to gender debates and women's issues? Although it remains to be seen if a male contribution to gender archaeologies can liberate itself from male-derived analytical categories, if we are to investigate critically the social construction of gender relations in the past, discussion must be directed towards perceptions of femininity *and* masculinity, and the place of such perceptions in social relations. Basically, what we require is a non-sexist archaeology; one which not only promotes different ways of speaking and acting, but different ways of listening. Our current working practices, structures of organization, employment and training may do little to inspire such a 'radical' shift in perspective, but if 'the open future rests on a new past' (Haraway 1978, cited by Conkey and Gero 1991: 3), then it rests equally on a new present.

Acknowledgements

Many thanks to Paloma Gay Y. Blasco and Lesley K. McFadyen for their help during the writing of this chapter.

References

Archaeological Review from Cambridge 1988, 7/1.

Bahn, P. (1992) 'Bores, bluffers and wankas: some thoughts on archaeology and humour'. *Archaeological Review from Cambridge* 11(2), 315–22.

Bauman, Z. (1992) *Intimations of Postmodernity.* London: Routledge.

Bloor, D. (1982) 'Durkheim and Mauss revisited: classification and the sociology of knowledge'. *Studies in the History and Philosophy of Science* 13, 267–97.

Claassen, C. (1992) 'Questioning gender: an introduction' in C. Claassen (ed.) *Exploring Gender Through Archaeology.* Monographs in World Archaeology no. 11. Wisconsin: Prehistory Press, pp. 1–9.

Claassen, C. (1994) *Women in Archaeology.* Philadelphia: University of Pennsylvania Press.

Conkey, M.W. and Gero, J.M. (1991) 'Tensions, pluralities, and engendering archaeology: an introduction to women and prehistory' in J.M. Gero and M.W. Conkey (eds) *Engendering Archaeology: Women and Prehistory.* Oxford: Blackwell, pp. 3–30.

Ehrenberg, M. (1989) *Women in Prehistory.* London: British Museum.

Engelstad, E. (1991) 'Images of power and contradiction: feminist theory and post-processual archaeology'. *Antiquity* 65, 502–14.

Gay Y. Blasco, P. (1995) *'Sex', 'gender' and the Gitanos of Madrid.* Unpublished PhD thesis. University of Cambridge.

Gero, J.M. and Conkey, M.W. (eds) (1991) *Engendering Archaeology: Women and Prehistory.* Oxford: Blackwell.

Gilchrist, R. (1991) 'Women's archaeology? Political feminism, gender theory and historical revision'. *Antiquity* 65, 495–501.

Gilchrist, R (1994) *Gender and Material Culture: The Archaeology of Religious Women.* London: Routledge.

Grillo, R.D. (1989) *Dominant Languages: Languages and Hierarchy in Britain and France.* Cambridge: Cambridge University Press.

Haraway, D. (1978) 'Animal sociology and a natural economy of the body politic. Part II. The Past is the contested zone: human nature and theories of production and reproduction in primate behavior studies'. *Signs: Journal of Women in Culture and Society* 4, 37–60.

Hodder, I. (1990) *The Domestication of Europe.* Oxford: Blackwell.

Seifert, D. (ed.) (1991) 'Gender in historical archaeology'. *Historical Archaeology* 25/4.

Shanks, M. and Tilley, C. (1987a) *Re-constructing Archaeology.* Cambridge: Cambridge University Press.

Shanks, M. and Tilley, C. (1987b) *Social Theory and Archaeology.* Cambridge: Polity Press.

Strathern, M. (1980) 'No nature, no culture: the Hagen case' in C. MacCormack and M. Strathern (eds) *Nature, culture and gender.* Cambridge: Cambridge University Press, pp. 174–222.

Walde, D. and Willows, N.D. (eds) (1991) *The Archaeology of Gender: Proceedings of the 22nd Annual Chacmool Conference.* Calgary: University of Calgary.

Wylie, A. (1991) 'Gender theory and the archaeological record: why is there no archaeology of gender?' in J.M. Gero and M.W. Conkey (eds) *Engendering Archaeology: Women and Prehistory.* Oxford: Blackwell, pp. 31–54.

3 Re-engendering gender: some theoretical and methodological concerns on a burgeoning archaeological pursuit

KURTIS S. LESICK

The influence of feminist thinking has profoundly affected general academic scholarship for the past two decades. Yet, it is only relatively recently that these concerns have infiltrated archaeology. Conkey and Spector's inaugural paper, 'Archaeology and the Study of Gender' written in 1984, the 1989 Chacmool Conference in Calgary, Canada on 'The Archaeology of Gender' (Walde and Willows 1990), and Gero and Conkey's (1991) now classic text, *Engendering Archaeology: Women and Prehistory*, all mark the beginning of a new and vibrant feminist-informed hermeneutic within archaeological inquiry. Since this time, 'gender oriented' studies in our discipline have multiplied at an astounding rate. Within these studies, the feminist pursuit of elucidating an archaeology of women has worked to highlight a number of fundamental inadequacies in general archaeological interpretation. Such a realization has allowed archaeology to transcend the once invisible barrier between examining the cultural residues of an amorphous society and examining those of a dynamic social community composed of groupings of individuals.

At this point, slightly more than ten years after Conkey and Spector's (1984) original article, we may ask how far along have we come toward an archaeology of gender? The abundance of conference papers dealing with so-called 'gender' issues would suggest that gender study in archaeology is very much alive. A closer look, however, reveals that the 'gender revolution' in archaeology is only just beginning now. What we have been experiencing in the last ten years was not a concentration on gender, but rather the development of a feminist archaeology. Though there are shared concerns between the two, they are not the same. Further, if we do not enact a theoretical separation between gender and feminism, then the conflation of terms will stifle development of both pursuits.

This, then becomes the starting point of the present inquiry. The purpose of this chapter is to bring into clearer resolution a number of theoretical and methodological concerns central to gender analysis. This is of necessity because, left unchecked, such concerns impede the effective development of gender study in archaeology. The objective of the present discussion, therefore, becomes three-fold. Firstly, the theoretical conflation of gender and feminism shall be considered, and as point of separation, a distinction will be drawn between the two. Secondly, the concept of gender will be developed as an analytical device which works, not only to organize and aid in the interpretation of archaeological data, but which also problematizes our notions of natural gender and sexual order. This, in essence, works to expose those *a priori* classifications which we mistakenly take as immutable. Finally, I shall discuss gender in terms of archaeology and, more specifically, in terms of material culture. I shall argue that rather than trying merely to 'find' gender in the archaeological record, archaeology must study the concept of gender from its own privileged standpoint. This is one characterized by an emphasis on material (cultural) forms as the primary focus of study. The lack of direct access to human subjects, far from being an impediment, works to filter out the anthropocentric bias inherent in much of social scientific research. Consequently, though gender is a schema for social ordering, it is culturally constructed, that is through the existence of, and interaction with, tangible objects. Hence, gender is accessible in prehistory because it is manifested primarily through material culture and then, secondarily, through social action.

Beyond the female gender

Whereas an archaeology of gender may be seen as developing from feminist epistemologies, feminism, in an archaeological context, can best be understood as a social by-product of archaeological practice. Historically, archaeology was – and some may argue still is – a predominantly male occupation. Though women had long participated, it was often in a role which reproduced the 'domestic female' stereotype; their contribution was often limited to laboratory, restoration, and cataloguing work (Reyman 1992: 74). One major hindrance was the fact that many project directors saw women as an 'unreliable element' because marriage and pregnancy were likely to interfere with their work (Babcock and Parezo 1988: v; Reyman 1992: 74). For women without a strong support base, pregnancy also placed practical constraints on post-graduate aspirations leading to a high attrition of women prior to achieving professional status. This is because 'women arrive at their penultimate childbearing years about the same time they are well into their PhD program or beginning the critical period of career development' (Kelley 1992: 86).

With a paucity of women fulfilling interpretive roles in archaeology, the development of a latent androcentrism was virtually undetectable. The male status quo believed that viewing material culture as social residue brought archaeology beyond the level of gender dynamics; gender neutrality was thought to be assured by focusing at a large-scale, societal level (Conkey and Spector 1984: 22–3). In reality, however, gender bias had prejudiced the interpretive process, for the very concepts through which archaeological inquiry was structured were, in fact, constructs of masculinity. As such, 'the past [became] written in terms of leadership, power, warfare, the exchange of women, man the hunter, rights of inheritance, control over resources, and so on' (Hodder 1991: 169).

As women moved into positions where it was they who were deciphering the archaeological record, there were fundamental inconsistencies between their interpretations of prehistoric groups and the traditional attempts at a 'gender-neutral' prehistory. This brought to the forefront much of the methodological naïveté of traditional archaeological thought and made clear the need for a conscious, explicit gender sensitivity in archaeological methodology. Beyond these immediate methodological concerns, feminist criticism also sought to resolve certain social inequities within archaeological practice by highlighting the vast shortage of women with interpretive influence, and the resulting inadequacies in archaeological understanding. In this way, the adoption of feminist philosophies into archaeology was motivated just as much by political intent, as academic. While arguing for a recognition of women in prehistoric contexts many feminists were, in fact, arguing for a similar voice within both contemporary archaeology and society.

Feminist archaeologies, then, tend to challenge the traditional, patriarchal conception of what it is to be a woman. This constitutes a rejection of the role of women as passive and secondary, and emphasizes 'women as agents and subjects' (Conkey and Gero 1991: 6). Importance is also placed on 'what are often considered the feminist issues: the situation of women and the analysis of domination' (Flax 1987: 622–3, quoted in Conkey and Gero 1991: 5). It then follows that one goal of feminism in academia is to heighten the representation of women in all gamuts of academic scholarship, infusing into the contemporary social psyche that women of the past had contributed to that which we know as the present. Such political conviction, though being integral to feminist pursuits, surpasses the requirements of an archaeology of gender. Indeed, it is at the level of politics where we must enact a methodological separation between the two pursuits. For feminist archaeologists to have power and political voice, they must view their studies in relation to contemporary male/female gender debate and dynamics. Consequently, as we have seen above, the use of feminist philosophies in archaeology is as much about exposing *current* women's issues, as those in the past. In doing so, however, we do not study what gender 'is', but rather the relationship between two reified concepts of gender – namely male and female.

Hence, the methodological defining point (as we will make it) is in the explicit subject of study. Where feminist archaeologies study 'women' as a heuristic category – problematizing the boundaries of the word and our conceptions of it – an archaeology of gender must do the same with the heuristic concept of 'gender'. This then suggests that, given a separation between the archaeologies of feminism and gender, the category of gender must be able to transcend the traditional dialectic of man and woman. Gender studies must go deeper than our current societal understanding of the word as a relationship between 'being' male and 'being' female.

By organizing gender studies solely in respect to 'women' defined in opposition 'men', gender archaeology is, to a great degree, guilty of the same oversights which created an androcentric representation of the past. Hence, many studies of gender in the archaeological record have been biased by the ideological boundaries of our Western concept of gender. This is to say that our primary schema for social (gender) ordering at *present* is in terms of a male/female polemic. To project this uncritically onto a prehistoric case-study is to potentially (once again) misrepresent any alternate patterns of gender dynamics.

A re-evaluation of gender: expanding definitions and potential

The proposition here, then, is that there is more to gender than 'male' and 'female'. We must not forget that these are only heuristic quantifications of our contemporary concepts of gender. Further, the concept of male/female duality has only been theoretically 'fixed' quite recently because of gender politics. This means, in all likelihood, that there are other gender categories – even within our present society – which are not overtly and politically recognized as such. We must, therefore, be careful not to lose sight of the fact that gender categories are *constructs*. As Maurer (1990: 414) warns:

> ... in universalizing what gender is, ... scholars constitute gender as an immutable fact, an ahistorical, unchangeable reality which once apprehended, can never be transcended. Gender, originally problematized as a cultural construct, becomes 'naturalized'.

It is the naturalized concept of gender which draws us into unrecognized bias. Thus, we must not look for quantifications of the masculine and feminine, as we know them, but create a broad analytical category of gender – one which problematizes our 'naturalized' view of it. It then becomes the role of the archaeological record to further define the extent of gender dynamics in prehistory. Before this can occur, however, we must re-evaluate the concept of gender and dissolve the myth that gender exists as a *dialectic* based on the two *binary* sexes.

It is generally agreed that 'gender is a system of cultural codes inscribed on biological sex' (Maurer 1990: 414). This would suggest that before we can understand the nature of gender, we must first delineate the role of 'biological sex' as a theoretical foundation for gender. This, however, is not as easy as one might think. Unfortunately, our concepts of biological sex turn out to be just as much socio-cultural construct as gender. As John Dupré (1986) reveals, there is little, if any, basis to ascribe an essential difference between the male and female sexes. There is nothing that occurs 100 per cent of the time in one sex, for which there is no potential in the other. Gamete size becomes the only primary difference between the two (Dupré 1986: 446), and what sex are those who cannot effectively produce mature gametes? Hence, our concept of sexual difference is based on a fluid collection of indicators, usually comprised of secondary sexual characteristics. Within this view of biological sex, we have the potentiality of, not two, but three sexes. These categories are generally delineated with regard to genitalia: males are those with a penis, females have a vagina, and hermaphrodites possess both.

Though the condition of hermaphrodism is viewed by many in the West with incredulity, in areas where it still endures, hermaphrodism has been shown to impact social conceptions of sex and gender (e.g. Herdt 1990, 1994). It is apparent that 'a hermaphroditic or intersexed body implicitly exposes and refutes the regulative strategies of sexual categorization' (Butler 1990: 96). Hence, for many of those groups where hermaphrodism occurs, gender and sex ideologies are 'polymorphous' rather than 'dimorphous' as in Western society (Herdt 1990: 435). Gender and sex constructs are, therefore, less rigid and one may conceptually (or physically) move between male, female and intersexed gender and sex categories. This brings to light the contingent nature of the social limitations which we, in Western society, place upon concepts of gender and sex. Hermaphrodism is one obvious example of a situation in which individuals may transcend the strict male/female dichotomy in gender. Even within dimorphous societies, hermaphrodites are often documented as shifting genders during certain periods in their lifetime (Foucault 1980; Trumbach 1994). Hence, biological sex is an inadequate foundation with which to statically 'fix' gender ideologies. Perhaps this should be taken as an indication that we cannot develop and use nomothetic concepts of sex-based gender to structure analyses of culture and society. It follows, that just as concepts of sex may be fluid and somewhat ambiguous to the Western eye, so is gender.

If gender cannot be conceptualized as strictly sex-based, then we must find a new structuring relationship between sex and gender. We are aware of the obvious gender constructs which follow from biological sex – namely male and female, or man and woman. These may be viewed as templates around which other genders are structured. Hence, one does not come from the womb equipped with a male or female gender. These must be developed and grown into. Gender, in this view, is patterned by sex in relation to the human, biological lifecycle. This renders a tripartite organization of gender:

Gender Class 1	Gender Class 2	Gender Class 3
Childhood	Adulthood	Old age
(Perhaps male and female)	(Male and female)	(Perhaps male and female)

Under this rationale, childhood, and perhaps even male and female children, may constitute different and separate genders. Here, concepts of 'male' and 'female' have a smaller role in organizing cultural experience, social action and identity. Marjorie Shostak (1981), for instance, discusses how male/female sex differences are of little consequence to gender categorization in !Kung childhood:

> !Kung children are not segregated by sex, neither sex is trained to be submissive or fierce, and neither sex is restrained from expressing the full breadth of emotion that seems inherent in the human spirit
>
> (Shostak 1981: 108)

It is only in their middle teens that boys and girls will start to separate into binary, gender-specific roles. Girls will go with their mothers to gather, while boys may be taken on hunting excursions with their fathers (Shostak 1981: 83, 105).

Childhood, then, constitutes a challenge to traditional gender thinking. Children are in an ambiguous phase before they reach sexual maturity, a defining point for binary gender. As the visible signs of sexual maturation come into being, children become re-engendered as adult male and adult female. Often at this stage, their childhood ambiguity is socially abolished within a ceremonial rite of passage (van Gennep 1960). This, if reinterpreted in terms of gender, may constitute an official process of re-engendering at whatever stage of life the ceremony takes place.

Old age is yet another situation of male/female gender ambiguity. This is especially evident when adult females reach menopause. This marks the end of their reproductive fitness and hence, for many, a transition in gender identity from female to elderly. At this stage, it becomes acceptable for elderly, post-menopausal women to engage in activities traditionally designated as 'male'. This includes a more active role in pursuits such as scavenging and hunting (Conkey and Gero 1991: 18). Male old age is a bit more problematic. There is no great biological marker to indicate a natural transition from one gender to another. In this situation, men may be re-engendered when they become incapacitated due to old age. They can no longer effectively fulfil male activities and, therefore, their responsibilities and gender identities shift. Elderly males may become more associated with the home-base and activities which might carry relatively 'feminine' connotations. These would include such responsibilities as child rearing, food preparation, and 'craft' production.

Both childhood and old age are two phenomena which are severely under-studied in archaeology. This is probably due to the fact that there is little archaeology done by the elderly, and even less done by children. As archaeologists, we have been caught, once again, ignoring that which is beyond our immediate experience and interest. By studying both these categories as genders we may take advantage of the quickly developing methodology within gender studies, which expedites interpretation at this more intimate level. The studies of childhood and old age also work to expose our contemporary, innate and adult dependency on male/female gender constructs. By looking at gender categories which are ambiguous in relation to the male/female dichotomy, we problematize this dependency and move toward abolishing both androcentric and gynocentric bias.

Such bias has also worked to effectively obscure from archaeological interpretation those adults in prehistory who may have been binary gender 'shifters'. This includes both formalized male/female gender transgression, such as institutionalized homosexuality (Whitehead 1981), ritualized transgendering (Nanda 1994) and individual gender crossing (Grémaux 1994), as well as more informal modes of homosexuality (Trumbach 1994), and transsexualism (Bolin 1994). These are situations where individuals negate aspects of their primary, social, male/female gender identity. Those who would ordinarily be typed as 'male' engage in behaviours and/or adopt identities which would class them as 'female', or vice versa. The problematization of male/female gender constructs are obvious in such instances of 'biological females wearing men's garb and often men's weaponry, performing men's jobs and enjoying, at least to some extent, public recognition as men' (Grémaux 1994: 241).

Though 'gender crossers' have traditionally been seen as 'defective' males and females in Western society, in other groups they are assigned separate gender identities recognizing their own set of gender attributes. Hence, the hirjas of India, a group of biological men who have been physically emasculated in devotion to the goddess Bahuchara Mata, 'are neither male nor female, man nor woman', but they are 'man plus woman, or erotic and sacred female men' (Nanda 1994: 373). This is reinforced, on one hand, by their preference for women's clothing, hairstyles and jewellery, and on the other by their smoking of the *hookah* or cigarettes – a male endeavour (Nanda 1994: 382–3). Hence, their group identity and alternative gender is supported through material means. Keith Matthews (1994) speaking on the archaeology of homosexuality has, therefore, argued that alternative genders should be identifiable in the archaeo-logical record through such material indicators, if only we chose to consider their potentiality.

Objects that engender

I have argued that if we are to incorporate the search for gender within archaeological methodology, then we must create a concept of gender which is self-critical and which problematizes the very Western ethnocentrism which has worked in the past to impede its study. For a true gender archaeology, however, we must go further and ensure that we understand the relationship between gender and material culture. As I have shown above, it is useful, and often necessary, to look for theoretical inspiration from other disciplines when ex-panding our own body of theory in archaeology. Nevertheless, as Alison Wylie (1991: 33) relates, it is also imperative for archaeologists to conceive of these theoretical constructs in terms of their own discipline, to create 'a body of linking principles' which expedites the usefulness of theory in archaeology. It follows, then, that because we do not have direct access to engendered individuals in the prehistoric record, we must compensate for this fact within our methodology. Hence, as archaeologists, we must take into account our methodological limita-tions and develop our own 'archaeology of gender' as opposed to a 'sociology' or 'anthropology of prehistory'.

Central to this sort of archaeology, is an understanding of the discipline's true object of study. Within archaeological methodology the primary focus of analy-sis is material culture and the material conditions of existence for past people. As objects of knowledge our access to the material form is direct and concrete. Our access to the human component, however, is indirect and strictly mediated through the existence of material forms. Archaeology, then, does not study humanity, but the *interaction between humanity and material forms*. Such an interaction is of paramount importance, for it is through experience with material forms that humans create knowledge, identity, and indeed reality. Material culture acts as a template to structure thoughts; it is the physical which grounds the abstract. Our experience as archaeologists reinforces this point: through the material record we construct abstract conceptions of past people. Our encounter with archaeological remains, in fact, creates the existence of the people which we hold in association with them. Hence, the interaction with the tangible material in archaeological contexts leads to a knowledge-creating venture. This becomes an analogue for our everyday experience with material culture. Rather than being a passive carrier of symbolic knowledge, the material form is active through cognitive process, and structures the nature of human experience.

Following from this, our concepts of gender must also take material culture as its foundation. Gender constructs are created, ordered and perpetuated in respect to associations with material culture. In Western society, gender is very much recognized in terms of material appearance. It matters little what genitalia one has if it is covered with clothing indicative of a different gender. Hence, we arrive at the problem of what to call a transvestite – 'he' or 'she'. In a similar vein, material culture can also be held in association with engendered activities. Again, in Western society if a male were to engage in *petit point* embroidery this activity may, to a degree, problematize his identity as a 'man'.

These isolated examples have meaning for us because we understand the social connotations of these engendered transgressions. Indeed, this poses a problem to archaeologists who cannot cross-reference their interpretations of an object with the people associated with them. Such a conundrum, however, can be resolved if we expand our inquiry to include the full gamut of available material culture. This would recognize that no one material form designates gender identity. Instead, tangible cultural forms must be seen as contributing to a 'material environment'. Gender, then embodies the nature of experience had within this environment. Under this rationale, gender is the schema by which our material environment orders our experience of life. Engendering, therefore, is when one becomes associated with a particular set of material forms. In this sense we are engendered by the objects around us; they pattern our experience of the world, while patterning how others experience us. In archaeological contexts it is these patterns which are of primary importance. Hence, gender archaeology must centre on the elucidation and analyses of such patterned sets of material culture which work to structure cultural experience and create social (gender) ordering.

Men, women, and beyond

The development of gender studies in archaeology has involved a number of theoretical revolutions, both in how we conceive of gender, but also in how we think of archaeology. This has called for, no less than a complete re-evaluation of archaeology's theoretical foundation. In this, it has been successful in exposing a succession of fundamental biases within archaeological thought. But it is still difficult to convince many archaeologists that studying gender in prehistory is a worthwhile pursuit. For them, gender is too abstract, too far removed from those more traditional and expedient methods of interpretation which are so established in archaeology. Yet as Conkey and Gero (1991: 7, 11–14) argue, gender is not any higher on the ladder of abstraction than any other heuristic categories used in archaeology. It is only when we limit our understanding of gender within our current, societal notion of the word, that the term lacks analytical power.

This is no surprise, however. We would not be so naïve as to expect to find evidence of a parliamentary administration in every archaeological context: ours is not the only form of government. Instead, our knowledge of past governing systems is constructed in relation to the evidence recovered in excavation. In the same way, gender constructs, just as much as 'political economy', 'matrilocality' or 'ritualized hoarding', are ways of ordering archaeological data so that they carry decipherable meaning.

Because gender studies have been so subsumed within the Western male/female gender struggle, it has taken too long for archaeology to realize that gender is *not*, in fact, 'men' and 'women'. The study of gender is not as simple as digging down until we come upon a big stone penis or vulva. Rather we must conceptualize gender as a structuring process, one where patterns in material culture help to create notions of identity. Using gender concepts to structure interpretation is no more artificial than relying on typologies based on perceived usage, form, or material composition. Gender, beyond the 'Western battle of the sexes' is, in fact, a useful and legitimate interpretive and classificatory device. In developing gender studies as a theoretically independent pursuit in archaeology it is no longer an issue of sexual politics. Rather, in the words of Conkey and Gero (1991: 23) 'gender *is* an issue of archaeology and prehistory'.

Acknowledgements

Many people deserve my thanks for their input on this chapter. Unfortunately, if I were to list them all, these acknowledgements would probably be longer than the chapter itself. Special thanks, therefore, go to Soren Blau, Seona Anderson and Jenny Moore for their feedback and support with the initial draft. I am also indebted to Mike Parker Pearson, Mark Edmonds, and Jenny (once again) for helping me to whittle down a much longer version of this chapter. In recognizing their efforts, I take full responsibility for the content, opinions and any short-comings of this composition. Finally, I dedicate this chapter to the memory of Anna Bilash – for over a century a woman of conviction, and an inspiration to me for all my life.

References

Babcock, B.A. and Parezo, N.J. (1988) *Daughters of the Desert: Women Archaeologists and the Native American Southwest, 1880–1980*. Albuquerque: University of New Mexico Press.

Bolin, A. (1994) 'Transcending and transgendering: male-to-female transexuals, dichotomy and diversity' in G. Herdt (ed.) *Third Sex, Third Gender: Beyond Sexual Dimorphism In Culture and History*. New York: Zone Books, pp.447–86.

Butler, J. (1990) *Gender Trouble*. New York: Routledge.

Conkey, M.W. and Spector, J.D. (1984) 'Archaeology and the study of gender' in M.B. Schiffer (ed.) *Advances in Archaeological Method and Theory 7*. New York: Academic Press, pp.1–38.

Conkey, M.W. and Gero, J.M. (1991) 'Tensions, pluralities, and engendering archaeology: an introduction to women and prehistory' in J.M. Gero and M.W. Conkey (eds) *Engendering Archaeology: Women and Prehistory*. Oxford: Blackwell, pp.3–30.

Dupré, J. (1986) 'Sex, gender, and essence'. *Midwest Studies in Philosophy* XI, 441–57.

Flax, J. (1987) 'Postmodernism and gender relations in feminist theory'. *Signs: Journal of Women in Culture and Society* 12 (4), 621–43.

Foucault, M. (1980) *Herculine Barbin: Being the Recently Discovered Memoirs of a Nineteenth Century French Hermaphrodite*. Translated by Richard McDougall. New York: Pantheon Books.

Gero, J.M. and Conkey, M.W. (eds) (1991) *Engendering Archaeology: Women and Prehistory*. Oxford: Blackwell.

Grémaux, R. (1994) 'Woman Becomes Man in the Balkans' in G. Herdt (ed.) *Third Sex, Third Gender: Beyond Sexual Dimorphism In Culture and History*. New York: Zone Books, pp.241–81.

Herdt, G. (1990) 'Mistaken Gender: 5-Alpha Reductase Hermaphroditism and Biological Reductionism in Sexual Identity Reconsidered'. *American Anthropologist* 92, 433–46.

Herdt, G. (1994) 'Mistaken sex: culture, biology and the third sex in New Guinea' in G. Herdt (ed.) *Third Sex, Third Gender: Beyond Sexual Dimorphism In Culture and History*. New York: Zone Books, pp.419–46.

Hodder, I. (1991) *Reading the Past: Current Approaches to Interpretation in Archaeology*, 2nd edn. Cambridge: Cambridge University Press.

Kelley, J.H. (1992) 'Being and becoming' in J.E. Reyman (ed.) *Rediscovering our Past: Essays on the History of American Archaeology*. Aldershot: Ashgate Publishing Ltd, pp.81–90.

Matthews, K. (1994) 'The Archaeology of Homosexuality'. Paper presented at the 1994 Theoretical Roman Archaeology Conference in Durham, England.

Maurer, B. (1990) 'Feminist challenges to archaeology: avoiding the epistemology of the "Other" ' in D. Walde and N.D. Willows (eds) *The Archaeology of Gender: Proceedings of the 22nd Annual Chacmool Conference*. Calgary: University of Calgary, pp.414–19.

Nanda, S. (1994) 'Hijras: an alternative sex and gender role in India' in G. Herdt (ed.) *Third Sex, Third Gender: Beyond Sexual Dimorphism In Culture and History*. New York: Zone Books, pp.373–418.

Reyman, J.E. (ed.) (1992) 'Women in American Archaeology' in *Rediscovering our Past: Essays on the History of American Archaeology*. Aldershot: Ashgate Publishing Ltd, pp.69–80.

Shostak, M. (1981) *Nisa: The life and Words of a !Kung Woman*. Cambridge, MA: Harvard University Press.

Trumbach, R. (1994) 'London's Saphists: from three sexes to four genders in the making of modern culture' in G. Herdt (ed.) *Third Sex, Third Gender: Beyond Sexual Dimorphism in Culture and History*. New York: Zone Books, pp.111–36.

van Gennep, A. (1960) *The Rites of Passage*, translated by M.B. Vizedom and G.L. Caffee. London: Routledge & Kegan Paul. First published in 1909.

Walde, D. and N.D. Willows (eds) (1990) *The Archaeology of Gender: Proceedings of the 22nd Annual Chacmool Conference*. Calgary: University of Calgary.

Whitehead, H. (1981) 'The bow and the burden strap: a new look at institutionalized homosexuality in native North America' in S. Ortner and H. Whitehead (eds) *Sexual Meanings: The Cultural Construction of Gender and Sexuality*. Cambridge: Cambridge

University Press, pp.80–115.

Wylie, A. (1991) 'Gender theory and the archaeological record: why is there no archaeology of gender?' in J.M. Gero and M.W. Conkey (eds) *Engendering Archaeology: Women and Prehistory.* Oxford: Blackwell, pp.31–54.

4 Ambivalent bodies: gender and medieval archaeology

ROBERTA GILCHRIST

Since its inception in the 1980s, the study of gender in archaeology has been concerned with the social construction of difference between men and women. Gender is socially created and historically specific, and, therefore, has been perceived as being distinct from fixed categories of biological sex (Gilchrist 1994: 2–5) Yet, gender is firmly located within the body: a society's construction of gender is rooted in its classification of sexual difference and ideas about the body. A distinctive archaeology of the medieval period emerged during the 1950s, devoted to the study of material culture dating roughly from the fifth century to the sixteenth century AD, although these chronological brackets vary between European regions. Despite the rich variety of medieval material culture, literature and documents, archaeologists have shown little awareness of the potential of these sources for commenting on gender. Medieval archaeologists have either ignored the issue of gender, by promoting interpretations which feature a gender-neutral medieval person, or approached it as a classification synonymous with biological sex. In this chapter I would like to explore definitions of sex, gender and the body, before turning to the issue of gender 'visibility' in medieval archaeology. Approaches to gender in medieval archaeology will be reviewed through three thematic case studies: the gift-exchange of medieval women, treatment of men and women in medieval burial and commemoration, and gender and housing.

Written on the body

As Alison Wylie has observed, the study of gender in archaeology has developed in three stages: first came feminist critiques of androcentrism in archaeological interpretations (Conkey and Spector 1984), leading to revised histories focusing on the role of women, and finally the development of studies which consider gender as a structuring principle active in shaping relations of power (Wylie 1991: 31–2). Gender archaeology has become a comparative study, evaluating male and female roles, relationships, cultural imagery, and definitions for masculinity and femininity. The social, as opposed to biological, definition of gender has been adopted in order to challenge interpretations that accepted modern gender stereotypes as timeless, objective and natural. This social definition has been a unifying factor in feminist research on gender archaeology (Gero and Conkey 1991; Gilchrist 1994; Seifert 1991; Wall 1994). Despite the acknowledgement that sex and gender are different, many studies have continued to propose binary gender structures, consisting of two balanced and inter-related halves: male and female.

It has been widely accepted, then, that biological sex is fixed while gender is constructed: one is born, the other made. But is this view ethnocentric, as deeply biased in its way as the androcentric ideas which preceded it? Recently there has been a return to the Foucauldian position that sex, as much as gender, is equally constructed by culture, serving as a means of grouping together biological functions into an artificial unity (Moore 1994: 12). Our western knowledge of biological sex derives from a particular discourse, a medical inheritance beginning with classical and biblical texts. In our own society we recognize that categories of sexual difference can be culturally variable: witness the growing awareness of androgeny, hermaphrodism and the 'third sex'. The work of Judith Butler has been especially influential in encouraging pluralism in academic debates, advocating that we resist the 'heterosexual hegemony' that has characterized discussions of gender. Butler considers sex and gender equally constructed concepts, and in an effort to move beyond the impasse of binary male/female categories, she has proposed the existence of any number of genders, sexualities and identities (Butler 1990: 142–9).

Historically we know of cases of cross-sex gender roles: the cross-dressing female saints of early Christianity, the eunuchs of early medieval Byzantium, and the well-cited Native American *berdache*, the term used to describe the young male or female transvestite who chose to assume the role and identity of their biological opposite (Whelan 1991; Whitehead 1981). Perhaps less fantastic are cases of gender ascription: societies that propose that gender develops and is modified through the course of a lifetime. Children may be considered genderless, or sexually neutral, until adolescence; and adults may experience transformations in their gender definition as their sexual potency or reproductive powers decline. The Hua of Papua New Guinea, for example, are classified as male or female according to their bodily fluids, which are understood to change through the ageing process (Moore 1994: 24). In a medieval context, the Galenic medical theory of the humours classified bodies according to the four basic elements, which it was believed also made up the universe. Water, or phlegm, was considered essentially female. But this humour dominated the complexions of children and eunuchs, and could alter the masculinity of men who lived certain lifestyles. In his text the *Chirurgie*, the fourteenth-century surgeon Henri de Mondeville wrote:

> There are also bodies and bodily parts which are soft: children, women, eunuchs, phlegmatic or effeminate men, freshwater fisherman, scholars, bourgeois, monks, and all those who spend most of their time in the shade, leading a quiet and leisured life.
>
> (quoted in Pouchelle, 1990: 112)

Ideas about physiology are central to a society's classification of sex and the gendering of the body. Categories of gender may be transmutable: constructed by sex, stages in the lifecycle, physical deportment, lifestyle and professional or religious status.

The invisible woman

Medieval archaeology presents an image of a gender-neutral past.[1] All genders and ages are encompassed in a single, genderless state, disrupted only when women or children are made visible through the presence of biologically sexed and aged skeletons. Although this neutral historical figure is referred to using male pronouns, both masculinity and femininity lose their historical resonances. This reticence to address gender is part of a wider flaw in the character of the discipline: medieval archaeology has often been regarded as the least theoretically informed of all branches of European archaeology (Champion 1991: 146). Yet the explanation posited for this lack of theoretical engagement is that medieval archaeology has allied itself too closely to the agenda of history (Austin and Thomas 1990). This premise bears little scrutiny in relation to the topic of gender.

The discipline of medieval history has a pedigree for studying women that extends back twenty years or more (see Power 1975), while more recent research on medieval gender has explored the social construction of masculinity, femininity, sex, sexuality and the body (e.g. Kay and Rubin 1994; Lees 1994; Partner 1993). Archaeological evidence linked with women in the Anglo-Saxon, Viking and later medieval periods has been surveyed, but such syntheses have been carried out by historians, *not* by archaeologists (Fell 1984; Hanawalt 1986; Jesch 1991). In contrast, the study of gender has found strong proponents amongst American historical archaeologists, with a number of detailed case studies published in recent years (for example: Seifert 1991; Wall 1994).

Occasionally this gender neutrality is disrupted by the mention of women in textbooks on medieval archaeology, but their portrayal recalls present-day stereotypes, such as John Steane's comment that the lack of floor deposits typical of excavated peasant houses results from 'constant sweeping by medieval housewives' (Steane 1985: 191). To use the term 'housewife' with no consideration of medieval gender relations or the economy of the peasant household, is to apply modern, capitalist gender stereotypes to the medieval past. Moreover, where archaeology provides contextual evidence that women's roles did not conform with such stereotypes, the meaning of the evidence is contested. For instance, Anne Stalsberg has discussed the presence of weighing equipment in women's graves in Russia, Birka and Norway as reflecting 'tradeswomen'. Previous scholars had concluded that the artefacts represented burials of merchants' wives, skeletons sexed incorrectly, or cases where the wife just happened to die while covering for an absent husband (Stalsberg 1991: 77).

Gender has been addressed only where burials of aged and sexed skeletons provide artefact correlates that can be linked to biological sexual difference. For instance, Klaus Randsborg is one of very few medieval archaeologists to have acknowledged that all societies possessed social distinctions based on gender and age. Yet, he proposed that such relations 'can often be identified only through grave goods', a problem in that 'the abundant jewellery of women often makes them more visible than men' (Randsborg 1991: 155). Gender is assumed to be a factor that occasionally becomes 'visible' in archaeological data, rather than as a concept which was active in structuring daily life and giving meaning to material culture. Strikingly, women's visibility in such contexts has been viewed as distorting and problematic, when their perceived invisibility in all other archaeological contexts is seldom questioned.

Medieval archaeologists have interpreted gender relations, and in particular the status of women, according to relative numbers of male and female burials. Randsborg has assumed that equal representation of men and women on the mortuary monuments of the Early Roman Empire reflected equality and 'the openness of the system' (Randsborg 1991: 151). He has interpreted equal numbers of male and female graves in Denmark (AD 200–400) as part of a shift towards lineage based agriculture which promoted greater equity between the sexes (Randsborg 1984). Parity of numbers is considered to reflect equality, while segregation of male and female burials is generally judged to show a disparity which disadvantaged women. In relation to the tenth-century phases at Raunds (Northants), for example, where women were placed towards the north of the cemetery, David Hinton commented that this may 'indicate status lowering' of women (Hinton 1990: 131). It is not clear why segregation should suggest lower status, rather than merely different treatment of men and women in death. Segregation of women's burials in contemporary contexts in Sweden, Iceland and Greenland also focused on the north of cemeteries, and held a particular meaning within the context of Christian belief (Gilchrist 1994: 134). The provision of separate cemeteries for women in early Christian Ireland (Hamlin and Foley 1983) and Iona, Scotland (O'Sullivan 1994: 359–60), attracted a long-standing tradition of segregated burial which was not considered to devalue either male or female, but instead respected the earlier veneration of religious women on the sites.

Occasionally archaeologists are alerted to the relatively low incidence of women's burials. David Hinton has observed that in some middle Saxon burial contexts women are under-represented: 'Was Southampton a male-dominated craft-working and trading centre existing outside the normal social and economic structures?' (Hinton 1990: 57). The lower occurrence of women's burials in early towns has been noted elsewhere (Randsborg 1991: 156). This negative evidence may imply that early trading places were inhabited largely by men, craftsmen and traders whose work may have brought them to towns on a seasonal or temporary basis. The place of gender in structuring major social transformations, such as urban development, merits further treatment.

The bartered bride

Medieval archaeology has made its greatest contribution in the study of physical landscapes, economic resources, agricultural systems and trade (Biddick 1984; Astill and Grant 1988). The absence of theorizing in medieval archaeology, and the reluctance to consider gender in particular, cannot be laid at history's door.

Instead, medieval archaeology appears to suffer from a general inability to engage with concepts, to problematize cultural categories, and to extend discussion beyond the level of description to that of explanation (Gilchrist 1994: 8–13). The historian Kathleen Biddick has criticized archaeologists for their undiscerning use of historical categories, showing little awareness of the way in which such categories have been created by the disciplines of history and anthropology (Biddick 1993: 1). Particularly in the work of Richard Hodges she has identified the tendency to regard categories of person, such as the peasant, and spatial entities, such as the toft or croft, as natural categories, as opposed to historically constructed concepts (Biddick 1993: 18).

Another inclination can be observed in the work of Hodges, and other medieval archaeologists, to treat social categories of person, such as peasants, children, or women, as single, unified groups, discussed as objects to be exchanged, bartered or buried. Such classifications objectify the body, and inhibit the exploration of agency, the potential of individual actors to engage in social practice. When issues of gender are implied, if never explicitly stated, it is in relation to the exchange and control of women as a strategy in maintaining economic resources. Hodges has proposed that women were part of a gift exchange of wives between Anglo-Saxon England and Frankish Europe, quoting Claude Levi-Strauss that women were 'the supreme gift among those that can only be obtained by reciprocal gifts' (Hodges 1989: 40–41; Levi-Strauss 1969: 65). This characterization negates the role of these high status women in building political alliances and initiating cultural exchange, such as their crucial role in the introduction of Christianity to the Anglo-Saxon Kingdoms. Hodges has suggested that the increasing status and number of grave goods associated with women's graves from the second half of the sixth century was linked with a movement away from the Celtic tradition of partible inheritance and 'resource polygyny', towards primogeniture, where right of inheritance belongs to the eldest son.

Controversially, Hodges noted that the legal rights of women improved in the tenth and eleventh centuries, but cited a limited amount of archaeological evidence to indicate a reduction in their life-expectancy and stature. He proposed that population expansion at the time would have been linked with an intensification in reproductive strategies:

> Women were needed to produce children, particularly in towns. Greater personal freedoms encouraged mobility, and must have led at the same time to the relaxation of existing attitudes to the age of marriage and intra-kin marriage. These changes in child-bearing and perhaps in nutrition may have contributed to worse conditions for women.
>
> (Hodges 1989: 178)

Leaving aside the validity of this interpretation and the evidence on which it is based, Hodges neglected the potential role of women in developing and maintaining alliances through marriage, nor did he consider the negotiating power that their greater mobility and reproductive value would have given them. His model treats all women as a single group, regardless of age, social position or ethnicity. Elsewhere, archaeological evidence has been used to suggest patri-locality. Harold Mytum has suggested that women in Early Christian Ireland can be linked with weaving through documentary evidence, and thus that imported spindle whorls recovered from archaeological contexts may indicate the move-ment of women upon marriage (Mytum 1992: 236). Such approaches imply that women are objects of exchange, without the possibility of their own agency. These models are unsatisfactory because they are incomplete: they have failed to consider women's strategies for maintaining some control over their role in economic production and their place in kinship networks.

The warrior child

The meaning of rituals surrounding death varies between societies. Objects placed in graves may comment more on mourners than on deceased, and may relate as much to the negotiation or transformation of gender in death, as reflect gender relations in life. Studies of early medieval burial in the Anglo-Saxon, Frankish and Germanic customs have frequently adopted gender as a term to describe sex, or as a classification denoted by a characteristic set of artefact correlates of biological sex. Sex correlates are certainly present: Anglo-Saxon weapon burials seem to have been exclusively male, and in the sixth century female burials had greater quantities and types of grave goods (Shephard 1979: 65–7). Rather than commenting on gender or other social constructions, grave goods have been used most commonly as an index to rank graves by wealth. The greater display of female graves was explained by Chris Arnold, 'that the wealth bestowed on a woman may be a reflection of her husband's status as much as her own' (Arnold 1980: 132). More recent studies have considered changes in the way in which male and female were signified in the seventh and eighth centuries (Geake 1992: 85); or have linked the decline of furnished burials to the lessening of differences based on gender and age in favour of those based on class, wealth and rank (Halsall 1992). The relationship between sex and gender has been left unresolved, however, and changing definitions of masculinity and femininity unexplored.

Where human remains have been sexed and aged independently of grave goods, studies have shown that there was a great deal of variation between regions, and even between individual cemeteries, in the degree of emphasis placed on distinctions of age and sex. The role of age, or stage within the lifecycle, seems to have been as important as gender in structuring identity. For women, age seems to have been a crucial factor in determining status. In Denmark, the quantity and quality of men's grave furnishings decreased with age, while the richest burials were those of women over 50 years of age (Sawyer and Sawyer 1993: 192). In the cemetery at Sewerby (E. Yorks), Susan Hirst concluded that certain grave goods represented the status of an important, adult woman, especially girdle hangers, girdle or purse rings and keys – the last symbolic of women as keepers of the household (Figure 4.1) (Hirst 1985: 102). At Holywell Row (Suffolk) only males over 12 years of age had spears included in their graves, and only adults were associated with shields (Pader 1982).

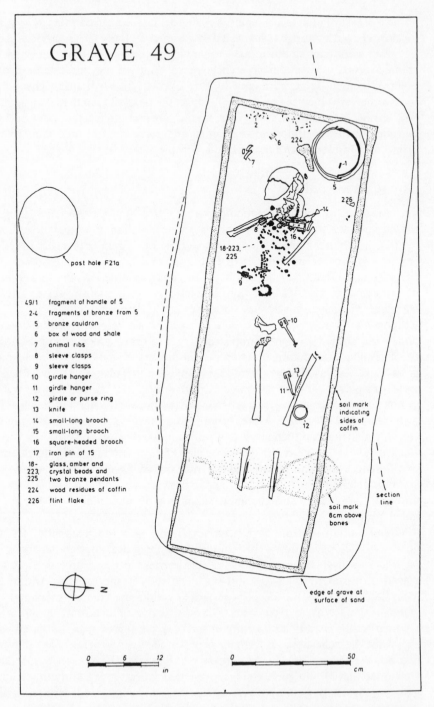

GRAVE 49

post hole F21a

49/1   fragment of handle of 5
2-4   fragments of bronze from 5
5   bronze cauldron
6   box of wood and shale
7   animal ribs
8   sleeve clasps
9   sleeve clasps
10   girdle hanger
11   girdle hanger
12   girdle or purse ring
13   knife
14   small-long brooch
15   small-long brooch
16   square-headed brooch
17   iron pin of 15
18-   glass, amber and
223,   crystal beads and
225   two bronze pendants
224   wood residues of coffin
226   flint flake

soil mark
indicating
sides of
coffin

section
line

soil mark
8cm above
bones

edge of grave at
surface of sand

N

0   6   12
in

0   50
cm

Figure 4.1 Inhumation burial (Grave 49) of an Anglo-Saxon woman from Sewerby (E. Yorks.) accompanied by girdle hangers and a purse ring, representative of the status of an important adult woman. (Reproduced with permission from S.M. Hirst (1985) *An Anglo-Saxon Inhumation Cemetery at Sewerby, East Yorkshire,* fig. 76, p. 163. York University Archaeological Publications 4.)

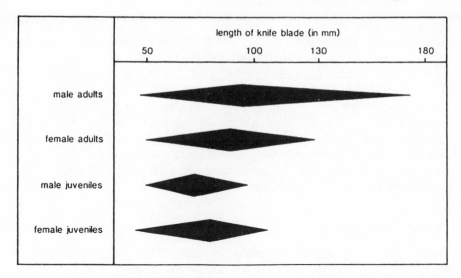

Figure 4.2 Blade lengths of knives in early Saxon inhumations from 47 English cemeteries. Reproduced with permission from H. Härke (1989) 'Knives in early Saxon burials: blade length and age at death'. *Medieval Archaeology* 33, fig. 1, p. 45.

Clearly grave goods were linked with age and gender, and the cultural status of being an *adult* man or woman.

The connection between cultural identity and gender has been clearly elucidated by the work of Heinrich Härke on weapon burials. Härke has examined the correlation between burial with a weapon, burial wealth and skeletal stature at 47 English cemeteries (Härke 1990), showing that weapons were associated with men with the tallest stature and strongest physique, and that the rite of weapon burial corresponded with periods of decline in actual military activity. He concluded that weapon burials did not directly reflect warriors, but rather 'warrior status', based on Anglo-Saxon ethnicity and descent. Although Härke has not discussed gender construction explicitly, his work suggests that the rite of weapon burial was connected with the construction of masculinity, and not necessarily with wealth or skill as a warrior, or even with incidence of warfare.

Härke has also examined the practice of burial with a simple iron knife, which occurred in 45–50% of fifth- to seventh-century burials (Härke 1989). He looked at 925 knives, and concluded that women were consistently buried with knives with shorter blade lengths (Figure 4.2). During the decline of the weapon burial rite during the seventh to eighth century, blade length became a symbol of masculinity. And yet, in juvenile burials, while males were more likely to have knives, females could have longer blades. This pattern has interesting implications for our understanding of gender. For example, until adolescence could some equivalent of the 'warrior status' have been earned equally by males or females? Before adolescence were children seen as another gender? To what extent did biological sex always dictate membership of a gender? At the cemetery of Buckland, Dover, 12% of the graves contained either weapons associated with female skeletons, or brooches or beads with male skeletons (Evison 1987: 123–7). At Spong Hill (Norfolk) one third of the inhumation graves did not contain sex-linked artefacts; this pattern, which is repeated in similar proportions at many cemeteries, has led Karen Brush to suggest that gender may *not* have been an important structuring principle in the living society (Brush 1988: 81). To the contrary, it seems to suggest that up to one third of the population may have constructed their gender identity without being strictly bound by material culture exclusive to one biological sex. At times, factors such as age, lifestyle or some aspect of social identity may have outweighed biological sex in contributing to the construction of gender.

The woman priest

The significance of artefacts in representing gender in the commemoration of the dead is confirmed by the very tenacity of the tradition. Long after the practice of accompanying burials with grave goods had ceased, Christian individuals were represented by symbols on medieval memorials. In England symbols were used on cross slab grave covers, dated primarily from the eleventh to fourteenth centuries, although earlier and later examples are known. Lawrence Butler has commented that 'the symbols are initially those of rank and by the thirteenth century those of trade and profession' (1987: 253). Yet, Butler notes the great continuity in the use of the sword, lance, shield and helmet to signify male military rank (1987: 250), and that of the key, buckle, purse and shears, which occur in Saxon cremations, as 'consonant with a female identity' (1987: 253). In this later medieval context, symbols appear which are indicative of religious status, such as the chalice, paten and book of the priest, the latter assumed to represent the Textus or Gospels. Others are representative of sex, an assumption proven for the emblem of the shears when it is accompanied by an inscription; in all cases these commemorate a woman.

But what if two gendered symbols are found together which conflict with this premise? For instance, while the book is generally found with the chalice or sword, clearly male symbols, it has been observed occasionally in association with the shears, a female symbol. There are six examples in the north-east and north Midlands of England: one in the Cathedral yard at Durham (Figure 4.3), one at Dearham (Cumbria), Bakewell (Derbys.), Hucknell (Notts.) (Butler 1987), Melmerby and Dovenby Hall (Cumbria) (Lees 1884). Butler originally suggested that, found with the shears, this (book-shaped) symbol must instead represent miniature wool bales or weights, thus commemorating a male cloth-worker. However, on the basis of assemblages of artefacts found together with female pagan Saxon cremations, he has since suggested that the symbol found with the shears may represent a 'workbox', or sewing kit, rather than a book. In other words, if the shears are proven by correlation with inscriptions to be a female emblem, it is inconsistent with our preconception of gender for the emblem which accompanies it to be a book. When found with a female symbol,

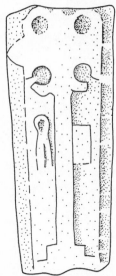

Figure 4.3 Medieval cross slab grave cover from the Cathedral yard at Durham, showing the shears (a female symbol), together with the book (a male clerical symbol). (After P.F. Ryder (1985) *The Medieval Cross Slab Grave Cover in County Durham.*)

a book is no longer a book, but a 'workbox'. But why should the book and shears together not symbolize some aspect of female religious status?

On a double slab at Chollerton (Northumb.) the book is the sole emblem accompanying the cross on the woman's side (Ryder 1985). The book overlies the cross shaft of the grave cover of a prioress from the site of the medieval nunnery of Ellerton, Swaledale (N. Yorks.), with the inscription *Petronile priorise* (Ryder 1985: 31), and accompanies the effigy of an abbess from Polesworth (Warwicks., *c.*1250), but is otherwise rare in female monastic contexts. The slab in the sanctuary floor at Melmerby (Cumbria), clearly depicts the shears, together with the symbols of the priest, the chalice and book, the latter shown with a distinctive book clasp (Figure 4.4). On no account can the Melmerby slab be dismissed as a workbox or sewing kit: here a woman was commemorated with clerical symbols. Could these slabs have represented some form of female religious status less orthodox than conventional nuns? Medieval records attest to the occasional deaconess or female assistant to the priest working in more remote areas. At Fairfield in the Romney Marshes (Kent), a *juvenculam*, or girl, was noted in 1294, when a representative of the Diocese of Canterbury was outraged by the presence of a young woman ministering at the altar (Woodruffe 1917: 161). Could these slabs commemorate deaconesses, or some category of chaste religious women, who, despite being biologically female, had attained a ritual status normally reserved for males? Medieval religion sometimes brought about syneisacticism, a situation in which men and women could live together in a single community and interact without reference to accepted sex roles. Such suspension of gender roles may have resulted in the perception of another,

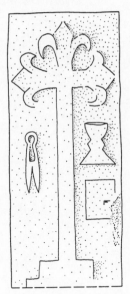

Figure 4.4 Medieval cross slab grave cover from the chancel of Melmerby parish church (Cumbria), showing the female symbol of the shears together with the male clerical symbols of the chalice and the book. (After an unpublished drawing by Peter Ryder.)

separate, gender, in this case a cultural category achieved by men and women who renounced their sexuality in pursuit of a virginal, religious status.

This ill-reputed house?

With few exceptions, archaeological approaches to medieval settlement and housing have been characterized by an empirical, descriptive tradition with little social interpretation. Without the presence of biologically sexed skeletons, it has been assumed that gender was not a factor in ordering space within houses. In relation to medieval and Tudor London, for example, John Schofield concluded that houses were not ordered 'explicitly or otherwise in this dimension' (Schofield 1994: 205), while it has been proposed that entire classes of medieval settlement, in particular the castle, were occupied only by men. Despite documentary and archaeological evidence to the contrary (for example: Pounds 1990: 86, 100, 197, 258), Tom McNeill observed that 'two species dominated castle life, men and horses' (McNeill 1992: 29).

Discussions of gender in relation to housing of all periods have displayed a striking similarity, suggesting in particular that women were associated with 'private', 'minor' or 'peripheral' areas, and men with 'public', 'major' or 'central' areas. A structuralist approach has been adopted which assumes that in all societies the symbolic and functional dimensions of gender are expressed through a system of signification that is composed of a series of binary oppositions. Artefacts, forms of decoration and space are considered to be organized

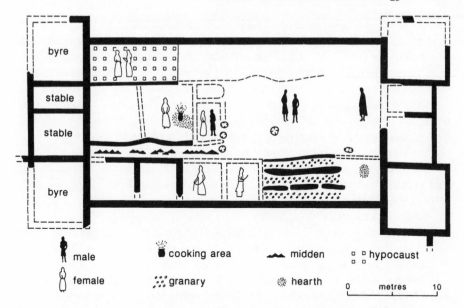

Figure 4.5 Interpretation of gender and space based on excavations at the Romano-British aisled hall at Warnborough (Hants.), suggesting that women were associated with areas of food preparation and the more peripheral, dark aisles. (After R. Hingley (1990) 'Domestic organization and gender relations in Iron Age and Romano-British households'.)

according to opposites such as male: female, public: private, cooked: raw, and so on. The structuralist model requires the use of cross-cultural laws and encourages the writing of historical narratives which emphasize continuity and inevitability. To take an example earlier than the period under review, in his chapter on gender in Iron Age and Romano-British households, Richard Hingley argued continuity with models proposed for Late Bronze Age settlement. Without any discussion of gender roles or evidence for a sexual division of labour, Hingley accepted that in Late Bronze Age and Early Iron Age settlements, 'women probably prepared the food and took it to the men for consumption – in other words there is a division of space within the compound according to gender' (Hingley 1990: 127). He went on to propose a structuralist model, in which male areas of houses and settlements were public, clean, light and associated with cooked food, and female areas were private, dirty, dark and associated with raw food (Hingley 1990: 133). Artefacts from the Romano-British aisled hall at Warnborough (Hants.), excavated in the 1920s, apparently confirmed his suggestion that women were associated with the aisles, the more peripheral areas (Figure 4.5), although Hingley provided no critical appraisal of the techniques or analysis used in the original excavation and report.

Hingley's interpretation assumed that static gender relations prevailed from the Late Bronze Age to the late Roman period, and his notion that the central area should be male and public was based purely on the positioning of the hearth. Central hearths and open halls were in use up until the mid-sixteenth century. Does this, therefore, suggest that gender was static from the Late Bronze Age until this time? In common with many structuralist models, Hingley's interpretation of gender and housing presented an essentialist view: that women, irrespective of their time or place, are linked with a private gender domain. In many cases women may indeed have been closely connected with the home, but studies such as Hingley's devalue the domestic domain by applying structuralist oppositions such as dirty and dark. By omitting to state explicitly the sources underpinning his interpretation, he implies that the female domain, and women's role in society, were secondary to the male and bound up exclusively with care of children and the home. The assumption that all social life is sharply divided between domestic and public limits our understanding of cultural variability and historical specificity.

In an innovative study, Matthew Johnson has explored the social meaning of traditional houses in later medieval and early modern Suffolk (*c.* 1400–1700). A structuralist approach to gender was adopted, with 'Man' defined as central, with 'everything beyond and outside Man's inner soul', namely servants, women and children, located as other, or 'Nature': elements to be tamed by Man (Johnson 1993: 134). The roles of the wife and female servants were suggested to be associated with the 'inner' and lower spaces of the house. Assymetrical relations of gender were said to have cut across those of social difference, so that both the mistress of the house and female servants moved 'within the "inside" domestic sphere' (Johnson 1993: 137). The transformation from open hall to closed house was linked with changing gender relations: 'the front/ back separation became more marked and with it the segregation between men's worlds and women's worlds' (1993: 138). Although Johnson acknowledged the possibility of alternative readings 'in terms of developing women's consciousness of their position and their "marking out" of areas of female control', his study privileged the male experience and perspective, situating woman as an essential category: the binary other to the essential category of Man.

In an interpretation of medieval settlement on Dartmoor (Devon), David Austin and Julian Thomas constructed a model of social relations and space for the long-houses of Okehampton Park (Austin and Thomas 1990). Nine houses were excavated which repeated a pattern in which the byre area was divided from the house by a cross-passage. The house was further divided between a 'public' area focused on the hearth, and a 'private' 'inner room'. They suggested that this spatial map represented hierarchical social relations in which the male head of the household maintained a private space at the upper end of the house, and held court over 'the children and the beasts' (1990: 59). The male head dominated the human space of the long-house and his private inner room. They noted from documents that occasionally the head of the household was female, but that this was rare. There was no further discussion of women, or gender relations, within the spatial map. They proceeded to suggest that the broader landscape was essentially male, with representation of the more diverse discourses of women and children only at church and market (1990: 75). Again, their model proposed sets of binary oppositions and static social relations.

In contrast, anthropological and historical evidence for the peasant household suggests a clear differentiation between male and female work areas, and a conceptualization of the house and hearth as female. Martine Segalen's anthropological study of nineteenth-century French peasantry suggested that in the traditional peasant home, the man was rarely in the house, but rather in the barns, cart-shed and byre, and when he was in the house, he was asleep. Certainly 'the communal room was not his kingdom' (Segalen 1983: 112). Instead this was a female common room, which was central, clean and public, for receiving visitors, rather than dirty, dark and private. A medieval spatial perspective is provided by the work of Barbara Hanawalt (1986). She has analysed accidental-death patterns in coroners' inquests and manorial court evidence. She argued that more women than men died in the house or toft (29.5% vs. 11.8%), perhaps confirming that women were more closely bound with the house. Men died in the fields, forests, mills, construction sites and marl pits, whereas women died around the village, at neighbours', gathering water from wells and doing laundry in ditches.

Other historians have demonstrated that medieval women enjoyed a high degree of mobility, both within the countryside and, in the case of young women entering servanthood, between the countryside and towns (Bennett 1987). Contrary to the perceptions of Austin and Thomas, the medieval countryside is unlikely to have been a stage exclusively for male discourse. In constrast to their model of social relations, the house seems to have been predominantly a female domain for much of the year. Gender domains in the medieval peasant household are likely to have been seasonal, with men in the house for greater periods during the winter months.

Conclusions: ambivalent bodies

In summary, gender has been considered in medieval archaeology only where sexual difference is visible. Where gender has been developed as a concept or structuring principle, for example in relation to housing, it has been reviewed according to binary oppositions which rely on universal categories and notions of male and female. Gender issues have been alluded to in discussions of economic structures, in particular referring to marriage patterns and the exchange of women. There has been little acknowledgement of either male or female agency, or of the construction of masculinity or femininity within medieval contexts. Tremendous potential remains to evaluate the place of gender in transformations surrounding the rise of urbanism, the conversion to Christianity, redefinitions of kinship, demographic shifts, political alliances and state formation; while critical considerations are urgently required of constructs such as the family and the household.

Perhaps the greatest challenge revolves around the interwoven issues of sex, gender and the body. Can we continue to assume that gender was always defined by the physical characteristics of biological sex? To what extent is gender ambiguous, defined as much by ritual or social role, or place within the lifecycle? Were different genders ascribed or achieved in some instances? Certainly the relationship of gender to the ageing process must be examined, and the possibility should be entertained that 'other genders' sometimes existed, perceived by their societies as neither conventionally male nor female. While genuine cases of institutionalized cross-sex roles may be rare, such as the *berdache*, some individuals may have attained a state that was beyond the usual definitions of male or female, such as the virginal man or woman of medieval Christianity. In moving beyond essentialist categories of male and female, medieval archaeology has the opportunity to rethink not just women or female agency, but also men and male agency. Beyond the gender-neutral lies the variability and ambivalence of masculinity and women, and femininity and men.

Note

1. Gender has been discussed in relation to medieval archaeology in Scandinavia (see *Medeltidsaakeologisk Tidskaift* 94, 1 (1994)), but to a far lesser extent than is the case for Scandinavian prehistory.

References

Arnold, C. (1980) 'Wealth and social structure: a matter of life and death' in P.A. Rahtz, T. Dickinson and L. Watts (eds) *Anglo-Saxon Cemeteries*. Oxford: British Archaeological Report 82, pp. 81–142.

Astill, G. and Grant, A. (eds) (1988) *The Countryside of Medieval England*. Oxford: Blackwell.

Austin, D. and Thomas, J. (1990) 'The "proper study" of medieval archaeology: a case study' in Austin, D. and Alcock, L. (eds) *From the Baltic to the Black Sea. Studies in Medieval Archaeology*. London: Unwin Hyman, pp. 43–78.

Bennett, J. (1987) *Women in the Medieval Countryside*. Oxford: Blackwell.

Biddick, K. (ed.) (1984) *Archaeological Approaches to Medieval Europe*. Kalamazoo: Medieval Institute Publications.

Biddick, K. (1993) 'Decolonizing the English Past: readings in medieval archaeology and history'. *Journal of British Studies* 32, 1, 1–23.

Brush, K. (1988) 'Gender and mortuary analysis in pagan Anglo-Saxon archaeology'. *Archaeological Review from Cambridge* 7, 1, 76–89.

Butler, J. (1990) *Gender Trouble: Feminism and the Subversion of Identity*. London: Routledge.

Butler, L. (1987) 'Symbols on medieval memorials'. *Archaeological Journal* 144, 246–55.

Carver, M.O.H. (ed.) (1992) *The Age of Sutton Hoo. The Seventh Century in Northwestern Europe*. Woodbridge: Boydell.

Champion, T. (1991) 'Theoretical archaeology in Britain' in I. Hodder, (ed.) *Archaeological Theory in Europe. The Last Three Decades*. London: Routledge, pp. 129–60.

Conkey, M.W. and Spector, J.D. (1984) 'Archaeology and the study of gender' in M.B. Schiffer (ed.) *Advances in Archaeological Method and Theory* 7. New York: Academic Press, pp. 1–38.

Evison, V.I. (1987) *Dover: Buckland Anglo-Saxon Cemetery*. London: HBMC Report 3.

Fell, C. (1984) *Women in Anglo-Saxon England*. Oxford: Blackwell.

Geake, H. (1992) 'Burial practice in the seventh and eighth century England' in

M. Carver (ed.) *The Age of Sutton Hoo. The Seventh Century in North-western Europe.* Woodbridge: Boydell, pp. 83–94.

Gero, J.M. and Conkey, M.W. (eds) (1991) *Engendering Archaeology: Women and Prehistory.* Oxford: Blackwell.

Gilchrist, R. (1994) *Gender and Material Culture. The Archaeology of Religious Women.* London: Routledge.

Halsall, G. (1992) 'Social change around AD 600: an Austrasian perspective' in M. Carver (ed.) *The Age of Sutton Hoo. The Seventh Century in North-western Europe.* Woodbridge: Boydell, pp. 265–78.

Hamlin, A. and Foley, C. (1983) 'A women's graveyard at Carrickmore, County Tyrone, and the separate burial of women'. *Ulster Journal of Archaeology* 46, 41–6.

Hanawalt, B. (1986) *The Ties that Bound. Peasant Families in Medieval England.* Oxford: Oxford University Press.

Härke, H. (1989) 'Knives in early Saxon burials: blade length and age at death'. *Medieval Archaeology* 33, 144–8.

Härke, H. (1990) 'Warrior Graves? The background of the Anglo-Saxon weapon burial rite'. *Past and Present* 126, 22–43.

Hingley, R. (1990) 'Domestic organization and gender relations in Iron Age and Romano-British Households' in R. Samson (ed.) *The Social Archaeology of Houses.* Edinburgh: University Press, pp.125–47.

Hinton, D.A. (1990) *Archaeology, Economy and Society. England from the Fifth to the Fifteenth Century.* London: Seaby.

Hirst, S.M. (1985) *An Anglo-Saxon Inhumation Cemetery at Sewerby, East Yorkshire.* York: York University Archaeological Publications 4.

Hodges, R. (1989) *The Anglo-Saxon Achievement. Archaeology and the Beginnings of English Society.* London: Duckworth.

Jesch, J. (1991) *Women in the Viking Age.* Woodbridge: Boydell.

Johnson, M. (1993) *Housing Culture. Traditional Architecture in an English Landscape.* London: UCL Press.

Kay, S. and Rubin, M. (eds) (1994) *Framing Medieval Bodies.* Manchester: Manchester University Press.

Lees, C. (ed.) (1994) *Medieval Masculinities. Regarding Men in the Middle Ages.* Minneapolis: University of Minnesota Press.

Lees, T. (1884) 'An attempt to discover the meaning of the shears combined with clerical symbols on incised grave-slabs at Dearham and Melmerby'. *Archaeological Journal* 41, 297–9.

Levi-Strauss, C. (1969) *The Elementary Structures of Kinship.* Boston, MA: Beacon Press.

McNeill, T. (1992) *Castles.* London: English Heritage/ Batsford.

Moore, H. (1994) *A Passion for Difference.* Cambridge: Polity Press.

Mytum, H.C. (1992) *The Archaeology of Early Christian Ireland.* London: Routledge.

O' Sullivan, J. (1994) 'Excavation of an early church and a women's cemetery at St. Ronan's medieval parish church, Iona'. *Proceedings of the Society of Antiquaries of Scotland* 124, 327–65.

Pader, E.J. (1982) *Symbolism, Social Relations and the Interpretation of Mortuary Remains.* Oxford: British Archaeological Report Int. Ser. 130.

Partner, N. (ed.) (1993) *Studying Medieval Women.* Cambridge, MA: The Medieval Academy of America.

Pouchelle, C. (1990) *The Body and Surgery in the Middle Ages.* Cambridge: Polity Press.

Pounds, N.J.G. (1990) *The Medieval Castle in England and Wales: a Social and Political History*. Cambridge: Cambridge University Press.

Power, E. (1975) (published posthumously, M.M. Postan ed.) *Medieval Women*. Cambridge: Cambridge University Press.

Randsborg, K. (1984) 'Women in Prehistory: the Danish example'. *Acta Archaeologia* 55, 143.

Randsborg, K. (1991) *The First Millennium* AD *in Europe and the Mediterranean. An Archaeological Essay*. Cambridge: Cambridge University Press.

Ryder, P.F. (1985) *The Medieval Cross Slab Grave Cover in County Durham*. Architectural and Archaeological Society of Durham and Northumberland Research Report 1.

Sawyer, B. and Sawyer, P. (1993) *Medieval Scandinavia. From Conversion to Reformation. circa 800–1500*. Minneapolis: University of Minnesota Press.

Schofield, J. (1994) 'Social perceptions of space in medieval and Tudor London houses' in M. Locock (ed.) *Meaningful Architecture: Social Interpretations of Buildings*. Aldershot: Avebury, pp.188–206.

Segalen, M. (1983) *Love and Power in the Peasant Family. Rural France in the Nineteenth Century*. Oxford: Blackwell.

Seifert, D.J. (ed.) (1991) 'Gender in Historical Archaeology'. *Historical Archaeology* 25.4.

Shephard, J. (1979) 'The social identity of the individual in isolated barrows and barrow cemeteries in Anglo-Saxon England' in B.C. Burnham and J. Kingsbury (eds), *Space, Hierarchy and Society*. Oxford: British Archaeological Report Int. Ser. 59, pp.47–79.

Stalsberg, A. (1991) 'Women as actors in north European Viking Age trade' in R. Samson (ed.) *Social Approaches to Viking Studies*. Glasgow: Cruithne Press, pp.75–83.

Steane, J. (1985) *The Archaeology of Medieval England and Wales*. London: Croom Helm.

Wall, D.D. (1994) *The Archaeology of Gender. Separating the Spheres in Urban America*. London: Plenum Press.

Whelan, M.K. (1991) 'Gender and historical archaeology: Eastern Dakota patterns in the 19th century' *Historical Archaeology* 25.4, 17–32.

Whitehead, H. (1981) 'The bars and the burden strap: a new look at institutionalized homosexuality in native North America' in S. Ortner and H. Whitehead (eds) *Sexual Meanings: the Cultural Construction of Gender and Sexuality*. Cambridge: Cambridge University Press, pp.80–115.

Woodruffe, C.E. (1917) 'Some early visitation rolls preserved at Canterbury'. *Archaeological Cantiana* 32, 143–80.

Wylie, A. (1991) 'Gender theory and the archaeological record. Why is there no archaeology of gender?' in J.M. Gero and M.W. Conkey (eds) *Engendering Archaeology: Women and Prehistory*. Oxford: Blackwell, pp.31–54.

5 Hearth and home: the timing of maintenance activities

MARINA PICAZO

Introduction

The ability of social groups to perpetuate themselves through time depends on biological reproduction as well as a series of activities and processes which collectively facilitate the persistence and survival of society. Since these activities are often summarily consigned to the realms of the 'domestic', it is argued here that there is consequently a need for an alternative approach; one in which the role of so called 'mundane' activities, essential to the well being and maintenance of the population, can be discussed. In what follows, therefore, I shall propose a more apposite category within which to address questions related to the day to day, routine, processes of food preparation, child care and socialization: for these we shall use the term *maintenance activities*.[1]

This term encompasses a set of practices concerning the sustenance and welfare of the individual members of the social group, as well as those tasks involved in generational replacement. Maintenance activities, thus, incorporate the sphere of the reproduction of individuals and they are related to the technological level as well as the specific values and norms operating within a particular society. They can be classed as habits of work whose benefits are shared by a group or community of actors although they can be – and frequently are – undertaken only by a section of the group.

From an archaeological perspective, the proposal for maintenance activities as an important category of social activities, underlines the need to draw attention to a field of human work and activity that normally is relegated either to the status of epiphenomena, or interpreted in a relatively marginal sense. Paradoxically, while the empirical evidence for these kinds of activities constitutes the most abundant part of any archaeological register, its importance as reflected in archaeological site reports and other publications, suggests that they are negligible and/or invisible.

Logically, we might assume that some of the most prominent maintenance activities were centred around the hearth, which for most societies until recent times, acted as an important material and symbolic focus in the life of the group. Moreover, the hearth as artefact, is often associated with specific food-related archaeological remains. These are the product of activities and practices that include the tasks of food preparation, distribution and consumption, refuse deposition, and food storage, as well as the tasks related to care and sustenance of the members of the group.

This latter set of activities not only involves the normal operations associated with childcare, but also concerns the care and welfare of those individuals unable (temporarily or permanently) to look after themselves by reason of illness, injury, and/or old age. An important aspect of maintenance activities are those tasks which involve the health, welfare and nutrition of the group, such as healing, hygiene, shelter, etc. An especially important aspect are the processes which are implicated in the socialization of children as future full members of the group. Maintenance activities, therefore, can be said to imply not only the creation or 'production' of social persons, but their constant re-creation by a continuous and interactive process of sustenance and socialization (Jónasdóttir 1993: 311).

In a sense, maintenance activities are generally consistent with the conventional definition of domestic labour in modern societies. But, as has been frequently pointed out (e.g. Tringham 1989), the term 'domestic work' is, of course, far from being neutral and has tended to be associated with the acceptance of a specific model of 'household' and kin group. In addition, this model assumes that maintenance activities can be identified with a particular social status, i.e., one which in contemporary societies has generally been regarded as being of lesser social importance.

There is clearly no necessary correlation linking the tasks of sustenance and care of individuals with any specific form of kinship organization (e.g. nuclear family structure). Moreover, it is doubtful whether maintenance activities can be identified with a particular sex, even though in most historical societies this kind of labour is generally the preserve of women and is seen in relation to the specific female context of biological reproduction. Doubtless, in different times and places, some of the tasks that we call maintenance activities were (and are still) done by men and/or women of different ages. However, perhaps the most plausible argument that can be made is, in most historical societies, women have normally been in charge of the various tasks related to the care and nurturing of the members of the group.

Work, time and maintenance activities

Until recently, most research in the social sciences relating to work – including much of Marxist anthropology – has been carried out from an explicitly male perspective; consequently, the role of production has been highlighted and that of reproduction neglected. On the other hand, since the 1970s, in the study of gender relations it has became clear that 'domestic work' is of decisive importance for the continuation of societal reproduction. However, existing research approaches have mostly focused on contemporary societies governed by market economics. For this reason the debate has frequently been centred on the question of the reproduction of the labour force, extending the notion to cover all activities that are implicated in the social reproduction of individuals (Daune-Richard 1988). In addition, it has been generally assumed that such 'invisible' labour is predominantly performed by women and that this domain of activities is articulated in a relatively autonomous way with respect to other spheres of production. In fact, since there is no *a priori* connection between the spheres of production and reproduction, but rather a series of connections which need to be analysed historically, it has been proposed that the structures of production and social reproduction must be seen as relatively independent and mutually interacting (Humphries and Rubery 1984).

Significantly, most of these studies question the different ways in which social theories conceptualize work. And for this reason, they attempt to reconceptualize the questions relating to the sexual division of labour between women and men. In relation to this idea, it is useful to consider the proposal of Hannah Arendt (1974) which expresses a different use of the terms *work* and *labour*; this is based on the fact that most modern European languages have maintained these two words of diverse etymology, but with similar meaning. Although in most languages they are used in some ways as synonyms, she has pointed out that the idea of 'labour' was originally related with the notion of effort; i.e. the difficulties associated with certain human activities (to be in labour, after much labour, etc.). Labour implies tasks that leave no residue (they have no product) and their effort or results lose their substance as quickly as they are produced. The substantive idea of 'labour' never designates the final product – though we might quote as an exception, the fact that in Spanish 'la labor' means needlework made by girls. Instead, Hannah Arendt emphasized that the notion of 'work' is always related with manual activities, including all the objects and products that are used and have *value*. Although she does not establish a relation between the two concepts, and the sexual division of labour, rather she emphasizes that the life of individuals depends on those labour activities that form the necessary requirements for the maintenance of life. We shall argue here, that this is a useful definition for most of the tasks related to the present concept of maintenance activities.

Another commonly used method to differentiate and establish a hierarchy of productive tasks, comes from the field of economics and is conventionally used in social science research. This involves the quantification of labour in terms of 'clock' time. The distribution of work time, is of course the corner stone of modern western society and is a product of the Industrial Revolution, the beginning of waged work and the confinement of workers in specific demarcated spaces (factories). All these factors facilitated an accurate control of the work time of individuals. In addition, the ordering of production time was fixed by gender criteria which reinforced the clear separation between work which was located in the factory and work undertaken by women as non-waged labour in domestic contexts. Control of time became characteristic, not just of capital enterprises but of most social activities in general: bureaucracy, schools, barracks, etc. 'Work' became identified with paid labour, sold on the labour market and thus all other forms of activity that were not mediated by this economic system, lost both value and recognition. This distinction is critical to any understanding of social and economic phenomena.

Moreover, it is important to stress that paid work and its time measurement have influenced the construction of the categories used in the historical analysis of different forms of organization of production – and, of course, reproduction – in past societies. In this context, the time spent on the countless small tasks by women in the home was not considered to be significant with respect to social activities, present or past. The work related to the maintenance and care of individuals is (and has always been), day-to-day activities with a routinized character, performed habitually in a continuous way, mostly without an evident material outcome (product) or with a product that is quickly consumed. What needs to be stressed in such a discussion is that the temporal rhythms which are resident in maintenance activities are different from the temporalities operating in other contexts (*domains*) of social life.

Time/times of history

Historical periodizations represent a selected cutting of the chronological *continuum*. For historians and archaeologists, the notion of historical periods is a crucial element in explanation and is generally given an 'objective' character. In fact, each historical work builds the temporal dimension of the past as an object and, using subjective criteria, selects an *absolute* time-scale from a vast array of possible temporalities. Any periodization, of course, implies by definition a form of interpretation, or explanation of past events. For example, the concept of a 'Dark Age' is frequently applied to those periods in the evolution of a society when central authority is lacking. Thus, our reading of Egyptian history is based on a chronological scheme in which the phases of so-called high points of civilization are marked by the absolute power of Pharaohs. By comparison, the intermediate periods – when the monarchical authority is weak – are represented as periods of cultural and social regression. The implication here is that a crucial aspect of a well-ordered society is the existence of hierarchical organization. Such a perjorative notion is also a central tenet of most models which describe the situation in Roman provinces after the exit of the Romans as a cultural reversal accompanied by the onset of a 'Dark Age'.

One of the important contributions of women's history, is that the accepted schemes of periodization have been called into question and generally found wanting. Events that have been considered to have had a significant effect on the development of societies, may in fact have affected women *adversely*. In this context we might cite Joan Kelly's (1977) comment on the question as to whether *women* had a renaissance in fifteenth-century Europe. Similar examples can be easily found from antiquity; for example, we might highlight the case of the Greek *polis* whose emergence as well as representing the birth of statehood in the classical world, also represented an increasing identification with a specifically male association that excluded women and slaves (Vidal-Naquet 1983: 242–3). This exclusion, which had been increasing from the seventh century BC, and in the case of the city of Athens, from the fifth century involved the actual seclusion of women within the house. Therefore, it needs to be remembered that the institution of democracy was founded on an exclusively male-centred network of socio-political relations.

These examples and many others which could be cited, do not imply that 'female' events are inevitably contradictory or opposed to 'male' events; clearly, all changes in the economic, social and political history of societies have of necessity, involved women also. The real problem lies in the different stages involved in the building of historical chronologies. Firstly, the selection of events, secondly, the ordering of these into coherent sets, and finally the act of cutting the series into discrete periods. In all these processes the historian or archaeologist imposes criteria of selection from a perspective that is generally masculine and hence, neglects or relegates the experiences of women. This must not be seen to imply that the solution lies simply in devising a complete alternative, i.e. a specifically 'female' chronological sequence. Nevertheless, what we are arguing is that historians and archaeologists must be more aware of the criteria, coherence and hierarchy of their chronological constructions. Moreover, conventionally historical research has been mainly the preserve of male researchers or conducted from a specifically masculine viewpoint. This has meant that the temporalities which define social activities and practices, have been ordered to conform to conventional hierarchical criteria. Those 'less relevant' practices such as routinized maintenance activities have been relegated to a marginal status. As with all classificatory systems, periodizations depend upon the questions being asked, and it must be emphasized that different *domains* of social activities are defined by their own intrinsic times or time scales. Therefore, it is clear that we must use differentiated analytical methods which will allow a richer explanation of temporalities.

In addition, recent feminist research has strongly emphasized the sexual differences which characterize the experience of time and especially of life times.[2] It is proposed here that this different 'timing' affected women and men in the past too, and that our present reflection on temporalities must take account of the gendered experience of time.

Time/times in archaeology

One of the most obvious, and problematic aspects of archaeological research, is that it imposes modern concepts of time and space on the past. Normally, we cannot readily come to terms with the complexities resident in time and spatial processes of the particular societies we are researching. Archaeology has traditionally built its chronological schemes based on intensive discussions of reputed typological successions and their respective temporal and geographical correlations. These data are used as sources with which to construct the 'timing' of the past. These processes involved focus on the selection of what are regarded as potentially the most informative artefacts, their subsequent ordering, and finally, their classification within the temporal context of a specific historical narrative.

Clearly the authors of these narratives are involved in the imposition of their own opinions and intentions, and these sometimes do not conform to conventional scientific criteria. Given the predominantly male orientation of most of the archaeological disciplines until recently, this has meant, effectively, that the artefacts used to define the temporalities of prehistoric periods are frequently restricted to items used or made (real or supposed) by men. It is common, for example, that the periodization of prehistoric groups is based on the processes of change in artefacts from male funerary contexts. In fact, artefacts of female graves of the same group can often be seen to exhibit an entirely different pattern of development.

This is the case of the chronology of the Argaric Bronze Age of south-east Spain, where recent research (González Marcén 1992) has re-established the archaeological description of the defined five periods based on statistical analysis of radio-carbon dates. The evolution of the characteristic Argaric pottery, the metal artefacts and, above all, their associations have become the primary elements in confering social and cultural meaning to the Argaric cultural assemblage. It has been possible to recognize differences in the associations between the metal items found in rich male graves, mostly weapons, and the rich female funerary furnishings in which there is a clear preference for the pairing of knife with chisel, probably associated with domestic activities. That which seems evidence of an assymetric ritual based on gender probably related to other social norms and habits in the subsistence and symbolic spheres of social reproduction.

Traditionally, the conventional chronology of the Argaric Bronze Age had been established solely on the basis of evidence provided by male artefacts, in this case, the weapons found in graves. However, Paloma González Marcén has suggested the possibility of a different pattern of change in the funerary rituals during most of the second millennium BC. For her, the fact that the group of artefacts related with female Argaric burials show an important longer duration than the male associations, potentially can be seen as indication of a different measure of historical time. If the rate of change in the evolution of the archaeological objects associated with men was based on some kind of political-ideological transformation, it is entirely plausible that women, as a group, were not affected by it in the same way.

While this represents a simple example, the message is that if we generate periodizations based only on the evolution of the male artefacts associations, we may be neglecting other possible temporal schemes, where the points of rupture will be clearly different. This example shows the importance of generating a variety of equally feasible chronological frameworks for prehistoric groups, depending on the particular criteria used in the process of selection. It is to such multiple readings of temporal meanings that we must direct our attention if we are to enrich the understanding of the dynamics of past societies.

In addition from a temporal perspective, the general tendency, especially within functionalist archaeology, has been to identify time with the diachronic or dynamic representation of change. On the other hand, a synchronic image of a social system, i.e. viewed as a timeless snapshot, effectively under-represents social reproduction – or at least takes it for granted. Moreover, the assimilation of time and change produces a spurious equation linking the static with stability. A major consequence of such a position is that the activities related to the sustenance of the members of the group have almost no relevance – they represent a 'taken for granted' element that never, or very slowly, changes. In fact, in systemic, functionalist archaeology, these changes are normally related to the general transformations of the system. They only have value (and meaning) when they can be explained as part of large-scale cultural processes. In this scheme, maintenance activities, or more generally gender structures, are considered irrelevant in explanations of societal change (Wiley 1991).

Given the obvious problems underlined by the previous discussion, it is clear that archaeology needs to generate a new consideration of social activities that emphasizes the role of multiple temporal dimensions in the structuring of social space.

Some final reflections

I have tried to present the idea that the temporal rhythms implicated in distinct social activities are very different and must be systematically identified before any interpretive frameworks are built. It has been pointed out (Hall 1983) that in most societies we can see two fundamental concepts of temporality; a unidirectional, lineal and cumulative time, and a dispersed time without an apparent productive objective. The first is regarded in contemporary society as 'productive time' and it is related to the concept of Newton's physics time, defined as an absolute, unidirectional measure of duration, motion and sequence (Adam 1994: 50–5). This has been the concept of time used by most historians to explain historical change (chronologies and periodizations). As already stated, it is this which, is erroneously applied to the analysis of most work processes in prehistoric and historic societies. On the other hand, cyclic and discontinous time, not cumulative, can be related to most of the tasks defined as maintenance activities. This kind of time has not usually been considered a social time and, for that reason, is ahistorical.

In this latter respect, it has been suggested that in most traditional cultures, ancient or modern, the temporalities of social activities have been expressed predominantly in cyclical terms; this is on account of the repetitive and routinization of most of the tasks related to social reproduction. Daily, weekly and annual periods of time maintain cyclical aspects in the organization of social activities (Giddens 1979: 201, 205). It has been proposed too, that the perception of time in these societies is rhythmical – a cadence in close connection with cosmic time, the lunar cycles, the seasons, the year, the day. Rhythmicity is fundamental to the natural world which includes human beings and is related to the processes involved in social life (Adam 1994: 70). There is a clear analogy between this kind of cyclic recurrence and the female body. For this reason, women (and their activities) present a more appropriate measure of human time. This idea, however, has no place in our contemporary society which is dominated by the notion of 'productive time' controlled by the clock.

Normally, conventional measures of time within processual archaeology – particularly with respect to social work – has centred on calculations of the amount of energy and labour expenditure involved in different activities. The idea of reducing human work to counts of kilocalories is a wholly inappropriate way in which to grasp the real dynamics involved in the sustenance and care of individuals; in such a scheme, time exists as a linear measure, when in fact, what we need to unravel are the complex temporalities at the root of maintenance activities, a *non-linear* concept of time (McGlade 1995). Only if we embrace such a flexible and discontinuous concept will we be able to encompass the myriad temporal rhythms and their attendant organizational levels which collectively are implicated in the production and reproduction of social life.

Another important aspect in coming to terms with the timing of maintenance activities is the question of periodization, i.e. the establishment of an understanding of differential rates of change. These changes are indicated in this case by the spatial transformations of the encounter places where the sustenance tasks are done. That is, the structural changes of the household (home), understood as the meeting point of the persons that undertake and/or receive the benefits of most of the maintenance activities. Generally, archaeological research has not been very interested in the analysis of households, but it is common to find in archaeological reports and monographs references to dwellings, storage and food preparation areas, based on the spatial patterns of artefacts. For example, in early Neolithic Thessalian villages, cooking facilities were usually located in open yards between houses, an arrangement which excavators suggested would have facilitated sharing of cooked food at least among neighbouring households or related kin. From the later fourth and third millennia BC onwards, there is an important change after which cooking structures were either placed indoors – in the 'kitchen' which formed a distinct part of many dwellings – or were set outdoors in a closed yard (Halstead 1989). The preparation and consumption of food was now done for a reduced number of persons in the different households. While this shift is dependent on other economic variables and is related to other production domains, it must be analysed in terms of the social and temporal consequences within which maintenance activities are embedded.

By way of summary, it can be suggested that the temporal concepts at the centre of archaeological discourse are inadequate descriptors of the multiple activities which collectively comprise those aspects of human work we define as maintenance activities. We must now initiate a research programme to address this issue, since it is of fundamental importance to a more accurate representation of the social dynamics which articulate society.

Notes

1. This category has been developed as part of a programme of research by a group of women archaeologists of the Universitat Autònoma de Barcelona: Eulalia Colomer, Silvia Gili, Paloma González Marcén, Sandra Montón, Marina Picazo, Cristina Rihuete, Mata Ruiz, Encarna Sanahuja y Montse Tenas.
2. Feminist proposal of a project of a law of times in the Italian Parliament: *Le Donne cambiano i tempi*.

References

Adam, B. (1994) *Time and Social Theory.* Cambridge: Polity Press.

Arendt, H. (1974) *La condición humana.* Barcelona: Paidos.

Daune-Richard, A.-M. (1988) 'Gender relations and female labor: a consideration of sociological categories' in J. Jenson *et al., Feminization of the Labour Force. Paradoxes and Promises.* Cambridge: Polity Press, pp. 260–75.

Giddens, A. (1979) *Central Problems in Social Theory: Action, Structure and Contradiction in Social Analysis.* London: Macmillan.

Gonzaléz Marcén, P. (1992) *Cronología del grupo argárico. Ensayo de fasificación radio-métrica a partir de la curva de calibración de alta precisión.* Tesi doctoral. Bellaterra: Barcelona, Universitat Autónoma de Barcelona, Microfitxes: ETD, SA.

Hall, E. (1983) *The Dance of Life.* New York: Anchor Press/Doubleday.

Halstead, P. (1989) 'The economy as a normal surplus: economic stability and social change among early farming communities of Thessaly, Greece' in P. Halstead and J. O'Shea (eds) *Bad Year Economics: Cultural Responses to Risk and Uncertainty.* Cambridge: Cambridge University Press, pp. 68–80.

Humphries, J. and Rubery, J. (1984) 'The reconstruction of the supply side of the labor market: the relative autonomy of the social reproduction'. *Cambridge Journal of Economics* 8, 56–69.

Jónasdóttir, A.G. (1993) *El poder del amor. ¿Le importa el sexo a la Democracia?* Universitat de Valéncia: Ed. Cátedra.

Kelly, J. (1977) 'Did women have a renaissance?' in R. Bridenthal and C. Koonz *Becoming Visible: Women in European History.* Boston, MA: Hough Mifflin.

McGlade, J. (1995) 'Archaeology and the ecodynamics of human-modified landscapes'. *Antiquity* 69, 262, 113–32.

Tringham, R.E. (1989) 'Households with faces: the challenge of gender in prehistoric architectural remains' in J. Gero and M. Conkey (eds) *Engendering Archaeology: Women and Prehistory.* Oxford: Blackwell, pp. 93–131.

Vidal-Naquet, P. (1983) *Formas de pensamiento y formas de sociedad en el mundo griego. El Cazador Negro.* Barcelona: Ed. Península.

Wylie, A. (1991) 'Gender theory and the archaeological record: why is there no archaeology of gender?' in J. Gero and M. Conkey (eds) *Engendering Archaeology: Women and Prehistory.* Oxford: Blackwell, pp. 31–56.

6 At home in the Long Iron Age: a dialogue between households and individuals in cultural reproduction[1]

ALEX WOOLF

I have always felt uncomfortable when approaching the problem of engendering the past. While it has for a long time been clear that the vast majority of literature dealing with social organization and practice in both the past and the present has been androcentric in its basic assumptions, the mechanisms and strategies necessary to redress this bias have not been at all obvious. An easy first step has been to familiarize oneself with 'women's history', but women's history is not the same thing as an engendered past and the risk is of falling into the 'women and other minorities' trope, in which women are considered as non-standard members of society alongside categories such as priests, immigrants and soldiers. It was not until relatively recently, as I became increasingly interested in medieval and ancient slavery, that I began to feel that there might be ways in which gender could be approached.

The dichotomy between slavery and freedom is, in some respects, analogous to that between male and female. In both relationships there appears to be a rigid division between the two categories and yet any observation of social practice in specific historical contexts shows that the 'rules' of society are constantly subverted. Thus in a slave-owning patriarchal society such as Republican Rome, in which all power is formally invested in free adult males, the slave and the wife of a powerful man may yet wield more influence in both the private and public spheres than the poorer free men; a reality running contrary to the dominant perception of the structuring of society. Slavery, like gender, creates invisible people. Frequently ignored by both ancient and modern commentators or marginalized unconsciously in the analytical literature, vast numbers of people, often the majority of any given community, disappear from sight. The literature is full of illustrations or discussions of the typical Roman or the typical Ancient Briton or the typical Anglo-Saxon which show him (*sic*) as a free man. The typical adult in all these societies was almost certainly a female slave. This is not to say that female slaves formed the majority group in Iron Age societies but they were probably the largest of the four categories of adults: free women, free men, unfree women, unfree men.

What I should like to do here is to sketch an impressionistic outline of household relationships based on my reading of early medieval literature and draw out, on the one hand, the similarities I see in the conditions of wives and slaves and on the other the blurred distinction between slaves and free folk in day to day practice. I shall then go on to discuss briefly whether such a society can be identified in the archaeological record and what light, if any, the material evidence might shed upon it.

To understand 'Barbarian Society' it is important to recognize that the most important unit of social reproduction was the household and that all economic activity was aimed, ultimately, at maintaining and reproducing the household. The typical member of society whom we meet in the literature is the primary male in such a household. Since Ancient Europe seems to have been comprised primarily of agnatic viripatrilocal populations the identity of the household is frequently linked to the identity of the primary male, a truth borne out by even a cursory familiarity with toponymy. Barbarian societies practised mixed agri-culture in which stock raising and cereal production predominated. As well as the agrarian chores necessary to maintain this subsistence regime other tasks such as cloth-making, metalworking, potting and so forth took place. Although it is unlikely that many farms were totally self sufficient, the percentage of the primary produce expended on goods bought in from outside was minimal. While excess land might have been rented out it is unlikely that many, if any, households subsisted upon the revenue from rents alone. It is this characteristic which principally distinguishes 'Barbarian Society' from the civilized societies of the Mediterranean, and from the feudal societies of the central and later Middle Ages.

Nineteenth-century visions of primitive democracy at work in Barbarian Society, including Marx's 'Germanic Mode of Production' (Hill 1990), were at fault in their patriarchal assumptions. Identifying the barbarian household with the householder (as we can conveniently label the primary male), the bourgeois Victorian proto-historians created an image of egalitarianism which subsequent generations of scholars have rejected. At its core, however, there was a level of accuracy in the nineteenth-century model. While it is clearly unacceptable to characterize a whole society with reference to the one member of each household alone, there was some truth in the notion that all the individuals within this category shared similar values and aspirations. The actual status of individual householders, relative to one another, would vary according to the size of their land holdings and their efficiency as social strategists and this in turn would be reflected in the size of their households.

Within each household we can infer from what little direct evidence we have, and also from ethnographic and historical analogs, that the division of labour was organized along lines of gender and age. Certain chores were regarded as lying within the female sphere and others within the male and within these two divisions tasks were divided once again as being suitable for the mature and the immature. Thus, for example, ploughing was a male preserve, the plough being guided by an adult while the oxen were led by a boy (Swanton 1975: 108).

The size of the household would vary according to the amount of land available but given the nature of the division of labour certain ratios of gender and age should remain broadly constant. 'Family planning', then, may well have been one of the householder's primary concerns. The poorest of households would not have been able to maintain such a rigid division of labour and their already tenuous position in society at large may well have been worsened through stigma associated with cross-labouring. Clearly even among better-off households the need to maintain a constant age and gender ratio, despite the ageing and mortality of its members, must have called for active measures to be taken.

In the British Isles in the early Middle Ages the optimum ages recommended for first marriage were the mid-twenties for a man and the mid-teens for a woman. In actuality many men may not have married until later as, unless well connected, they will have had to wait until their father died or retired before they could enter into land-holding and house-holding themselves (Charles-Edwards 1993: 175–81). Clearly at this age the couple are in their prime and would be able to supply many of the labour needs of the household themselves but it will be some time before their own children will be able to help them. A number of strategies were available to make up this labour shortfall; slavery, concubinage, fosterage and hired labour. A word should be said first about hired labour. Concepts of wages were unknown in barbarian societies, which were largely without money or with only a partially monetarized economy. In early medieval Europe labourers of either sex were taken on at certain regular dates in the year and undertook to join the household for a specific period of time, usually a full year. During that time they were not paid but lived with the household as one of the family. At the time that their term of service expired they might receive a gift from the householder the value of which would reflect his assessment of the individual concerned (Miller 1990: 120–2). Fosterlings were in much the same situation except that as minors the contract would be settled between the fosterer and the natural parents, again with an exchange of gifts, and the period of fosterage was usually several years (Charles-Edwards 1993: 78–82, 311–12; Miller 1990: 122–4).

Concubinage and slavery were somewhat different. Fosterlings and hirelings were frequently kinsfolk or the offspring of near neighbours and their residence in the household was generally of a relatively short duration. For them it was a transitional period between leaving the parental home and setting up house on their own. Wives and slaves, at least in theory, were permanent additions to the household, and they were rarely, if ever, close kin. Polygyny of one sort or another was fairly common in Barbarian Europe, unfortunately our assumptions about it have been coloured by modern perceptions of the seraglio, or of Koranic insistence of the equality of wives, just as our images of slavery have been unduly informed by our familiarity with the *latifundia* of the ante-bellum South. In early Irish law it is quite clear that there were different grades of wife and that any householder would have a primary wife who was lady of the house, and such distinctions were probably to be found elsewhere (Kelly 1988: 70). Indeed, were we to attempt to create objective distinctions between certain forms of polygyny, concubinage and the simple abuse of female slaves and hirelings we should probably fail, but this is not to say that in any specific social setting it would be unclear when such lines had been crossed.

Slaves in Barbarian Society were almost invariably foreigners. This is one of the fundamental features of the slave trade which has often eluded those who attempt economic reconstruction, who have sought a gradient of exchange and tried to distinguish slave producing from slave consuming regions. As the early plantation owners in America discovered, natives make poor slaves. They are familiar with the region and with the ecosystem, they have friends and kin within reach and they speak the language and know the customs of the land. Wherever enslavement originally takes place, the slave will be most pliable where she or he is an alien. The Latin word *servus*, a slave, derives from the verb *servare* meaning to 'save' or 'protect' and this etymology is not merely euphemistic. Household slavery of the sort we are interested in here (for the idea of vast *laifundia* with their separate slave quarters is alien to Barbarian Society) operated through a social contract between the householder and the slave. The new slave had no kin or friends in the district and would probably have had difficulty with the local language. As such she, or he, was an outlaw with no one to stand surety for her, and was also most probably very young and without much experience of the world. Her, or his, position in the household was much like that of the fosterling and hireling. She, or he, received free board and lodging in return for fulfilling the chores allocated by the master. Without wishing to present slave owning as a philanthropic activity, it should be clear that once the slave had arrived in her new home the household offered more security to her than any of the other available options.

The proposition which I would like to present now is that, in Barbarian Society, marriage and slavery were conditions analogous to childhood. In these, mixed agrarian, rural communities the household was the basic unit of social reproduction. Successful households maintained and reproduced themselves, sometimes several-fold. They did this by recruiting new members to fulfil essential social and economic roles. We have reviewed briefly a number of the ways such recruitment can take place but have so far ignored that method of recruitment which was regarded as most normal by ancient writers; biological reproduction. The Barbarian world was a high mortality/high fertility society with an easy come, easy go attitude to babies. Philippe Ariès (1965) has argued that children were not loved before the seventeenth century and, while this extreme view is probably not tenable (Arnold 1980), it is acceptable to assume that couples were resigned to the fact that many of their children would not survive infancy. As the child grew and thrived it would earn for itself a place in the affections of those who cared for it. While a death in the first year of life might be regarded as a regrettable but unavoidable turn of events, a death in the fifth year, when the 'creature' had had time to develop a distinct personality, and become a person, would have been a tragedy.

I would like to float the proposal that in the household, which represented a microcosm of the universe to its inhabitants, wives and slaves, entering from outside the community of the kin, underwent a similar process to children. Entering the community without a social identity and unfamiliar with the rules of the house, their happiness and personal security were at a very low premium. As the years dragged by, those who survived would gradually build a society around themselves in which they had particular friends among their cohabitees and neighbours and an increasing wealth of shared experiences with all those around them. The majority of the households in northern Europe in the period from 1000 BC to AD 1000 lived in one or two room buildings and excessive familiarity with individuals of all classifications would have been unavoidable. The biological children of the primary male would also play a major role in socializing their carers since wives and slaves would have had a large role in their upbringing and education. As their wards achieved maturity, and attained more significant roles within the household and the community at large, the status of the carers is also likely to have been enhanced, a state of affairs that can be visibly observed whenever the literature is available; the matriarch and the aged nurse are stock figures the world over. Nor need such characters be so advanced in age. When her eldest daughter married the mother might still be in her early thirties, and the child minder a few years younger.

The image of a society I have conjured here is based largely on a variety of diverse documentary and literary evidence ranging from Anglo-Saxon, Welsh and Irish law codes to Icelandic sagas and Tacitus' *Germania*. Archaeology has so far contributed little to the construct save the physical description of the house itself, but this is not negligible. Despite the differences of ascribed status, all the kinds of people we have considered were living in very close proximity, eating sleeping and working together. The age constraints on labour division will have entailed the free man carrying out tasks at one point in the house's history which a slave may have performed at another and similarly mistress and maid will have taken their turns at the butter churn. One of the failings of our politically correct society has been to idealistically place love and abuse at opposite ends of some kind of behavioural spectrum when an understanding of the world based on observation might suggest something quite different. A level of identification of interest between members of such a closely integrated community, whatever their ascribed status, must have been unavoidable.

But all of this is a fantasy. Some rather dubious and far from unequivocal medieval documents have been used to construct a generalized vision of Barbarian Society, a Long Iron Age. Where is the beef? We were asked to look at invisible people, so is it any surprise that there is no evidence for their existence? The concept of invisibility in fiction and film is fatally flawed. It is easy to imagine how one could invent something that could not be seen and that could be used to make a garment to cover the entire human body. The visual image is merely the result of light being reflected from the surfaces in the field of vision onto the retina of the observer, if we could create a surface that was completely non-reflecting then we would not be able to see it. The flaw however, which is always ignored in fiction and film, is that however invisible a person or object might be it would not create light conditions that would allow us to see through them. This is how black holes were identified by astrophysicists, they cannot be seen but stars and other heavenly bodies disappear when they pass behind them. In this fashion we should be able to locate invisible people in the past by identifying the negative evidence for their existence.

What we are looking for is evidence for a period of greater economic independence of individual households, and for distinctions of status existing within the household but being disarticulated from labour specialization. The large one-roomed Iron Age house standing alone, or with only one or two other similar structures within a demarcated enclosure, is the central feature of this social formation. The lack of internal divisions within the house may well point to the integrated nature of the community within. Other features which may mark the emergence of this kind of society in the last couple of centuries of the Bronze Age are the relative decline in monumentality and the increased investment in weaponry and armour. Both these phenomena may be linked to a relative rise in slavery. In societies in which slavery is less important and households are largely made up solely of the biological family of the householder there is, necessarily, a greater dependence upon the co-operative labour of other households. At the end of our period this can be identified in the appearance of nucleated villages at precisely the period when we know that slavery is becoming less common. Although the day to day workings of labour organization in the Neolithic and the early to mid-Bronze Age are unknown, current trends in interpreting the awesome monumentaltiy of these periods stress the rôle monument construction played in reinforcing communal relations over a relatively wide area (Parker-Pearson 1993). The increase in weaponry in the archaeological record of the Long Iron Age might also be explained with reference to slavery. We need not interpret the increased incidence of arms in the record as necessarily indicating an increased incidence of violence for what we are seeing are the results of structured deposition. What has happened is that weapons have become important signifyers and this must indicate that there is a status division between the man with weapons and the man without.

From another perspective we have a period of relatively stable population density in the Long Iron Age (the transitory aberration of the Roman intervention in some areas excepted) when compared to the population explosions of the Neolithic and Feudal Ages. This may be linked to the micro-demography which we have been examining. Our Barbarian households are, by and large, quite substantial establishments in which the reproductive biological family of the householders are in the minority. In the nucleated villages of the Feudal era, and perhaps in the communities of the Neolithic and Early Bronze Age, most households are comprised almost entirely of the biological family of the householder. This means that in such societies a far higher proportion of the labour force is involved in biological reproduction.

A third perspective is that of unstructured deposition. In much of the north of Europe over the period I have designated the Long Iron Age there is a general paucity of finds. Recent work, such as that of J.D. Hill (e.g. 1990), has argued that much of what we do find from Iron Age occupation sites is the result of structured deposition; the deliberate laying down of materials in some specific and conscious ritual practice. Such theses argue that the apparent absence of material from some regions does not necessarily indicate relatively poor economic conditions but merely differing traditions of deposition. This leaves us with the altogether different question; why was there so little unstructured deposition (dumping) in the Iron Age and Early Medieval periods? Above I have argued that Barbarian Society is characterized by a very high degree of self-sufficiency as a result of labour concentration in individual households. Under such conditions it could be argued that not only production but also consumption were fully socialized and that, like wives and slaves, artefacts were also part of the family. If this were the case then non-utilitarian or less than fully efficient objects might be retained far longer than in a market oriented society. Their eventual deposition, like that of the human members of the community, might be more likely to be structured.[2]

So this contribution comes to an end. What has it added to the debate? Perhaps only one idea, and that not revolutionary. That the household is a kingdom of itself and that none can enter into it unless they be born again.

Notes

1. For the purposes of this chapter I shall adopt the concept of the Long Iron Age as short hand for the kind of societies that seem to have dominated northern Europe between about 1000 BC and AD 1000. This classification includes the last few generations of the Bronze Age and the Roman period away from the Mediterranean. I will also sometimes use the phrase 'Barbarian Society' with reference to the social formations covered in this definition.
2. I have been told that a similar theory has been published by a Hungarian archaeologist in German but have so far been unable to track this work down.

References

Ariès, P. (1965) *Centuries of Childhood*. New York: Jonathan Cape.
Arnold, K. (1980) *Kind und Gesellschaft im Mittelalter und Renaissance*. Paderborn and Munich: Schoningh and Martin Lurz.
Charles-Edwards, T.M. (1993) *Early Irish and Welsh Kinship*. Oxford: Oxford University Press.
Hill, J.D. (1990) 'Reconsidering Iron Age societies: Iron Age Wessex without "Celtic societies" or prestige goods economies', unpublished paper circulated in draft.
Kelly, F. (1988) *A Guide to Early Irish Law*. Dublin: Dublin Institute for Advanced Studies.
Miller, W.I. (1990) *Bloodtaking and Peacemaking: Feud Law and Society in Saga Iceland*. Chicago: University of Chicago.
Parker-Pearson, M. (1993) *Bronze Age Britain*. London: Batsford.
Swanton, M. (ed.) (1975) *Anglo Saxon Prose*. London: Dent.
Tacitus (ed. H. Mattingly, 1948) *On Britain and Germany*. Harmondsworth: Penguin.

Commentary: The gender screen

IAN HODDER

Several of the authors in this introductory section (e.g. Lesick in Chapter 3 and Gilchrist in Chapter 4), pay homage and tribute to the article by Conkey and Spector (1984). Indeed the notion that this article played a seminal and originary role in the growth of an archaeology of gender seems to have become part of the canonical history of gender archaeology. This view is held despite the fact that a lively debate on gender issues was well underway by that time in Norway (e.g. Dommasnes 1982). But as Olsen (1991) has cogently argued, Norwegian archaeology is out of the mainstream. Its language, among other things, make it invisible. A gender debate, seeking to make gender and childhood visible, serves further to confirm other groups as marginal.

However sensitive to gender issues, bias remains. As another example, Hurcombe (Chapter 1) discusses a scene of tomb building in a colour magazine. There might be expected to be more children than are depicted. There should be, she suggests, 183 children causing havoc somewhere outside the scene. In many non-Western societies, the concept of childhood and children has little meaning. Young people, sometimes very young, often work either inside or outside the home. The assumption that children cause havoc is specific to contemporary Western societies. A more contextual understanding of age is suggested by Woolf.

My aim here is not to point the finger of bias; not to be the self-appointed arbiter of political correctness. Rather, it is to point out that bias is an unavoidable and essential part of interpretation. We need a perspective through which to view the archaeological record. One of the problems surrounding gender archaeology is that it can give the impression of changing one bias (male sexist) for another (female centred). By moving from sexism (of one kind or another) to gender it is often argued that bias is removed.

Many writers on gender archaeology have tried to argue that both male and female should be included in theoretical and analytical approaches. But even the use of the term 'gender' would appear to involve defining or assuming some universal, essentialist category. The very notion of gender, even the question of whether 'it' can be discerned as a distinct category of relationship or identity or domain may have varied through time. Lesick emphasizes in his chapter that 'gender' must be problematized in radical ways. Gender categories are constructs. Boyd (Chapter 2) also argues that outside Western intellectual traditions gender is not a principle, a concept, a 'useful category of analysis'. This may be true, but it is necessary to go further. There is still a bias in stating in universal terms that gender is not always a useful category of analysis. The bias is of a constructivist or contextualist kind. At some historical moments the category 'gender' may have been well defined, and that definition might (for all we can presume) have been close to 'ours'. A fully anti-essentialist position would have to accept that gender may or may not be a useful category at different historical moments.

The same can be said for sex. Gilchrist and Lesick refer to Judith Butler and Foucauldian ideas that sex, as much as gender, is constructed. Gilchrist provides interesting examples of cases in the medieval archaeological record where juveniles might have had different gender identities to adults. Certainly we need to consider that there may have been more than one sex defined in the past. But few of the discussions in archaeology which recognize the need to reconsider sex as a fixed and neutral foundation for gender archaeology have explored the potential for a radical reappraisal of the 'engendering' process.

Perhaps because of the interpretivist background to most gender theory and research, criticism has stopped before it reaches the supposed bedrock of scientific biological analysis. There appears to have been little questioning of the 'engendering' processes when it comes to attributing sex to human skeletal remains. Yates (1993) has discussed the variable biological criteria that can be used to define sex, and the continuous nature of most variables thought to be relevant in distinguishing sex.

But if sex is indeed (at least sometimes) historically constructed, then there is an enormous potential for archaeologists to explore such issues. This is only possible once the absolute separation between biological science (the sexing of bones by morphological criteria) and socio-cultural interpretation (the study of gender relations, identities, ideologies) is broken down. At present the normal methodological procedure is that the human remains are sexed independently of the cultural evidence. Correlation between sexed bodies and artefact associations in graves is then sought. But such artefact associations could be used in a very different way – as part of the initial 'identification' of sex.

The particular historical construction of sex in any one community might be examined in the following way. Human bones could be ordered according to various biological criteria (e.g. size, ratios, dimensions which appear generally to correlate with sex). It is these separate variables (rather than any average or summary definition of male and female) which are then correlated with artefactual and contextual variation. Thus, certain biological variables might correlate more closely with artefactual patterning than others. This might indicate that, *in the specific historical group being studied*, sex was defined in a particular way, and that certain boundaries between points on the biological continua were marked by artefactual or contextual differences. Here 'culture' is being used to help define 'biological' sex.

It might also be shown, following such a method, that sex had different meaning at different social levels or in relation to different ages. For example, the definition of 'woman' or 'man' might occur at a different point on the biological continuum or in relation to different biological variables in high status and low status contexts. The potential is enormous. The category 'old' or 'young' might differ among high status men and women when compared with low status men and women. The categories of age and gender might be endlessly dissected in such ways, in some cases down to individual idiosyncracies and interpretations. Once we are freed from the assumption that biology is fixed and gender is constructed, the archaeological record can be used to explore the numerous subtle ways in which sex and gender are defined at specific historical moments.

We have tended to reify the concept of sex in the same way that we tend to reify gender. Rather than seeing the concepts as infinitely malleable and redefinable we have wanted to hang on to some certainty – whether that be some general definition of gender, or the supposed biological fixity of sex. But the gender debate, along with many others over recent decades throughout the social sciences, has pushed many towards a full realization of the constructed and contextual nature of human action. We tend to forget too easily that terms like gender are only provisional – they are initial attempts to grasp something through the fog of understanding that separates us from the past. They are provisional and temporary starting points. They allow us to know what we are talking about, but they act not only as a passport but as a screen. They need to be used and then, in any analysis, be redefined or even discarded.

In most objects of study in archaeology (as in any discipline), the terms we use can only withstand so much critical analysis. Whether it be power, settlement or agriculture, critical reflection tends to end in the total dissolution of the concept. Power ends up everywhere and in everything. The definition of 'settlement' dissolves into arbitrary decisions about types and duration of activities taking place in different types of place. The origins of agriculture or domestication quickly become lost in the continuities of different types of human-environment relationships. The specialist so often ends up despairingly saying 'it depends what you mean by ... '. Bloch (1994) has pointed nicely to the fact that even what we mean by 'meaning' is historically contingent, dependent on language and culture for example. Thus, the French and English words for 'meaning' do not precisely coincide, and still less do the English and Malagasy terms correspond. When we confidently talk about what the past 'means', we do so through a screen of words, biasses and assumptions.

The terms in the screen should be provisional starting points, always open to critical re-evaluation in relation to interaction with 'other' worlds, whether ethnographic, historical or archaeological. But so often, as with gender, the provisional terms become reified. Essentialism and reification involve the mistake of confusing the provisional starting point with what is beyond the screen when in fact it is only a constructed concept (in 'our' language) which helps us to begin to understand associations and constructs different from our own.

Picazo (Chapter 5) makes the point that time and periodization may have been experienced differently by men and women in the past. There is nothing we can assume or take for granted. This contextualism which I espouse is my own bias. Gender is another. These are the screens, the biasses, the languages, through which we look at the world and at the past. There is nothing essential about gender, or about a contextualized approach to gender. This group of chapters stimulate an important debate. But in the end the problem is to get beyond the screen of gender to look at the way in which identities, selves and bodies were constructed in the past (Meskell 1996).

References

Bloch, M. (1994) 'Questions not to ask of Malagasy carvings' in I. Hodder and M. Shanks *et al.* (eds) *Interpreting Archaeology*. London: Routledge.

Conkey, M. and Spector, J. (1984) 'Archaeology and the study of gender' in M. Schiffer (ed.) *Advances in Archaeological Method and Theory 7*. New York: Academic Press, pp.1–38.

Dommasnes, L. (1982) 'Late Iron Age in western Norway: female roles and ranks as deduced from the analysis of burial customs'. *Norwegian Archaeological Review* 15, 70–84.

Meskell, L. (1996) 'The somatisation of archaeology: discoveries, institutions, corporeality'. *Norwegian Archaeological Review* 29, 1–16.

Olsen, B. (1991) 'Metropolises and satellites in archaeology' in R. Preucel (ed.) *Processual and Postprocessual Archaeologies*. Southern Illinois University.

Yates, T. (1993) 'Frameworks for an archaeology of the body' in C. Tilley (ed.) *Interpretatve Archaeology*. London: Berg.

Part 2

Writing Gender

7 Skin scrapers and pottery makers? 'Invisible' women in prehistory

LYNNE BEVAN

> There were distinctive territories, marked by different styles of pottery and bronze axes which pre-figured the Iron Age tribal areas. Each of these may have been controlled by chiefly dynasties or equivalent kinds of autocratic authority. Alternatively, they may have been organized as relatively egalitarian tribal groups. The relative status of women is hard to gauge but they may have become increasingly tied to the settlement compound and the duties of preparing and serving food.
>
> (Parker-Pearson 1993: 134)

Thus ends *Bronze Age Britain* with women confined to hearth and home and obliged to perform various low-status 'duties', relegated to second place, a prehistoric postscript. Although 'different styles of pottery and bronze axes' are put forward as territorial indicators (Parker-Pearson 1993: 134) and the author has already suggested the presence of pottery 'specialists' (1993: 112), no attempt is made to link women with this craft. Women were capable of producing the food that went into the pots and serving it as part of their 'duties', but incapable of making and decorating the pots.

The relative status of women appears no higher in Bronze Age Italy. From the cemetery of Osteria dell'Osa (near Rome) women's roles 'were less numerous, and socially less important than male ones, although their funerary outfits are usually richer both in fine decorated pottery and personal ornaments . . . ' (Bietti-Sestieri 1994: 255). Female funerary outfits which included evidence of weaving, spinning and possible 'ritual' equipment attest to textile craft specialization and participation in some form of socially-recognized ritual. It is difficult, therefore, to find any support for the assumption that objects ascribed to females were inherently inferior to 'male' objects and that female roles were correspondingly limited and of lower status.

This chapter is an attempt to decode the meanings of certain objects, commonly associated with women and found in domestic and funerary contexts. Such elements of material culture will be re-contextualized within an overall cultural milieu, rather than simply within an economic and craft framework. We should, however, remember the lost components of material culture which tend to perish, except under exceptional circumstances. Such materials might include leather goods, basketry and textiles, all of which are frequently associated with the creative endeavour of females. A wide range of activities constitute the fabric of women's lives, and the relationship of material culture with its makers and users is seldom a simple or purely economic one. Symbolism is central to the experience of non-industrialized societies, and often integral to the relationship between men-women, home-wild, and inside-outside, Hodder's *domus* and *agrios* (1990). These relationships, the subject of detailed discussion in anthropological literature, should not necessarily be seen in opposition, a possibility overlooked in the simplistic male-hunting and female-gathering models frequently used in archaeological interpretation.

One reason suggested for the perceived female/hearth, male/hunting sexual division of labour is sedentism 'associated with increased female fertility and with higher birth and infant survival rates', resulting in larger social groups including numbers of pregnant women, nursing mothers and older people; 'those adults who did not go out on a stalking type hunt ... [who] must have assumed the responsibility for performing hearth-centred tasks and for overseeing the activities of "dependent" youngsters excluded from the hunt' (Leibowitz 1983: 138). Such 'hearth-centred tasks' would have included preparing and cooking animal and vegetable foods, the manufacture of equipment, including vessels in a number of perishable and non-perishable materials, and tools such as flint scrapers and awls used in the processing of skins and hides. The material culture associated with such activities, including ceramics (both vessels and other objects), often survives archaeologically.

Whatever the relative values of female/male and hearth/hunting in the multiplicity of archaeologically-known societies, women's early hearth-based, and later more general settlement-based, activities have always been presented in archaeological accounts as secondary to those of men. The latter have been regarded as operating outside the home in a larger, more dangerous, more important and a potentially heroic sphere. Almost patronisingly, revisionists have conceded certain 'safe' craft activities to women of the archaeological past in the mistaken belief that control of these implies no degree of social or economic power or status for women. Such views are often supported by ethnographic accounts of gender division, among which specific studies of women are rare and, in any case, have often been misunderstood. For example, Hayden concedes certain tasks involving low-investment stone tools to women, including 'the almost universal role of women in scraping and preparing hides in societies without specialists, in grinding foods and in processing fish for storage' (1992: 35). The common assumption that women cannot have been lithic specialists has recently been challenged by Gero (1991). Hayden, using a few isolated examples from recent native American Indian groups in which women processed the carcasses of animals hunted by men, goes on to conclude that 'in these societies, and I suspect in the rich reindeer based societies of the French Upper Palaeolithic, women's status was not particularly high, and the wealth that was generated supported hierarchal polygynous social structures' (Hayden 1992: 36). Thus, an ideological leap is made from a possible sexual division of labour to a judgement of relative social values. This judgement, based upon data collected from societies undergoing change as a result of the economic demands of white contact, cannot effectively be applied to prehistoric situations and well illustrates the practice of introducing women only to denigrate them.

What is the basis for such a practice? In the West, several contemporary factors contribute to the widely-accepted view of prehistoric women being dominated by men. Factors involved in this are the devaluation of crafts such as potting, embroidery or weaving to mere middle-class art centre hobbies; the view of housework and cooking as menial; and the break-down of the extended family, resulting in the peripherization of motherhood. Although perceived as natural and desirable, suffused by the media with a romantic worthy glow, child-rearing is often socially-isolating and rarely compatible with work outside the home.

While it is often true that menstruation taboos, procreation, and ensuing childcare responsibilities tend sometimes to restrict women's movements to a limited domestic area, our understanding of motherhood in non-western societies has recently been questioned. Criticism has been directed at the emphasis placed by anthropologists on the role of young mothers to the exclusion of all other female roles, as well as the application of western constructions of extended 'childhood' to such societies (Bolen 1992). Non-western mothers' childcare responsibility is often of shorter duration and in any case is often shared with other women. Post-partum sexual taboos, longer lactation periods, and high infant mortality rates limit family size in non-industrialized societies. A number of nineteenth and early twentieth century observers have contrasted high western birthrates, resulting in more than 10 children per family, to the birthrates of so-called 'primitive' peoples which were usually less than half that amount (Reed 1975).

Writing about female weavers among the Aztecs, Brumfiel has criticized the application of 'our own customary separations of "private" and "public", "homemaking" from "work", and "maintenance" from "production"' to the Aztec culture (Brumfiel 1991: 225–6). Numerous ethnographic studies attest to female potters and weavers. These crafts are often essentially home-based, combined with childcare and domestic 'duties' in the context of an extended family. Such skills can provide women with control of a means of production and thus some degree of financial independence. Additionally, in socio-cultural terms, such skills provide a means of forming 'group solidarity' and 'achieving social strategies through the silent discourse of their decorated pots and cala-bashes' (Braithwaite 1982; Hodder 1982). Within apparently male-dominated societies pottery production can, therefore, subvert social organization, and when highly-decorated Neolithic and Bronze Age pottery is considered, the implications are obvious.

If social information can be transmitted through the form and decoration of pottery vessels, the symbolic potential of ceramic models, often depicting human and animal forms in both prehistoric and ethnographically-known contexts, is greater. For this reason, a close examination of the form and usage of ceramic figurines among African societies of the recent past can prove in-structive. I am not proposing to take such figurines, perhaps too readily dis-missed as mere toys or 'teaching aids' by both Ehrenberg (1989) and Hodder (1990), out of their cultural contexts and to relate them directly to the European Neolithic and Bronze Ages. Yet the similarities between certain recurring images are undeniable. Additionally, the documented meanings of such figures can provide alternative explanations to the potentially anti-feminist fixation with goddesses which has dominated recent literature, implying nostalgia for a matriarchal golden age which may never have existed. Instead, women's ritual lives can be dynamic, exclusive, and central to the transmission of culture from one generation to the next, at the heart of society and not separate from daily life or activities.

Despite the secrecy inhibiting the study of clay images in African puberty rites, Hans Cory, a sociologist, assisted by local informants, investigated the underlying meanings of over 2000 such figurines used by four tribes living around Lake Tanganyika in the 1940s. Both male and female rites using similar figurines were recorded, the general message being one of social control, reinforcing traditional male-female roles and warning against innovation. Popular images referred to menstruation taboos, the duties of marriage, and the importance of rest in pregnancy. A recurring image was the clay phallus, common in artefact assemblages in prehistoric Europe where it has generally been interpreted as a fertility symbol. Cory noted that in this instance it represented the male neophytes who embarked upon the puberty rites as boys and left them as young men (Cory 1955).

In female rites among the Bemba, of the north-eastern plateau of Zambia, such images were intended to introduce young women to the concept of the penis, the behaviour of which would be explained by midwives and ritual specialists. These mature women produce a variety of clay images, often easily recognizable as human figures, domestic equipment such as miniature pots, and animals with specific meanings, for example the crocodile which warns against adultery. Such images were used as *aide memoires* in female nubility rituals – 'chisungu' – when girls are brought to the initiation hut hearth and 'shown the fire' at the time of their first menstruation. Certain images provide warnings, such as the ithyphallic figure, a jaunty young man back from the mines 'all penis and no domestic virtues', as Brain (1980: 238) has so succinctly described him, and the figure of an armless man, a worthless creature who stays in the house all day and will not work to support his family. Both kinds of men are, as in any culture, to be avoided. Other images are indicative of fertility, such as those of pregnant women, yet often the underlying message is one of warning, an example being the pregnant woman who risks bewitchment by gossiping too long at market. During the 'chisungu' rites the young women receive instruction in all aspects of sexuality and reproduction, to prepare them for their future life as sexual beings as well as mothers. Yet these secret women's rituals often involve punishments and endurance tests, rites left over from more dangerous times when young people of both sexes had to survive in the bush. The form and meaning of these clay images are believed to have been passed down from the ancestors, and they are not merely 'teaching aids' but vital to the transmission of cultural knowledge. Although men have political control among the Bemba, the society is matrilineal and Bemba women are known for their ferocity and strength.

While separate male and female roles and ritual lives are a common feature of many ethnographically-known societies, the interplay between the sexes is seldom simply based upon an unequal relationship of dominance and subservience. Even when feasting is an important manifestation of male social competition, as it is among the head-hunting Naga tribes of north-eastern India, females play a pivotal role in the preparation and organization of these feasts. Without his wife's 'co-operation in production, the man is unable to gain status. He is unable to amass the necessary rice, or indeed the cotton, which the wife tends and then fashions into the cloths which portray his (and her) high status as Feast-givers' (Jacobs 1990: 132). Whereas males are dominant in taking the heads of enemies, a form of killing that confers sacred fertility upon the head-taker and allows him the right to wear certain ornaments, females may acquire similar rights through their role in feast-giving which is at once practical and sacred. It is in this arena that 'male-female interdependence' is emphasized with the joint opportunity to 'share in the high ritual status acquired' (Jacobs 1990: 132). 'A nice illustration of this complementarity is seen, for instance, in the tug-of-war found in a number of communities during argicultural feasts. In the Ao Moatsu festival, after sowing, in addition to dancing, men and women form teams and pull a length of creeper; neither side "wins", but rather both sides give and take in turn' (Jacobs 1990: 132).

Nagas' sexual symbolism, expressed in both stone and wooden statuary, the latter in the form of female Y-shaped wooden poles, counterbalancing male stone 'phallic' posts and stones, is of particular relevance to this study. The potential archaeological implications are obvious. In considering the lost components of material culture, evidence of vital concepts will be lost as perishable materials such as the female Y-shaped wooden posts deteriorate, leaving only the resilient 'phallic' stones. And what of the feasts, the symbolic beer-brewing performed by the ornament-wearing, high-status women, the textiles, the agricultural production, even the symbolic tug-of-war? Archaeologically, none of these would be recognizable, but the weapons and the skulls, the work of warriors, would be more resilient, negating, as ever, 'female' status.

The Nagas demonstrate the difficulties involved in interpreting gender relations in economically simple but symbolically-complex societies of the present and recent past. Assumptions are made as to past relationships of dominance and subordination, based upon modern pre-conceptual baggage, from a small archaeologically-resilient portion of material culture.

Now let us briefly examine the links between women and material culture in funerary contexts. Ethnographic studies often focus upon funerary ritual and the embedded social meanings manifest in the actions of the participants. These actions, documented in examples of grave good deposition – the deliberate placing of certain items in burials – are rarely observed and usually viewed in a simplistic way. In fact, objects in non-western societies can be imbued with meaning as repositories of social information. The inclusion of specific items in female or male graves can be significant on a number of levels, the least important of which may relate to the deceased's involvement in a particular craft or domestic activity, but instead may represent underlying themes of sexual and social conflict or potential danger. One such example is found among the

Lugbara of north-western Uganda and north-eastern Zaïre, a farming people documented by Middleton in 1982. Among the Lugbara, death is the central rite of passage, with the accompanying rituals outnumbering those connected with birth and marriage. Death rituals are complex, elaborate and lengthy. In contrast, grave goods are deposited with the body in an almost casual way – a woman is accompanied by her beads, the firestones from her hearth and one of the stones she has used for grinding flour; a man by his quiver, his drinking-gourd and his stool. These represent his or her status while alive; there is no belief that they are to accompany the deceased on a journey to the world of the dead. These items reveal a certain amount of information about their owners – the grinding stones and firestones indicate the domestic and agricultural spheres in which the women operate and beads are personal adornments but may indicate marital or childbearing status. The quiver indicates the men's role as warriors/protectors and the drinking gourd and stool their socio-political role among other men. It is worth noting that in Bandkeramic graves of Neolithic Europe there are half a dozen or so categories of grave goods among which quern stones have been found exclusively in female graves (Whittle 1985).

In contrast to the correlation between women and the hearth, the Lugbara 'men are said to be "inside" as ... people of the home and women to be "outside" ... things of the bushland': women are ambiguous 'belonging both to the bushland and also to the home' (Middleton 1982). Devoid of social power derived from authority, which the men possess, the women's power – that of procreation – comes from divinity and is considered evil and dangerous to society unless controlled by men – the women's husbands and fathers. This most feared part of women's nature is believed to belong to the world outside the compound, the wild. The Lugbara believe that there is a parallel between sexuality and fire: both are dangerous but when tamed are at the centre of ordered social life. This concept echoes the aforementioned Bemba nubility rites in which young women about to embark upon their adult lives are 'shown the fire' where they are taught to conduct their sexual lives in a socially acceptable way. Perhaps this association with fire would also account for the inclusion of firestones in the Lugbara female graves, symbolizing the extinguishing of both forces in death. Although a rare example, Lugbara symbolism shows how women can be perceived as being both inside and outside, perhaps ideally functioning and securely contained within the home, Hodder's *domus* (1990), yet with part of their nature originating from the wild to which it might return at any time. Conversely, males with their shaft-hole axes and adzes, so prevalent in the burials of the Linear Pottery Culture of prehistoric Europe, for instance, may have operated within the wild and sought to tame it, but even then they may not have monopolized this dangerous sphere.

One of the most interesting contrasts apparent from this study is the few and largely dismissive representations of women's lives as opposed to the extensive writing on the social significance of their deaths. The study of material culture associated with mortuary literature allows women to be placed within a social and cultural construction of considerable complexity, in glaring contrast to their seemingly passive, simplistic and socially-dislocated role in craft and in the home. In this arena non-utilitarian stone and ceramic objects, including figurines, are associated with women, without any attempt being made, until recently, to understand the purposes of such items within a social context. Yet the activities of these 'handmaidens of the hearth' involving the skin scrapers and pottery makers of my title, can be seen from recent studies to be highly-skilled and powerful both on economic and symbolic levels, at the very heart of society and vital to its continuance and the transmission of culture.

Acknowledgement

With thanks to Iain Ferris for his comments on this chapter.

References

Bietti-Sestieri, A. M. (1994) 'Osteria dell'Osa'. *Current Archaeology* 139, 253–7.

Bolen, K. (1992) 'Prehistoric construction of mothering' in C. Claassen (ed.) *Exploring Gender through Archaeology*. Monographs in World Archaeology II. Madison WI: Prehistory Press, pp.49–62.

Brain, R. (1980) *Art and society in Africa*. London & New York: Longman.

Braithwaite, M. (1982) 'Pottery as silent ritual discourse' in I. Hodder (ed.) *Structural and Symbolic Archaeology*. Cambridge: Cambridge University Press.

Brumfiel, E. M. (1991) 'Weaving and cooking: women's production in Aztec Mexico' in J. M. Gero and M. W. Conkey (eds) *Engendering Archaelogy: Women and Prehistory*. Oxford: Blackwell, pp.224–54.

Cory, H. (1955) *African figurines, their ceremonial use in puberty rites in Tanganyika*. London: Faber & Faber.

Ehrenberg, M. (1989) *Women in Prehistory*. London: British Museum Press.

Gero, J. M. (1991) 'Genderlithics' in J. M. Gero and M. W. Conkey (eds) *Engendering Archaelogy: Women and Prehistory*. Oxford: Blackwell, pp.163–93.

Hayden, B. (1992) 'Observing prehistoric women' in C. Claassen (ed.) *Exploring Gender through Archaeology*. Monographs in World Archaeology 11. Madison, WI: Prehistory Press, pp.33–47.

Hodder, I. (1990) *The Domestication of Europe*. Oxford: Blackwell.

Jacobs, J. (1990) *The Nagas*. London: Thames and Hudson.

Liebowitz, L. (1983) 'Origins of the sexual division of labour' in M. Lowe and R. Hubbard (eds) *Woman's Nature: Rationalizations of Inequality*. Oxford: Pergamon Press, pp.123–47.

Middleton, J. (1982) 'Lugbara death' in M. Bloch and J. Parry (eds) *Death and the Regeneration of Life*. Cambridge: Cambridge University Press.

Parker-Pearson, M. (1993) *Bronze Age Britain*. London: Batsford.

Reed, E. (1975) *Women's Evolution from Matriarchal Clan to Patriarchial Family*. New York: Pathfinder Press.

Whittle, A. (1985) *Neolithic Europe: a survey*. Cambridge: Cambridge University Press.

8 Body imagery in the Aegean Neolithic: ideological implications of anthropomorphic figurines

DIMITRA KOKKINIDOU AND MARIANNA NIKOLAIDOU

The problem of ideology is central to historical – as to all social – understanding. If men govern the rest of nature in virtue of their reason and technological power, they are themselves governed by their beliefs. All human action ... belongs to a frame of reference, however, unconsciously formulated. It is this framework of assumptions and intentions, habits and ends, interests and ideas, values and knowledge which constitutes an ideology.

(Leff 1969: 155)

Introduction

Ideologies, active in many aspects of cultural reality, are especially manifest in the ways that power is established and negotiated in a society. The issues of power and ideology are, in turn, closely related to the construction of gender. Feminist research over the last decades has drawn attention to the fact that cultural aspects of masculinity and femininity are both parts of and preconditions for the creation of power relations (for example, di Leonardo 1991; Gero and Conkey 1991; Moore 1988; Walde and Willows 1991). As an important parameter for understanding power, gender can, therefore, be best considered by reference to specific ideological contexts. From the archaeological point of view, a gender-aware study of material culture and art has the potential of illuminating ideologies and the concomittant social relations (Braithwaite 1984; Conkey 1991; Hodder 1984, 1991a). The study of human representations, in particular, may be expected to provide important information on how people of the past understood their gender identities and manipulated associated roles and interaction.

This chapter addresses the above issues with focus on anthropomorphic figurines of the Aegean Neolithic. Although these artefacts have been frequently dealt with by archaeologists, little attention has been paid so far to their possible ideological role for the construction of gender and the interplay of power relations in the Neolithic communities of the Aegean region.

We begin with a brief presentation of the archaeological evidence, namely the figurines and their findcontexts, and an overview of the interpretations suggested so far about the meaning of this material. In the discussion that follows we argue for gender-specific ideological implications of these statuettes, and for their ritualized functions, by paying closer attention to:

(i)   their style and iconography
(ii) the loci of discovery
(iii) their systemic context
(iv) ethnographic examples.

The concluding section stresses the role of body imagery as an organizing principle in the conceptual frameworks, communication systems, symbolic behaviours, and social negotiations of Neolithic peoples in the Aegean.

The archaeological evidence

The figurines

Figurines dating from all phases of the Neolithic period (*c.* 6500–3000 BC) are found all over the Aegean, including mainland Greece, the Cyclades and other islands further north, and Crete (Aslanis 1992; Chourmouziadis 1994; Gimbutas 1991; Marangou 1992; Talalay 1993; Theocharis 1973; Ucko 1968). Small in size and relatively easy to make (see Talalay 1993: 29–33), they are mainly manufactured of clay, while various stones (marble, alabaster, steatite, river pebbles), shell, bone, and probably wood were occasionally used. A special category consists of the so-called 'acrolithic' figurines, that is idols with a clay body and an inserted head of other material, usually stone. A large number of figurines depict humans, female and male, as well as children and figures of indeterminate sex. Other pieces, very rare ones, show hermaphrodite or hybrid beings with zoomorphic features. Several curious fragments of what have been termed 'split-leg figurines' (Talalay 1987) have been found in the Peloponnese; these are half-fragments of the lower body including leg and buttock, and it is suggested that they were originally attached to complementary and matching halves (Talalay 1987, 1993: 45). Effigies of animals (Toufexis 1990, 1994), models of houses and ovens, loaves of bread, and miniatures of furniture and utensils (Marangou 1992; Theocharis 1973) are also present. Figurines are usually free-standing and modelled in the round, but anthropomorphic or zoomorphic relief attachments on pots are not uncommon either, and vessel parts like the neck or the handle sometimes assume a plastic quality as well.

Although the above range of plastic forms is present all over the Aegean and Helladic area, there are considerable regional differences in typology and style as well as in the frequency of certain types. To give an example, the 'split-leg figurines' seem to be restricted to the north-eastern Peloponnese (Talalay 1987), while comparable isolated legs are far less common further north (see Chourmouziadis 1994; Gimbutas 1986, 1989a; Marangou 1992). On the other hand, an ongoing study of a large body of Thessalian figurines strongly indicates that anthropomorphic imagery in this particular area of mainland Greece is clearly distinct from equivalent creations in other regions, like Macedonia, the Cyclades or Crete (Gallis and Orphanidis 1994).

Concerning the typology and style of anthropomorphic figurines, we must note the numerical preponderance of the female among the examples that can be safely sexed, although the male-female ratio can vary regionally or chronologically. Women are portrayed standing, seated or reclining, often with accentuated sexual features. Representations of women holding babies (so-called *kourotrophoi* in Greek), or being involved in everyday tasks such as carrying items or preparing food, are known as well, albeit sporadically. Male imagery is similarly varied, despite its comparatively limited occurrence: characteristic types include men seated on a stool, standing figures dressed or naked, phallus-shaped objects, and a few examples of ithyphallic idols. Anthropomorphic idoloplastic throughout the Neolithic is characterized by the co-existence of abstraction and 'naturalism'; a third tendency consists in the exaggeration of the prototype in the form of overemphasized bodily parts and/or facial features. In Thessaly at least, researchers have recognized a general preference for naturalistic or exaggerated representations in the Early and Middle Neolithic, whereas the advanced phases of Middle Neolithic see the beginnings of stylization which can reach great schematism during the Late Neolithic phase (see Gallis and Orphanidis 1994). The modelling of figurines is often enriched with painting, incisions and plastic additions to point up anatomical or decorative details, or to denote dress and ornaments.

Find contexts and proposed functions

In the excavations figurines are usually retrieved from habitation deposits associated with dwellings: they occur either inside the house or in pits and yards outside domestic structures. In southern Greece they are usually found singly, whereas further north groups of statuettes are often recovered from a single context, as for example at Achilleion, Tsangli and Rachmani in Thessaly, Nea Nikomedeia and Sitagroi in Macedonia, in a fashion similar to the Balkans (for Balkan examples see Gimbutas 1991; Marangou 1992).

Already in the Early Neolithic settlement of Nea Nikomedeia in West Macedonia (late seventh and early sixth millennia BC) a large central building with a tripartite arrangement of parallel rows of heavy timbers yielded five steatopygic female effigies. Along with these was found a number of special artefacts including two outsize greenstone axes, two large caches (of hundreds) of unused flint blades, two gourd-shaped ceramic vessels and several hundred roundels of baked clay (Rodden 1962: 285–6, 1964: 114, 1965: 88–9). Based on the substantial construction of the building itself and the exceptional nature of the objects, the excavators described the area as a shrine which contained representations of the Goddess of Fertility (Rodden and Rodden 1964). In Thessaly similar assemblages are known from Early and Middle Neolithic houses at Achilleion (seventh and early sixth millennia BC, Gimbutas 1989a: 171–227) as well as from the Middle Neolithic House T at Tsangli (Wace and Thompson 1912: 115–17, 123–4). The Achilleion finds have also been associated with the cult of the Goddess, and a sacred character has been ascribed to the buildings with which they were associated (Gimbutas 1989a: 171–227).

During the Late Neolithic (*c.* 5300–4500 BC) figurines still occur in domestic contexts. That at least some of these images could have had a ritual function is hinted at by a foundation offering underneath the floor of a house at Plateia Magoula Zarkou in Thessaly. The find consists of a baked clay model of an unroofed structure which contained eight human effigies, adult males and females as well as children (Gallis 1985, 1990: 17–19). Although several house models are known from Greece, in no other case is a whole 'scene' with figurines in a building depicted, nor are there other clear examples of foundation offerings. The find from Plateia Magoula, unique for the Aegean Neolithic in terms of its iconography and context, can best be paralleled with plastic groups and foundation deposits from the Balkans (for the latter see Gimbutas 1991: figs 7.53–59).

Towards the end of the Neolithic period, in the phase known in the Balkans as Final Neolithic or Chalcolithic (*c.* 4500–3200 BC), there appear remarkable regional differences in terms of the find context. Central and northern Greece, on the one hand, continue the long tradition of domestic associations of the figurines. Again they occur either individually, or in groups as, for example, at Rachmani in Thessaly (Wace and Thompson 1912: 39–41). On the other hand, new patterns of distribution are evident further south, with human idols accompanying burials at Kephala on the Cycladic island of Keos (Coleman 1977). Based on ethnographic parallels Talalay (1991: 49, 1993: 74–5) argues that the latter practice alludes to some kind of ancestral cult. We may interpret the contextual variability in the figurine corpus as part of a general trend towards cultural diversity that has been recognized in the distinct social trajectories which are evident among different regions of the Aegean at this time (Demoule and Perlès 1993: 406–7; van Andel and Runnels 1988).

The problem of meaning(s)

There has been a long discussion in the archaeological literature concerning the use and meaning of Stone Age figurines in the Mediterranean and the Balkans. The proposed interpretations range from religiocentric views at one end of the scale to scepticism as to any cultic purpose at the other (see review in Talalay 1993: 37–44). Even more, the interpretive value of these portrayals has been challenged as a whole (Hayden 1992: 38).

The greater number of female as compared to male idols initially led to the hypothesis that the former, in particular those with overemphasized sexual features, are early indications of a religion which focused on the worship of the Great Mother Goddess or Fertility Goddess, known from later textual and archaeological documents of the Near East. The Great Mother model has been widely used to designate a variety of divinities and symbols connected with life-giving and regenerative forces such as fertility, sexual union, birth, nurturing, and the growing cycle (see especially Gimbutas 1982, 1986, 1989a and b, 1991). The belief in the Mother Goddess archetype was deeply influenced by psychoanalytic theories which have been rejected (Bailey 1994a), perhaps too dogmatically, as having absolutely no relevance to what the archaeological record may reveal about the beliefs and rituals of Neolithic people. Certainly we should not underestimate Gimbutas' pioneering research on the symbolic potentials of prehistoric art. Nevertheless, her decontextualized arguments, especially the uncritical association of Neolithic imagery with the so-called prehistoric matriarchy, have rightly been challenged as archaeologically untenable (Barnett 1992; Chourmouziadis 1994; Fagan 1992; Hayden 1986; Marangou 1992; Talalay 1991, 1993).

Current scholarship has adopted a broader perspective and applied a multiplicity of working hypotheses for 'reading' this category of Neolithic art. Specifically, attention has been drawn to a number of variables which can help establish a rigorous approach, namely to the figurines themselves, their archaeological and systemic contexts, as well as ethnographic analogies (Talalay 1991: 49, 1993: 44). From this standpoint there would be no incompatibility with parallel or cross-cutting uses and meanings of these early images including symbolic signification, ceremonial or cultic content, decoration or even daily use. Instead of the all-encompassing and thus problematic Mother Goddess theory, a range of alternative functions and symbolic values has been suggested on the basis of the morphological, typological, stylistic, and thematic variability of the figurines. These have been collectively considered as ritual and magical objects, teaching devices, charms, tokens, toys, and ornaments (Talalay 1993; Ucko 1962, 1968); portraits of prehistoric individuals (Bailey 1994a; Gallis and Orphanidis 1994); depictions of personal desires or even rudimentary signs of a 'proto-script' (Chourmouziadis 1978: 50–1, 1994).

Discussion

Allowing for a 'multivocal' character of the anthropomorphic figurines, we have chosen in this chapter to treat them as material symbols of a complex of notions and values interwoven with gender arrangements. In the following sections we will discuss possible uses of these artefacts which, we think, may shed some light on the ways that Neolithic peoples in the Aegean perceived, shaped and 'acted out' their genders.

Depicting the body: 'archetypes', 'portraits' and ambiguous forms

Many figurines, both 'naturalistic' and abstract, provide evidence for a selection of, and emphasis on, certain aspects of femininity and masculinity (Hodder 1990: 60–70). Specifically, a consistent concern for the erotic and reproductive areas of the human body can be recognized in both cases. To begin with 'naturalistic' representations, a group of corpulent female images are characterized by an exaggerated modelling of the breasts, belly and buttocks (Figure 8.1), whereas the facial features are not executed in detail or may even be missing. Frequently the very posture of the statuette, holding or supporting her breasts with her hands (Figure 8.2), is suggestive of a special meaning ascribed to this part of the body which is closely connected with nurturing and sexuality. Indicative are also some figurines in what can be interpreted as a birth-giving position, from Achilleion (Gimbutas 1989a: fig. 7.46, p.1.7.11) (Figure 8.3) and Sitagroi (Gimbutas 1986: figs 9.51, 9.146–9). On the other hand, even in cases

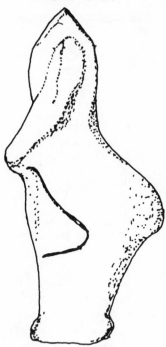

Figure 8.1 Female figurine. Early Neolithic, Prodromos, Thessaly (after Chourmouziadis 1994: pl. 27)

of considerable schematization the pubic triangle (Figure 8.4) or the breasts are often clearly shown. As far as the male body is concerned, it is the phallus that receives similar attention (Marangou 1991). In several abstract examples it is the only anatomical feature depicted, while in more 'naturalistic' pieces it constitutes an explicitly marked trait; characteristic are figures of either style which are shown touching their genitals. The phallus is also modelled as an autonomous form (Figure 8.5), or attached on pots, and the whole body of some idols has a phallic shape (Figure 8.6).

The above examples of what may be described as an 'iconography of sexuality' seem to echo an attempt of Neolithic people to understand and interfere symbolically in the phenomenon of fertility. We can imagine that the very experiences, anxieties, and wishes of everyday life would have inspired the themes and aesthetics of Neolithic idoloplastic (Chourmouziadis 1994: 222–31), as well as they would have been felt in the ritual sphere (Barrett 1991) with which several of those effigies were possibly associated. The woman's body, in particular, is likely to have been envisaged as participating in a more obvious and essential way in the creation and sustaining of life (Chourmouziadis 1994: 82). This may be one of the reasons that the female image is most 'visible' in the art of this period.

A peculiar manifestation of the interest in the mysteries of human biology may be recognized in a series of women's statuettes with emphasized breasts and/or buttocks and a phallus-shaped neck (Figure 8.2). Although an elongated,

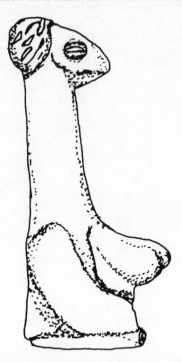

Figure 8.2 Torso of a woman supporting her breasts with her hands. Early Neolithic, Ayia Anna, Thessaly (after Chourmouziadis 1994: pl. 39)

Figure 8.3 Female figurine in a birth-giving posture. Early Neolithic, Achilleion, Thessaly (after Gimbutas 1989a: fig. 7.46(1))

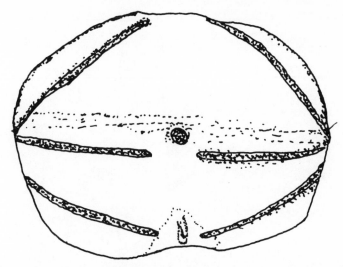

Figure 8.4 Schematized figurine with emphasized pubic area. Early Neolithic, Prodromos, Thessaly (after Chourmouziadis 1994: pl. 11)

Figure 8.5 Painted phallus. Thessaly (after Chourmouziadis 1994: pl. 2 low left)

phallic-looking stem is often used as neck in figurines of both sexes (see Chourmouziadis 1994: 197–8), in this particular group of expressly 'female' representations such an iconographic convention could perhaps be 'read' as an amalgamation of reproductive qualities within the body of the woman-mother. Female fertility symbolically transgresses, we suggest, the boundaries of sexual dimorphism and the division between 'man' and 'woman'. In other words, it rises to the level of an 'archetypical' image, an epitome of Neolithic people's ontology which was deeply embedded in the agricultural mode of life.

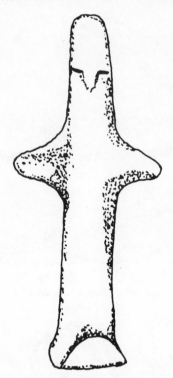

Figure 8.6 Phallus-shaped figurine. Early Neolithic, Prodromos, Thessaly (after Chourmouziadis 1994: pl. 3)

Far beyond biological determinants, human procreative capacities embrace cultural phenomena, especially notions of sexuality, personal identity, child care, social organization of power (see Bolen 1992; Chourmouziadis 1994: 135–6). In early farming communities, reproduction and maternity could be metaphorically parallel to agriculture, both phenomena consisting in the dramatic transformation of natural elements into life by human – biological *and* cultural – interference. This idea is suggested, among other things, by the occurrence of several female figurines within or near hearths and storage spaces (Marangou 1992: 222–3; Papaefthymiou-Papanthimou 1987: 175). Moreover, the rendering of the eyes of some female figurines in the shape of corn grains (so-called 'coffee-bean eyes') (Chourmouziadis 1994: 93; Theocharis 1973: 67) (Figure 8.2) might echo similar symbolic associations, even if such plastic modelling of the eyes is not limited to 'naturalistic' female images (see Chourmouziadis 1994: 93). Interestingly the idol of a seated woman from the Early Neolithic site of Prodromos in Thessaly preserves an impression of wheat grain on its shoulder. This find led the excavator, G. Chourmouziadis (1994: 70–3), to the hypothesis that many figurines were originally decorated with real grains which would in other cases be imitated by clay pellets that were applied as eyes or as decorative elements on the body and head of several statuettes (Figure 8.7).

The emphasis on the reproductive functions of the human body is counter-

Figure 8.7 Fragments of figurine decorated with grain-shaped pellets. Middle Neolithic, Achilleion, Thessaly (after Gimbutas 1989a: fig. 7.37(1))

balanced by two other iconographic types of Neolithic idoloplatic which point to different avenues of communication via anthropomorphic imagery: (i) the so-called 'portraits', a series of realistic heads, each one of particular style and morphology that can be taken as representations of actual persons (see especially Gallis and Orphanidis 1994), and (ii) the a-sexual or ambiguous images, namely idols with no clear indication of sex or of a totally abstract form.

(i) A considerable number of broken realistic heads have come to light in Thessaly. In these faces we may recognize a purposeful deviation from the standard modelling of the human image. The makers chose instead 'to convey age, physical deformation or the facial expressions of real persons' (Gallis and Orphanidis 1994: 159; cf. Chourmouziadis 1994: 212). These creations raise puzzling questions: what are the reasons for this interest in realistic imitation? What was so special in the persons portrayed to deserve depiction? Many heads are characterized by an outstanding plastic quality and such an expressive power that they have been tentatively interpreted as portraits of important members of Neolithic society (Gallis and Orphanidis 1994: 156). This may be true but then we must realize that 'importance' does not seem to exclude ugliness. Indeed the range of portraits suggests that wrinkles, wounds, or even physical deformities might stimulate as vivid an interest as faces of outstanding expressive strength; the so-called 'hydrocephalous' (Chourmouziadis 1994: 212) or 'mongol child' (Theocharis 1973: 80) provides a striking example of the former group. Unfortunately, most of the heads do not preserve their body so that it is not possible to reconstruct the original image. There are, however, a few better preserved figurines that show a comparable interest in the deformities of the body: women with 'humps' are known from Kara Mourlar and Stefanovikion, while the so-called 'old woman' from Tzani Magoula depicts a body and face that have suffered from age and/or some anatomical problem (Chourmouziadis 1994: 27; Theocharis 1973: figs 203, 205). Would such images have been made in a mocking mood or as an expression of awe? It is impossible to tell. It may be helpful to note that several of the 'portrait'-heads were perhaps originally attached to large vases or placed on top of house models that would be similar to the models surmounted by anthropomorphic heads from Porodin and other Balkan sites (Chourmouziadis 1994: 212; for Balkan examples see Gimbutas 1991: figs 7.53–56).

Figure 8.8 Acrolithic figurine. Final Neolithic, Thessaly (after Chourmouzia-dis 1994: pl. 64 upper right)

(ii) The type of a-sexual figurine occurs all over the Aegean, and the earliest examples already date in the Early Neolithic (for example, Talalay 1993: 12, 23–4). In the later Neolithic phases there are two characteristic variations of schematic acrolithic figurines with no indication of sex. The first includes stone cross-shaped forms, head and torso that end in a pointed protuberance by means of which it was probably inserted into a clay core (Theocharis 1973: figs 208, 227). The second variation consists of stone triangular, oval or trapezoidal heads that were inserted into a roughly shaped clay body (Gallis and Orphanidis 1994: figs 19–21; Theocharis 1973: fig. 198). How are such utterly simplified forms to be explained? The expressive abilities of Neolithic idol-makers, evidenced in the 'portraits' as well as in the large number of 'naturalistic' figurines discussed above, do not allow for the hypothesis that people switched to abstract representation because they did not know otherwise. For instance, in the Late Neolithic we also have examples of acrolithic female figures from Mandalo in West Macedonia with very eloquently modelled buttocks and pubic area (Papaefthymiou-Papanthimou 1987: figs 1–5). Indeed the co-existence of naturalistic 'gendered' images and abstract a-sexual figures throughout the Neolithic, suggests that we should consider the latter as deliberate a choice as the emphasis on gender and sexuality might have been in the former case (Talalay 1993: 12). In other words, schematic images may have been intended to convey the general concept of human without further specification (Chourmouziadis 1994: 190–1). In fact several of them are characterized by technical competence in execution and by a particular aesthetic quality: the cross-shaped torso is some-times brilliantly decorated (Theocharis 1973: fig. 227) while the many stone geometric heads can have facial features vividly painted in a highly stylized fashion (for example, Gallis and Orphanidis 1994: figs 19–20) (Figure 8.8). In the painted heads the face again becomes the focus of interest and formal elaboration (Chourmouziadis 1994: 211), in a way comparable with and yet radically different from facial treatment in the 'portrait' series examined earlier. Whatever reasons may have dictated the concentration on the human face in some figurines – while lively preoccupation with the 'sexual' and 'gendered' human body is apparent in others – are not easy to decipher from the available data. At the moment we can only assume that both phenomena allude to important concepts and ideals.

Neolithic households: symbolic elaboration and social reproduction

As has already been noted, the majority of the figurines derive from habitational contexts. In Achilleion, for example, they were 'omnipresent in human activity areas inside and outside the house' (Gimbutas 1989a: 213): within the houses they were recovered at or on benches, or in areas used for food preparation, pottery-making and other workshop activities. In open-air courtyards they occurred at the extended platforms of ovens or hearths, and on benches adjoining these constructions. Several came from pits some of which Gimbutas has described as ritual, others as garbage. Figurines were often found in groups of as many as 14 pieces, while a single house yielded a total of 30. Together with these statuettes was found a whole array of artefacts ranging from plain and decorated pottery; bone awls, querns, and chipped stone tools, the latter including a lot of obsidian blades; stone palettes; clay utensils, such as ladles and discs; spindle whorls and spools; zoomorphic figurines, anthropomorphic vessels, and other fragmentary plastic forms; models of furniture and ceramic axes; and an alabaster seal (Gimbutas 1989a: 213–18). The figurines from the earliest strata at this site (*c.* 6300–6200 BC) provide 'the earliest evidence so far in Europe for the association of figurines with the house, oven and bench' (Gimbutas 1989a: 214).

Figurines from systematically excavated floor layers, like those at Achilleion and other comparable contexts (see review in Talalay 1993: 72–9), support the idea that these items were primarily associated with the *domus*, to use Hodder's term (1990: 38). He defines the *domus* as involving, on the one hand, a range of practical activities carried out in the domain of the Neolithic household, the basic social unit. These include the construction of dwellings and domestic facilities; storage, processing, serving and consumption of food acquired through agricultural production and animal herding, as well as fishing, hunting, and gathering; the manufacture of bone and stone tools, such as awls, spatulae, querns, and blades; various crafts, like spinning and weaving, basketry, mat-making, hide-processing, ceramic production, and ornament-making. On the other hand, the symbolic connotations of such practices have been stressed: the house has been treated as a focus for symbolic elaboration and as a metaphor for social and economic strategies and relations of power (Hodder 1990: 44–5).

It is reasonable to assume that negotiations of time, space, resources, energy, and knowledge would be required in order to carry out the productive tasks of Neolithic domestic economy and to manipulate their end products. Negotiations would have involved decision-making on an intra-household, intra- or

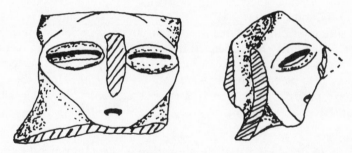

Figure 8.9 Human face attached on a vessel. Middle Neolithic, Achilleion, Thessaly (after Gimbutas 1989a: fig. 7.54)

inter-community level, affiliations between individuals and social groups, inter-marriages, the exchange of raw materials, goods, information, and expertise. Accordingly we may argue that the Neolithic household would have provided an appropriate framework for the materialization of ideologies, including gender roles, both among its members and between the various household-based groups (families?) in the community and beyond (Chapman 1991; Tringham 1991). The available archaeological data allow the hypothesis that such strategies of social reproduction would not rely on the fulfilment of social duties alone, but also on the integration of daily practices into a symbolic framework of references, including cosmological beliefs, ritual performances, and the production and use of art forms (Conkey 1991). We might then imagine that Neolithic men, women or children created and used their material symbols, including figurines, within the context and as a key element of the *domus*-centred action and interaction. The foundation offering from Plateia Magoula Zarkou, recovered under a house floor and possibly depicting adult and younger members of the same family (Gallis 1985), indeed points to this direction.

The evidence discussed so far suggests that the cosmological perceptions of Neolithic people were inextricably linked with the daily experience of transforming natural resources into cultural benefits. Thus, the depiction of the human body in its sexual and procreative capacity is likely to have acquired ideological importance. Such an idea is suggested, among other things, by the depiction or attachment of human forms upon ceramic vessels (Figure 8.9), a category of artefacts closely connected with basic practices of Neolithic domestication, like storage and food serving. Sometimes the whole pot is made in the shape of a figurine. Talalay (1993: 35) has drawn attention to possible conceptual links between Neolithic pots, figurines and the human body, which can be deduced from the use of the same decorative motives on pottery and figurines as well as the incorporation of anthropomorphic elements in vessel forms; Gimbutas (1989a, b) has discussed further the ritual and symbolic implications of such metaphoric links. It is interesting to note that anthropomorphic attachments appear on a variety of pots, ranging from storage jars to serving receptacles to what has been described as 'social ceramics' (Elster 1986), namely plastic vessels and tripods of probable ceremonial function.

A powerful imagery: figurines and social negotiation

Having thus far argued for the symbolic significance of anthropomorphic figurines in relation to the *domus*, we can now turn to their rôle in the construction of power within the household and beyond. We would like to propose that the visual emphasis on the female element may be interpreted as a possible source of power. Ian Hodder has remarked that representation, whether overt or muted, can itself be a form of power (Hodder 1991a: 14). Such a symbolically encoded power, as we may recognize with regard to female figurines from the Aegean, should be understood as power from within, or, to use Miller and Tilley's (1984: 5) definition, as 'power to'. They discuss this form of power as an integral and recursive element of social interaction: it is only manifested through its effects on individuals, groups and institutions, and therefore should be distinguished from 'power over' which involves coercion and asymmetrical forms of social domination. This does not mean, however, that 'power to' is not subject to challenges and does not need reconfirmation. On the contrary, in studying prehistoric ideologies we should be alert to ' ... different types of power which overlap and conflict and are continually being negotiated between different interest groups. Power is not simply a "reality" of force but is also linked to meanings, values and prestige' (Hodder 1991b: 170).

From this perspective the central symbolism of the feminine in Neolithic idoloplastic should not necessarily be taken as an implication of women's authority (Bailey 1994b). Instead, we should allow for the possibility that certain aspects of femininity were conceptually central, and as such they could have become appropriate vehicles for the communication of important cultural information and ritual knowledge. As suggested earlier, the transmission of such messages may often have been a matter of negotiation. If we accept Bender's argument (Bender 1985) that control of ritual knowledge lies at the roots of social differentiation, we begin to appreciate the ideological significance of figurines, especially of female imagery, as material symbols in the power dynamics of the household and by extension of Neolithic society as a whole (Chapman 1991).

Other aspects of power discourse can perhaps be discerned in a group of seated figurines of both sexes. Commenting on male figures seated on a stool (Figure 8.10), researchers chose to view them as depictions of resting farmers (Chourmouziadis 1994: 91) or 'images of social power' (Chourmouziadis 1994: 82), namely representations of esteemed members of the community (Marangou 1991: 19). Both 'readings' are plausible, although images of women seated on the ground or on a stool (Figure 8.11) have also to be taken into account if we hope to understand why certain figurines are shown in a seated posture. What we find more difficult to be reconciled to is the idea of Gimbutas (1982) that those male figures represent leaders, priests or gods. Social organization in the Aegean Neolithic world, as can be traced in the archaeological record, does not appear to have been based on any type of institutionalized authority (Demoule and Perlès 1993: 406). Consequently, the notion of an official, fully developed pantheon cannot be substantiated, for such a form of religion is

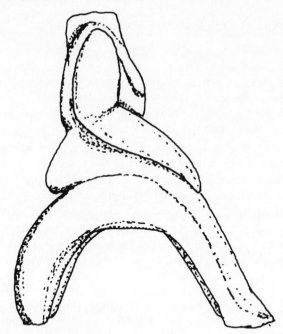

Figure 8.10 Male figurine seated on a stool. Pyrassos, Thessaly (after Chourmouziadis 1994: pl. 8)

Figure 8.11 Figurine of a seated woman. Middle Neolithic, Achilleion, Thessaly (after Gimbutas 1989a: fig. 7.38(1b))

connected to a social order more complex than that prevailing in the period under consideration. Instead, Neolithic cult would have been primarily domestic and pretheistic (Theocharis 1981: 63), focused on ancestral veneration and permeated by beliefs in general superhuman and supernatural forces rather than personified deities (Anati 1986; Talalay 1993: 75). Be that as it may, figurine groupings in certain areas of Thessalian and Macedonian sites (Achilleion, Nea Nikomedeia, Tsangli) imply the existence of special ritual loci within the village. This possibility is reinforced by Balkan parallels where similar concentrations of statuettes have been interpreted by Chapman (1989) as marks of areas which housed communal gatherings or ceremonies of primary ideological importance. Some forms of ritual control and 'centralization' seem to have operated further north in the Balkans (Whittle 1985), but it is still hard to reconstruct similar processes for the Aegean cultures with equal confidence. However, we should not preclude any form of social differentiation within Aegean farming communities either. It is not unlikely that 'hierarchies' related to individual or family position, gender, age, and experience were at play. It might not be accidental that representations of elderly individuals of both sexes do occur throughout the Neolithic: they are portrayed seated or standing, dressed or naked, with fleshy but not so firm bodies and faces sometimes marked by wrinkles and other signs of advanced age (see Chourmouziadis 1994).

Possible functions

The material discussed above allows us to view Neolithic idoloplastic in its iconographic variety as a material code of communication through which people tried to represent and shape cultural realities (cf. Talalay 1993: 50). As essential components of this communicative apparatus, the depictions of men and women would have encompassed and, in turn, produced concepts and values embedded in social and gender identities. Consequently, the ideological role of these artefacts should have involved a diversity of meanings and possible functions. An interesting function of figurines as tokens has been proposed with regard to the 'split-leg figurines' from the north-eastern Peloponnese. Because they have been found only in a limited number of settlements not very far from each other, it is believed that these detached half-fragments were used as symbols of recognition by trading or other partners, each partner keeping one of the two matching halves (Talalay 1987, 1993: 45–6).

As indicated by ethnographic data, figurines can have various uses ranging from initiation ceremonies to magic. At the 'mundane' end of the scale they are simply toys. They can also serve as pedagogic items in puberty rites, with the aim of explaining the biological functions of the human body. It is likely that the Neolithic statuettes with accentuated sexual features, as well as the effigies of pregnant women, of women in the posture of giving birth or of others holding babies (*kourotropoi*), and the phallus-shaped objects were especially appropriate for this purpose. In addition to these categories, messages relating to social roles may have been conveyed by means of seated or reclining figures (Figure 8.12) and those involved in daily tasks (Figure 8.13). Furthermore, figurines bearing dress (Figures 8.14, 8.15) and head-dresses (Figure 8.16a and b), ornaments (Figure 8.17), or tattoos (Figure 8.18) on their bodies and faces may denote individual styles, or else could have helped impart a communal ethos both on an intra- and an inter-site level. The evidence for dress, adornment and bodily decoration (Figure 8.19) of Neolithic figurines is quite varied, possibly alluding

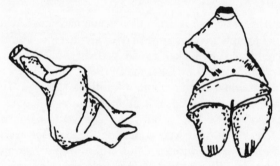

Figure 8.12 Figurine of a reclining woman. Middle Neolithic, Achilleion, Thessaly (after Gimbutas 1989a: fig. 7.35(1))

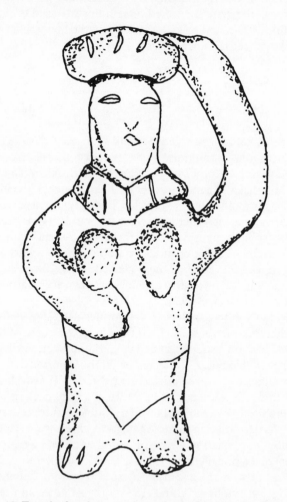

Figure 8.13 Female figurine carrying a loaf of bread (?). Early Neolithic, Prodromos, Thessaly (after Chourmouziadis 1994: pl. 81)

to a multiplicity of cultural messages, and certainly deserves a future comprehensive study.

Equally, figurines may depict mythical personages or ancestors (Chapman 1991). In the realm of sympathetic magic they were possibly employed in order to enhance human procreation and the fertility of nature or as apotropaic amulets. Noteworthy is a group of phallus-shaped pendants, some of them modelled in a very 'naturalistic' fashion, which have been interpreted as erotic charms (Chourmouziadis 1994: 87–9). Finally, ethnographic reports (Talalay 1993: 40–4) warn us that a single figurine can have multiple functions, according to its context of use.

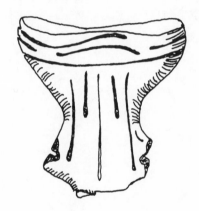

Figure 8.14 Female figurine with incisions possibly indicating dress. Late Neolithic, Sitagroi, Macedonia (after Gimbutas 1986: fig. 9.12)

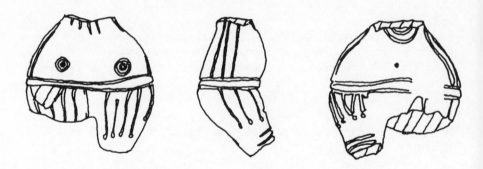

Figure 8.15 Female figurine with incisions possibly indicating dress. Late Neolithic, Sitagroi, Macedonia (after Gimbutas 1986: fig. 9.21)

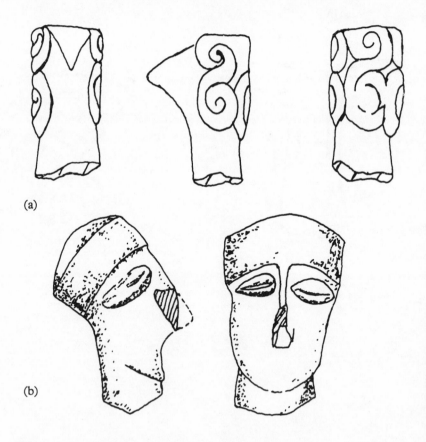

(a)

(b)

Figure 8.16 Figurines with head-dresses from Sitagroi (a) and Tsangli (b) (after Gimbutas 1986: fig. 9.24 and Gimbutas 1989a: fig. 7.22(2) respectively)

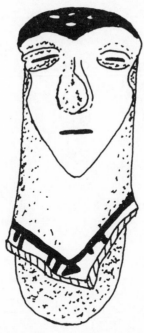

Figure 8.17 Phallus-shaped head wearing necklace. Middle Neolithic, Achilleion, Thessaly (after Gimbutas 1989a: fig. 7.51 right)

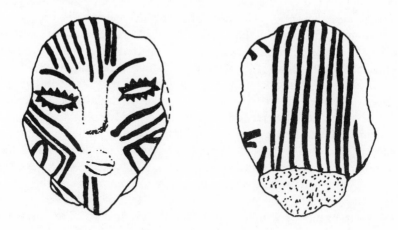

Figure 8.18 Figurine head with tattoo. Late Neolithic, Sitagroi, Macedonia (after Gimbutas 1986: fig. 9.27)

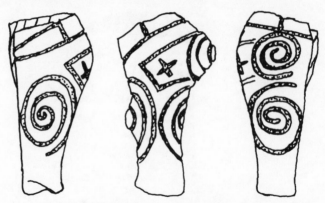

Figure 8.19 Figurine fragment with rich incised decoration on tne ıegs and buttocks. Late Neolithic, Sitagroi, Macedonia (after Gimbutas 1986: fig. 9.18)

Conclusion: depicting the body, constructing ideologies

We have attempted to outline the gender and other social implications of anthropomorphic idoloplastic in the Aegean Neolithic. We have proposed that the human body may have functioned as one of the organizing metaphors by which the world of Neolithic people was ordered and understood. In concluding, we wish to argue that this category of material culture possibly operated within a framework of symbolically and ritually encoded behaviours, on a collective or a personal level. Following Bell (1992: 182–223), ritualization of social practices can be best considered as a strategy for the construction of certain types of power relations, which makes it ideologically effective. Accordingly, we suggest that Neolithic body imagery was perceived and used within an ideological setting which underlies the construction of gender identities, the performance of cultural roles, and the creation of social bonds among Neolithic people.

Admittedly, the current state of Neolithic figurine studies, as outlined in this chapter, does not yet provide definite answers to basic questions related to the manufacture and use of these images. By whom were they produced, and for whom? Where, how, and why were they made? How was shared information attested by stylistic similarities in the figurine corpus of different geographical regions transmitted? Who was controlling the production of figurines? Who was organizing the ritual events in which they may have been used? Was production and/or use gender-, age- or otherwise-specific? Was figurine-making always as purposeful as we imagine, or should we also allow for humorous moods and last-minute decisions to account for the production of at least some figurines in moments of leisure? Puzzling as these issues may be, we can still suggest some symbolic content for these artefacts and explore their ideological implications in the social context of the Aegean Neolithic. Far from being exhaustive, our discussion has hopefully highlighted some of these implications which are now beginning to ripen for future research.

Acknowledgements

Many thanks to Eleanor Scott and Jenny Moore for inviting us to contribute to this volume and for their editorial comments. Dr Ernestine S. Elster has provided many helpful suggestions and encouragement. We are also indebted to 'Vanias Publications' (Thessaloniki, Greece) and the Office of Publications, UCLA Institute of Archaeology, for permission to reproduce illustrations from Chourmouziadis 1994 and Gimbutas 1986 and 1989a, respectively. The figures were drawn by Marianna Nikolaidou.

Earlier versions of this chapter were presented as follows: 'Gender ideology and Neolithic figurines: the Aegean evidence', session on 'Ideologies of Gender in the Past', 15th Annual Conference of the Theoretical Archaeology Group, Department of Archaeology, University of Durham, 13–16 December 1993; 'Body imagery in the Neolithic: ideology, sexuality and anthropomorphic figurines from the Aegean', session on 'Sexuality, Society and Archaeology', 16th Annual Conference of the Theoretical Archaeology Group, Department of Archaeological Sciences, University of Bradford, 14–16 December 1994.

References

Anati, E. (1986) 'The question of fertility cults' in A. Bonnano (ed.) *Archaeology and Fertility Cult in the Ancient Mediterranean: Papers Presented at the First International Conference on Archaeology of the Ancient Mediterranean, The University of Malta, 2–5 September 1985.* Amsterdam: B.R. Gruner, pp.2–15.

Aslanis, I. (1992) *I proistoria tis Makedonias I: i Neolithiki epochi* (The prehistory of Macedonia I: the Neolithic Age). Athens: Kardamitsa.

Bailey, D.W. (1994a) 'Reading prehistoric figurines as individuals'. *World Archaeology* 25 (3), 321–31.

Bailey, D.W. (1994b) 'The representation of gender: homology or propaganda?'. *Journal of European Archaeology* 2 (2), 189–202.

Barnett, W. (1992) 'Review of Marija Gimbutas "The Language of the Goddess"'. *American Journal of Archaeology* 96, 170–1.

Barrett, J.C. (1991) 'Towards an archaeology of ritual' in P. Garwood, D. Jennings, R. Skeates and J. Toms (eds) *Sacred and Profane: Proceedings of a Conference on Archaeology, Ritual and Religion, Oxford 1989.* Oxford University Committee for Archaeology, Monograph 32, 1–9.

Bell, C. (1992) *Ritual Theory, Ritual Practice.* New York and Oxford: Oxford University Press.

Bender, B. (1985) 'Prehistoric developments in the American Midcontinent and in Brittany, NW France' in T.D. Price and J.A. Brown (eds) *Prehistoric Hunter-Gatherers: The Emergence of Cultural Complexity.* New York: Academic Press.

Bolen, K.M. (1992) 'Prehistoric construction of mothering' in C. Claassen (ed.) *Exploring Gender through Archaeology: Selected Papers from the 1991 Boone Conference.* Monographs in World Archaeology 11. Madison WI: Prehistory Press, pp.49–62.

Braithwaite, M. (1984) 'Ritual and prestige in the prehistory of Wessex, c. 2200–1400 BC: a new dimension to the archaeological evidence' in D. Miller and C. Tilley (eds) *Ideology, Power and Prehistory.* Cambridge: Cambridge University Press, pp.93–110.

Chapman, J.C. (1989) 'The early Balkan village' in S. Bökönyi (ed.) *Neolithic of Southeast Europe and its Eastern Connections.* Varia Archaeologica Hungarica II, Budapest, 33–53.

Chapman, J.C. (1991) 'The creation of social arenas in the Neolithic and Copper Age of S.E. Europe: the case of Varna' in P. Garwood, D. Jennings, R. Skeates and J. Toms (eds) *Sacred and Profane: Proceedings of a Conference on Archaeology, Ritual and Religion, Oxford 1989.* Oxford University Committee for Archaeology, Monograph 32, 152–71.

Chourmouziadis, G. Ch. (1978) 'Eisagogi stis ideologies tis ellinikis proistorias' (An introduction to the ideologies of Greek prehistory). *O Politis* 17, 30–51.

Chourmouziadis, G. Ch. (1994) *Ta Neolithika eidolia* (Neolithic figurines). Proistorika Anagnosmata 4, Thessaloniki: Vanias.

Coleman, J.E. (1977) *Keos I. Kephala: A Late Neolithic Settlement and Cemetery.* Princeton: American School of Classical Studies at Athens.

Conkey, M.W. (1991) 'Contexts of action, contexts for power: material culture and gender in the Magdalenian' in J.M. Gero and M.W. Conkey (eds) *Engendering Archaeology: Women and Prehistory.* Oxford: Blackwell, pp.57–92.

Demoule, J.P. and Perlès, C. (1993) 'The Greek Neolithic: a new review'. *Journal of World Prehistory* 7 (4), 355–416.

di Leonardo, M. (ed.) (1991) *Gender at the Crossroads of Knowledge: Feminist Anthropology in the Postmodern Era.* Berkeley, Los Angeles, and London: University of California Press.

Elster, E.S. (1986) 'Tripods, plastic vessels and stands: a fragmentary collection of social ceramics' in C. Renfrew, M. Gimbutas, and E.S. Elster (eds) *Excavations at Sitagroi: A Prehistoric Village in Northeast Greece, vol. 1.* Monumenta Archaeologica 13. Institute of Archaeology, Los Angeles: University of California, pp. 303–44.

Fagan, B. (1992) 'A sexist view of prehistory'. *Archaeology* 45 (2), 16–18, 66.

Gallis, K.J. (1985) 'A Late Neolithic foundation offering from Thessaly'. *Antiquity* 59, 20–4.

Gallis, K.J. (1990) 'Prosfates erevnes sti neolithiki Thessalia' (Recent investigations in Neolithic Thessaly). *Archaiologia* 34, 9–20.

Gallis, K. and Orphanidis, L. (1994) 'Twenty new faces from the Neolithic society of Thessaly' in *Thessalia: Dekapente chronia archaiologikis erevnas, 1975–1990, Apotelesmata kai prooptikes. Praktika Diethnous Synedriou Lyon, 17–22 Apriliou 1990* (Thessaly: Fifteen years of archaeological research, 1975–1990, Results and perspectives. Proceedings of the Lyon International Conference, 17–22 April 1990). Athens: Ministry of Culture, pp. 155–62

Gero, J.M. and Conkey, M.W. (eds) (1991) *Engendering Archaeology: Women and Prehistory.* Oxford: Blackwell.

Gimbutas, M. (1982) *The Gods and Goddesses of Old Europe, 7000 to 3500 BC: Myths, Legends and Cult Images.* Berkeley and Los Angeles: University of California Press.

Gimbutas, M. (1986) 'Mythical imagery of Sitagroi society' in C. Renfrew, M. Gimbutas and E.S. Elster (eds) *Excavations at Sitagroi: A Prehistoric Village in Northeast Greece, vol. 1.* Monumenta Archaeologica 13. Institute of Archaeology, Los Angeles: University of California, pp.225–301.

Gimbutas, M. (1989a) 'Figurines and cult equipment' in M. Gimbutas, S. Winn, and D. Shimabuku (eds) *Achilleion: A Neolithic Settlement in Thessaly, Greece, 6400–5600 BC.* Monumenta Archaeologica 14, Institute of Archaeology, Los Angeles: University of California, pp.171–250.

Gimbutas, M. (1989b) *The Language of the Goddess.* San Francisco: Harper and Row.

Gimbutas, M. (1991) *The Civilization of the Goddess: The World of Old Europe*. New York: HarperCollins.

Hayden, B. (1986) 'Old Europe: sacred matriarchy or complementary opposition?' in A. Bonnano (ed.) *Archaeology and Fertility Cult in the Ancient Mediterranean: Papers Presented at the First International Conference on Archaeology of the Ancient Mediterranean, The University of Malta, 2–5 September 1985*. Amsterdam: B.R. Gruner, pp.17–30.

Hayden, B. (1992) 'Observing prehistoric women' in C. Claassen (ed.) *Exploring Gender through Archaeology: Selected Papers from the 1991 Boone Conference*. Monographs in World Archaeology 11, Madison WI: Prehistory Press, pp. 33–47.

Hodder, I. (1984) 'Burials, houses, women and men in the European Neolithic' in D. Miller and C. Tilley (eds) *Ideology, Power and Prehistory*. Cambridge. Cambridge University Press, pp. 51–68.

Hodder, I. (1990) *The Domestication of Europe: Structure and Contingency in Neolithic Societies*. Oxford: Blackwell.

Hodder, I. (1991a) 'Gender representation and social reality' in D. Walde and N.D. Willows (eds) *The Archaeology of Gender: Proceedings of the Twenty-Second Annual Conference of the Archaeological Association of the University of Calgary*. The University of Calgary, Archaeological Association, pp. 11–16.

Hodder, I. (1991b) *Reading the Past: Current Approaches to Interpretation in Archaeology*. Cambridge: Cambridge University Press.

Leff, G. (1969) *History and Social Theory*. London: Merlin Press.

Marangou, Ch. (1991) 'Eikonografia tis neolithikis epochis kai tis proimis chalkokratias: i (fainomeniki) spaniotita tis andrikis parousias' (Iconography of the Neolithic and Early Bronze Age: the (deceptive) rarity of male presence). *Archaiologia* 41, 15–23.

Marangou, Ch. (1992) Ειδωλια: *Figurines et miniatures du néolithique récent et du bronze ancien en Grèce*. Oxford: British Archaeological Reports International Series 576.

Miller, D. and Tilley, C. (1984) 'Ideology, power and prehistory: an introduction' in D. Miller and C. Tilley (eds) *Ideology, Power and Prehistory*. Cambridge: Cambridge University Press, pp. 1–15.

Moore, H. (1988) *Feminism and Anthropology*. Cambridge: Polity Press.

Papaefthymiou-Papanthimou, K. (1987) 'Tria neolithika eidolia apo to Mandalo tis Makedonias' (Three Neolithic figurines from Mandalo in Macedonia) in *Eilapini: Tomos timitikos gia ton kathigiti Nikolao Platona* (Eilapini: Studies in honour of Professor Nikolaos Platon). Herakleion: Vikelaia Dimotiki Vivliothiki, Dimos Irakleiou, 171–7.

Phelps, W. W. (1987) 'Prehistoric figurines from Corinth'. *Hesperia* 56, 233–53.

Rodden, R. J. (1962) 'Excavations at the Early Neolithic site at Nea Nikomedeia, Greek Macedonia (1961 season)'. *Proceedings of the Prehistoric Society* 28, 267–8.

Rodden, R. J. (1964) 'Recent discoveries from prehistoric Macedonia: an interim report'. *Balkan Studies* 5, 109–24.

Rodden, R. J. (1965) 'An Early Neolithic village in Greece'. *Scientific American* 212 (4), 83–91.

Rodden, R. J. and Rodden, J. M. (1964) 'A European link with Çatal Hüyük: the 7th millennium site at Nea Nikomedeia in Macedonia. Part II: Burials and shrine'. *Illustrated London News*, 18 April, 604–7.

Talalay, L. (1987) 'Rethinking the function of clay figurine legs from Neolithic Greece: an argument by analogy'. *American Journal of Archaeology* 91, 161–9.

Talalay, L. (1991) 'Body imagery of the ancient Aegean'. *Archaeology* 44 (4), 46–9.

Talalay, L. (1993) *Deities, Dolls and Devices: Neolithic Figurines from Franchti Cave, Greece.* Excavations at Franchti Cave Fascimile 9, Bloomington and Indianapolis: Indiana University Press.

Theocharis, D. R. (ed.) (1973) *Neolithic Greece.* Athens: National Bank of Greece.

Theocharis, D. R. (1981) *Neolithikos politismos: syntomi episkopisi tis Neolithikis sto elladiko choro* (Neolithic culture: A brief overview of the Neolithic in the Helladic area). Athens: National Bank of Greece.

Toufexis, G. (1990) *Neolithika eidolia zoon apo ti Thessalia* (Neolithic animal figurines from Thessaly). Postgraduate thesis, Thessaloniki, Department of History and Archaeology: Aristotle University of Thessaloniki.

Toufexis, G. (1994) 'Neolithic animal figurines from Thessaly' in *Thessalia: Dekapente chronia archaiologikis erevnas, 1975–1990. Apotelesmata kai prooptikes. Praktika Diethnous Synedriou Lyon, 17–22 Apriliou 1990* (Thessaly: Fifteen years of archaeological research, 1975–1990, Results and perspectives. Proceedings of the Lyon International Conference, 17–22 April 1990). Athens: Ministry of Culture, pp. 163–8.

Tringham, R. E. (1991) 'Households with faces: the challenge of gender in prehistoric architectural remains' in J.M. Gero and M.W. Conkey (eds) *Engendering Archaeology: Women and Prehistory.* Oxford: Blackwell, pp. 93–131.

Ucko, P. J. (1962) 'The interpretation of prehistoric anthropomorphic figurines'. *Journal of the Royal Anthropological Institute of Great Britain and Ireland* 92, 38–54.

Ucko, P. J. (1968) *Anthropomorphic Figurines of Predynastic Egypt and Neolithic Crete with Comparative Material from the Prehistoric Near East and Mainland Greece.* Royal Anthropological Institute Occasional Paper 24. London: Andrew Szmidla.

van Andel, T. H. and Runnels, C. N. (1988) 'An essay on the "emergence of civilization" in the Aegean world'. *Antiquity* 62, 234–47.

Wace, A. J. B. and Thompson, M. S. (1912) *Prehistoric Thessaly: Being Some Account of Recent Excavations and Explorations in Northeast Greece from Lake Kopais to the Borders of Macedonia.* Cambridge: Cambridge University Press.

Walde, D. and Willows, N. D. (eds) (1991) *The Archaeology of Gender: Proceedings of the Twenty-Second Annual Conference of the Archaeological Association of the University of Calgary.* The University of Calgary Archaeological Association.

Whittle, A. (1985) *Neolithic Europe: A Survey.* Cambridge: Cambridge University Press.

9 Engendering domination: a structural and contextual analysis of Minoan Neopalatial bronze figurines

LOUISE A. HITCHCOCK

We need to analyse artefacts in terms that go entirely beyond them.
(Michael Shanks and Christopher Tilley 1987)

Introduction

As in other areas of Minoan archaeology, consensus, agreement and certainty regarding the overall status of women and their relationship to Minoan social, religious and political structures is lacking. Generally speaking, representations depict women of high status and seem to fall into certain categories: goddesses/ priestesses, or a goddess impersonator whose image takes many forms; and attendants, worshippers, and protagonists in festivals and rituals believed to revolve around rites of passage and various aspects of fertility. Women occur in idealized depictions as young girls, as adolescents, and as mature women. The media of representation for women in the Neopalatial period (c. 1700–1450 BCE) includes the frescoes, seal iconography and bronze figurines which are the subject of this chapter.

Previous research on Cretan bronzes has resulted in the production of an empiricist catalogue and typology that distinguished eight different types of gestures (Verlinden 1984). Six of these are attested in Minoan bronzes from the Neopalatial period. These six gestures form the analytical background for this chapter and may be described as follows:

Gesture 1   This is the so-called 'Minoan Salute' with variations in the form of sub-types a–d discussed in Verlinden (1984: 90–1), in which the right hand touches or is directed toward the forehead and the left arm remains at the side or is bent across the chest (Figures 9.1 and 9.2).
Gesture 2   Both hands are bent toward the face (Figure 9.3).
Gesture 3   Both hands are placed on the hips (Figure 9.4).
Gesture 4   Both hands are folded on the chest (Figure 9.5).
Gesture 5   The hands are crossed on the chest (Figure 9.6).
Gesture 6   The right hand is folded on the chest, the left hand remains at the side (Figure 9.7).

In order to attempt to work out the relationship of the figurines to social practice in my study, I selected gender, gesture and context as significant traits,

Figure 9.1 Gesture 1 (from Tylissos, House A, Crete)

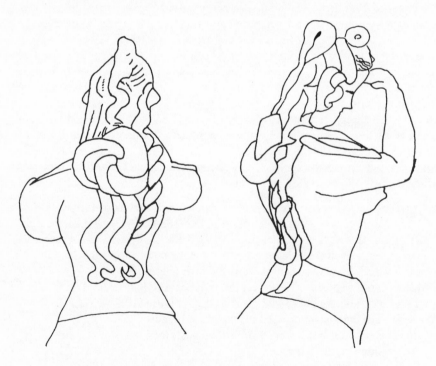

Figure 9.2 Gesture 1 variation 1b (from Troad, Turkey)

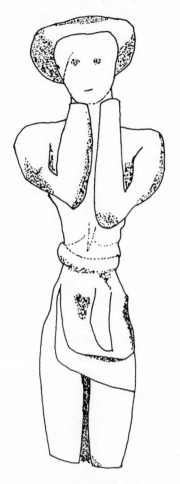

Figure 9.3 Gesture 2 (from the environs of Phaistos, Crete)

thereby introducing gender as one of the analytical concepts used (Gero and Conkey 1991: 9ff.). My data consisted of 114 out of 116 published Neopalatial bronze figurines depicting adult humans (Verlinden 1984; Lebessi and Muhly 1990: fig.14).

My analysis of the figurines was carried out on several levels: at the level of the objects themselves to tabulate the traits and examine their numerical breakdown (Tables 9.1–9.3); followed by a detailed descriptive analysis of the network of associations produced through archaeological context. I also searched the corpus of seal representations in the *Corpus der minoischen und mykenischen Siegel* (*CMS*) for gestures that were similar or identical to those made by the figurines, thereby introducing another level of context (Table 9.4). In attempting to interrelate all three levels of analysis, new networks of associations came into play, creating an ever-widening hermeneutic spiral (Hodder 1992; Shanks 1992) of contextual associations that I believe are relevant to documenting social

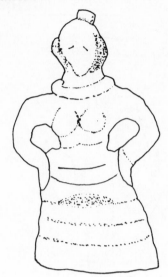

Figure 9.4 Gesture 3 (from Palaikastro, room 41, region X, Crete)

practice. This chapter presents a summary of a more detailed, unpublished study (Hitchcock 1991) along with a detailed discussion of gesture 4 where the hands are folded on the chest.

Gesture, power and authority

I would suggest that gestures 3 and 4 were used to express power and authority by females and males respectively. Although few in number, a broader range of gestures is made by the female figurines (Table 9.3). Multiple explanations for this are possible. They include: the use of certain gestures by females to define their own ideological sphere (Handsman 1991: 329ff.), the indication of a system of social ranking within a religious hierarchy acted out through ritual action for females who had access to bronze, and finally, a greater diversity of roles for women within the social and religious spheres of Minoan life. The vast majority of males as well as a significant percentage of the females tended to cluster in gesture 1a, the Minoan salute (Table 9.1). Here males greatly outnumber females (Table 9.3) by a margin of more than five to one (5.5 to 1 or 50 males to 11 females). The contextual and iconographic evidence clearly indicates that these represented a group or class of worshipper (Figure 9.8). The greater overall numbers of male figurines in proportion to female figurines (a two to one margin, see Table 9.2) further suggests engendered differences in social position as indicated by the asymmetrical distribution of resources (Miller and Tilley 1984: 7), namely bronze. Such disparities in the controlled distribution of a commodity for individual use, seems to be at odds with the portrayal of women in fresco imagery.

Only a single female bronze figurine makes gesture 3 (Figure 9.4). It was found at Palaikastro in a deposit of white ashes, pottery, clay bull heads, lamp

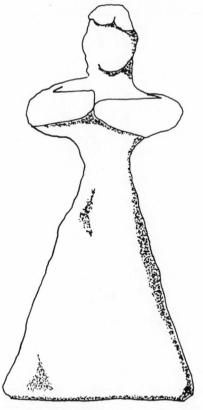

Figure 9.5 Gesture 4 (from the Dictaean Cave, Lassithi, Crete)

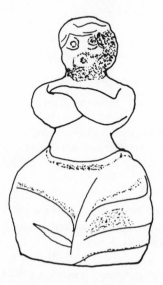

Figure 9.6 Gesture 5 (from Lyttos, Pedias, Crete)

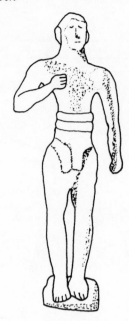

Figure 9.7 Gesture 6 (from Tylissos, Crete)

Table 9.1 Minoan bronzes, context by gesture

Gesture	PS	C	M	V	T	R	No Prov.	Total
1a	4	10	–	8	–	2	37	61
1b	–	–	–	1	1	–	5*	7
1c	–	1	2	–	–	1	6	10
1d	–	–	–	–	–	–	2*	2
2	–	–	–	2	–	1	1	4
3	–	–	–	–	–	1	–	1
4	2	5	–	3	–	–	3	13
5	–	1	–	–	–	–	2	3
6	–	–	–	–	–	–	5	5

PS = Peak sanctuary, C = Cave, M = Megastructure, V = Villa, T = Temple,
R = Rural find, Prov. = Provenance
* One figurine counted twice because it incorporated elements of sub-types b and d.
Verlinden (1984) classified it as 1b. The distinctions in Gesture 1 sub-types were made
by Verlinden. It is not clear whether the Minoans would have made the same distinc-
tion.

fragments, bovine bones and horn cores (Dawkins 1904–5: 287). Facial features
are selectively rendered, the skirt has horizontal folds and the hair is in a great
curl on top of the head that falls down the back. It is one of only two female
figurines wearing jewellery (a necklace), such display being more common to the
male figurines. Based on the gesture, Verlinden (1984: 52, n. 119) suggested
that it might be a priestess.

The rarity of the gesture, the material, namely bronze, its particular context,

Table 9.2 Minoan bronzes, context by gender

Gender	PS	C	M	V	T	R	No Prov.	Total
M	6	12	2	8	1	2	46	77
F	2	10	–	6	1	2	16	37
Total	8	22	2	14	2	4	62	114

PS = Peak sanctuary, C = Cave, M = Megastructure, V = Villa, T = Temple, R = Rural find, Prov. = Provenance

Table 9.3 Minoan bronzes, context by gender and gesture

Gender	PS	C	M	V	T	R	No Prov.	By gesture
M	3	8	–	8	–	1	28	1a
F	1	2	–	–	–	1	7	1a
M	–	–	–	–	1	–	1	1b
F	–	–	–	1	–	–	4*	1b
M	–	–	2	–	–	1	6	1c
F	–	1	–	–	–	–	–	1c
M	–	–	–	–	–	–	–	1d
F	–	–	–	–	–	–	2*	1d
M	–	–	–	–	–	–	1	2
F	–	–	–	2	–	1	–	2
M	–	–	–	–	–	–	–	3
F	–	–	–	–	–	1	–	3
M	1	–	–	–	–	–	1	4
F	1	5	–	3	–	–	2	4
M	–	–	–	–	–	–	1	5
F	–	1	–	–	–	–	1	5
M	–	–	–	–	–	–	4	6
F	–	–	–	–	–	–	1	6

PS = Peak Sanctuary, C = Cave, M = Megastructure, V = Villa, T = Temple, R = Rural find, Prov. = Provenance
* One figurine counted twice because it incorporated elements of sub-types b and d. Verlinden (1984) classifies it as 1b. The distinctions in Gesture 1 sub-types were made by Verlinden. It is not clear whether the Minoans would have made the same distinction.

and evidence from three seals would tend to support Verlinden's interpretation and my proposition that it was a female gesture of authority. In two instances, there is a central figure rendered in hierarchic scale flanked by two smaller figures. All are making gesture 3 (Figure 9.9). The possible roles of the flanking figures could be attendants, priestesses, worshippers, or minor deities. In addition to the small flanking figures, another example includes a built structure with an associated tree. Similar, though not identical, relationships can be observed in yet another seal in which the flanking figures are not rendered in hierarchic scale, but are both bent over in contrast to the central figure who is still positioned above them by virtue of her posture (Figure 9.10). Both of the flanking figures are associated with built structures associated with columns and vegetation, common Aegean religious symbols.

Table 9.4 Minoan bronzes, iconographic parallels for gestures 1–6*

Gesture	Male	Female	Seal parallels
1a	50	11	M-1
1b	2	5	M-2; F-3
1c	9	1	M-2; F-2, 2?
1d	–	2	F-1; 1?
2	1	3	F-2?
3	–	1	F-3
4	2	11	M-1
5	1	2	–
6	4	1	F-1; 1?

* Parallels which do not derive from seals are not tabulated. Neither are seal parallels which depict the figures gesturing in isolation as these do not provide enough contextual information to permit any kind of interpretive analysis.

Figure 9.8 So-called Mistress of the Mountains seal from the 'Palace' at Knossos, Crete (after Evans)

Figure 9.9 Gesture 3, Seal from Mycenae, Greece (after CMS I no. 159)

Figure 9.10 Gesture 3, Seal from Mycenae, Greece (after CMS I no. 126)

Context

Males and females are equally well represented in caves and 'villas' (large well-constructed houses incorporating 'palatial' design features; however, their function is not well understood) (Table 9.2). Since males usually greatly outnumber females, the almost equal numbers of females in cave and villa contexts is particularly significant: it suggests that both males and females were taking part in the activities at caves. A number of different functions can be suggested for the figurines found in villas including storage, ritual and personal use. In each case, these interpretations are heavily dependent upon context, and are too detailed to be elaborated here.

In contrast to gesture 1, females making gesture 4 outnumber males by more than five to one (Table 9.3), although in fewer numbers (actually 5.5 to 1, or 2 males to 11 females). Both gesture 1a and 4 occur in the peak sanctuary context (Table 9.1). Based on this, I would like to suggest that gesture 4 is a female gesture of worship employed alternately with gesture 1a. However, females making gesture 4 occur more frequently in cave contexts (Table 9.3). They account for half of the executions of gesture 4 among females. This may be significant, since gesture 4 is one of the two most frequent gestures made by females and more than one quarter of the female bronzes with known provenance occur in caves. Females overall, regardless of their gesture, are rarely attested in peak sanctuary contexts where there are three males for each female. However, at eight, the total number of bronzes from peak and outdoor sanctuaries is so small, little else can be said.

Both of the males that make gesture 4 are unusual. One is a male bronze without provenance (Verlinden 1984, no.93) and wearing a tall, conical cap (Figure 9.11). It is one of only two Neopalatial bronze male figurines which wear headgear. The conical cap connoted divinity or ruler status in the Near East where such caps typically included horns. The Mesopotamian ruler might have himself portrayed with divine attributes such as the conical cap in order to enhance his status, as is depicted in the Akkadian Stele of Naram Sin (Figure 9.12).

The other male bronze figurine making gesture 4 (Figure 9.13) comes from the peak sanctuary at Kato Symi (Lebessi 1988: 154; Lebessi and Muhly 1990: fig.14) and is stylistically dated to the Neopalatial period (Verlinden 1984). It is highly detailed: the eyes are rendered with incised pupils; nose, mouth, and ears

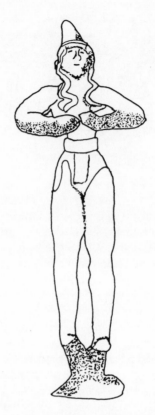

Figure 9.11 Gesture 4, male with conical cap, from Katsaba, Crete

as well as hair falling on the chest and the back are depicted. The largeness of the ears and eyes may have constituted individuating features. The Symi figurine was found in an area referred to as the 'Sacred Enclosure', although the precise location is unclear.

The site of Kato Symi is located in south-eastern Crete on the slopes of Mount Dikte where it overlooks the south coast. The date of the Neopalatial sanctuary is Late Minoan I (*c.* 1650–1450 BCE). This period is represented by three architectural phases and includes a 'monumental complex' open to the sky and composed of three distinct elements as summarized from Lebessi and Muhly (1990). The complex incorporates a massive enclosure wall defining a rectangular area (approximately 530 sq. m), a paved road (2 m wide) leading to the interior of this area and a rectangular, unroofed built structure lacking internal supports (12.20 × 7.7 m) in the middle of the area. The road follows a dog-leg approach.

Associated material from the 'Sacred Enclosure' included cups, pots and faunal remains in a midden deposit. The excavators suggest that ritual feasting was taking place. They interpret the ground plan of the rectangular structure as conforming to the representation of the tripartite shrine on the so-called 'Peak

Figure 9.12 Akkadian Stele of Naram Sin, originally Sippar, Babylonia, later Susa, Mesopotamia

Sanctuary' rhyton from Kato Zakro as reconstructed by J.W. Shaw (1978). The enclosure wall distinguishes Kato Symi from Shaw's reconstruction. Its presence around the rectangular built structure and the location of the midden deposit between the two architectural features indicates that participants would have been free to either move back and forth, or circumambulate the rectangular structure in the performance of ritual action.

Elite and cult connections

At least five bronze figurines, one 'libation' table with a Linear A inscription, and the absence of human and animal terracottas that were a common offering at peak sanctuaries in the earlier 'Old Palace' or 'Middle Minoan' period (*c.* 1900–1700 BCE) were found in association with the sacred enclosure. This suggests an élite status for those moving about the enclosure (Lebessi and Muhly 1990: 334–5). The relationship between luxury materials and peak sanctuaries indicates palatial control (Peatfield 1987). This is further indicated by the

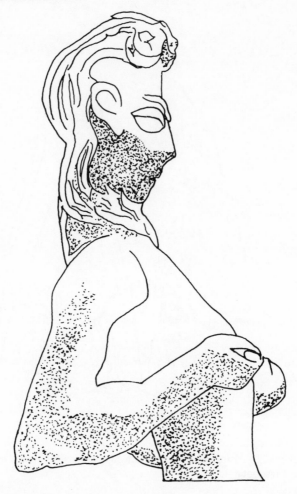

Figure 9.13 Gesture 4 (from the sanctuary at Kato Symi, Crete (after Lebessi and Muhly, 1990))

regulatory role which the so-called 'Palaces' played in the production and distribution of goods such as bronze to the stratum of society that had access to them, and the proliferation of villas in the Neopalatial period. This indicates an élite stratum of Minoan society that was predominantly male which was procuring bronze figurines and making offerings at the peak sanctuaries. The presence of the male figurine making gesture 4 within the enclosure further emphasizes this élite connection. Bronze was the material favoured for dedicatory figurines in the Late Minoan I period. The use of bronze, the high degree of workmanship, the individuating features and the rarity of gesture 4 in the male sphere would tend to indicate that this particular figurine placed in Kato Symi represented a specific individual of higher status than the dedicants of two of the other male bronze figurines (Verlinden nos 51 and 115) which are making the more common gesture 1, the so-called 'Minoan salute'.

Figure 9.14 Gesture 4 (from Kydonia, Crete (after CMS I no. 201)

Although gesture 4 is made predominantly by female bronze figurines occurring mainly in caves and villas, in its only occurrence on a seal (CMS I no. 201), it is being made by a male (Figure 9.14). In this composition, he stands between 'horns of consecration' and is flanked by a winged goat and a Minoan genius (Betts 1965, 1978: 18, n. 4; Pini 1978: 142–5). Sir Arthur Evans (1921–36: IV, 467) has interpreted this figure as a 'Youthful Male God' based on his relationship to the horns, his centrality, and the flanking by supernatural animals which places him in what Nanno Marinatos (1984: 61–2) calls the 'realm of the fantastic'. MacGillivray *et al.* (1988: 267, 1989: 426–7) have noted that the gesture of the figure in the seal is identical to the gesture of the chryselephantine male figurine recently discovered at Palaikastro (Figure 9.15). Based on Evans' interpretation of the seal figure as a divinity, they interpret the Palaikastro statuette as a cult figure, and not as votive. Sackett and MacGillivray (1989: 26–31) have gone so far as to suggest that the Palaikastro statuette may have represented a youthful Zeus. Their interpretation is based on classical Greek myth, archaeological evidence that the Roman temple site of Diktaian Zeus overlies Minoan Palaikastro where an Archaic Greek 'Hymn to the Kouros' was found, and on four offering tables from the peak sanctuary at Petsophas overlooking Palaikastro on which DI-KI-TE was inscribed in Linear A (Sackett and MacGillivray 1989: 30–31). Does the evidence suggest continuity of cult or the projection of a homeostatic idealized Greek past onto a dynamic, changing pre-Greek Bronze Age?

In trying to determine whether the status of males making gesture 4 is divine, I want to consider two other examples of supernatural animals flanking human figures. In the so-called 'Throne Room' at Knossos, the occupant of the throne was flanked by griffins. A similar, though not identical (McCallum 1987) situation can be found at Mycenaean Pylos. It has been suggested that a re-enactment of an epiphany took place in the Knossian throne room with a priestess occupying the throne (Niemeier 1987) and that a female occupies the throne because the stone seat is carved to suit a woman's anatomy (Peatfield pers. com., 1988). Still, it remains uncertain whether the occupant of the Knossian 'throne' was a male or a female, a king or a queen, a priest or a priestess, or some other type of official.

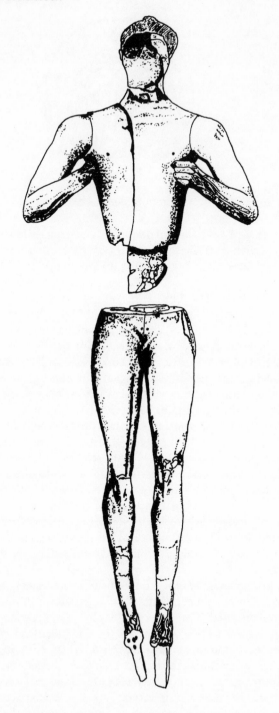

Figure 9.15 Palaikastro Statuette, from Palaikastro, Building 5, Crete (after MacGillivray and Sackett 1991)

The situation at Pylos is somewhat different. The title 'wanax' or king is attested in the Pylos tablets [Na58; Ta711; La622; Un03], as is the word for throne: to-no [Ta707]. What, then, happens to a ruler who is placed in association with supernatural animals? Does this make the wanax divine or place him under divine protection? How strongly do the secular and the religious become conflated? In ancient Sumer, kingship was handed down from heaven (Kramer 1963: 328–31), whereas in Egypt, Pharaoh was god.

Discussion

Now that our hermeneutic spiral has led us to Sumer and back, I wish to state that I am not raising these questions to suggest that the situation in Minoan Crete was necessarily identical to those in Pylos, Mesopotamia, or in Egypt. Rather, I am trying to demonstrate that the status of a figure placed between supernatural animals is not as simple as Evans, Sackett, MacGillivray, Marinatos and others would have us believe. Do the male bronze figurines, the seal example and the Palaikastro statuette all making gesture 4 represent Minoan deities or do they represent early examples of Minoan ruler portraiture? How do we relate all of these strands of contextual meaning back to the question of gender?

I want to reiterate the high degree of workmanship and the careful rendering of facial details in the piece from Kato Symi (Figure 9.13). There are also other differences in our male examples of gesture 4. The long, 'snaky' locks of hair that are typical of mature Minoan males are absent on the seal example and the Palaikastro statuette (Figures 9.14, 9.15). The stippling on the Palaikastro statuette suggests the shaved head that is an indication of youth in the Bronze Age Aegean (Marinatos 1984). In contrast, both Verlinden no. 93 and the Kato Symi statuette have long locks and detailed workmanship. (Figures 9.11, 9.13). Verlinden no. 93 is further distinguished by the cap. Both of the male examples can be distinguished from all of the females making gesture 4, which are simply rendered and lack facial detail (Figure 9.15). Despite their greater numbers, the female figurines making gesture 4 received less effort and artistic workmanship. Their context in caves and villas rendered them less visible. Of the female figurines making gesture 4 from 'villas', only the one from Palaikastro House X (see Dawkins 1904–5: 272ff) has a well documented context (Bosanquet and Dawkins 1939: 122–3). As an example, it effectively serves to underscore significant differences from the male figurines. In terms of workmanship, facial features are not rendered, other details are not clearly visible, and the back of the figurine is practically flat (Verlinden 1984: 55). In terms of context, it was found with an ivory comb in a narrow cubicle decorated with painted plaster. Its location eight thresholds and a corridor from the reconstructed external portico (Preziosi 1983: 400ff.) ensured its seclusion.

The gendered contrasts in the figurines making gesture 4 might be further illustrated by the following oppositions: male/female, detailed/simple, individual/common, presence/absence, peak sanctuary/cave, outside/inside, public/personal. These oppositions underlie the social relations that were cunningly acted out in the production and use of these figurines by the Minoans. For a term, in this case gesture 4 used in the male context, to become dominant, it needed to devalue another term (Derrida 1976, 1978; Ulmer 1985). The transference of gesture 4 in the male sphere is thus built upon the repressed female. The less visible context of caves and villas for female figurines making gesture 4 served to place them under erasure through the creation of an ideology of separate spaces. As a result, the status of females making gesture 4 does not seem to be as high within the female sphere as those making gesture 3.

Gesture 4 was primarily associated with females, as its distribution among the bronzes indicates (Table 9.3). However, I would suggest that its enhanced visibility, prominent display and restricted use by males indicates a gradual transference of power relations between males and females through the appropriation of a gesture popular among a particular class of female worshipper. Among males, its use was restricted to males of rank, status, power, and possibly divinity, or a combination of these, as further demonstrated by the much greater degree of detail in males making gesture 4.

Gesture 4 further combined elements of rank and reverence which were played out in the sphere of public and perhaps private ritual action as indicated by its contextual associations. These include peak sanctuaries and caves where it was made only by females. If the bronze example from Kato Symi represented a ruler, then it also served a polysemous function as a representation of a powerful ruler who chose to demonstrate his reverence for the divine. This demonstration was carried out by using a gesture that was predominantly used by female worshippers. By appropriating a known sign of worship, placing it into a slightly different context, and bringing it into a visible public discourse of social practice, he thus engendered his dominant role in Minoan society.

Acknowledgements

The research for this chapter could not have been carried out without the enthusiastic support of Professor David Gordon Mitten of Harvard. Its further development was greatly encouraged by the comments of Marianna Nikolaidou and Mike Shanks. Bill Sillar made the fateful suggestion that I perform the gestures as I read the original paper. Thanks are due to Claire Lyons for comments on an earlier draft.

References

Betts, J. (1965) 'Notes on a Possible Minoan Forgery'. *Annual of the British School at Athens* 61, 203–6.

Betts, J. (1978) 'Some Early Forgeries: The Sangiorgi Group'. *Corpus der minoischen und mykenischen Siegel* Suppl. I. Berlin: G. Mann Verlag, 17–35.

Bosanquet, R.C. and Dawkins, R.M. (1939) *The Unpublished Objects from the Palaikastro Excavations, 1902–1906*. London: Macmillan and Co. Ltd.

Dawkins, R.M. (1904–5) 'Excavations at Palaikastro'. *Annual of the British School at Athens* 11, 258–92.

Derrida, J. (1976) *Of Grammatology*. Baltimore: Johns Hopkins University Press.

Derrida, J. (1978) *Writing and Difference*. Chicago: University of Chicago Press.

Evans, A.J. (1921–36) *The Palace of Minos at Knossos I-IV*. London: Macmillan and Co. Ltd.

Gero, J. and Conkey, M. (eds) (1991) *Engendering Archaeology: Women and Prehistory*. Oxford: Blackwell.

Handsman, R.G. (1991) 'Whose Art Was Found at Lepenski Vir? Gender Relations and Power in Archaeology' in J. Gero and M. Conkey (eds) *Engendering Archaeology: Women and Prehistory*. Oxford: Blackwell, pp. 329–65.

Hitchcock, L.A. (1991) *Towards a Method for Recovering Meaning and Function in Minoan Bronze Figurines*. Athens: Unpublished Paper of the American School of Classical Studies.

Hodder, I. (1992) *Archaeology: Theory and Practice*. London: Routledge.

Kramer, S.N. (1963) *The Sumerians*. Chicago: University of Chicago Press.

Lebessi, A. (1976) 'A Sanctuary of Hermes and Aphrodite in Crete'. *Expedition* 18, 3, 2–13.

Lebessi, A. (1988) 'Syme Viannou'. *To Ergon tes en Athenais Archaiologikes Hetaireias*.

Lebessi, A. and Muhly, P. (1990) 'Aspects of Minoan Cult. Sacred Enclosures. The Evidence from the Syme Sanctuary (Crete)'. *Archaeologischer Anzeiger* 3, 315–36.

McCallum, L.R. (1987) *Decorative Program in the Mycenaean Palace of Pylos: The Megaron Frescoes*. Philadelphia, Pennsylvania. Unpublished PhD Dissertation, University of Pennsylvania.

MacGillivray, J.A., Sackett, L.H., Driessen, J., MacDonald, C. and Smyth, D. (1988) 'Excavations at Palaikastro, 1987'. *Annual of the British School at Athens* 83, 259–82.

MacGillivray, J.A., Sackett, L.H., Driessen, J., Farnoux, A. and Smyth, D. (1989) 'Excavations at Palaikastro, 1988'. *Annual of the British School at Athens* 84, 417–45.

MacGillivray, J.A., Sackett, L.H., Driessen, J., Bridges, R. and Smyth, D. (1991) 'Excavations at Palaikastro, 1990'. *Annual of the British School at Athens* 86, 121–47.

Marinatos, N. (1984) *Art and Religion in Thera*. Athens: D. and I. Mathioulakis.

Miller, D. and Tilley, C. (eds) (1984) *Ideology, Power and Prehistory*. Cambridge: Cambridge University Press.

Niemeier, W.-D. (1987) 'On the function of the "Throne Room" in the palace at Knossos' in R. Hägg and N. Marinatos (eds) *The Function of the Minoan Palaces*. Stockholm: Svenska Institutet i Athen, pp. 163–8.

Peatfield, A. (1987) 'Palace and peak: The political and religious relationship between palaces and peak sanctuaries' in R. Hägg and N. Marinatos (eds) *The Function of the Minoan Palaces*. Stockholm: Svenska Institutet i Athen, pp. 89–93.

Pini, I. (ed.) (1964–74) *Corpus der minoischen und mykenischen Siegel*. Berlin: G. Mann.

Pini, I. (1978) 'Echt oder falsch? – Einige Falle'. *Corpus der minoischen und mykenischen Siegel* Suppl. I. 135–57.

Preziosi, D. (1983) *Minoan Architectural Design*. Berlin: Mouton.

Sackett, H. and MacGillivray, S. (1989) 'Boyhood of a God'. *Archaeology* 42, 5, 26–31.

Shanks, M. (1992) *Experiencing the Past: On the Character of Archaeology*. London: Routledge.

Shanks, M. and Tilley, C. (1987) *Social Theory and Archaeology*. Cambridge: Polity Press.

Shaw, J.W. (1978) 'Evidence for the Minoan Tripartite Shrine'. *American Journal of Archaeology* 82, 429–48.

Ulmer, G.L. (1985) *Applied Grammatology*. Baltimore: Johns Hopkins University Press.

Verlinden, C. (1984) 'Les statuettes anthropomorphes crétoises en bronze et en plomb, du IIIe millenaire au VIIe siecle av. J.-C.'. *Archaeologia Transatlantica* IV Louvain-la Neuve, Belgium: Art and Archaeology Publications, Collège Érasme.

10 Changing gender relations in the later prehistory of Eastern Hungary

JOHN CHAPMAN

Introduction

With few exceptions, Hungarian prehistory has been the stronghold of an apparently gender-free, and, therefore, implicitly male-dominated, paradigm. There is a long and distinguished record of male scholarship in Hungarian prehistory, stretching back to the foundation of the National Museum in 1802. In this record, it is exceptional to find women such as Baroness Zsófia von Torma, the discoverer of Tordos in the 1870s, who published and excavated widely (Gyula 1972). The male achievement continued into the twentieth century through strong schools of archaeology in Budapest and Szeged (Laszlovszky and Siklódi 1990) and with increasing attention paid by non-Hungarians to the wealth of the local archaeological heritage. Since there were few female professionals in Hungary until after the Second World War, the narratives of Hungarian prehistory are, for the most part, both replete with male achievers and male achievements and bereft of a gendered perspective about major foci of change.

Previous studies

There is a strong tendency for male prehistorians to exclude females from their discussions, unless the topics of figurines or burials are under consideration. In his review of Neolithic and Copper Age studies, entitled 'Clay Gods', Kalicz (1970) takes the standard line on Neolithic art and ritual: 'Quite naturally, the female became the symbol of fertility, as the source of life' (Kalicz 1970: 15). Similarly, major recent surveys of the Late Neolithic and the Bronze Age in eastern Hungary, all edited by males (Kovács 1994; Meier-Arendt 1992; Raczky 1987), consistently avoid discussion of gender except in the context of burials and figurines. A male-dominance position is also adopted by Sherratt in his processual research programme on social organization, settlement and exchange in eastern Hungary (Sherratt 1982a, 1982b, 1983). Here, males and females are related in a hierarchical manner, with males possessing the 'power within the group (which) consisted in control over marriageable women' (1982b: 22). Women are fetishized as exchange commodities, such as valuables and trade items, while men are regarded as the pivotal points in lineage relationships and alliances.

It is when we turn to the work of Ida Bognár-Kutzian that gender perspectives make their first real impact in recent Hungarian prehistory. In her classic study of the Copper Age cemetery of Tiszapolgár-Basatanya (Bognár-Kutzian 1963), the author uses ethnographic parallels and multi-disciplinary research to produce innovative conclusions about the mortuary population of the Polgár region. Three aspects of her gendered account are significant: the assessment of gendered status from grave goods; the investigation of the conditions of women's life from sex ratios and grave goods; and the assessment of the gendered division of labour from the distribution of tools.

Amalia Mozsolics has had a major impact on Hungarian Bronze Age metalwork studies (Mozsolics 1943, 1967, 1973, 1985). However, the fact that most of Mozsolics' research concerns assemblages of weaponry has limited her opportunities for the development of gendered perspectives on the Bronze Age. As her eminent contemporary, the late Marija Gimbutas, remarked in an interview about the Bronze Age: 'weapons, weapons, weapons; it's like TV – war, war, war whatever channel'. It is the work of Gimbutas which we now consider, since it is based on a strongly gendered approach.

In her later syntheses, Gimbutas argued for a total opposition between 'Old Europe' – the Late Neolithic and Copper Age climax societies of South East Europe – and the warrior pastoralist invaders from the Pontic steppes who brought this civilization to an abrupt end (Gimbutas 1978, 1979, 1989). Two incompatible social structures and ideologies confronted each other: a matrilinear, egalitarian and peaceful Old Europe, whose ritual foundations were birth, death and regeneration through the female principle of the Goddess; and a patriarchal, ranked and warlike Kurgan horde, dominated by virile male heroic warrior gods of the shining and thunderous sky (Gimbutas 1979: 114).

The main reason for Gimbutas' popularity among Californian and other feminists (Knaster 1990) is surely her depiction of a vision of a peaceful matrilinear world before Indo-European males destroyed women's creativity through unceasing warfare. The upshot of the rejection of Gimbutas' exaggerated gender opposition and the domination of male archaeologists in the narration of Hungarian prehistory is the almost total absence of integration of gendered perspectives into mainstream archaeological writing. In this article, I attempt to make a preliminary assessment of the role of gender contrasts and oppositions in the Neolithic and Copper Age of eastern Hungary. This assessment forms part of an attempt to write a variety of narratives about an archaeology of social power from differing viewpoints, in order to make sense of the results of our collaborative fieldwork in north-east Hungary (the 'Upper Tisza Project').[1]

Theoretical perspectives

The appearance of gender and age differentiation may be taken, *inter alia*, as a set of changes in social power relationships. The types of social power in question may be defined, *pace* Michael Mann (1986, 1993) as ideological and economic, with little emphasis on military power and no evidence for state (i.e.

political) power. The context of gender differentiation is the time-space framework of social action set within contemporary social structure. The differentiation of a neutral physical space, not yet colonized by human communities, into a series of places associated with specific functions leads to the emergence of place value and a narrative of peoples' pasts inscribed onto that landscape. As place values accrue, places become arenas of social power in which important and quotidian cultural activities are carried out by individuals and groups in pursuit of their own cultural and social goals (Chapman 1988, 1993, 1994). The definition and explanation of time-space sequences of arenas of social power (ASPs), therefore, constitute an important goal in prehistory.

The appearance of new ASPs in a given region is always an important change and requires explanation. It has been proposed that one way to resolve otherwise unmanageable contradictions within an existing social structure is a spatial displacement which allows different forms of social action, of a nature otherwise inappropriate or impossible in traditional time-space contexts (Chapman 1994). Three common contradictions have been defined: (1) new potential for the accumulation of personal wealth in social groups with strongly collective traditions; (2) the expansion of social networks, whether by colonization or exchange network linkage; and (3) changes in gendered power relations. There are several criteria for the identification of one of these contradictions rather than any other, or a combination of several at once. The most important is a new range of material phenomena occurring in a new ASP but not in coeval ASPs or previous ASPs (e.g. a new kind of mortuary site with evidence for accumulation of rich grave goods). The second is an unambiguous linkage between the new material phenomena and the proposed cause (e.g. different associated symbols found only in female graves). The third is evidence for contrasts in the material record of traditional ASPs coeval with new ASPs (e.g. minimal material differentiation in domestic contexts in contrast to a rich and varied mortuary record). In this approach, the questions 'what is the evidence for gendered power relations and changes in such relations?' can best be answered within a time-space context of power relations. In the following example, the archaeological record of Neolithic and Copper Age communities in eastern Hungary is explored in an attempt to identify the extent to which gender is explicitly used as a structuring principle.

The Neolithic and Copper Age of eastern Hungary

Eastern Hungary forms part of the middle Danube basin, one of the largest lowland basins in Eastern Europe (Figure 10.1). However, within an apparently uniform topography, there is marked diversity in soils, vegetation and subsistence potential, only partly related to the annual or seasonal inundation of much of the Plain. The sequence of ASPs in eastern Hungary in the period 5800–2500 cal. BC may be summarized as an overall preponderance of generally short-term, open, flat settlement sites, punctuated with the periodic but long-term use of tells – settlement mounds consisting of occupational debris of vertically built-up settlement layers. Burial was predominantly intramural throughout the Neolithic, while extramural mortuary sites in the Copper Age

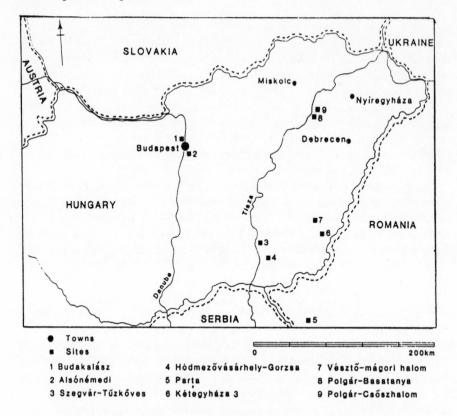

Figure 10.1 Location map of eastern Hungary, showing the location of sites and monuments mentioned in the text.

varied between large, flat cemeteries and mortuary barrows, often termed 'kurgans'. This sequence of ASPs (Figure 10.2) represents a series of contrasting site types, in which the appearance of new ASPs often contrasts with pre-existing site types (Chapman 1994). This discussion will be structured by the division of site types into the two overall classes of ASPs – domestic and mortuary.

Domestic arenas of social power

The Neolithic of eastern Hungary is dominated by the settlement record. Hamlets and villages, as well as single farmsteads, are known from the outset. Timber-framed wattle-and-daub houses are found from the Early Neolithic through to the Late Neolithic (Raczky 1988). In the Early and Middle Neolithic, artefact assemblages regularly include items of ritual paraphernalia. Few artefacts except the figurines have strong associations with a specific gender; the vast majority of gendered figures are female. It is assumed that females controlled many of the household activities, including care of the fire and, by extension, potting, bread-making and cooking. Small-scale hoe agriculture is documented,

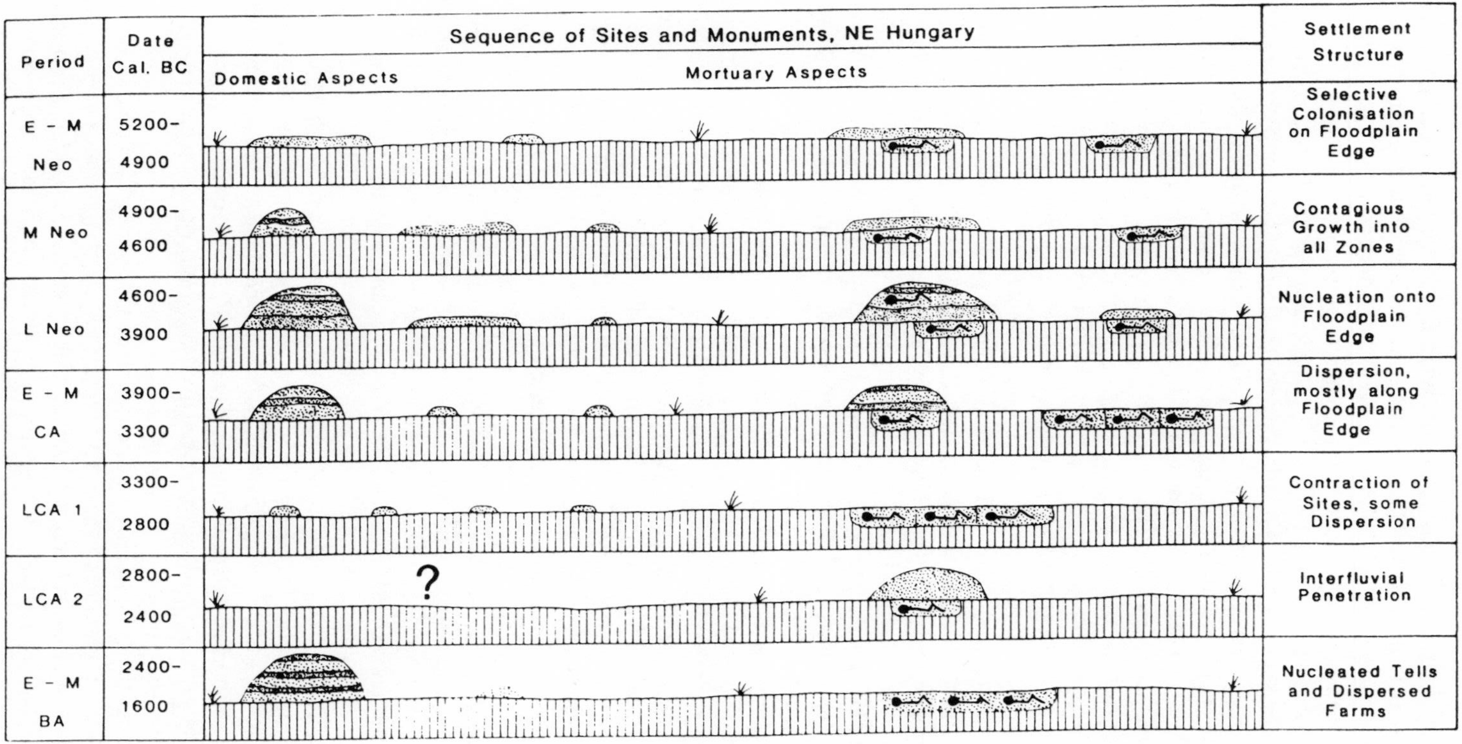

Figure 10.2 Dated sequence of the settlement structure of domestic and mortuary arenas of social power in eastern Hungary.

together with broad-spectrum hunting, gathering, shell-collecting and fishing; many of these activities relied on women's work (Brumfiel 1991; Claassen 1991). It is unclear whether domestic ritual was controlled by females or by males making use of female imagery; but there is little doubt that females possessed much economic and ideological power.

In the later part of the Middle Neolithic and especially in the Late Neolithic, tell villages emerge, characterized by increasingly diverse and elaborate material culture. An ancestor ideology is embedded in the structure of these settlements, where houses are often built directly above those where the ancestors once lived (Chapman 1991). The houses of the Late Neolithic are particularly large, durable and elaborate (Raczky 1987). Ritual artefacts are more common than before, with a majority of female figurines, some males and a few hermaphrodites. In the Late Neolithic, pottery decoration resembles textile patterns and the clothing on figurines, making multiple links in female production. The subsistence strategies pursued were broadly similar to those of the earlier period. However, the nucleation of up to 200 people or 30 families in tell co-residence had many social advantages to offset the heightened potential for disruptive aggression and violence. These included the potential for more elaborate socialization of children in contrast to the relative isolation of a farmstead, the increased development of supra-household groupings as a counterpoise to household units and the opportunities for richer social interaction. If the elaboration of material culture is related to such social possibilities, the roles played by women, men and children would be critical. Two areas where women's social power could have been expressed were in food and clothing, which are considered as idioms of political negotiation in the open, competitive environs of a tell community (Brumfiel 1991). The existence of domestic shrines at tells such as Vésztő-mágori halom (Hegedüs and Makkay 1987) and a public shrine at the tell of Parţa (Lazarovici 1989) indicates the increasing significance of private and public ancestor ritual but there is still no clear indication of whether ritual was controlled by males or females.

In the Copper Age, the occupation of tells declined gradually, with very few settled in the Middle Copper Age. The main settlement unit in this period is the dispersed farmstead, with its nucleus of an extended family at the centre of the family landholdings. The decreased diversity in material culture seen on the farms stood in contrast to that of those few surviving tell communities such as Vésztő. Maintenance of social reproduction required the participation of a substantial number of farmsteads (perhaps as many as 50) in an extensive breeding network focused on those few tells still in use and on other communal places. Social actors in this network also exchanged exotic items obtained through inter-regional exchange (Sherratt 1982b). An increasingly important role in such networks was played by household heads, whether male or female.

One of the most significant changes in the Copper Age was the transition from subsistence practices based on primary products (animal meat) to practices based on animal secondary products. The so-called 'Secondary Products Revolution' highlights the linked adoption of five innovations – the plough, animal traction, woolly sheep, dairy products and equid domestication – in a neo-diffusionist package originating in the Near East *c.* 4500 cal. BC and said to appear in Europe after 3500 cal. BC (Sherratt 1979). In fact, there is convincing evidence from Hungary for the emergence of woollen textiles, dairy produce, domestic horses and possibly the plough before 3500 cal. BC (Chapman 1982). What would be the expected impact of parts of the Secondary Products Revolution in the Early Copper Age in the Carpathian Basin on gendered power relations?

One way of approaching this question is the examination of cross-cultural ethnographic data on task differentiation. This approach has been justly criticized as being ultimately sterile if used in isolation (Spector 1991) but, if carefully targeted, can lead to valuable insights. The Human Relations Area Files study in question lists seven activities in which there is a very strong preponderance of female involvement: collecting wild vegetal food; dairy production; spinning; laundering; water fetching; cooking; and preparation of vegetal foods (Murdock and Provost 1973). It is not difficult to appreciate the potential for the increase in female economic power through control of the production of woollen textiles and the development of a range of new dairy foods. It is suggested that the potential increase in female economic power in these two innovations matched the potential increase in male economic power through the development of animal traction, horse-riding and ploughing, at any rate prior to military exploitation of the horse. Thus, the onset of secondary products created new opportunities for the consolidation of economic power, but in spatially differentiated and gender-contrasting sectors – the *domus* and the *agrios*.

In the early part of the late Copper Age, there is little evidence for any settlement unit other than the farmstead. Settlement remains are increasingly dispersed across the plains landscape, with small-scale, often undifferentiated material remains. This increased settlement dispersion is matched by an expansion of social networks documented through the enormous distribution of Baden pottery and by the inter-regional trade in metals.

In the later part of this period, settlement evidence becomes almost invisible in eastern Hungary. It may be hypothesized that increased levels of budding-off from extended family farms led to the foundation of smaller farms in increasingly marginal locations, with a higher proportion of unsustainable farms ending in abandonment. It is paradoxical that so little evidence for farmstead stability exists from the period when secondary products-based subsistence strategies became more widespread. The increasing importance of secondary products would have presumably led to the strengthening of both male and female economic power bases proposed for the earlier Copper Age.

In summary, a series of settlement transformations, from selective colonization, to site nucleation, to maximum site dispersion, was mediated by the presence of the single farmstead as a key element in the social landscape. In comparison with the Neolithic, the increased divergence of economic resources in the Copper Age stimulates the emergence of a more gendered division of labour, with prestige gained from the production of food and clothing available to females controlling the *domus* as a counterpoise to male prestige in the *agrios*. In any period of increasing gender differentiation, the self-identities of the two genders led to self-definition of prestigious activities, materials and lifestyles capable of expression only by members of that gender.

The mortuary domain

The mortuary domain is a key spatial arena of public performance, in which appropriate ways of treating the dead are negotiated, including the definition of gender categories and roles (Chapman 1994; Mosko 1989; Pollock 1991). Major changes in mortuary ASPs are observed in the Neolithic and Copper Age of eastern Hungary.

In the Early–Middle Neolithic, intramural burial in settlements was typical for the region and as yet no extramural cemetery has been located (Chapman 1983; Kalicz and Makkay 1977; Kutzian 1944; Trogmayer 1969). No explicit rules of gender differentiation were observed whether relating to grave goods, burial mode or orientation. In the Late Neolithic, intramural burial continued to be dominant, on both tells and flat sites, but with new rules emphasizing gender separation. A very high proportion of all tell burials were contracted inhumations in small clusters, often in timber coffins, with few grave goods. There was a strong tendency for females to be laid out on the left side, and males on their right side (Horváth 1987). The total absence, or small number, of child burials on the tells is also striking (an exception is Szegvár-Tüzköves: Korek 1987).

The Late Neolithic developments signify an increased distancing of the living from the dead on tells but the inclusion of the dead in ancestral places is still maintained. If the serological analysis of one of the Gorzsa clusters is correct, and the deceased are members of a single genetic unit going back several generations (Horváth 1987), we may conclude that the newly dead are included on tells so as to maintain and strengthen links with the ancestors. Thus kin groups pursuing an ideology of cyclical time are in control of the mortuary spaces of tells, thereby maintaining control over traditional customs in the domestic domain.

The first appearance of discrete, bounded cemeteries in eastern Hungary can be dated to the Early Copper Age. These bounded areas imply, *pace* Saxe (1970) and Goldstein (1981), the operation of lineage principles, a notion supported by the recognition at one of the largest cemeteries – Tiszapolgár-Basatanya (henceforth Basatanya) – of lines of burials suggested to be family groupings (Bognár-Kutzian 1963). However, it is important to note that intramural burials on tells still continue in this period, as at Vésztö. I now turn to a more detailed analysis of the Basatanya Cemetery, since it spans the Early–Middle Copper Age and is the largest excavated sample of Copper Age graves in eastern Hungary.

The Basatanya cemetery was excavated in 1929 before the main excavation in 1950–54 by I. Bognár-Kutzian (1963). A total of 154 Copper Age graves were identified, 67 from the Early Copper Age (Period I) and 87 from the Middle Copper Age (Period II). The total duration of the cemetery has been estimated to be 900 years, from 4500 to 3600 cal. BC (Forenbacher 1993). While the sex

Table 10.1 Presence–absence chart of non-ceramic grave goods in Period I at the Tiszapolgár-Basatanya cemetery by age and gender

Grave good	Male	Female	Child	Adult & child
Deer tooth	–	★	–	–
Auroch bone	–	–	–	★ (Female)
Shed antler	★	–	★	–
Pig/boar's tusk	★	–	★	★ (Male)
Other wild animal bones	★	–	–	–
Mussels	★	★	–	–
Snails	★	–	–	–
Cattle metatarsal	★	–	–	★ (Male)
Other cattle bone	★	★	–	–
Pig mandible	★	–	★	★ (Male)
Complete dog	★	–	–	–
Other domestic animal bones	★	–	★	–
Bone awl	★	★	–	–
Bone spoon	–	★	–	–
Antler artefact	★	★	★	★ (Male)
Pebble	–	★	–	–
Flint blade	★	–	★	★ (Male & female)
Flint scraper	–	–	★	–
Obsidian	–	–	★	–
Ground stone	–	★	–	★ (Male)
Limestone beads	★	★	★	★ (Male & female)
Limestone disc	★	–	–	–
Clay loom-weight	★	–	–	–
Ochre lumps	★	–	–	–
Copper bead	★	★	★	–
Copper ring	★	★	★	–
Copper bracelet	★	–	★	–
Traces of fire	★	★	★	–

ratio is more or less equal in Period II, males outnumber females in Period I by almost 2:1. Children are under-represented in both Periods (Némeskeri and Szathmári 1987). The range and quantity of grave goods deposited at Basatanya and the size of the burial population offers the opportunity for many kinds of analyses. In this chapter, discussion is limited to qualitative analyses of non-ceramic grave goods and their age-sex associations, which leads to an exploration of the creation of the social identities of males, females and children.

The non-ceramic grave goods fall into 39 types, 28 of which appear in Period I and 29 in Period II (Tables 10.1 and 10.2). On the basis of Némeskeri's physical anthropology (in Bognár-Kutzian 1963), seven age-sex classes can be distinguished, including those double graves where association of grave goods with skeleton is unclear. In Period I (Table 10.3), the largest number of associations defines the identities of males and children: 15 out of 28 (54%) of categories are associated with these two classes; 7 out of 28 types (25%) occur with all age-sex classes, while females, and females with children have few associations. Period II has no equivalent to Grave 67 from Period I, where a complete dog skeleton is found, together with joints of meat from six species, in the grave of an adult male. Maleness is reinforced through the repeated combinations of raw materials, tools and food remains. In Period II (Table 10.4), a

Table 10.2 Presence–absence chart of non-ceramic grave goods in Period II at the Tiszapolgár-Basatanya cemetery by age and gender

Grave good	Male	Female	Child	Adult & child	Found in Period I
Deer tooth	–	–	–	–	★
Auroch bones	–	–	–	–	★
Shed antler	–	★	–	–	★
Pig/boar's tusk	★	–	–	–	★
Other wild animal bones	–	–	–	–	★
Mussels	–	★	–	–	★
Snails	★	–	–	–	★
Fishbones	–	★	–	–	–
Bos metatarsal	–	–	–	–	★
Other *Bos* bone	★	–	–	–	★
Pig mandible	★	★	–	–	★
Complete dog	–	–	–	–	★
Other domestic animal bones	–	–	–	–	★
Bone awl	–	★	–	–	★
Bone spoon	–	★	–	–	★
Antler artefact	★	–	–	–	★
Pebble	–	★	–	–	★
Flint blade	★	★	★	–	★
Flint scraper	★	★	–	–	★
Obsidian	★	★	–	–	★
Lithic core	★	★	–	–	–
Ground stone	★	–	–	–	★
Limestone beads	–	★	–	★ (Adult male)	★
Limestone disc	–	–	–	–	★
Polished stone plate	–	★	–	–	–
Polished stone hammer-axe	–	★	–	–	–
FC loom weight	–	–	–	–	★
FC spindle whorl	–	★	–	–	–
Clay stud	–	★	–	–	–
Clay funnel	★	–	–	–	–
Ochre lumps	★	★	–	★ (Adult male)	★
Traces of fire	★	–	–	–	★
Copper bead	–	–	–	–	★
Copper ring	–	–	–	–	★
Copper bracelet	–	★	–	–	★
Copper ingot	–	★	–	–	–
Copper awl	★	–	–	–	–
Copper pin	★	–	–	–	–
Copper dagger	★	–	–	–	–

very different picture emerges: gendered adult identities rather than those of children are reinforced by means of artefact associations (12/29 artefact types for women only plus 10/29 for men only, or 76% combined).

What is even more striking is the change in the choice of grave goods for creating social identities between Periods I and II (Figure 10.3). Only 4 out of 28 types used in Period I maintain the same age-sex class association in Period II. While 11 out of 29 types found in Period II are new, half of the Period I symbols are associated with new age–sex classes (Table 10.5), mostly for adult women and men. The main change concerns the switch from joints of meat, with a symbolic emphasis on hunting, to productive artefacts; such as spindle whorls,

Table 10.3 Diagnostic non-ceramic artefacts in Period I of the Tiszapolgár-Basatanya cemetery by age and gender

Child only	Flint scraper, obsidian
Adult male only	Wild animal bones, snails, complete dog, limestone disc, loom-weight, ochre lumps
Adult female only	Deer tooth, bone spoon, pebble
Adult male & child only	Auroch bone, shed antler, boar's tusk, cattle metatarsal, pig mandible, domestic animal bones, copper bracelet
Adult female & child only	
Adult male & adult female	Mussels, cattle bones, bone awl
All categories	Antler artefacts, flint blade, ground stone, limestone beads, copper bead and ring, fire

Table 10.4 Diagnostic non-ceramic artefacts in Period II of the Tiszapolgár-Basatanya cemetery by age and gender

Child only	
Adult male only	Tusk, snails, cattle bones, antler artefact, ground stone, clay funnel, fire, copper awl, copper pin, copper dagger
Adult female only	Shed antler, mussels, fishbone, bone awl, bone spoon, pebble, polished stone plate, polished stone hammer-axe, spindle-whorl, clay stud, copper bracelet, copper ingot
Adult male & child only	
Adult female & child only	Limestone beads
Adult male & adult female	Pig mandible, flint scraper, obsidian, lithic core
All categories	Flint blade, ochre lumps

metal ingots and flint cores, or status artefacts, such as stone hammer-axes and metalwork, often now found to indicate femaleness. While the associations with hunting do not disappear in Period II, their decline suggests that other activities are perhaps beginning to gain equal status.

The window which Basatanya opens onto gendered power relations in the Early–Middle Copper Age remains relatively opaque for lack of comparative cemetery material. In these analyses, an attempt has been made to study the horizontal axes of social differentiation rather than the vertical wealth/status dimension. While this record is difficult to interpret in detail, the overall picture is unambiguous – major changes in the representation of gender relations are occurring between Periods I and II – the major period of transition between subsistence strategies based on primary products and those based on secondary products. While it may be noted that no obvious symbols associated with female production of dairy foods or woollen clothing were found, neither the funeral costumes nor the contents of the pottery has survived. The main axes of change

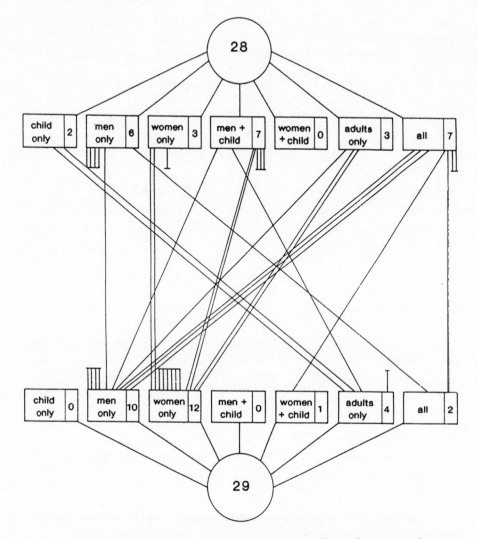

Figure 10.3 Changes in the age-gender associations of non-ceramic grave goods between Periods I and II, Tiszapolgár-Basatanya cemetery. Each line represents a different class of grave goods.

in mortuary identities are the symbols of the *domus* and those of the *agrios*, but neither of these are confined to the genders that archaeologists may have predicted! More fundamentally, the categories of maleness, femaleness and childness are in the process of redefinition over this 900-year-long period. It is consistent with the theory of ASPs that such redefinition could only take place away from the traditional ancestral places – the tells.

A valuable comparison with the mortuary record of a cemetery comes from the 23 Early Copper Age burials on Vésztö-mágori halom (pers. com. K. Hegedüs). All the burials were contracted inhumations, oriented SE–NW; 12

Table 10.5 Changes in associations of non-ceramic grave goods by age and gender between Periods I and II, Tiszapolgár-Basatanya cemetery

Period I	Period II	Grave good
Children only	Adults only	Flint scraper, Obsidian
Men only	All	Ochre lumps
Women only	All	No finds
Adult male & child	Men only	Boar's tusk
Adult male & child	Adults only	Pig mandible
Adults only	Men only	Domestic cattle bones
Adults only	Women only	Mussel shells, Bone awl
All	Men only	Antler artefacts, Ground stone, Fire
All	Adult male & child	Limestone beads

males, 5 females and 6 children were found. Almost all of the burials were placed in wooden coffins, and most burials were wrapped in osier shrouds, which had red ochre sprinkled on them. Gender differentiation cannot readily be analysed at Vésztö, since only rather general categories of grave goods were recorded. Pottery was found with women and children only; necklaces of limestone and other beads with men and childen only; and tools with both men and women but not children. The picture from Vésztö confirms the close similarities to Late Neolithic tell burials, the continuation of traditional practices rather than the social flux identified at Basatanya.

The mortuary record of the early phase of the Late Copper Age is poorly documented in eastern Hungary, for there are few large Baden cemeteries in the Plain. It is a matter of considerable importance whether or not the Plains communities had developed as clear a set of gender-based rules and categories in their cemeteries as were visible in the large Baden cemeteries of the Danube valley (Banner 1956), where potent symbols of ploughing and animal traction, as well as most fine metalwork, are unambiguously associated with maleness.

In the late phase of the Late Copper Age, a new mortuary ASP appears in the Great Hungarian Plain – the mortuary barrow or kurgan (Ecsedy 1979). These barrows are found in two contrasting locations: within previous settlement concentrations or on marginal, dry interfluves. The traditional explanation of this new ASP, with its new mortuary rite and set of novel grave goods is the invasion of Pontic steppe nomads into eastern Hungary (Gimbutas 1979). An alternative explanation is that the barrows represent an imitation of a tell – the ideological transformation of a symbol of domestic power into a mortuary arena (Chapman 1994).

The gender implications of kurgan burial are considerable, since every single excavated Copper Age kurgan has contained an adult male as the primary burial deep beneath the level of the Plain (Ecsedy 1979). Since no other burials are known as yet from this phase of the Late Copper Age, we are left with the unambiguous conclusion that females have been made invisible, while a potent male symbol of burial dominates views over the Plain. An important point concerns the grave goods typically deposited with the primary male. In previous periods, ochre has had as much a female as a male association and the same is true for long flint blades and copper beads; the textile offerings were probably also produced by females. Thus, it appears that dominant males have manipulated female production and/or association of prestige grave goods in the Late Copper Age to their own advantage in legitimizing their right to high-status barrow burial. The associations with the ancestors so characteristic of tells has also been taken over by males in this period in an ideological coup of unrivalled boldness. A series of rules establishing the centrality of the male category has been created through the public incorporation of elements symbolizing both females and males, both individuals and the community.

To summarize, the mortuary record has been subject to a variety of gendered rules and categorizations in the Neolithic and Copper Age of eastern Hungary. The nodal periods are the Early and Middle phases of the Copper Age. Before that, rules of mortuary behaviour which were balanced for both females and males were beginning to crystallize in the Late Neolithic in the ancestor-dominated environment of the nucleated tell. In the Late Copper Age, male control of public mortuary rites became clearer than ever before, reaching a peak in the barrow burial tradition. Between these two periods of stable mortuary rules lay the Early–Middle Copper Age – a period of instability and social change, in which notions of what constituted maleness, femaleness and childness were negotiated in a time of economic and ideological change.

Patterns in the Plain: discussion

The Neolithic and Copper Age of eastern Hungary embody one of the strongest contrasts in the central European archaeological record – the maximal settlement nucleation and elaboration of material culture of the Late Neolithic tells and maximal population dispersion with minimal elaboration of material culture at the end of the Copper Age. Social life on the tells was dominated by links with the ancestors; the place value of the tell was an intimate expression of the past of its residents, their identities and the cultural performances that marked those identities. The richness of social interactions on the tells had, however, a price – the lack of flexibility within ancestral conventions and practices, which constrained novel forms of social action, whether personal accumulation of wealth or new gender relations.

There were two routes open to changes in gendered social power. The first focused on male appropriation of female resources in the household or the denial of social value to such activities. There is as yet no clear evidence that this route was followed. The second route led to the establishment of alternative contexts for the development of male power. In the Late Neolithic, there is no evidence for the appearance of new ASPs, but it remains possible that resistance to the ancestor-dominated tell lifeways was practised on the small farms of the surrounding areas. Increases in female social power were possible through stronger control over household production and reproduction, as well as in greater participation in public ceremonial and exchange. On these developments, the evidence is ambiguous.

It is in the Early–Middle Copper Age that we find abundant evidence for new

ASPs in the form of flat cemeteries spatially distinct from settlement zones. Ancestral values are still maintained on the few tells still occupied but a rival ideology of power is developed centered on the new cemeteries. The changes in the earlier Copper Age may be summarized in three trends: (1) an increased divergence of female and male economic power with the expanded importance of secondary products in the domestic domain; (2) an increasing spatial separation between the living and the dead; and (3) increasing distinctions drawn between gender identities in the mortuary domain. It is the proposal of this study that the three trends are interdependent and that the second route was chosen by males to further their power strategies outside the domestic domain. However, the Basatanya analyses indicate that this new ASP was the stage for the negotiation of gendered power relations for many centuries. The increased emphasis on the production of goods rather than on foodstuffs by both females and males underlines the importance of surplus exchangeable commodities in the Copper Age, a period of increasing circulation of prestige gold and copper artefacts.

After the intense negotiations of gender relations in the earlier Copper Age, the gender struggle appears to have been convincingly won through the male domination of the mortuary domain in the kurgan phase. The invisibility of the domestic domain complicates any understanding of female power in household production, although this must have continued and probably increased, together with the importance of secondary products. The contrast in physical scale between mortuary barrows and domestic settlements can be read as a metaphor for ideological power struggles and it is in this form that gendered power relations are negotiated in the later Copper Age. The exclusion of females from the Late Copper Age burial domain is a vivid sign of the appropriation of that domain by males but single farmsteads must still have been the locus of female economic and perhaps ideological power.

Conclusions

Definite conclusions hardly seem appropriate in this study, which has attempted to produce a narrative of a hitherto largely ungendered prehistory of eastern Hungary. Several clear trends have been observed, which may perhaps act as a foundation for further considerations. In the social power model used here as the main theoretical framework, I outlined three possible causes of the appearance of new arenas of social power: changes in accumulation, network expansion and gender relations. While the main focus has been on the third, it should not be forgotten that accumulation of copper and gold prestige goods also prompted questions about new values in the Copper Age, while the colonization of new interfluvial terrain as much as the consolidation of inter-regional exchange networks indicate that network expansion cannot be excluded from our consideration.

Nonetheless, changes in gender relations are apparent from the ambiguities of the Early and Middle Neolithic, to the Late Neolithic, when clear-cut gender rules first appear in the mortuary domain. In the Copper Age, the mortuary record provides a contrast in spatial contexts, with traditional conventions still observed on tells and unstable and shifting negotiation of new gender relations apparent in new flat cemeteries. Qualitative analysis of non-ceramic grave goods at Tiszapolgár-Basatanya provides a picture of fluctuating representations of gender identities, with increasing emphasis on artefact production rather than hunting and pastoralism in the Middle Copper Age. The impact of secondary products-based subsistence strategies is apparent in the earlier Copper Age, with the increased potential for female economic power in textile and dairy production contrasting with the male economic power derived from ploughing, horse riding and animal traction. These alternative routes to economic and ideological power run on into the later Copper Age, where the domestic domain becomes increasingly restrained in the archaeological record, which is dominated by the mortuary barrow, male burial and the exclusion of females from burial. The Late Copper Age contrast between visible male barrows and invisible female farmsteads seems an appropriate metaphor on which to conclude my contribution to this book.

Note

1. The Upper Tisza Project is an inter-disciplinary Anglo-Hungarian research project, in which a collaboration between the University of Newcastle upon Tyne and Eötvös Loránd University, Budapest aims to define and explain changes in the landscape, settlement and social structure over the last 10,000 years in north-east Hungary (Chapman and Laszlovszky 1992, 1993, 1994). The Project is funded by the British Academy, National Geographic Society, the Society of Antiquaries of Newcastle, the Prehistoric Society and the two Universities.

References

Banner, J. (1956) *Die Péceler Kultur*. Archaeologia Hungarica 35. Budapest: Akadémiai Kiadó.

Bognár-Kutzian, I. (1963) *The Copper Age Cemetery of Tiszapolgár-Basatanya*. Archaeologia Hungarica 42. Budapest: Akadémiai Kiadó.

Brumfiel, E.M. (1991) 'Weaving and cooking: women's production in Aztec Mexico' in J.M. Gero and M.W. Conkey (eds) *Engendering Archaeology: Women and Prehistory*. Oxford: Blackwell, pp. 224–53.

Chapman, J.C. (1982) 'The secondary products revolution and the limitations of the Neolithic'. *Bulletin of the University of London Institute of Archaeology* 11, 119–41.

Chapman, J.C. (1983) 'Meaning and illusion in the study of burial in Balkan prehistory' in A. Poulter (ed.) *Ancient Bulgaria Volume 1*. Nottingham: University of Nottingham Press, pp. 1–45.

Chapman, J.C. (1988) 'From "space" to "place": a model of dispersed settlement and Neolithic society' in C. Burgess, P. Topping and D. Mordant (eds) *Enclosures and Defences in the Neolithic of Western Europe*. International Series 403. Oxford: BAR, pp. 21–46.

Chapman, J.C. (1991) 'The creation of social arenas in the Neolithic and Copper Age of

South East Europe: the case of Varna' in P. Garwood, P. Jennings, R. Skeates and J. Toms (eds) *Sacred and Profane*. Oxford Committee for Archaeology, Monograph 32, pp. 152–71.

Chapman, J.C. (1993) 'Social power in the Iron Gates Mesolithic' in J.C. Chapman and P. Dolukhanov (eds) *Cultural Transformations and Interactions in Eastern Europe*. Worldwide Archaeology Series 5. Aldershot: Avebury, pp. 61–106.

Chapman, J.C. (1994) 'The living, the dead, and the ancestors: time, life cycles and the mortuary domain in later European prehistory' in J. Davies (ed.) *Ritual and Remembrance: Responses to Death in Human Societies*. Sheffield: Sheffield Academic Press, pp. 40–85.

Chapman J. and Laszlovszky, J. (1992) 'The Upper Tisza Project 1991: report on the first season'. *Archaeological Reports 1991*. Durham: University of Durham, pp. 10–13.

Chapman J. and Laszlovszky, J. (1993) 'The Upper Tisza Project: the September 1992 season'. *Archaeological Reports 1992*. Durham: University of Durham, pp. 13–19.

Chapman, J. and Laszlovszky, J. (1994) 'The Upper Tisza Project – September 1993 season'. *Archaeological Reports 1993*. Durham: University of Durham, pp. 1–7.

Claassen, C.P. (1991) 'Gender, shellfishing, and the Shell Mound Archaic' in J.M. Gero and M.W. Conkey (eds) *Engendering Archaeology: Women and Prehistory*. Oxford: Blackwell, pp. 276–99.

Ecsedy, I. (1979) *The people of the Pit-Grave kurgans in Eastern Hungary*. Fontes Archaeologici Hungariae. Budapest: Akadémiai Kiadó.

Forenbacher, S. (1993) 'Radiocarbon dates and absolute chronology of the central European Early Bronze Age'. *Antiquity* 67, 235–56.

Gimbutas, M. (1978) 'The first wave of steppe pastoralists into Copper Age Europe'. *Journal of Indo-European Studies* V, 4, 277–338.

Gimbutas, M. (1979) 'The three waves of the Kurgan people into Old Europe, 4500–2500 BC'. *Archives suisses d'anthropologie générale* 43, 2, 113–37.

Gimbutas, M. (1989) *The language of the goddess*. London: Thames & Hudson.

Goldstein, L. (1981) 'One-dimensional archaeology and multi-dimensional people: spatial organization and mortuary analysis' in R. Chapman, I. Kinnes and K. Randsborg (eds) *The Archaeology of Death*. Cambridge: Cambridge University Press, pp. 53–69.

Gyula, P. (ed.) (1972) *Torma Zsófia Levelesladajbol*. Bucharest: Kriterion Konyvkiadó.

Hegedüs, K. and Makkay, J. (1987) 'Vésztö-mágor. A settlement of the Tisza culture' in P. Raczky (ed.) *The Late Neolithic in the Tisza Region*. Budapest-Szolnok: Szolnok County Museums, pp. 85–104.

Horváth, F. (1987) 'Hódmezövásárhely-Gorzsa. A settlement of the Tisza culture' in P. Raczky, (ed.) *The Late Neolithic in the Tisza Region*. Budapest-Szolnok: Szolnok County Museums, pp. 31–46.

Kalicz, N. (1970) *Clay Gods*. Budapest: Corvina.

Kalicz, N. and Makkay, J. (1977) *Die Linienbandkeramik in der Grossen Ungarischen Tiefebene*. Budapest: Akadémiai Kiadó.

Knaster, M. (1990) 'Raider of the lost Goddess'. *East West* (December), 36–44.

Korek, J. (1987) 'Szegvár-Tüzköves' in P. Raczky (ed.) *The Late Neolithic in the Tisza Region*. Budapest-Szolnok: Szolnok County Museums, pp. 47–60.

Kovács, T. (ed.) (1994) *Treasures of the Hungarian Bronze Age*. Budapest: Hungarian National Museum.

Kutzian, I. (1944) *The Körös Culture*. Budapest: Akadémiai Kiadó.

Laszlovszky, J. and Siklódi, Cs. (1990) 'Theoretical archaeology without theory' in I. Hodder (ed.) *Archaeological Theory in Europe: The Last Three Decades*. London: Routledge, pp.272–98.

Lazarovici, Gh. (1989) 'Das neolitische Heiligtum von Parţa'. *Varia Archaeologica Hungarica* II, 149–73.

Mann, M. (1986) *The Sources of Social Power. Volume 1. A History of Power from the Beginning to* AD 1760. Cambridge: Cambridge University Press.

Mann, M. (1993) *The Sources of Social Power. Volume 2. A History of Power from* AD 1760 to AD 1914. Cambridge: Cambridge University Press.

Meier-Arendt, W. (ed.) (1992) *Bronzezeit in Ungarn. Forschungen in Tell-Siedlungen an Donau und Theiss*. Frankfurt-am-Main: Museum für Vor-und Frühgeschichte–Archaeologische Museum Szolnok.

Mosko, M. (1989) 'The developmental cycle among public groups'. *Man* (N.S.) 24, 470–84.

Mozsolics, A. (1950) *Der Goldfund son Velem-Szentvid Praehistorica I*. Basel: Prometheus Verlag.

Mozsolics, A. (1967) *Bronzefunde des Karpatenbeckens. Depotfundhorizont von Apa und Hajdúsámson*. Budapest: Akadémiai Kiadó.

Mozsolics, A. (1973) *Bronze- und Gold-Funde des Karpatenbeckens. Depotfundhorizont von Forró und Opályi*. Budapest: Akadémiai Kiadó.

Mozsolics, A. (1985) *Bronzefunde aus Ungarn*. Budapest: Akadémiai Kiadó.

Murdock G.P. and Provost C. (1973) 'Factors in the division of labor by sex: a cross-cultural analysis'. *Ethnology* 12, 203–25.

Némeskeri J. and Szathmári L. (1987) 'An anthropological evaluation of the Indo-European problem: the anthropological and demographic transition in the Danube Basin' in S.N. Skomal and E.C. Polomé (eds) *Proto-Indo-European. The Archaeology of a Linguistic Problem. Studies in Honor of Marija Gimbutas*. Washington, DC: Institute for the Study of Man.

Pollock, S. (1991) 'Women in a men's world: images of Sumerian women' in J.M. Gero and M.W. Conkey (eds) *Engendering Archeology: Women and Prehistory*. Oxford: Blackwell, pp.366–87.

Raczky, P. (ed.) (1987) *The Late Neolithic in the Tisza region*. Budapest-Szolnok: Szolnok County Museums.

Raczky, P. (1988) *A Tisza-Vidék Kulturális és Kronológiai kapcsolatai a Balkánnal és az égeikummal a neolitikum, rézkor időszakában*. Szolnok: Szolnok County Museum.

Saxe, A.A. (1970) *Social dimensions of mortuary practices*. PhD thesis. Ann Arbor: University of Michigan.

Sherratt, A. (1979) 'Plough and pastoralism: aspects of the secondary products revolution' in I. Hodder, N. Hammond and G. Isaac (eds) *Patterns in the Past*. Cambridge: Cambridge University Press, pp.261–305.

Sherratt, A. (1982a) 'Mobile resources: settlement and exchange in early agricultural Europe' in C. Renfrew and S.J. Shennan (eds) *Ranking, Resources and Exchange*. Cambridge: Cambridge University Press, pp.13–26.

Sherratt, A. (1982b) 'The development of Neolithic and Copper Age settlement in the Great Hungarian Plain: Part 1 The regional setting'. *Oxford Journal of Archaeology* 1, 3, 287–316.

Sherratt, A. (1983) 'The development of Neolithic and Copper Age settlement in the Great Hungarian Plain: Part 2 Site surveys and settlement dynamics'. *Oxford Journal of Archaeology* 2, 1, 13–41.

Spector, J. (1991) 'What this awl means: towards a feminist archaeology' in J.M. Gero and M.W. Conkey (eds) *Engendering Archaeology: Women and Prehistory.* Oxford: Blackwell, pp.308–405.

Trogmayer, O. (1969) 'Die Bestattungen der Körös-Gruppe'. *A Mora Ferenc Múzeum Evkönyve* 1969, 2, 5–15.

11 Housewives, warriors and slaves? Sex and gender in Anglo-Saxon burials

S. J. LUCY

Introduction

In southern and eastern England, the archaeological evidence from the fifth to the seventh century AD consists predominantly of inhumation and cremation cemeteries, identified by the distinctive metalwork and pottery with which both types of burial were often furnished. In the inhumation burials from these areas, the metalwork found consists mainly of decorative jewellery and dress-fastenings and of weapons and other iron and bronze implements.

The jewellery and ornaments have traditionally been attributed to female graves, and the weapons and tools to male ones, and these two assemblages have been uncritically accepted as true indicators of biological sex. This rigid division of adults into two distinct groups does not facilitate critical enquiry into the historical reality of sexual roles and relations in the Anglo-Saxon period, but merely lends itself to a crude caricature, in which women reside in the home dressed in their finery, while men go out to work and to fight. The parallels between this view and the traditional late Victorian ideal of the middle-class family suggest that perceptions of the past have been influenced by cultural stereotypes about 'natural' gender roles.

Feminist critique, which has developed in social anthropology and other social sciences since the 1970s, has, until now, had very little impact on the agendas of Anglo-Saxon archaeology. In contrast, studies of the Scandinavian Iron Age, the chronologically equivalent period on the other side of the North Sea, have been in the forefront of the development of feminist and gender archaeologies (Dommasnes 1982, 1987, 1991; Gibbs 1987; Hjørungdal 1991, 1994; Høgestøl 1986; Stalsberg 1984, 1987a, b). Such divergent interests obviously have very little to do with the nature of the archaeology being investigated, for both the Anglo-Saxon period and the later Scandinavian Iron Age deal mainly with burial evidence, and with settlement evidence to a lesser extent. The difference, therefore, must lie in the traditions of scholarship, rather than being inherent in the data itself.

This chapter will attempt to relate the theoretical perspectives developed by archaeologists working in other chronological periods and geographical areas to the archaeology of early Anglo-Saxon England. These perspectives all hold as a central tenet the idea that gender relations are important in the structuring of society and the maintenance of social relations within that society (Barrett 1988;

Conkey 1993; Conkey and Spector 1984; Gero and Conkey 1991; Gilchrist 1991; Sørensen 1991, 1992). By being receptive to the possibility of variation and change in gender relations (rather than the static bi-polar models of male and female which until now have been current) one can pave the way for a more dynamic understanding of the nature and development of Anglo-Saxon society. To these ends, the variation within two Anglo-Saxon cemeteries in Yorkshire will be investigated.

Anglo-Saxon archaeology

Part of the explanation of current practice of Anglo-Saxon archaeology lies in its history. Until the 1920s, when the first domestic structures were excavated (Leeds 1923, 1927), Anglo-Saxon archaeology consisted mainly of burial evidence. This had first been correctly identified as Anglo-Saxon by Reverend James Douglas, who published the results of his excavations in Anglo-Saxon Kentish cemeteries from 1779 to 1793 as *Nenia Britannica* (1793). The long-standing bias towards mortuary evidence in archaeological remains from this period is made apparent by the fact that by the late 1940s, while approximately 1130 cemeteries were known, just six settlement sites had been identified (Webster 1986: 123).

The uses to which this evidence was put were determined by the historical preoccupations of the day. Anglo-Saxon archaeology was seen from its inception as a 'handmaid' to history, and was often used by historians as evidence to support interpretations made from documents (for example, Kemble 1849, 1856; Stenton 1943). It therefore sought to answer the questions posed by historians, rather than developing its own interests and agendas (Champion 1990). This contrasts strongly with the situation in Scandinavia where, with no Roman Period to separate it from the earlier Iron Age, this period was regarded as truly prehistoric (Champion 1990: 89). The over-riding concern of Anglo-Saxon archaeologists from the start of the nineteenth century was to chart the progress of the Anglo-Saxon 'invasions' and 'migrations' documented in the histories of Bede and Gildas (see Lucy 1995 for a detailed critique of this). In this respect too it differed from work on the Scandinavian Iron Age, which had no such 'historical' invasions, and, therefore, concentrated on developing theories to explain internally-driven change in the archaeological evidence (e.g. Hedeager 1993).

In Anglo-Saxon archaeology there was thus little interest in the social arrangements which the material elucidated. The cemeteries were seen merely as evidence for the progress of the newcomers across the country, and contents of graves could be used to date this. Therefore, the main thrust of research was the development of artefactual chronologies and typologies (Åberg 1926; Evison 1979; Leeds 1913, 1936; Myres 1937, 1969, 1977; Swanton 1973). This still remains a current research interest, albeit with more sophisticated methods (Hines 1984, 1992; Palm and Pind 1992). Such research is situated within a prescriptive historical framework based on ethnic and racial identities; identities which have recently undergone extensive critique (Amory 1993; Austin 1990;

Champion 1987, 1990, 1991: 146; Geary 1983; Hedeager 1993; MacDougall 1982; Wormald 1983). Agendas were also determined by perceptions of the past moulded by the interests of modern nation states (Champion 1991: 142; Lucy 1995). The aims of such approaches were perfectly summed up in a quote from Collingwood and Myres (1937: 359): 'There are two ways in which archaeology may help us to understand the settlement [of the incoming Anglo-Saxons]: the distribution of the pagan cemeteries may reveal the areas which were first or most thickly populated, and the grave-goods which they contain may throw light on the cultural affinities of those who used them'.

In contrast to this approach, Anglo-Saxon archaeology in the 1960s and 1970s was characterized as being more concerned with economics, social structures and settlements than previous work, leading to a decline in cemetery research (Dickinson 1979: 12), exemplified by the absence of any funerary research from Wilson (1976). Calls were made at this time for an increase in the use of stratigraphic and spatial analyses of cemeteries, to supplement the traditional areas of typology and chronology and thus reinvigorate the subject and make it more relevant to present concerns (Dickinson 1979: 17–19). It was not widely realized that the application of new methods to the data could not compensate for the lack of critique (Hodder 1982). In the 1980s some scholars held the belief that social and political arrangements could be 'read off' directly from the archaeology. The forays of 'processual' archaeologists such as Richard Hodges (1989a, b) and Chris Arnold (1984, 1988) (both students at South-ampton when Colin Renfrew was professor) thus sought overarching principles which structured the Early Anglo-Saxon evidence, seeking to formulate general-izations about the nature of social, political and economic arrangements. There seemed to be no consideration in this theorizing of the impact of the actions of real people, who were capable of taking decisions, and influencing these arrangements.

Occupants of Anglo-Saxon burials were, therefore, seen as representing larger entities: 'Germanic immigrants', 'native British' (but only in rare cases, where the burial was 'unusual'), or 'aristocratic élites'. In a similar vein, they were identified as 'women' (if buried with jewellery or ornaments), 'men' (if with weapons), and frequently 'slaves' or 'servants' (if accompanied by a 'poor' assemblage, or by no grave goods at all). Little interest was paid by scholars to these various roles, beyond assuming stereotypic traits for them.

Some recent research has, however, displayed new attitudes towards the nature of material culture, and consequently the interpretation of cemetery evidence. An important work was that of Pader (1982), who looked at East Anglian cemeteries from a structural and symbolic perspective, concluding that sex-based relations could be seen to be articulated by constraints placed on the distribution of artefact classes, artefacts and skeletal positioning, and that these relations differed between cemeteries (1982: 129). This work, although based on only three cemeteries with poor skeletal preservation, demonstrated the advantages of employing a detailed contextual approach to such evidence. A more considered perspective of the significance of mortuary evidence is appar-ent in other work also: 'Mortuary ritual reinforces cultural differences and helps classify Anglo-Saxon society. It provides a means of describing social identity' (Richards 1992: 135). It is with relation to these emerging perspectives, viewing Anglo-Saxon cemetery evidence as something which can inform about the creation and maintenance of social relations, rather than just ethnic identity and population movement, that this chapter is situated.

Engendering archaeology

This chapter is also informed by the rich tradition of feminist debate which has arisen over the last twenty years, problematizing the previously 'common-sense' ways in which sex and gender have been dealt with. Such critique developed first in social anthropology and some of the other social sciences (see for example, Kessler and Mackenna 1978; Ortner and Whitehead 1981; Rosaldo and Lamphere 1974; and other works cited in Conkey and Spector 1984). Archaeologists in Scandinavia began to take this critique on board in the mid-1970s, a notable event being the 'Were They All Men?' conference which took place at Bergen in 1979; and their counterparts in Anglo-American prehistoric archaeology joined the debate in print in the early 1980s, with the Gender Archaeology session at the 1983 Theoretical Archaeology Group Meeting, Conkey and Spector's 1984 article and the gender issue of *Archaeological Review* from Cambridge in 1988. There were three facets to this discussion: the position of women in the archaeology profession, the development of gender theory, and historical revision of the presentation of women in the past (Conkey and Spector 1984; Gilchrist 1991).

An important early stage in these discussions was the critique of the way women had been dealt with (or, rather, had not been dealt with at all) in archaeological interpretation (Bertelsen *et al.* 1987; Conkey and Spector 1984; Gero and Conkey 1991). This was a necessary first step in combating versions of the past which accepted modern day gender stereotypes as timeless, objective and natural (Conkey and Spector 1984), and it thus paved the way for archaeological interpretations which had been reworked in the light of feminist research (Conkey and Spector 1984: 28). Part of this project was 'finding' women in the past, specifically in those fields which had traditionally been seen as male preserves, such as hunting, technology and production. Challenging stereotypes of female behaviour was also an issue.

This feminist critique fed into an emerging school of archaeological thought (if it can be characterized as such a holistic entity), 'post-processualism' (Barrett 1988: 12), with its emphasis on the active nature of material culture, the importance of context and, recently, the ideas drawn from structuration theory (Giddens 1984) which see the individual as an active social agent. The agendas of feminist archaeology and post-processualism highlighted the importance of self-critical reflection in archaeological enquiry, as both explored the influence of social and political factors on supposedly 'objective' investigation (Barrett 1988; Hodder 1982, 1986; Shanks and Tilley 1987). Although not identical in their objectives (see, for example, Engelstad's criticisms of post-processual archaeology (1991a, b)), dialectic between the two positions has led, in recent years, to a growing emphasis on the archaeology of gender (i.e. on the relations among and between men and women, rather than the feminist position of dealing with women alone).

It was realized that the feminist 'add woman and her perspectives' approach (Dommasnes 1992: 8), assigning women their own place in the archaeological record, merely served to obscure fundamental and problematic assumptions about men and women, gender and gender relations (Gero and Conkey 1991: 11). These assumptions have thus been subjected to a detailed critique which has included close examination of the concepts of sex and gender (Hjørungdal 1994; Nordbladh and Yates 1990; Sørensen 1991, 1992). One of the aims of gender archaeology (and other post-processual archaeologies) is to develop a body of theory and the requisite conceptual frameworks for archaeological enquiry (Conkey 1993: 4), recognizing that archaeological theory is a product of dialogue with one's data, and that that data is at the same time generated by theory (Dommasnes 1992: 11). This self-critical tradition does not produce radically different feminist versions of the past (Sørensen 1992: 31), although it does reject entrenched nineteenth century gender roles (Sørensen 1992: 32). It will hopefully, however, contribute to the development of a different archaeology: 'one that is richer, humanized, and tuned to understanding how differences are not just socially constructed but historically contingent and changing' (Conkey 1993: 10).

This engendered perspective (i.e. literally 'produced by union of the sexes' (Conkey 1992: 30)) can contribute to the interpretation of Anglo-Saxon burials, by seeing gender as something:

- which is not 'given', nor even necessarily rigidly tied to biological sex;
- which is actively created, both by an individual and by a society;
- which can change throughout an individual's lifetime;
- which can vary from society to society and over time;
- which is intimately involved in the construction and maintenance of social relations;
- and as something which pertains to males as much as to females.

The possibility thus arises of interpretations of the past which are centred around people and variation in human behaviour, rather than being driven by present-day sexual stereotypes. The implications of this approach for Anglo-Saxon burial archaeology will be explored in the next section, following which the case study of the Yorkshire material will be described.

Sex, gender and burials

It is highly indicative of attitudes towards sex and gender in Anglo-Saxon burial archaeology that a determination of gender based on associated grave goods is almost always preferred over biological sexing of the skeleton. For example, Hirst (1985: 33–4) states of the burials at Sewerby, East Yorkshire that 'The sex determinations used here are based on an amalgamation of the biological and cultural data. Where these data disagree ... the cultural determination has usually been preferred'. At the Buckland, Dover cemetery, Evison (1987: 123) concurs with this view: 'When ... a skeleton is provided with grave goods exclusively attributable to one sex, e.g. brooches and beads for a woman and a sword or spear for a man, it is regarded reasonable here to assume that the grave goods are a true indication of sex'. This view is, however, reliant on a bi-polar view of both sex and gender: there is no recognition that more than two categories of either may exist (*contra* Nordbladh and Yates 1990). It also assumes a direct equation between sex (as a biological fact) and gender (as represented by the grave-goods). The power of this idea is such that, when the data disagrees, as in the cases above, the 'scientific' findings are rejected in favour of the stereotype.

It is possible that grave goods may not give a clear indication of the sex or gender of the person buried. The traditional linking of jewellery with women and weapons and tools with men can be traced back to its origins in mid-nineteenth century German/Danish antiquarian circles (Hjørungdal 1994: 144), and should thus be viewed as a nineteenth century construction which has been uncritically accepted by modern archaeologists. If the engendered perspective outlined above is taken, it becomes impossible to see such correlations as 'natural' and 'timeless' any longer. It is ridiculous to use grave goods to 'sex' a body (Henderson 1989: 81). Rather, the relationship between grave goods, gender and sex must be investigated, not assumed.

If biological sex is rejected as the determining feature of behaviour in both life and death, the way is opened for a more dynamic understanding of the Anglo-Saxon period. This can include looking at the role of symbolism in burial rites. Härke's work on the weapon burial rite (1989a, b, 1990, 1992), for example, has demonstrated that the symbolism of grave goods is often more powerful than their assumed practical function: 'neither the ability to fight, nor the actual experience of fighting were relevant for the decision as to who was buried with, or without, weapons' (1992: 153). A different perspective also allows one to investigate other aspects of the burial rite, such as orientation, positioning and grave structure, without ignoring the majority of the burials which cannot be 'sexed' by their grave goods, and therefore given a gender-related identity. In the next section I intend to examine one of the most basic assumptions used in previous analyses of Anglo-Saxon burials – that males are buried with weapons and females with jewellery – and that these associations reflect gender roles and relations.

Anglo-Saxon burials in Yorkshire

There is a long tradition of Anglo-Saxon cemetery research in East Yorkshire (see Figure 11.1). This county was an area in which two of the most prolific barrow-diggers of the later nineteenth century, J. R. Mortimer and Canon Greenwell, were active, both of whom were unusual for their time in that they published detailed records of their excavations (Greenwell and Rolleston 1877; Mortimer 1905). Although the main targets for their activities were the numerous Bronze Age barrow cemeteries situated on the chalk Wolds which run

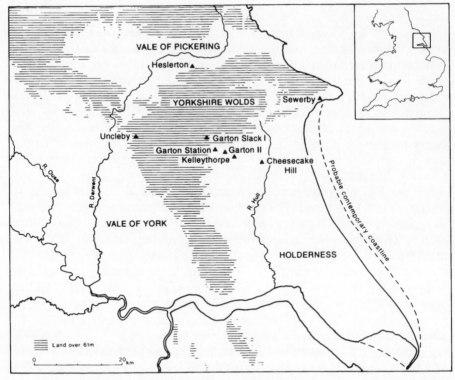

Figure 11.1 Location of Early Anglo-Saxon cemeteries in East Yorkshire (redrawn by Yvonne Beadnell, after Hirst (1985)).

through the county, Anglo-Saxon inhumation cemeteries were sometimes found to be centred on such barrows. These too were, in general, carefully excavated and recorded, for example, the cemeteries at Uncleby (Smith 1912), Garton Slack, Cheesecake Hill, and Kelleythorpe (Mortimer 1905). There have also been some modern cemetery excavations in the area, notably those at West Heslerton (Powlesland 1986, in press) and at Sewerby (Hirst 1985), both of which date from the mid-fifth to the early seventh century. Although neither are complete (burials at Heslerton remain under a major road, and those at Sewerby under farm buildings), both excavations are believed to form representative samples of the whole cemetery.

It is these last two sites which were used in this brief analysis, as it is a feature of both excavations that the skeletal remains underwent independent biological sexing by bone specialists, which has been noted as an unusual practice in Anglo-Saxon research (Henderson 1989: 81), although this is rapidly becoming standard practice. This deserves some comment here. Skeletal sexing is carried out by observation of a number of different morphological features, notably those present on the cranium and pelvis. For most physical characteristics, adult humans share around 95 per cent of the total range of variation (St Hoyme and Isçan 1989: 59), yet for a cemetery with excellent adult skeletal preservation as many as 97 per cent of the burials will be sexed with a reasonable degree of certainty (Molleson and Cox 1993: 91) (children cannot be sexed with any accuracy, as their sexually dimorphic features do not diverge until puberty (El-Najjar and McWilliams 1978; Krogman 1962; Stewart 1979)). At sites with less than perfect skeletal preservation, this figure will be dramatically decreased (Henderson 1989: 79).

The association of jewellery and ornaments with biological females and weapons with biological males is assumed and not proven. A preliminary stage in the analysis is to test whether these goods really did form part of separate assemblages. The next stage of investigating the correlations of these goods with biological sexing may then be undertaken. Methods used in this analysis incorporate spreadsheets, statistical comparisons and visual observation.

Results

Observation of the breakdown of both cemeteries by grave and assemblage constituents (see Figure 11.2) shows that the assemblages can be separated into four groups: those containing jewellery or ornamentation of some sort (notably brooches, bead strings, pendants, sleeve clasps and waist-hangings such as girdle-hangers, latch-lifters or girdle-rings – see Figure 11.3 for illustration of types); those containing weapons (at the least a spear, but sometimes also accompanied by a shield and rarely by a sword – see Figure 11.4); those containing goods which do not fall into these previous two categories (including individual beads, knives, buckles or belt-fittings, vessels and animal bones); and those containing no surviving artefacts at all. No graves containing weapons contained items from the jewellery assemblage, and no graves with jewellery contained items from the weapon assemblages. Both, however, contained items from the 'neutral' assemblage.

The relative proportions of these assemblages are surprising. Figure 11.5 shows the percentage of burials within each assemblage at the two sites. At Sewerby over half the burials do not contain a weapon or jewellery assemblage (57.6% = 20 neutral and 14 no goods assemblages from a total of 59), and at Heslerton this is true for just under half (44.6% = 43 neutral and 39 no goods assemblages from a total of 184 burials). This emphasizes the point that current methods of categorizing burials are unable to deal with the majority of the burials. At both sites there are many more graves with jewellery than weapon assemblages (at Sewerby there are four times as many, while at Heslerton there are about 3.3 times as many – see Figure 11.5).

Comparison of the four assemblages with biological sexing of the skeletons generated some interesting results. A glance at Figures 11.6 and 11.7 clearly shows just how few burials, in proportion, are biologically sexed at both sites (due to poor bone preservation). This gives rise to the fact that at Heslerton only 10.9% of the total number of burials actually conform to the stereotypes of males with weapons (N = 6/184) and females with jewellery (N = 14/184). At Sewerby the figure is even lower, at 10.2% (two male and four female burials out of a total of 59). If the probable/possible sexings are included in this, the

GRAVE NO	BIOLOGICAL SEX	BROOCH	NECK ORNAMENT	OTHER DRESS FAST.	WAIST ORNAMENT	1-4 BEADS	KNIFE	BUCKLE/BELT	VESSEL	STONE/FLINT	ANIMAL REMAINS	SPEAR	SHIELD	SWORD
G15		Δ	Δ	Δ			Δ	Δ	Δ					
G35B	F	Δ	Δ	Δ	Δ		Δ	Δ						
G28		Δ	Δ											
G38	M?	Δ	Δ	Δ	Δ		Δ							
G50		Δ	Δ	Δ										
G54		Δ	Δ	Δ	Δ		Δ	Δ	Δ					
G17		Δ	Δ						Δ					
G19	M?	Δ	Δ	Δ				Δ	Δ					
G29		Δ	Δ											
G41	F?	Δ	Δ			Δ	Δ	Δ	Δ	Δ				
G8	F	Δ	Δ				Δ							
G12	F	Δ	Δ				Δ							
G49	F?	Δ	Δ	Δ	Δ		Δ		Δ	Δ	Δ			
G57		Δ		Δ		Δ	Δ	Δ						
G42	F?	Δ		Δ			Δ							
G23	F	Δ					Δ	Δ	Δ					
G51		Δ				Δ					Δ			
G16				Δ		Δ								
G24	F?	Δ												
G31	M?	Δ												
G27	M						Δ	Δ	Δ					
G56							Δ	Δ	Δ					
G5							Δ		Δ					
G52							Δ		Δ					
G34	F?						Δ	Δ	Δ					
G40							Δ	Δ						
G48	M						Δ	Δ						
G25	F						Δ							
G39							Δ							
G58							Δ							
G2									Δ					
G32									Δ					
G36									Δ					
G46									Δ					
G53	M?								Δ					
G9	M								Δ					
G26	F								Δ					
G33	M					Δ								
G35A						Δ								
G21								Δ						
G1	M													
G13	F													
G14														
G16B														
G20														
G22														
G3														
G4	M?													
G43														
G44	M													
G47														
G50A	M?													
G6														
G7														
G10	M?						Δ	Δ				Δ		
G11	M							Δ				Δ		
G37	M						Δ					Δ		
G45	M?						Δ					Δ	Δ	
G55							Δ	Δ				Δ		Δ

Figure 11.2 Constituents of assemblages at Sewerby

percentages rise to 12.0% at Heslerton (16 female and 6 male burials from a total of 184) and 20.3% at Sewerby (8 females and 4 males from a total of 59): still not a solid base on which to build a rigid dichotomy.

Turning to the question of whether jewellery is found with males and weapons with females (see Henderson 1989 for research on some cemeteries outside

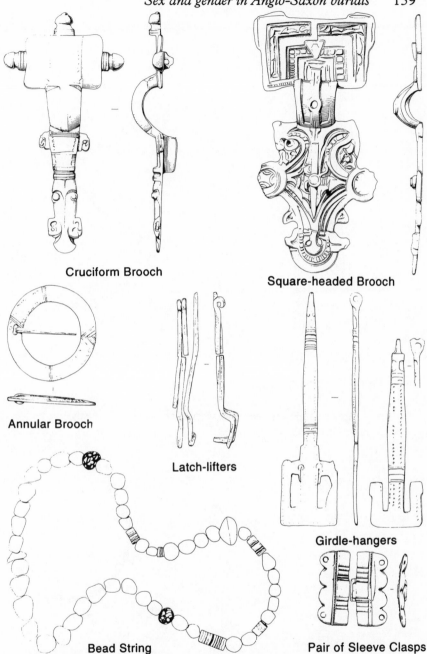

Cruciform Brooch

Square-headed Brooch

Annular Brooch

Latch-lifters

Girdle-hangers

Bead String

Pair of Sleeve Clasps

Figure 11.3 Illustration of jewellery assemblage (redrawn by Yvonne Beadnell, after Hirst (1985))

Yorkshire), at Heslerton, although no male graves (definite or possible) contain any items from the jewellery assemblage, 12.5% (N = 3/24) of the weapon burials were sexed as certainly or possibly female. At Sewerby the opposite

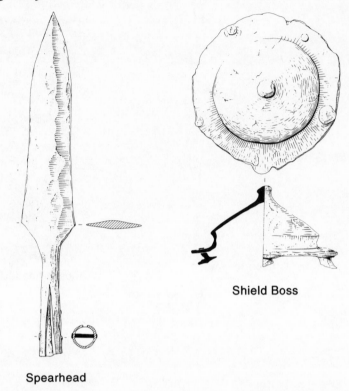

Shield Boss

Spearhead

Figure 11.4a Illustration of weapon assemblage (redrawn by Yvonne Beadnell, after Hirst (1985))

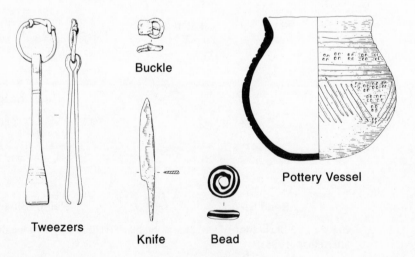

Buckle

Tweezers

Knife   Bead

Pottery Vessel

Figure 11.4b Illustration of neutral assemblage (redrawn by Yvonne Beadnell, after Hirst (1985))

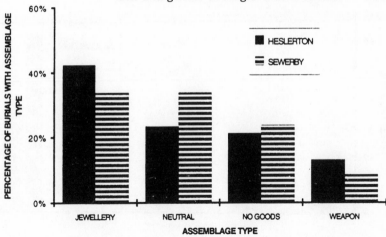

Figure 11.5 Relative proportions of assemblage types at Sewerby and Heslerton

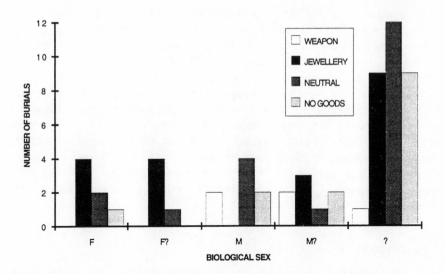

Figure 11.6 Breakdown of assemblage by biological sex at Sewerby

picture is seen, with no female weapon burials, but 15% of the jewellery burials (N = 3/20) being sexed as possibly male. It is illogical to try to cast doubt on these results by questioning the validity of the biological sexing, for example Evison (1987: 126) who preferred to interpret a double weapon burial as evidence for homosexuality, rather than accept the sexing of one of the skeletons as possibly female. If the validity of some sexing is rejected, then the validity of all other sexing must also be questioned, including those burials where the stereotype does hold true.

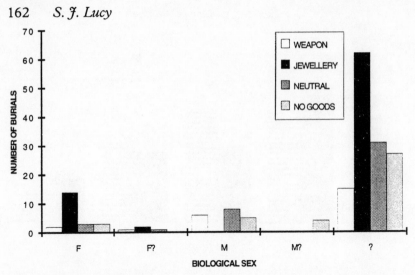

Figure 11.7 Breakdown of assemblage by biological sex at Heslerton

To summarize, in the above analysis it was demonstrated that four distinct assemblages were present in the Yorkshire cemeteries of Sewerby and Heslerton. These consisted of a jewellery assemblage, a weapon assemblage, a 'neutral' assemblage, and one with no surviving goods. At both sites there were vastly more burials with jewellery assemblages than those with weapons, and an extremely small percentage of burials could be shown to conform with the traditional gender stereotype of males buried with weapons and females with jewellery (although at a site with better bone preservation, many more may do so). A small number of burials at each site were found to be associated with the 'wrong' assemblage for their probable sex. Most notable, however, was the extremely high proportion of burials at both sites which were not associated with weapons or jewellery, a fact which throws doubt on the whole basis of the weapon–jewellery dichotomy.

Discussion

Anglo-Saxon burials can no longer be divided equally into males and females (with none left over), but rather the variation evident in the archaeology must be explored. At both sites discussed above, there are vastly more jewellery than weapon burials, and an extremely high proportion of 'neutral' burials, or those with no surviving goods. This variation in burial practice emphasizes that each community actively created its own burial rite, rather than grave goods being determined by the biological sex of the deceased. This, therefore, suggests that the rite helped communicate certain things to the observers of the burial. At a certain point in the burial rites, with the body laid out in the grave, symbolism associated with the grave goods would have been highly important. Hedeager (1993) has suggested that the weapon burial rite may have been employed in the creation of a Germanic origin myth. The presence of weapons in a grave may have been an attempt to signify to the observers of the burial that the occupant was a member of a 'Germanic' lineage, possibly as a way of establishing the authority or status of the deceased's descendants.

Jewellery may also have played a similar role in indicating cultural affiliations or other social signifiers, as it has been shown that no part of the assemblage was essential for holding a costume together (Brush 1993: 139–40). Some constituents of the jewellery assemblage, namely girdle-hangers and latch-lifters, have yet to be attributed a certain function at all, which emphasizes the symbolic nature of such decoration. In a similar vein, there are suggestions that some dress-fastenings, particularly large brooches, may have been too heavy for the cloth to which they were attached (Loveluck pers. com.), and thus could not have been worn this way in life. The greater variation within the jewellery assemblage, compared to the weapon set, suggests that its role may have been different, possibly signifying more specific social affiliations to the mourners.

If this is the case, those burials without such strong statements could be interpreted as communicating different messages to the participants in the funeral, rather than just being too 'poor' to afford the appropriate goods for their sex. They may have been burials of people for whom the rest of the community felt it was inappropriate to be buried with a 'significant' assemblage. Alternatively, the classification of an assemblage as 'neutral' may be denying the symbolic meaning of grave goods such as vessels and animal bones, which are usually ignored because they cannot be placed within the male-female dichotomy, and, therefore, seem unimportant. In a similar way, those burials with no surviving goods should not be dismissed as 'poor' or 'slaves'. There are many things with which a person could be buried which would not survive, such as wood, food, cloth and other organic materials. It, therefore, must be taken into consideration that present-day evaluations of what is 'valuable', 'beautiful' or 'significant' may be entirely innappropriate when attempting to interpret archaeological material from centuries ago.

Regardless of the various interpretations which can be put upon the different assemblages, each can be seen to be attempting to communicate a message (or messages) to the mourners. The next step in this work is to investigate different aspects of the burial rite, in order to get closer to what the significance of the goods might be. Assemblages may, in fact, have very little to do with biological sex, or even gender, but much to do with other factors such as age, social position and familial lineage.

The above analysis is part of a larger body of work which looks at the structuring of the burial rite in all its aspects, including the positioning of the body in the grave, its orientation, the physical structure of the grave itself, the laying out of grave goods around the body, and changes over time, as well as skeletal characteristics such as age at death and biological sexing (Lucy 1995). By considering these variables in relation to the four different assemblages, it is possible to pull out differences in the treatment of different groups within the burials, to identify different ways of burying people at different cemeteries, and to trace changes in burial rites through time.

Conclusions

By using evidence from two recent cemetery excavations in Yorkshire which had independent biological sexing of the skeletons, it was possible to test the validity of the traditional practice in Anglo-Saxon burial archaeology of ascribing 'sex' on the basis of the grave goods associated with the burial. It was shown that the factual basis for the traditional stereotype of males with weapons and females with jewellery was actually very small, and that this dichotomy failed to account for roughly half the total number of burials which were not associated with these assemblages. By showing the existence of two other, equally significant assemblages in numerical terms, the interpretation of grave goods was cast in a new light. It was demonstrated that the basic classifications which are used in cemetery analysis must be carefully examined, and questioned if they can be seen to be reliant on uncritical assumptions. It is only in this way that the variation of burial practice can be fully explored, and assigned its true importance in the creation and maintenance of social structures.

The symbolism associated with various assemblages, and their constituent parts, was seen as being more important than their ability to supply information about the 'sex' of the person buried, and therefore group them into the passive categories of 'housewife', 'warrior', and the genderless 'slave'. Contextual investigation of this symbolism, exploration of the variation within and between graves and cemeteries and study of how they change over time can furnish Anglo-Saxon archaeology with more dynamic interpretations of pre-Christian burial rites. These interpretations will be rooted in the method and theories of gender archaeology, but they will not be radical revisions of the past. Rather, they will be detailed studies of a phenomenon – the Anglo-Saxon furnished (or non-furnished) inhumation burial – which can throw some light on the realities of social organization and gender relations, rather than relying on sexual stereotypes which explain nothing, because they are not based on reality, but on misconception. Ultimately, the unquestioned authority of the sexual stereotype must be challenged: why is it so distressing if gender relations and expressions in the past do not conform to entrenched nineteenth century expectations?

Acknowledgements

I am extremely grateful to the Director of the Heslerton Parish Project, Dominic Powlesland, for all the assistance he has given me, and the willingness with which he made the Heslerton data available. I would also like to thank Catherine Hills and J.D. Hill for commenting on previous drafts of this chapter, and Eleanor Scott for her encouragement.

References

Åberg, N. (1926) *The Anglo-Saxons in England*. Uppsala: Almquist och Wicksells Boktryckeri.

Amory, P. (1993) 'The meaning and purpose of ethnic terminology in the Burgundian Laws'. *Early Medieval Europe* 2, 1, 1–28.

Arnold, C. (1984) *Roman Britain to Saxon England*. London: Croom Helm.

Arnold, C. (1988) *An Archaeology of the Early Anglo-Saxon Kingdoms*. London: Routledge.

Austin, D. (1990) 'The "proper study" of medieval archaeology' in D. Austin and L. Alcock (eds) *From the Baltic to the Black Sea: Studies in Medieval Archaeology*. London: Unwin Hyman, pp. 9–42.

Barrett, J. (1988) 'Fields of Discourse: reconstituting a social archaeology'. *Critique of Anthropology* 7, 3, 5–16.

Bertelsen, R. Lillehammer, A. and Naess, J.-R. (1987) *Were They All Men? An Examination of Sex Roles in Prehistoric Society*. Stavanger: Arkeologisk Museum i Stavanger.

Brush, K. (1993) *Adorning the Dead: The Social Significance of Early Anglo-Saxon Funerary Dress in England (Fifth to Seventh Centuries AD)*. Unpublished PhD Dissertation. Cambridge: University of Cambridge.

Champion, T. (1987) 'The European Iron Age: assessing the state of the art'. *Scottish Archaeological Review* 4, 98–107.

Champion, T. (1990) 'Medieval archaeology and the tyranny of the historical record' in D. Austin and L. Alcock (eds) *From the Baltic to the Black Sea: Studies in Medieval Archaeology*. London: Unwin Hyman.

Champion, T. (1991) 'Theoretical archaeology in Britain' in I. Hodder (ed.) *Archaeology in Europe: The Last Three Decades*. London: Routledge, pp. 129–60.

Collingwood, R.G. and Myres, J.N.L. (1937) (2nd edn) *Roman Britain and the English Settlements*. Oxford: Clarendon Press.

Conkey, M.W. (1992) 'Does it make a difference? Feminist thinking and archaeologies of gender' in D. Walde and N.D. Willows (eds) *The Archaeology of Gender: Proceedings of the 22nd Chacmool Conference*. Calgary: The University of Calgary.

Conkey, M.W. (1993) 'Making the connections: feminist theory and archaeologies of gender' in H. du Cros and L. Smith (eds) (1993) *Women in Archaeology: A Feminist Critique*. Occasional Papers in Prehistory 23. Canberra: Department of Prehistory, Research School of Pacific Studies, The Australian National University.

Conkey, M.W. and Spector, J. (1984) 'Archaeology and the study of gender'. *Archaeological Advances in Method and Theory* 7. New York: Academic Press, pp. 1–38.

Dickinson, T. (1979) 'The present state of Anglo-Saxon cemetery studies' in P. Rahtz, L. Watts and T. Dickinson (eds) *Anglo-Saxon Cemeteries*. Oxford: British Archaelogical Reports (British Series) 82.

Dommasnes, L.H. (1982) 'Late Iron Age in western Norway: female roles and ranks as deduced from an analysis of burial customs'. *Norwegian Archaeological Review* 15, 1–2, 70–84.

Dommasnes, L.H. (1987) 'Male/female roles and ranks in Late Iron Age Norway' in R. Bertelsen, A. Lillehammer and J.-R. Naess (eds) *Were They All Men? An Examination of Sex Roles in Prehistoric Society*. Stavanger: Arkeologisk Museum i Stavanger.

Dommasnes, L.H. (1991) 'Women, kinship and the basis of power in the Nowegian Viking Age' in R. Samson (ed.) *Social Approaches to Viking Studies*. Glasgow: Cruithne Press, pp. 65–73.

Dommasnes, L.H. (1992) 'Two decades of women in prehistory and in archaeology in Norway: a review'. *Norwegian Archaeological Review* 25, 1, 1–14.

Douglas, J. (1793) *Nenia Britannica: or a sepulchral history of Great Britain*. London: John Nichols.

El-Najjar, M.Y. and McWilliams, K.R. (1978) *Forensic Anthropology*. Springfield, Ill.: Charles C. Thomas.

Engelstad, E. (1991a) 'Feminist theory and post-processual archaeology' in D. Walde and N.D. Willows (eds) *The Archaeology of Gender: Proceedings of the 22nd Chacmool Conference.* Calgary: The University of Calgary.

Engelstad, E. (1991b) 'Images of power and contradiction: feminist theory and post-processual archaeology'. *Antiquity* 65, 502–14.

Evison, V. (1979) *A Corpus of Wheel-Thrown Pottery in Anglo-Saxon Graves.* Leeds: Royal Archaeological Institute.

Evison, V. (1987) *Dover: The Buckland Anglo-Saxon Cemetery.* London: HBMC Report 3.

Geary, P.J. (1983) 'Ethnic identity as a situational construct in the Early Middle Ages'. *Mitteilungen der Anthropologischen Gesellschaft in Wien* 113, 15–26.

Gero, J.M. and Conkey, M.W. (eds) (1991) *Engendering Archaeology: Women and Prehistory.* Oxford: Blackwell.

Gibbs, L. (1987) 'Identifying gender representation in the archaeological record: a contextual study' in I. Hodder (ed.) *The Archaeology of Contextual Meanings.* Cambridge: Cambridge University Press, pp. 79–89.

Giddens, A. (1984) *The Constitution of Society: Outline of the Theory of Structuration.* Cambridge: Polity Press.

Gilchrist, R. (1991) 'Women's archaeology? Political feminism, gender theory and historical revision'. *Antiquity* 65, 495–501.

Greenwell W. and Rolleston, G. (1877) *British Barrows.* Oxford: Clarendon Press.

Härke, H. (1989a) 'Early Saxon weapon burials: frequencies, distributions and weapon combinations' in S. C. Hawkes (ed.) *Weapons and Warfare in Anglo-Saxon England.* Oxford: Oxford University Committee for Archaeology, Monograph 21.

Härke, H. (1989b) 'Knives in early Saxon burials: blade length and age at death'. *Medieval Archaeology* 33, 144–8.

Härke, H. (1990) ' "Warrior Graves". The background of the Anglo-Saxon weapon burial rite'. *Past and Present* 126, 22–43.

Härke, H. (1992) 'Changing symbols in a changing society: the Anglo-Saxon weapon burial rite in the seventh century' in M. Carver (ed.) *The Age of Sutton Hoo. The Seventh Century in North-Western Europe.* Woodbridge: Boydell, pp. 149–62.

Hedeager, L. (1993) 'The creation of Germanic identity – a European origin myth' in P. Brun, S. van der Leeuw and C. R. Whittaker *Frontières d'Empire – Nature et Signification des Frontières Romaines – Actes de la Table Ronde Internationale de Nemours 1992.* Mémoires du Musée de Préhistoire d'Ile-de-France 5.

Henderson, J. (1989) 'Pagan cemeteries: a study of the problems of sexing by grave goods and bones' in C. A. Roberts, F. Lee and J. Bintliff (eds) *Burial Archaeology – Current Research, Methods and Developments.* Oxford: British Archaeological Reports (British Series) 211.

Hines, J. (1984) *The Scandinavian Character of Anglian England in the pre-Viking period.* Oxford: British Archaeological Reports (British Series) 124.

Hines, J. (1992) 'The seriation and chronology of Anglian English women's graves: a critical assessment' in L. Jorgensen (ed.) *Chronological Studies of Anglo-Saxon England, Lombard Italy and Vendel Period Sweden.* Arkaeologiske Skrifter 5. Copenhagen: Institute of Prehistoric and Classical Archaeology, University of Copenhagen.

Hirst, S. (1985) *An Anglo-Saxon Cemetery at Sewerby.* York: York University Archaeological Publications 4.

Hjørungdal, T. (1991) 'Det skjulte kjønn. Patriarkal tradisjon og feministisk visjon i arkeologien belyst med fokus på en jernalderkontekst'. *Acta Archaeologica Ludensia Series in 8* 19, 1–188.

Hjørungdal, T. (1994) 'Poles apart. Have there been any male and female graves?'. *Current Swedish Archaeology* 2, 141–9.

Hodder, I. (1982) *Symbolic and Structural Archaeology*. Cambridge: Cambridge University Press.

Hodder, I. (1986) *Reading the Past: Current Approaches to Interpretation in Archaeology*. Cambridge: Cambridge University Press.

Hodges, R. (1989a) *Dark Age Economics: The Origins of Towns and Trade* AD 600–1000. London: Duckworth.

Hodges, R. (1989b) *The Anglo-Saxon Achievement – Archaeology and the Beginnings of English Society*. London: Duckworth.

Høgestøl, M. (1986) 'Endringer i sosial posisjon hos jernalders kvinner'. *Kvinner i Arkeologi i Norge* 3, 49–58.

Kemble, J. M. (1849) *The Saxons in England*. London.

Kemble, J. M. (1856) *Horae Ferales; or Studies in Archaeology of the Northern Nations*. London.

Kessler, S. and MacKenna, W. (1978) *Gender: An Ethnomethodological Approach*. New York: John Wiley and Sons.

Krogman, W. M. (1962) *The Human Skeleton in Forensic Medicine*. Springfield, Ill.: Charles C. Thomas.

Leeds, E. T. (1913) *The Archaeology of the Anglo-Saxon Settlements*. Oxford: Clarendon Press.

Leeds, E. T. (1923) 'A Saxon village near Sutton Courtenay, Berks'. *Archaeologia* 73, 147–92.

Leeds, E. T. (1927) 'A Saxon village near Sutton Courtenay, Berks.' *Archaeologia* 76, 59–80.

Leeds, E. T. (1936) *Early Anglo-Saxon Art and Archaeology*. Oxford: Clarendon Press.

Lucy, S. J. (1995) *The Anglo-Saxon Cemeteries of East Yorkshire*. Unpublished PhD Dissertation. Cambridge: University of Cambridge.

MacDougall, H. A. (1982) *Racial Myth in English History – Trojans, Teutons and Anglo-Saxons*. Montreal: Harvest House.

Molleson, T. and Cox, M. (1993) *The Spitalfields Project. Volume Two: The Anthropology: The Middling Sort*. York: CBA Research Report 86.

Mortimer, J. R. (1905) *Forty Years Researches in British and Saxon Burial Mounds of East Yorkshire*. London: A. Brown and Sons.

Myres, J. N. L. (1937) 'The present state of the archaeological evidence for the Anglo-Saxon conquest'. *History* n.s. 21, 317–30.

Myres, J. N. L. (1969) *Anglo-Saxon Pottery and the Settlement of England*. Oxford: Clarendon Press.

Myres, J. N. L. (1977) *A Corpus of Anglo-Saxon Pottery of the Pagan Period*. Cambridge: Cambridge University Press.

Nordbladh, J. and Yates, T. (1990) 'This perfect body, this virgin text: between sex and gender in archaeology' in I. Bapty and T. Yates (eds) *Archaeology after Structuralism: Post-Structuralism and the Practice of Archaeology*. London: Routledge, pp. 222–37.

Ortner, S. B. and Whitehead, H. (1981) *Sexual Meanings: The Cultural Construction of Gender and Sexuality*. Cambridge: Cambridge University Press.

Pader, E-J. (1982) *Symbolism, Social Relations and the Interpretation of Mortuary Remains*. Oxford: British Archaeological Reports (British Series) 130.

Palm, M. and Pind, L. (1992) 'Anglian English women's graves in the fifth to seventh centuries AD – a chronological analysis' in L. Jørgensen (ed.) *Chronological Studies of Anglo-Saxon England, Lombard Italy and Vendel Period Sweden*. Arkaeologiske Skrifter

5. Copenhagen: Institute of Prehistoric and Classical Archaeology, University of Copenhagen, pp. 50–80.

Powlesland, D. (1986) 'Excavations at Heslerton, North Yorkshire 1978–82'. *Archaeological Journal* 143, 53–173.

Powlesland, D. (in press) *West Heslerton: The Anglian Cemetery.*

Richards, J. (1992) 'Anglo-Saxon symbolism' in M. Carver (ed.) *The Age of Sutton Hoo. The Seventh Century in North-Western Europe.* Woodbridge: Boydell, pp. 131–47.

Rosaldo, M.Z. and Lamphere, L. (1974) *Woman, Culture and Society.* California: Stanford University Press.

St Hoyme, L.E. and Isçan, M.Y. (1989) 'Determination of sex and race: accuracy and assumptions' in M.Y. Isçan and K.A.R. Kennedy (eds) *Reconstruction of Life from the Skeleton.* New York: Alan R. Liss, pp. 53–93.

Shanks, M. and Tilley, C. (1987) *Social Theory and Archaeology.* Cambridge: Polity Press.

Smith, R.A. (1912) 'The excavation by Canon Greenwell F.S.A., in 1908, of an Anglo-Saxon cemetery at Uncleby, East Riding of Yorkshire.' *Proceedings of the Society of Antiquaries* 24, 146–58.

Sørensen, M.L.S. (1991) 'The construction of gender through appearance' in D. Walde and N. D. Willows (eds) *The Archaeology of Gender. Proceedings of the 22nd Chacmool Conference.* Calgary: The University of Calgary.

Sørensen, M.L.S. (1992) 'Gender archaeology and Scandinavian Bronze Age studies'. *Norwegian Archaeological Review* 25, 1, 31–49.

Stalsberg, A. (1984) 'Skandinaviske Vikingetidsfunn fra Russland med saerlig vekt på kvinnefunnere. Et bidrag til kvinne-arkeologien'. *Unitekst fagskrift* 6, 68–102, University of Trondheim.

Stalsberg, A. (1987a) 'The implications of the women's finds for the understanding of the activities of the Scandinavians in Russia during the Viking Age'. *Kvinner i Arkeologi i Norge* 5, 33–49.

Stalsberg, A. (1987b) 'The interpretation of women's objects of Scandinavian origin from the Viking period found in Russia' in R. Bertelsen, A. Lillehammer and J–R. Naess (eds) *Were They All Men? An Examination of Sex Roles in Prehistoric Society.* Stavanger: Arkeologisk Museum i Stavanger.

Stenton, F.M. (1943) *Anglo-Saxon England.* Oxford: Clarendon Press.

Stewart, T.D. (1979) *Essentials of Forensic Anthropology.* Springfield, Ill.: Charles C. Thomas.

Swanton, M.J. (1973) *Spearheads of the Anglo-Saxon Settlements.* London: Royal Archaeological Institute.

Webster, L. (1986) 'Anglo-Saxon England AD 400–1100' in I. Longworth and J. Cherry *Archaeology in Britain since 1945: New Directions.* London: British Museum Publications.

Wilson, D. (1976) *The Archaeology of Anglo-Saxon England.* Cambridge: Cambridge University Press.

Wormald, P. (1983) 'Bede, the Bretwaldas and the origins of the *Gens Anglorum*' in P. Wormald (ed.) *Ideal and Reality in Frankish and Anglo-Saxon Society.* London: Blackwell.

12 Female into male, won't go! Gender and early Christian asceticism

MARY HARLOW

Introduction

The substance of the argument in this chapter is based on the discourse of early Christian asceticism. It uses texts as the primary source of evidence and for this reason perhaps, it requires some justification for its inclusion in an 'archaeology' volume. There are two main reasons why I think it has a place in such a collection, the first is theoretical, the second is subject specific. Firstly then, to feel the need at all to justify an entry that is text based implies a perceived dichotomy between the disciplines of ancient history and archaeology. It is a false dichotomy that is often encouraged by the academic structures of university courses, wherein ancient history is often the poor relation to either archaeology and/or classics, rather than the integral link that bridges both disciplines. Texts are, after all, fundamental aspects of material culture and essential, where extant, to the understanding of past societies. Archaeology and ancient history must be embedded within each other, each integral to the findings and thinking of the other and to the reconstruction of past societies and the ways in which those societies constructed themselves. Secondly, this chapter is concerned with the discourse of asceticism and its implications for the social construction of gender. Ascetic lifestyle, by its very nature, leaves little in the archaeological record so discussion must be primarily text-based. In wider terms the discourse becomes essential as a framework behind the construction of early monastic communities and for the excavation of sites such as those of the desert monks of Egypt. It may be helpful to know how a given group constructed themselves, albeit in ideal terms, when attempting to reconstruct their habitations and lifestyle from other material remains.[1] What we say about how we live can often quite innocently misconstrue the actual way we live and the same can be said of the historical record, so rather than sit on either side of an academic divide, archaeology and ancient history must interact to enhance the reconstruction of the past.

Towards a gendered spirituality?

The central issue this chapter seeks to address is: the implication for the construction of gender within the early Christian ascetic movement. The chronological timescale is that of the late fourth and early fifth centuries AD, a time when Christianity had 'triumphed' and was no longer a persecuted faith but a growing political, social and economic force in late Roman society. Ascetic lifestyles were far from unknown in the pre-Christian ancient world, but here they are discussed solely within the Christian context. Asceticism is defined, in this context, as the suppression of ordinary bodily needs and desires in order to liberate the spirit; as subduing the physical and thus allowing the spirit/soul/mind to draw closer to the divine. Here, the implications of this in a world view that aligned the rational and spiritual with the male, and the irrational and physical with the female are explored. Was spirituality always defined as an attribute of the male, and did women therefore have to 'become manly' to achieve spirituality? If this was the case, was female spirituality always inferior to male? In addition, how did this separation of the physical and the spiritual fit into the context of a religion, one of whose central tenets is that of the Incarnation, the unity of body and spirit in the person of Christ, spirit become man?

The theological, social, historical and cultural implications of the ascetic movement in the early Christian period are well documented by modern scholarship.[2] The actual practice of the ascetic life involved numerous physical deprivations of varying degrees, ranging from isolation, fasting and lack of sleep to the wearing of rough clothing. It also included time spent in prayer, scripture study, sometimes physical labour and charitable activities. In much of the Church Fathers' writings on the subject a great proportion of the discussion was predicated on celibacy, chastity and the denial of sexuality, these being the fundamentals of ascetic life. The suppression of desire became one of the first tasks of the novice ascetic. Virginity became the preferred option for both men and women, though a great part of the writing was aimed at women, since they were perceived of as more physical beings, more tied to the body.

The social implications for women choosing the ascetic life over traditional family expectations has been explored over the past decade. Within this patristic rhetoric, certainly, women only attained the highest ascetic virtue, spirituality, by denying all that was perceived to construct them as female and by acquiring certain 'manly' virtues. In ideal terms it was necessary for women to remove themselves from the traditional nexus of family, marriage and children if they wished to attain salvation. As Jerome, one of the most vociferous supporters of the ascetic life, stated:

> As long as woman is for birth and children she is as different from man as body is from soul. But when she seeks to serve Christ more than she does the world, she will cease to be a woman and will be called a man.
>
> Commentary on Epistle to the Ephesians III.V (*PL*.26.567)

Women had to ignore traditional gender roles and also discard other attributes that defined them as women – material things such as dress and jewellery and emotional attitudes seen as particular to females, such as light-mindedness, frailty and vanity. Jerome quotes Paula, a wealthy Roman matron, as stating her intentions, when planning to take up the ascetic life on the death of her husband:

I must disfigure that face which contrary to God's commandment I have painted with rouge, white lead and antimony. I must mortify that body which has been given up to many pleasures. I must make up for my long laughter by constant weeping. I must exchange my soft linen and costly silks for rough goat's hair.

Ep.108.15. (*PL*22.891).[3]

Although we must be suspicious of the use of the first person here, this is at least an example of the lifestyle expected of these women.

Such women were encouraged to deny their bodily needs to the extent that they suppressed their own sexuality and were no longer likely to tempt men to desire them. Women were perceived of as more closely linked to the physical and material world, a closeness that was rooted in biological function. Through their capacity for reproduction women were perceived of as inextricably linked with sexuality and, therefore, to the material world. In theological terms women, as descendants of Eve, were responsible for bringing about the Fall of Man. In one interpretation of the creation story,[4] Eve through her inability to contain her desire brought about punishment on men and women in the form of sexual awareness and sexuality. For woman the penalty tied her eternally into a subordinate role defined by her ability to reproduce:

I will multiply your pains in childbearing, you shall give birth to your children in pain. Your yearning shall be for your husband, yet he will lord it over you.

(Genesis 3:16)

A man's woman and manly women

According to those Church Fathers who supported asceticism, women's main hope of salvation was to transcend their sex: perpetual virginity and the ascetic life were offered as ways of avoiding the tie to the material world inherent in femaleness. Celibacy and virginity thus became linked to the notion of spirituality. Married couples could also achieve this state if they lived a life of shared continence and austerity. As Jerome wrote to Lucinius concerning his wife Theodora, once they had made such a decision:

You have with you one who was once your partner in the flesh but now in spirit, once your wife, now your sister; once a woman, now a man; once an inferior, now an equal.

Ep. 71.3. (*PL*.22.670)

The aligning of spirituality with maleness had been part of the Christian world view since Paul. I Cor. 11:3–7, demonstrates the desired hierarchy within which society should exist:

However, what I want you to understand is that Christ is the head of every man, man is the head of every woman, and God is the head of Christ.

This is a sentiment that is reflected in classical assumptions about gender roles that justified and legitimated all sorts of social roles.

The status quo is justified, God at the top and woman at the bottom. For John Chrysostom, another advocate of the ascetic life, it was part of the natural order that man should be the 'head' and woman the 'body'.[5]

In patristic writings spirituality is often defined in opposition to the physical, and implies the corresponding alignment of male with spiritual and female with physical. This is significant and has implications not only for gender roles and expectations but also for patristic assumptions about them. For Christian writers like Jerome, John Chrysostom, and Augustine, these oppositions were 'natural', that is ordained by God, and not, in any way, cultural. To quote Augustine, echoing Aristotle, (*Politics* 1):

> What therefore is to be found in one person, the rational mind and desire – the one rules and the other is ruled, the one has power and the other is subdued – this is also to be found in two people, the man and the woman.
>
> (De opere monachorum 40. PL. 40.580)

Spirituality then is understood within a context of asceticism that held that one could not be fully spiritual until one subdued the needs of the physical body. As the male was held 'naturally' to belong to the rational, cerebral realm, spirituality became invested with male qualities. Women could, therefore, only acquire it, in this context, by becoming like men, otherwise they were 'naturally' identified with the irrational, corporeal realm. By setting the body and spirit in opposition to each other, one stresses the other and both are defined by interaction with the other.

Definition by opposition – male : female, rational : irrational, spiritual : physical, head : body, public : private[6] – informed much of the writing of the Church Fathers and amounted to a validation of women's inferior position. It is further exemplified by the fact that asceticism was given a positive press as an escape from that other traditional female area, domestic life, as opposed to the public, male realm. It offered freedom from 'the drawbacks of marriage, such as pregnancy, the crying of infants, the torture caused by a rival, the cares of household management' (Jerome: Ep.22.2. *PL*.22.395). It is fair to say that men suffered within the same context, but paradoxically they could never be seen to acquire attributes of femaleness. In his treatise, *Instruction and Refutation Directed Against Those Men Cohabiting With Virgins*,[7] John Chrysostom lists the dangers for men who have to attend to women's needs, though it has to be said, these are not virgins that either John Chrysostom himself, or Jerome would have approved of: they appear to require mirrors and perfume and all sorts of unsuitable accoutrements. These women have a terrible debilitating effect on their male companions, as John succinctly describes:

> They render them softer, more excitable, shameful, thoughtless, more prone to temper, insolent, importunate, ignoble, abject, cruel, ungenerous, reckless, nonsensical, and, to sum it up, the women take all their corrupting feminine customs and stamp them into the souls of these men.
>
> (Ag. Cohab. Virg. 10. PG. 47.510)

After this list of derogatory adjectives Chrysostom goes on to say that men who live with women end up by being able to talk only of wool and weaving, i.e. women's things, and become servile and, therefore, not fit for that most masculine of physically and symbolically gendered space, the civic sphere. And being unable to manage civic affairs he will be even less able to manage spiritual matters. This is a splendid example not only of misogynistic writing and male opinions of characteristic female traits, but also of aligning male with the spiritual, and here also, with the traditional male sphere, the civic and public. Where women have to cross the boundaries of oppositions to achieve the desired aim, men must stay firmly within them.

Discussion

If women have to cross traditional gender boundaries to achieve spirituality, are we to assume that the ideal Christian woman was a man? Not so: women undertaking the ascetic life did not, of course, become men. On the contrary, I would argue that what they did was to offer a new ideal of woman. However much they might denigrate their bodies, even to the extent that they might suppress menstruation,[8] the most obvious sign of their femaleness and of their tie to reproduction, they remained, physically and symbolically, women. They did not, therefore, inhabit an ambiguous, blurred 'degendered' area. They cannot be compared to say, modern-day transexuals, who though they may acquire the attributes of their preferred sex are rarely fully admitted to society. Ascetic Christian women were replacing the traditional Roman female ideal of wife and mother with a new ideal, that of virgin. And those who took up the ascetic life as widows became, as it were, born-again virgins.

However, they were still acting within a patriarchal system which defined the female sex as falling anywhere between the two extremes of virgin and whore. Their choice of lifestyle, while denigrating their sex and sexuality, at the same time redefined it, but within a context of unquestioned patristic assumptions about the nature of women. It seems too that women internalized this ideal and defined themselves within that context – as far as we can tell. The tiny percentage of women's voices we have record the use of the same imagery. Perpetua, one of the first women martyrs, dreams that she 'was made a man' the night before she is thrown to the beasts in the arena at Carthage.[9] Amma Sarah, one of the Desert Mothers says to some other hermits that '*It is I who am a man, you who are women.*'[10] Christian women then, were framing their lives within a male context and conforming to male ideas about femaleness. If, by living ascetic lives, they hoped to transcend their sex and return to the time before the Fall and so redeem the guilt of Eve, they were colluding in the reasoning that held Eve, and, therefore, women, responsible for original sin. However extreme their deprivations, by their very self-denial they were embodying an ideal of what constituted femaleness.

Within the given context of asceticism then, we have an opposition between male and female, spiritual and physical. Women obviously do have the capacity for spirituality as defined in the terms of the ascetic movement, and it should be acknowledged that this notion of spirituality was very real to the early Christians.[11] How then do we evaluate female spirituality? Must it, given the established hierarchy, be inferior to male spirituality? Because women are associated more closely with the physical realm do they have to work harder at bodily suppression than men? Men have less suppressing to do as the body is not so dominant in the male as it is in the female, and anyway men, or stoic Roman men at least, were more used to the idea of a regime of self-control. Can male and female spirituality amount to the same thing, if male and female are perceived to be in opposition to each other? Must female spirituality be inferior? Jerome and John Chrysostom considered that women could become their equals, on some levels, but this equality was defined by categories other than ascetic denial, although it could never have existed at all outside of that context. Clark[12] has shown that the women who became the protégées of Jerome and John were educated and wealthy; they had established, high social status before they ever took to self-denial. They also – despite, as ascetics, denying their sexuality – acted within traditional expectations of female behaviour, looking to their (male) spiritual mentors for guidance, putting themselves voluntarily inside male control. Marcella, another one of Jerome's patrons in Rome, studied and interpreted the scriptures but, according to Jerome, when she answered questions she gave her opinion not as her own but as if from himself.[13] Equality is then a relative term, and spiritual equality is subject to the same outside factors that control social equality. Dedicated ascetic women were recognized by their male counterparts as holy and spiritual, with holiness/spirituality always linked to chastity.

The pure body was necessary for approaching the divine. Holy virginity represented the purity of pre-Fall intactness. This is the central paradox of the whole body/spirit debate, that it remained rooted in the body, even if it was a redefined 'unsexed' body. Virginity, whatever else it may symbolize,[14] is an intensely physical state of body. My final question therefore is: how did this movement, so predicated on the body and sexuality, come to terms with the central Christian belief in the Incarnation? This is the unity of body and spirit in the person of Christ, a unity that is both divine and human and at the same time the antithesis of the ascetic aim. While asceticism sought to separate the spiritual from the physical in order to come closer to the divine, the divinity has celebrated the physicality of the human body by joining with it. There seems to be a surprising contradiction here between Christian belief and the Christian way of life. Again, virginity is the key link. Christ entered the world, born of a virgin. There was no stain of sexuality on his creation, for, like Adam in Eden, he was a pre-sexual being. Christ's creation was untouched by the sin that had caused the Fall of Man. In the person of Christ human and divine were united, but his was a special non-sexual state. Human beings could only hope to attain that unity of body and spirit by getting their bodies back to a pre-Fall condition, that is by extreme ascetic practice. Self-denial and close sexual control, not only the suppression of desire but the lack of it altogether, were seen as essential to this aim. The body that had experienced post-Fall sensuality could not unite with the spirit and achieve that purity that was the Incarnation. What Christians required in fact, was the right sort of body, a better, purer body that was devoid of sexual characteristics. Baptism, a sacrament that wipes away the stain of original sin, could be construed as a ritualization of the notion of rebirth. After this cleansing one could take on a new body, the right sort of body suitable for the final resurrection. As we know, many early Christians deferred baptism until the last possible moment, so they had little chance of defiling these 'new bodies' even in their thoughts!

Conclusion

In the final analysis the body appears triumphant, as in one form or another it will continually get in the way of any ultimate ascetic aim of transcending it. Women encounter an additional difficulty in that they are perceived as more tied to the body than men. Within the ascetic discourse spirituality does seem to be essentially defined as a male trait, but one that was attainable by women if they behaved in certain prescribed ways. These teachings would appear to sharpen the gender boundaries of society for Christians, at the very least to bring them into sharp focus for men and women. This aesthetic of the ascetic justified woman's inferior status through a series of associations that linked her with the physical/domestic/material realm and held her responsible, through her sexuality, for the loss of paradise. Woman could not, of course, even through ascetic practice, become man, she could at best conform to male Christian ideas about what an ideal woman was. Within the early Christian cosmology male and female were not equal in life, nor was female spirituality equal to male spirituality, for however much a woman might attempt to transcend her sex, she remained physically a woman with all the inherent implications of her sexuality. This is not to say that women were not considered capable of spirituality, but that female spirituality was defined in different terms. Paul's claim 'there are no more distinctions between Jew and Greek, slave and free, male and female, but all are one in Christ Jesus',[15] may have been a comforting thought but had little bearing on women's lives, any more than it did on other disparaged groups.

Notes

1. For example on the diet of the Desert Fathers see Dembinska, M. (1985) 'Diet: A comparison of food consumption between some eastern and western monasteries in the 4th-12th centuries'. *Byzantion* 35, 431–62. Smith, W. (University of Leicester, forthcoming), on seed remains in Egyptian monastery sites. For the rhetoric of the Desert Fathers see Ward, B. (trans.) (1975) *The Sayings of the Desert Fathers*.

2. See for example: Brown 1988; Clark, E.A. 1983, 1986; Clark, G. 1993; Drijvers 1987; Pagels 1988; Rouselle 1983; Salisbury 1991.

3. All following extracts of Jerome from (1893) *Jerome: Letters and Selected Works*, in Select Library of Nicene and Post-Nicene Fathers of the Church, vol. VI. Oxford and New York.

4. For interpretations of the Genesis story and its social implications see Pagels (1988).

5. John Chrysostom, Homily 17 on Genesis 4 and 9. *PG*.53.139. Clark, E.A. 1979.

6. For more on the theory of binary opposition and construction of society see Lovibond 1994: 88–101 and Moi 1985: 104–26, on Cixous.

7. Trans. and ed. Clark, E.A. (1979) *Jerome, Chrysostom and Friends.*

8. For a concise summary of the effects of semi-starvation on the body see Crisp 1980: 13–18.

9. Musurillo 1972: 119.

10. Ward 1975: 230.9.

11. Brown 1986: 427–43.

12. Clark, E.A. 1979, 1986.

13. Jerome, Ep. 127.7.

14. See for example, Douglas, M. (1966) *Purity and Danger: An Analysis of the Concepts of Pollution and Taboo.* London: Ark.

15. Paul *Galatians* 2.28.

References

PL Patrologia latina
PG Patrologia graeca

Jerome. *Letters and Selected Works* (trans. 1893) in Library of Nicene and Post-Nicene Fathers, Oxford and New York

Brown, P. (1986) 'The Notion of Virginity in the early Church' in B. McGinn, J. Meyendorff and J. Leclercq (eds) *World Spirituality Vol. 16. Christian Spirituality: Origins to the Twelfth Century.* London: Routledge, pp. 427–43.

Brown, P. (1988) *The Body and Society: Men, Women and Sexual Renunciation in Early Christianity.* London: Faber.

Clark, E.A. (1979) *Jerome, Chrysostom and Friends: Essays and Translations.* Studies in Women and Religion. New York: Edwin Mellen.

Clark, E.A. (1983) *Women in the Early Church.* Minnesota: The Liturgical Press.

Clark, E.A. (1986) *Ascetic Piety and Women's Faith: Essays on Late Ancient Christianity.* New York: Edwin Mellen.

Clark, G. (1993) *Women in Late Antquity: Pagan and Christian Lifestyles.* Oxford: Oxford University Press.

Crisp, A.H. (1980) *Anorexia Nervosa: Let Me Be.* London: Academic Press.

Dembinska, M. (1985) 'Diet: a comparison of food consumption between some eastern and western monasteries in the 4th–12th centuries'. *Byzantion* 35, 431–62.

Douglas, M. (1966) *Purity and Danger: An Analysis of the Concepts of Pollution and Taboo.* London: Ark.

Drijvers, J. W. (1987) 'Virginity and asceticism in late Roman western elites' in J. Blok and P. Mason (eds) *Sexual Asymmetry.* Amsterdam: Gieben, pp. 241–73.

Lovibond, S. (1994) 'An ancient theory of gender: Plato and the Pythagorean Table' in L. J. Archer, S. Fischler and M. Wyke (eds) *Women in Ancient Societies: An Illusion of the Night.* London: Macmillan, pp. 88–101.

Moi, T. (1985, repr. 1993) *Sexual/Textual Politics.* London: Routledge.

Musurillo, H. (1972) *The Acts of the Christian Martyrs: Introduction, Texts and Translation.* Oxford: Oxford University Press.

Pagels, E. (1988) *Adam, Eve and the Serpent.* London: Penguin.

Rouselle, A. (1983) *Porneia: On Desire and the Body in Antiquity*. Oxford: Blackwell.
Salisbury, J. (1991) *Church Fathers, Independent Virgins*. London: Verso
Ward, B. (ed. and trans.) (1975) *The Sayings of the Desert Fathers*. London: Mowbray.

Commentary: Writing Gender

BARBARA BENDER

The strength of the chapters in this section is mainly methodological. They focus attention on the relationship between gender and material culture and the multiplicity of ways in which the record can be addressed.

Three of the archaeological chapters play off each other. Kokkinidou and Nikolaidou (Chapter 8), Hitchcock (Chapter 9) and Chapman (Chapter 10) all address questions of gendered relations and gendered power in the Neolithic and Early Bronze Age of the Aegean and Balkans. Kokkinidou and Nikolaidou look at the corpus of Aegean Neolithic figurines, but instead of simply focusing on the figurines, they move between figurine and pottery, between figurines and household economy, and they don't fudge the variability and ambiguity of many of the figurine forms. They suggest that the frequent emphasis on female fertility is part of a reiterative process that encompasses many aspects of social reproduction within a modest, household-orientated agricultural way of life. They note the way in which a figurine might combine breasts and an elongated phallic neck: 'Female fertility symbolically transgresses the strict boundaries of sexual dimorphism and the division between "man" and "woman"'. They note with interest, but could perhaps have discussed further, figures that portray deformities and the process of ageing. It might have been worth considering the ways in which gendered social divisions may be transformed, cross-cut or superseded by divisions based on age, kin affiliation, healing powers etc.

Kokkinidou and Nikolaidou make it clear that they are talking about gendered ideologies rather than gendered authority. Hitchcock, working with Cretan Early Bronze Age figurines is able, through a very detailed examination of materials used, craftsmanship, context, and precise figural analysis to distinguish female and male gestures of supplication and authority, and then to suggest ways in which the female authoritative gesture is increasingly co-opted within the male arena.

John Chapman, in his chapter on 'Changing gender relations in the later prehistory of eastern Hungary' seems to think that if there were more women archaeologists working in Hungary there would be more gendered archaeology. Would that the equation were so simple! This chapter considers a long time range and a wide sweep of settlement and burial evidence. Chapman's argument is that in the transition from Neolithic to Copper Age there is a burgeoning of crafts and activities, a greater division of labour, 'a strengthening of both male and female power bases' and, therefore, increasing gender differentiation. There are a fair number of questionable assumptions built into this scenario, including the correlation of increased labour input with increased authority. Recourse to ethnographic tabulations culled from the Human Relations Area File are also less than convincing. The changes he charts in burial patterns and grave goods are much more interesting, although, again, the apparently unproblematic sexing of the burials seems open to question. Quite apart from the acknowledged difficulty of sexing skeletons, the biological reductionism end-stops many questions before they are even posed. We have to recognize that in trying to interpret a gendered past all the assumptions and methodologies built into earlier accounts have to be re-examined, nothing can be taken for granted. Nonetheless, with the very rich Hungarian burial materials available, one can begin to catch a glimpse of a world of fluid, cross-cutting and changing gendered, status- and age-related identities and relationships. We might also suspect that other sorts of cemetery information on placement of plots, groupings, orientations, construction etc. would allow for even more detailed correlations and negations to be explored.

Just as these three chapters demonstrate very satisfactorily that, despite Gimbutas' best attempts, there are no easy equations to be made between female figurines and matrilineal societies or Mother Goddess cults, so Lucy's chapter (Chapter 11) shows that the frequent assumption that men = weapons and women = jewellery is equally unsatisfactory. In an analysis of two East Yorkshire Anglo-Saxon cemeteries Lucy shows that around half the burials have neither jewellery nor weapons, that of those graves that do contain them between three and four times as many contain jewellery as contain weapons, and that at one cemetery 15 per cent of the probable male graves contain jewellery, while at the other over 12 per cent of the certain or probable female graves contain weapons! All this suggests that something much more nuanced than a bimodal sexual division is at work here, that multiple strands of identity, and complex relations to the past and present wind their way into the grave.

Archaeologists frequently feel that the material record is recalcitrant, and so it is, but all these studies show how much more there is that can be said about the past. The written word provides another material medium which needs to be played off against archaeological information. Harlow (Chapter 12), using written sources, gives a very strong account of Early Christian attitudes to women, and the way in which (high status) women could redeem themselves through a negation of their sexuality. Giving up the pleasures of the flesh they are reclassified as men. This is a wonderful example of how gender is culturally constructed, but it is somewhat undermined by Harlow's comment that, nonetheless, they remain women. Surely not: if they conceive of themselves as men, and if men treat them as non-women, then clearly they are 'other'. Her study cries out for work on other material dimensions: how were such ascetes buried? What grave goods were they given? Where and how were they housed? Where were they located in pictorial presentations? How were they dressed?

Finally, Bevan's chapter (Chapter 7), which is mainly based on ethnographic material, makes many useful cautionary points: that burials are only part of the long process of talking to and about the dead; that material culture may convey gendered messages that cannot be spoken; that our binary categories – men: women, home: wild, inside: outside, domestic: ritual – are *our* binary categories. At other times and places they may not be oppositional. Among the Lugbara the grave goods associate women with the domestic and agricultural spheres, but in the ritual and mythology men are 'inside' – the people of the home – women are 'outside' – the people of the bushland. Women's procreative power is 'natural' and, therefore, 'dangerous'. Bevan notes, and the above chapters support her contention, that we tend to assume that certain arenas and activities are more symbolically loaded – more powerful – than others. This again tallies with our own sense of ritual and non-ritual occasions and places. But these divisions do not hold. If we want to find out more about people and how they construct a sense of identity and relate to each other we have to recognize that all places and all aspects of material culture form part of a ritualized creative process and part of the shifting fields of power.

Of the six case-studies in this section, one is text-based, one primarily ethnographic, and the rest are based on archaeological materials. This wide gamut should permit some interesting comparisons of the strengths and weaknesses of different data-sets, methodologies and theoretical approaches to questions of gender within the different disciplines. But, with the exception of Sam Lucy's chapter, such comparative issues are hardly addressed. Indeed, perhaps more surprisingly, the authors, with the exception of Kokkinidou and Nikolaidou, spend little time on gender theory. Perhaps this is due to the constraints of length, or perhaps because the more 'theoretical' chapters are elsewhere in the volume, but I wonder whether it also represents a disinclination to tangle with the often quite difficult abstractions of gender theory, or conversely, a belief that 'We've done the theory, now it's time to think about the data and method'. I would suggest that a lack of theoretical contextualization is premature. Archaeologists have been remarkably slow to enter the debate on gender issues, we are still building on very slender theoretical discussions, and deeply entrenched gender-blind and gender-biased views of the past still dominate the literature. I suspect that most readers have only a hazy notion of the heated and often contentious cross-disciplinary debates that surround questions of sexuality, the gendered politics of everyday encounters, or the cross-cultural and intra-cultural *variability, permeability, changeability and ambiguity* of gender construction and negotiation. I think that we still have to wrestle with the theoretical arguments over and over again.

Part 3

Writing Children and Childhood

13 Invisibility as a symptom of gender categories in archaeology

MARY BAKER

I am the awkward sorceress of the invisible: my sorcery lacks power to evoke, without the help of your sorcery. Everything I evoke depends on you, depends on your confidence, on your faith. I gather words to make a great straw-yellow fire but if you do not put in your own flame my fire will not start, my words will not burst into yellow sparks. My words remain dead words. Without your breath in my words there will not be any mimosa.

(Cixous 1991: 196)

I am committed to the concept of 'writing into European prehistory' as a political activity, but I believe that such writing will change the stories of prehistory only if we approach the research from very different conceptual frameworks than those which are currently used to work through representations of social relations. My feminist perspective is informed by gender theory which takes the reappropriation of the concept of the feminine as its grounding. In the context of this chapter, I explore how children have been defined as feminine, and as such have been invisible in interpretations of prehistory. By rewriting archaeology in ways which acknowledge the multiplicity of genders, our stories about the past can more effectively portray the complexity of past societies.

Anglo-American feminist politics of equality have perpetuated the dominance of androcentric and phallocentric binary interpretative frameworks. When feminist archaeologists have addressed issues of social relations, sexual and gender divisions in prehistory, they have been informed by contemporary feminist practice which has usually taken equality as its defining goal. This has confined the debate within masculist bounds. Equality is understood in relation to maleness and to male knowledge, our claims are restricted to: 'women can be as good as men' 'as strong', 'as intelligent' etc. If, instead, we follow the French feminist philosophical traditions (Cixous 1991 and Irigaray 1989), we take gender and difference as our conceptual frameworks. This allows us to work with the multiple possibilities of fluid and flexible combinations of gendered categories. We can then understand the non-masculine as more than Other. In this way, we address the bigger problem of how it has been possible to people the past with adult males, instead of gendered people of different ages and sexes. These were people who understood their lived mediations of gender categories in unfixed multiple ways through the diverse contexts of day to day interactions with people, in social and cultural contexts.

By reappropriating knowledge of the lived experience of genders, I propose that we can think about the past in ways which avoid the presuppositions informed by masculist heterosexual norms. We must think beyond the choice of being male/masculine or being as good as male/masculine. It is these frameworks which require the exclusion of some to produce and sanction the significance of others. The concept of gender as multiple possibilities and differences offers disruption of the dominion of dichotomous value systems. Gender is not simply a choice of fixed male or female. As a social understanding of biologically defined sex, it is not reduced to one of two static, unchanging, and obvious phenomena, but is both; always a choice of many, and also always changing. We are never just one gender – our genders are series of mediations of contextual behaviours, referencing culturally and temporally located gender categories. If we understand this in relation to a number of widely accepted oppositional dichotomies, we have:

Visible	Invisible
Public	Domestic
Culture	Nature
Active	Passive
With access to power	Without access to power

When we recognize that lived experience of gender categories is never a choice of just two, we do not live *a* gender but negotiate the categories in multifarious ways, we can think of more flexible statuses and consider social roles in ways which do not rely on binary oppositions and their embedded values. If we apply this to the ways we understand prehistoric roles we can see that we confound dichotomies such as public/domestic, hunter/gatherer, active/passive, adult (male)/child, visible/ invisible, etc.

Gender as social category has been subconsciously assimilated into dualisms fused to phallocentric binary conditions of have or lack. As Moira Gatens says, 'it is the male body, and its historically and culturally determined powers and capacities, that is taken as the norm or the standard ... ' (Gatens 1991: 125). In archaeology we have interpretations of the past which exclude categories of people that do not conform to masculine ideals. This exclusion has resulted in accounts which in effect make some members of society invisible: women, the elderly, the weak, the sick, and children. They are invisible in the archaeological record because of the binary, phallocratic, interpretive framework used by archaeologists. We can give existence to these 'missing people' if we interpret the social as part of the fabric of gender categories which are flexible and plural, and as such, do not need to be defined within as positive or negative, visible or invisible. Different interpretive frameworks are possible when we use gender perspectives *actively*.

To do this we must first problematize some of the taken-for-granted under-standings of 'gender', and acknowledge the historical locations of understand-ings of 'sex'. 'Sex is not simply what one has, or a static description of what one is' (Butler 1993: 2). It is an historical and contingent construct. In under-standings of sex and gender within binary thought, sex is to nature as gender is

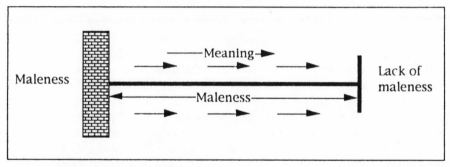

Figure 13.1 Male Meaning

to culture. As Judith Butler (1993) says, sex is no more 'natural' than gender. We are never any closer to 'reality' than our located experiences of it. Our knowledge of what it means to physically be a sex is constructed and constrained by cultural frames of reference. In social archaeology today we often find that the most dominant of these 'knowledges' is that of the potential of women being limited by their capability to be pregnant and, therefore, less able to do other tasks. Women are defined by this capacity and by contemporary (i.e. post-Victorian) understandings of motherhood, childhood and the nuclear family, and with their input into representations of the social in the past being assessed with these presuppositions explicitly to the fore.

The binary nature of this interpretive framework has also allowed the concept of 'neutral gender' to conceal implicit masculine norms, as in the use of generic term he/man language. In contemporary masculist culture there is no such position. Texts written as though they are gender neutral, are representing universal, central maleness, and result in the production of accounts in which already-there male adults are assumed. This works because gendered dichotomous understandings of difference are explained as a choice between two, with the distance between the two being linear and subsumed by male meanings. The feminine end of the opposition only exists because it is not the male and the meaning of the feminine only happens at the end of the line; all meaning is bounced off the wall of the dominant meaning which is always maleness.

When we look at this apparent choice between two we recognize that the representative dichotomy of masculine/feminine, or maleness and lack of maleness, encompasses values of gender which are social and cultural measurements of 'worth'. In the phallus-centred contemporary academic discourse, these are measured in relation to access to power in the dominant masculist system of value. Gender is the understandings of age, size, marital status, etc. and is linked to sex through the interpretive framework centred on the symbolic reference points of the phallus and penis. In Figure 13.1 the area of meaning marked as 'lack of maleness' includes all those who are disqualified from membership of the 'Phallus Club'. The complexity and fluidity of the judgement process is disguised by this simple depiction in the way that the taken-for-granted nature of binary opposition disguises the self-supporting logic of interpretive frameworks based on the symbolic phallus and its metonymic partner, the penis. The slip between the two has both informed categories of opposition and in a circular movement, been underpinned by this binary reasoning. The multiplicity of gender has been subsumed in the two of sex, fixed male or female as choice of definition deny the possibilities of fluid and changing gender. When understood in this dichotomy the male meaning in the diagram defines the meaning of all else, that which lacks, is understood as feminine. If we reclaim sex as multiple we can recognize the complex and flexible nature of the content of the 'non-masculine' package and also recognize that the package is actually composed of fragmented and multiple combinations of categorized members of society with contextual significance. The status of children is most often defined as non-male, within the complex categories of gender evaluation but paradoxically when 'gender' is subsumed by 'sex' they become even more invisible. Within the binary option of sex when they are categorized as not male, for example by age, or role, or by their relationship to the domestic and women, they disappear from specific representation into the opposite of male, i.e. the feminine. When categorized as 'with masculine value', for example, by their role in association with work defined as 'male work', they disappear into the category of maleness, they are invisible because they are denied their gendered specificity.

In archaeology, we can see the results of this framework of presuppositions in the status assigned to tasks both for archaeologists working today and for the tasks of people living in the past. The unresearched is predominantly that which is defined feminine. Little attempt has been made to examine the lives of women and children in the far past and yet it is assumed that we know they were inactive, home-based, less inventive, subordinate people. Most archaeology continues to be written in this way with the simultaneous use of generic term 'he', with the prelocation of women, children in the domestic sphere reinforcing masculist social frameworks. In order to claim space which represents women, children and the elderly positively, with their multiple possibilities, we must make the androcentric and phallocentric practices explicit. We can create meanings which can be understood outside of valued, *a priori* notions of status which are informed by phallocentric ideology.

These suppositions which inhibit the imagined potential of women and children's social roles are possible because of the phallocratic nature of academic discourse. Cocks (1989: 153) defines this: 'The cultural reserves that the masculine self finds at his disposal are so great that the moment he steps out from those close intimate quarters into an airier public space, he sees his vision of desire confirmed wherever he looks while the feminine sees her vision constantly negated.' Binary oppositions work against the norm of male/man and are sustained by phallocentric valorization which is informed by epistemological groundings in the understandings of men as complete, others as incomplete. Men produce semen containing the soul, women were the fertile vessel after Aristotle, and Freudian theories of penis envy, i.e. man/masculine equals has and is, woman/feminine equals lack and is not. These work to pathologize women and also to locate women and the feminine in nature, in the static timelessness of the 'natural', as opposed to in culture and in history.

If we recognize these restrictions on the way we read people in the past we can see that phallocratic reasoning with the phallus as central, and as access to knowledge and public (valued) power, allows only the male adult and masculine visibility in the archaeological record. I do not envisage this recognition only as a way to find women, nor as a simple way to give feminine meanings to material culture. Neither do I see 'children' as connected to 'women' in an ahistorical way. The invisibility of children and the absence of accounts about women results from male-centred interpretations which have been informed by phallo-centric ideologies. As such children have been both absent/invisible from the archaeological record, and invisible, unknowable at the conceptual level. Contemporary culturally constructed social knowledge, embedded as it is in masculist ideologies, fits 'children' in the interpretative framework as incomplete humans, that is, not male/masculine. Children are defined as feminine and understood as lacking in this phallus/symbolic power structure and as such are simultaneously included and excluded from the accounts of the past, they exist as the negative, non-public, non-authoritative, weak, subordinate, unknown. They are absent as active, knowledgeable agents in their own history. Contemporary understandings of children are: invisible (silent unless spoken to), non-public, part of the domestic, women's accessories, unknowledgeable, small, weak, illogical and subordinate. They are, as such, Other or non-male, as the feminine has been.

As I have said above, this interpretive framework relies on the taken-for-granted central complete male. Helene Cixous and Luce Irigaray disrupt this assumption when they write in ways which situate their theoretical perspective in rewritten embodiedness, both as women and as feminine. This offers the possibility of rewriting other social categories. They declare that they are women *and* they are complete, Helene Cixous has described her task as 'To confront perpetually the mystery of the there-not-there. The visible and the invisible.' (Cixous 1991: 3). Her embodied experience informs her that she exists as an active, intelligent member of society, yet her cultural knowledge informs her that she exists in relation to men, defined by masculist ideology. Irigaray argues that we should reclaim the feminine as complete by expressing joyous pleasure in our own experiences of our bodies, thus undermining the centrality of the penis/phallus in understandings of the world (Irigaray 1985). Both Cixous and Irigaray speak of actively writing and reading texts in ways which offer much to us as embodied archaeologists in our engagement with the material culture of the past. Irigaray describes a hermeneutic engagement with text which offers a potentially enriching dialogue with the material culture of prehistoric societies.

> The only reply that can be given to the question of the meaning of the text is: 'read: perceive, feel' . . . Who are you? would be a more pertinent question, provided that it does not collapse into a demand for an identity card or an autobiographical anecdote. The answer would be, and who are you? Can we meet? Talk? Love? Create something together? Thanks to which milieu? What between us?
> (Irigaray 1989: 192).

My excitement about the possibilities offered by Irigaray and Cixous to read and write as feminist political activity are, however, checked by my experience of the discipline of archaeology. Writing of this kind cannot be written in the generalized, technical language of the sort usually used in archaeological accounts. This imaginative approach will not sit easily within the traditions of the discipline of archaeology. I cannot 'imagine' a reading of the material culture of prehistory which includes people of all ages and both sexes playing active roles in their society which would live up to empiricist standards. We can argue that empiricism:

> embodies the most common beliefs about successful science and scientists ... crude empiricism assumes that the scientist is a sort of *spectator* of the object of inquiry. In other words, reality is presumed to exist externally to scientists and its structure and content are seen to be independent of their beliefs and desires.
>
> (Doyle and Harris 1986: 2)

I realize that few archaeologists in 1995 still believe that this scientific objectivity exists in a pure form, but inherent in the discipline is a level of acceptability of what can be 'reasonably' said about the past which remains deeply embedded in empiricist values (Shanks and Tilley 1989). Contemporary archaeology has not escaped its dependence on the authority of Western science. Patterson notes that 'Descartes drew an absolutely unbridgeable distinction between matters of faith and matters of fact' (Patterson 1995: 6). The fact/faith dichotomy represents a paradox in archaeology which is evident in Wylie's 'lack of faith' when she says that:

> Unlike other social sciences where the tangible presence of women poses a direct challenge to androcentric theorizing, in archaeology the very identification of women subjects and women's activities is inherently problematic; they must be reconstructed from highly enigmatic data.
>
> (Wylie 1990: 31)

We treat as fact the assumption that the material we find was used by men, we have faith that men were there, while women must be found. My embodied experience of the world, and of academia informs me that it is only by the 'leap of faith' that we can work against androcentric and phallocentric perspectives and change the stories we tell. Without such a change in our interpretative frameworks women and children will inevitably remain invisible.

Janet Spector offers an example of a different way of representing a past way of life in her story, *A Time of Loss One Summer Day at Little Rapids* (Spector 1991). In this she:

> wrote the narrative based on the archaeology at Little Rapids, documentary and oral accounts, my relationships with Mazomani's family, information from the Dakota-English dictionary, and my general impressions from having worked 4 summers at the same place that the Wahpeton people had their planting village 150 years earlier.
>
> (Spector 1991: 397)

In it Spector quite explicitly writes children into her account.

Spector's less conventional form of interpretation of material culture allows her to break free of some of the more usual presuppositions informed by masculist dichotomous interpretative frameworks. She begins with women and children as central, the men are described as being far from the village (1991: 397). The men's work is not awarded more status than the work of the women and children at the sugar camps. We are told of mother, grandmothers, and daughters in relation to their own positive feminine roles rather than as negative to the superior male position. Women are active in the social dynamics of the group. The central tool, the awl, is owned and used by a girl (a child) who 'had a reputation ... for hard work, creativity, and excellence through her skills in quill and bead work' (1991: 398). Women are portrayed as having social networks and are active in public spaces and situations, taking part in exchange and feasting. The main character is a female child. By writing in this way she actively denies any pretence of aiming for objectivity; the inherent interpretative nature of archaeology was explicit without being dressed in the guise of 'matters of fact'. In doing this she breaks implicit historic rules. This attempt by Spector to write alternatively does unsettle the embedded androcentric assumptions, without creating dominant Amazonian women. She has told a story based on the evidence which contests the oppositional dichotomies usually informing social readings of material culture.

In 1990–91, in an attempt to think about the past differently, I asked children aged 8–11 to write about some Neolithic people who might have lived near Bryn Celli Ddu, the burial monument site within view of their village school. (This project took place in conjunction with The Anglesey Archaeological Landscape Project, Edmonds and Thomas, 1991.) The children took part in a week of archaeology in which they were involved in the excavation of a causewayed enclosure and they were encouraged to take part in discussions and interpretations of the site and the evidence. They showed no hesitation in depicting active children, women and men in their stories. Interestingly, while their written work showed stereotypical sex role divisions, it did not reflect phallocentric values. Bethan wrote of people of all ages in her story:

> I live in a big tent in Wales with my mum, dad, three brothers, and two sisters and I'm the third in the family. Also my aunt, uncle and four cousins two boys and two girls live in the same tent. I'm twelve, my sisters are eight and ten and my brothers are six, seven and eleven. My girl cousins are four and nine and my boy cousins one eight and ten. I've had a busy day today. My mum taught me and my ten year old sister how to sew with a needle made out of bone. My uncle taught my eleven year old brother and my nine year old girl cousin how to collect animal skin and cut it. My aunt took the rest of the girls to collect nuts and my dad took the rest of the boys except the six and seven year olds who went with my aunt. I made five coats and so did my ten year old sister. . . .

Leah wrote:

> The people who lived about two thousand years BC in Bryn Celli Ddu had no money so they had to eat nuts and blackberries and the meat from animals. . . . I think the women would have cooked and prepared the food as the men would have made a mess of it probably. The children would go and collect nuts and berries close by as it would be an easy job for them to do. . . .

The children have informed their stories from their located positions in society and in so doing have engaged in interactive reading and writing. By presupposing social groups which include children, women and men, and by not referencing back onto phallus-centred symbolic power structures for their evaluation of social roles, the children have not been restrained by *a priori* absence/invisibility. In their interpretations of the evidence which included lectures, discussions, flint knapping demonstrations and their excavation experience, they write themselves into history. It simply did not make sense to the children to have a past without children represented in it. The children were writing from their located positions as 'not-yet-adults', which positioning is inevitably short lived. This brief example, and that of Spector, shows how it is possible to make a difference by engaging with the past through interpretative frameworks of gender in order to write stories which include people of all ages and of both sexes.

To do so means that we write in ways which are not sanctioned by, and cause discomfort to academia. Androcentrism and phallocentrism are deeply embedded at the root of contemporary dominant interpretative frameworks. Our stories do not make sense when referenced to these frameworks and are too easily understood as nonsense and as misinformed. Caroline Whitbeck warns us that: 'One is always at the risk of having one's statements construed either as nonsense, or as quaint phrasing of what are familiar truths according to the old ontology.' (Whitbeck 1989: 61).

Phallocentrism informs and sanctions the invisibility of the feminine. We feminists who try to change this are being unreasonable, we are trying to topple the metaphorical phallus. The negative binary column which includes hidden, unknown, unknowable, unreasonable, illogical, and unknowing, represents the social space conventionally inhabited by women and children. By claiming intellectual space and by engaging with the past through the concepts of gender theory we can, in that activity, disrupt the authenticity of phallocratic reason. By refusing the authority of the phallus and by repeating our claims to other ways of reading the past we can write gendered accounts which include children.

References

Butler, J. (1993) *Bodies That Matter*. London: Routledge.

Cixous, H. (1991) in D. Jensen (ed.) *Coming to Writing and Other Essays*. Cambridge, MA: Harvard University Press, pp. 1–58.

Cocks, J. (1989) *Oppositional Imagination: Feminism, Critique and Political Theory*. London: Routledge.

Doyle, L and Harris, R. (1986) *Empiricism, Explanation and Rationality, an introduction to the philosophy of the social sciences*. London: Routledge and Kegan Paul.

Edmonds, M. and Thomas, J. (1991) *The Anglesey Archaeological Landscape Project: Interim Report 1990*. Lampeter: St David's University College.

Gatens, M. (1991) *Feminist and Philosophy: perspectives on difference and equality*.Cambridge: Polity Press.

Gero, J. and Conkey, M. (1991) *Engendering Archaeology: Women and Prehistory*. Oxford: Blackwell.

Irigaray, L. (1985) *This Sex Which is Not One*. trans. C. Porter. Ithaca: Cornell University Press.

Irigaray, L. (1989) 'Equal to whom?' *Differences* 1, 59–76.

Patterson, T. (1995) *Towards a Social History of Archaeology in the United States*. Orlando: Harcourt Brace College Publishers.

Shanks, M. and Tilley, C. (1989) *Reconstructing Archaeology*. London: Routledge.

Whitbeck, C. 1989. 'A Different Reality: Feminist Ontology' in A. Garry and M. Pearsal (eds) *Women, Knowledge and Reality: Explorations in Feminist Philosophy*. London: Unwin Hyman.

Wylie, A. (1990) 'Gender theory and the archaeological record: why is there no archaeology of gender?' in J.M. Gero and M.W. Conkey (eds) *Engendering Archaeology: Women and Prehistory*. Oxford: Blackwell, pp. 31–54.

14 Engendering children, engendering archaeology

JOANNA SOFAER DEREVENSKI

Chief of our aunts – not only, I,
But all your dozen of nurslings cry –
What did the other children do?
And what were childhood, wanting you?

(*To Auntie*, R.L. Stevenson 1885)

Since the inception of gender archaeology in the 1970s, archaeologists have succeeded in highlighting a variety of methodological problems and prejudices within the discipline. Importantly, they revealed the extent of androcentric bias in archaeological interpretation and in doing so, pushed for recognition of the value of women's contributions to ancient and modern societies (Gero 1988). An initial emphasis on the 'finding of women' gradually translated into greater awareness of their socio-economic contributions, manifest in the growing number of studies of the gendered division of labour (Conkey and Spector 1984; Gero 1991; Hollimon 1992; Joyce 1992; Spector 1982, 1991). However, the range of activities attributed to women has often been influenced by assumptions of logistical or biological constraints derived from controversial cross-cultural anthropological models (Peacock 1991). Women's activities were defined as those compatible with child care, confined to limited areas in and around settlement sites. These interpretations proved unacceptable to feminist scholars who opposed sociobiological perceptions of sex and gender as interchangeable concepts, arguing that gender differences and male/female power relations were not the natural and inevitable product of biological difference (Fausto-Sterling 1985; Lorber 1994).

Under feminist influence the terms 'male' and 'female' were increasingly questioned. Concepts of biological sex (concrete and categorical), were separated from gender (the social construction) as researchers demonstrated enormous cultural diversity in fe/male tasks and roles (Collier and Yanagisako 1987; Conkey and Spector 1984; Hess and Ferree 1987; Moore 1986, 1988; Ortner and Whitehead 1981; Wylie 1991). Others saw sex itself as a socio-political construction (McDonald 1989) or as a function of discourse (Foucault 1984).

Yet, paradoxically, the feminist-inspired reaction against the emphasis on 'woman as mother' and associated assumptions regarding the need to feed and nurture infants, did not precipitate an interest in the socio-economic roles or gender development of children – the very individuals who were deemed axiomatic to the development of gender systems. This is perhaps even more surprising given the recent anthropological emphasis on kinship relations as gendered structures (Collier and Yanagisako 1987; Howell and Melhuus 1993). A number of basic questions necessary to the project of an engendered archaeology which might have been addressed through an examination of children were, therefore, left unexplored. For example: what is the relationship between sex and gender? If gender is not biologically defined, then how are gender structures actively constructed, mediated and passed on from generation to generation? How might this be recognized in the archaeological record? What are the socio-economic roles of children in relation to the gendered division of labour?

The reasons for this apparent reluctance to explore an archaeology of children are twofold. First, it is often argued that the under-representation of children in the archaeological record, particularly in cemeteries, precludes their examination (Boddington 1987; Moore *et al.* 1975). Nonetheless, we know that just as women and men existed in the past, children must also have existed. Lacking the evidence of the body from which to construct evidence of the person, the development of a theoretical frame of reference within which the roles or perceptions of children as human beings could be accommodated, was rather perversely deemed unnecessary. This 'under-representation' argument follows strikingly similar lines to that advocating a need to 'find' hidden women and render them visible. Yet, it is now increasingly recognized that the activities of women have always been part of the archaeological record, a realization which should also be extended to children. Bonnichsen (1973) and Hammond and Hammond (1981) have emphasized the role of children in site-formation processes. Thus the perceived difficulty lies not in the invisibility of children but in the identification of their activities as opposed to other agents in the archaeological record.

The second reason lies in the concepts 'childhood' and 'child' themselves. These only exist in relation to the concepts 'adult' and 'maturity' and western notions of the compartmentalization of the human lifecycle (Burman 1994; MacCormack 1980a). Backwards inference from our own culturally specific concepts of childhood, as a prolonged period of dependence on the parent and an age of innocence, leads to an assumption that it is adults (i.e. fertile and sexually mature individuals) who have political and social control over the production of material culture and social ideologies. Nonetheless, the activities of children are often vital to communal economic survival in traditional societies (Claassen 1992; Draper 1975; Friedl 1975). It is therefore plausible that the experiences of children also moulded the past.

The term 'children' is culturally loaded and the product of western culture which marginalizes their activities. By universal extension 'children' are, therefore, rendered invisible in the archaeological record. The modern western usage of the term 'child' is problematic in that it is a blanket term for individuals at a variety of stages of development with widely differing levels of dependence and independence. This need not be congruent with age categories and conceptions of maturity or immaturity in other societies. There is a need to problematize the investigation of children along with a reconceptualization of the concept of 'child'. Age and sex classifications alone cannot account for cultural variation in attitudes and classifications of children (Friedl 1975; MacCormack and Strathern 1980). One possibility lies in regarding not only age and dependence, but also the development of gender sensibilities as defining parameters of childhood. A child may be regarded as a cultural *tabula rasa* gradually engendered as s/he develops an awareness of gender identity, gender roles and gender ideology. These evolve and change as the individual absorbs, learns and complies with culturally defined gender rules. At the same time, society's gendered perceptions of that individual may change in line with his or her development. Even if an individual is assigned to a sex based gender category at birth (Scheffler 1991) s/he must still learn and accept gender appropriate behaviours.

I therefore suggest that the study of gender in the archaeological record may benefit from a discussion of the gender development of children. I do not wish to discuss notions of *socialization per se*. This concept is often associated with Freudian theories of suppression, assuming that children need to be moulded to a certain pattern, along the same lines as the primitive eventually becomes civilized (Burman 1994). Indeed, the notion of socialization may itself be culturally specific, existing in some cultures, but not in others (MacCormack and Strathern 1980). Instead, I wish to link models drawn from developmental psychology and gender theory to argue that it is possible to theorize about the activities of children by examining the mediation of gender within the archaeological record. Children can be regarded as learners and practisers of gender.[1]

The assumption that aspects of material culture act as repositories of gender symbolism and thus that artefacts behave as contextually determined gender markers, underlies much of the project of an engendered archaeology. This assumption is necessary if archaeologists are to be successful in interpreting gendered social structures in the past. Used in conjunction with post-processualist concepts of the active object (Hodder 1982, 1987), everyday items such as clothing, have been regarded as media for gendered communication and mediators of ideology, producing some of the most successful attempts at engendering archaeology (Gibbs 1987; Sorensen 1991).

Yet material culture may function not only as a communicative vehicle for the maintenance of symbolic structures or social values, but may also be instrumental in actively constructing the world of the individual on the most fundamental level. Cole *et al.* (1971) found that different interactions and observations of interactions may lead to culturally specific learning outcomes and world perceptions. When asked to organize piles of food and household items, the Kpelle of Liberia consistently distributed the objects in terms of functional relations reflecting the way the items were used (potato-pot : food-tool). When asked how 'a fool' would carry out the task, participants demonstrated a typical western classification system based on type (potato-orange : food-food). Thus, it is through observing the behaviour of his/her elders interacting with material culture and through his/her own interaction with it, that the child learns abstract principles, is stimulated and learns about the nature of the world. The nature of individual interaction need not follow the western pattern of children playing with toys and the result of this interaction is not 'given' or germane, otherwise universal 'laws' would be applicable to all cultures.

This perspective assumes that children make sense of their world in qualitatively different ways at different points in their development. Thus, children's understanding of gender may be quite different at different ages, with the development of gender understanding paralleling the development of children's growing abilities to reason about other aspects of the world (Golombok and Fivush 1994). In their book *Gender Development*, Golombok and Fivush (1994) describe Kohlberg's (1966) findings regarding children's developing concept of gender in western society. He argued that the major developmental task facing children is coming to understand that gender is constant and cannot be changed regardless of superficial characteristics.[2] Children develop through three stages in coming to understand gender. In the beginning children do not use gender to categorize themselves or others at all. If asked if they are female or male, they may respond 'female' when asked the first time and 'male' when asked again. He interpreted this as a lack of understanding of gender as an unchanging characteristic of an individual. At about two years of age children enter stage one called *gender identity*. They are now able to consistently label themselves and others as male or female, but base this categorisation on physical characteristics. Thus a person is female because she has long hair and wears skirts, and a person male because he has short hair and wears a tie. If external appearance changes, then gender changes as well. Similar gender identifications with different objects or aspects of dress are possible in other non-western cultures and need not be limited to bipolar associations with biological sex. Thus in cultures with more than two genders, where these are 'marked' in some way, for instance by clothing or jewellery (Sorensen 1991), children might learn to identify them in a similar way.

At about three to four years children move on to stage two called *gender stability*. They now understand that if an individual is fe/male at the present time then s/he was fe/male earlier in life and will later remain so. Stage two children understand that gender is stable across time but do not yet understand that gender is constant across situations. If a male engages in female typed activities, stage two children believe that the male might change into a female. In Kohlberg's model children progress to stage three, called *gender constancy*, at about age five. Bem (1989) related this to an understanding of the biological basis of gender identity. Children now understand that gender is constant across time and situations. They assert that gender will not change regardless of the clothes worn or the activities engaged in. They have come to realize that gender is an underlying, unchanging aspect of identity.[3]

Even very young children know a great deal about culturally defined stereotypes and 'may only need to know some very basic information about gender to begin to use gender as a way of thinking about the world' (Golombok and Fivush 1994: 95). This knowledge is intimately linked to gendered associations with material culture. Two types of tasks have been used to assess western children's understanding of gender: gender knowledge tasks and gender preference tasks. Gender knowledge tasks measure how much information children know about gender and gender stereotypes. Typical versions of these tasks include examining children's knowledge of gender-typed clothing and toys. Children are shown pictures of a boy and a girl and asked to match the items with the 'appropriate' person. In gender preference tasks children are asked to rate how much they would like to play with toys that are either gender consistent (e.g a truck for a boy) or gender inconsistent (e.g. a doll's house for a boy). These tasks indicate that gender knowledge and gender preferences do not appear to be interdependent. A child may know a lot about gender but show little preference for gender-typed activities and vice versa.

While neither of the tasks described above are free from problems and limitations (Golombok and Fivush 1994), they reveal the role and power of aspects of material culture as signifiers and mediators of gender. Material culture influences gender development since it acts as a reflector of gender and is associated with culturally defined gender stereotypes from a very early age. It is, therefore, of great importance as a repository of cultural values with which the child and those around him/her interact. Shanks and Tilley (1987a, 1987b, 1989) describe the individual as an active social agent. Thus, children actively engage in the creation and maintenance of gender structures through material culture, while an individual's experience of the world is in turn, described by gendered interactions with a material culture which itself actively constructs social relations. Material culture is vital in perpetuating gender differences and similarities as the child continues to develop his/her knowledge of gender throughout childhood and provides a framework for the organization of that knowledge as objects become associated with gendered behaviours.

Gender identity is not developed solely as the result of genital identification (Nordbladh and Yates 1990) or linguistic involvement (Vygotsky 1962, 1978) but is also a consequence of interaction with gender specific forms of material culture. If it is possible to examine gender in the archaeological record through the identification of gender markers, then by extension, those markers are also perpetuators of gender. They are symbolic messengers passing on gendered meanings and constructs to the next generation. Interaction and observation of interaction with those objects conveys that gendered meaning to other individuals, including children, who learn socially defined gender structures and socially acceptable gendered behaviours from those interactions. Acceptance of those meanings leads to their perpetuation. Material culture constructs and maintains gender interactions on a macro societal level, but may also construct gender awareness on an individual level from a very early age. The logical extension to this is that gender structures cannot be present or relayed without the existence of a gendered material culture. Hence, material culture in gendered societies must carry gendered nuances.

The engendering of children is, therefore, the development of an understanding of the use of material culture as a repository of gendered symbolic meanings, followed by the decoding and learning of those embedded meanings and finally, the organisation of that symbolic knowledge.[4] The developing child imports, transfers, and ascribes gendered meanings to objects and actively transforms them into the gendered world in which s/he lives. Those objects are recoverable as archaeological artefacts. I am not advocating artefact association as an archaeological methodology. The fallacy of this has already been well demonstrated (Conkey and Gero 1991). However, by following current archaeological assumptions regarding the gender symbolism of artefacts, it is possible to pursue a chain of logic which uses the engendering of children to examine gender in the archaeological record and, therefore, to include children and view the archaeological record in a new light.

How then is it possible to account for a variety of gendered behaviours within a single society and for the complexity of gender systems, given that individuals may be born into the same cultural milieu? Social learning theory suggests that children engage in behaviour for which they are rewarded, with differential reinforcement acting on individuals to produce different genders. Gender-typed behaviour is initially guided by children's anticipations of the responses of others. Children are more likely to imitate behaviour which will be favourably received (Bussey and Bandura 1992).

> Girls and boys learn[ed] the symbolic behaviour appropriate to their future adult gender status. Where there is significant separation of women and men, much of this symbolic behaviour relates the person to the members of the other status and is age graded. That is, girls and boys had to be taught not only how to work as women and men but how to behave toward girls and boys their own age and toward women and men their parents' and grandparents' age. They also learned how women and men were supposed to act toward each other as well as how everyone actually did act toward each other. In the process, the children identified with the members of their gender category, and because they were rewarded for it, they came to want to act in the prescribed ways. In this way gender statuses were reproduced in daily activity.
>
> (Lorber 1994: 130)

The influence of gendered parenting in providing such models is unconfirmed, although in western society parental choice, provision and promotion of gender typed activities appear to be important aspects of gender development (Golombok and Fivush 1994). Nonetheless, gender influences may come from other than parental sources since the care and teaching of children may be assigned to individuals who are not their biological parents (Yanagisako and Collier 1987).

Children often display a preference for their own sex-typed activities and display more knowledge about their own gender (Golombok and Fivush 1994). Cognitive developmental theories attribute this to 'schema driven memory bias', whereby children pay more attention to information that conforms to their stereotyped beliefs and predictions about gender. Younger children show greater attachment to gender stereotypes than older children (Golombok and Fivush 1994). As children grow older and acquire more complex, problematic and ambiguous knowledge they incorporate this and show increasing flexibility in their gender schemas. Individuals will display different degrees of flexibility and schemas will be culturally specific. As children get older they build personal standards based on their cognitive understanding of gender and on their history of reinforcements. They start to evaluate their own behaviour and gender appropriateness becomes an important dimension of children's own self-evaluations. We therefore see children participating in, practising, or being allowed and encouraged to carry out gender appropriate predominantly 'adult' tasks (Friedl 1975). This has implications for archaeological analyses of the gendered division of labour which may be more complex than is currently perceived.

In western culture childhood is generally regarded as one continuous block of undivided time with adulthood attributed to an individual upon the attainment of a birthday between the ages of 16 and 25, depending on the law of an individual country. Yet in other societies individuals may pass through stages in the achievement of maturity through rites of passage or initiation rituals. The importance of different age stages in the social accomplishment of gender has been ignored in archaeology because western culture views all sub-adults as children, although Friedl (1975: 82) explicitly refers to 'age as a modifier of sex roles'. Gender learning may be informal or formal. Many initiation rituals exist specifically to teach or test gendered skills or gendered behaviour. Moogk (1991) has described the construction of 'woman' in the Nuu-chah-nulth girls' puberty ceremony. The Laymi Indians view growth to maturity through language and gender attributed language skills (Harris 1980). In Sherbro society children are considered to be proto-social. 'They talk a great deal about children who do not have "sense" and who need "training"' (MacCormack 1980b: 95). MacCormack describes sexual division of labour in productive tasks in which children are intensively and carefully trained, especially during their liminal status in the initiation ritual. During this period adolescent males learn masculine farming skills and other male skills such as weaving cloth. Adolescent females demonstrate mastery of feminine farming skills and spin cotton. The complementary nature of these tasks demonstrates the interdependence of the genders. 'Both men and women, after initiation, are designated "those who may procreate" and are publically recognized as having a minimal level of "adeptness" in adult roles' (1980b: 95).

> Gendering extends to children because men and women separately train them in order to reproduce themselves socially. This training is an investment in the children's future labor, a 'lien over time, the claim of both men and women over the future production of children' (Siskind 1978: 864). Unless they are strictly segregated, however, girls and boys can learn each other's work. If they persist in doing the work of the other gender, and the work is strictly divided between women and men with little overlap, they will be ostracized unless their society permits gender shifts, as happens when boys become berdaches; they will be women and do women's work when they grow up.
>
> (Lorber 1994: 131–2)

Yet gender related knowledge goes further than merely to describe 'who does what'. Gender schema theory describes developmental differences in gender related knowledge. It divides gender knowledge into a number of components including behaviours, roles, occupations and traits (Martin 1993). In western culture, therefore, 'male' is stereotypically associated with playing football, father, engineer and aggressive. Knowledge is organized and distinct so that knowing the gender label 'male' or 'female' leads to clear links about its gender related components and associations. Each component of knowledge is independent so one might know a great deal about female related behaviours but little about female related occupations. Knowledge becomes organized so that associations are made both within and across components, allowing increasingly complex predictions about gender attributes to be made as the complexity of knowledge increases (Martin 1993; Martin and Halverson 1981). This theory has parallels in archaeology where Renfrew (1994: 10) proposed the concept of the 'mappa', in which each individual possesses, 'a cognitive map of the world, built up in the light of one's own experience and activities, so that this map or world-view serves as the referant used by the individual in determining his or her future activities.'

This chapter has been intended as an exploration of some of the issues, problems and potential that an investigation of children raises for the examination of gender in archaeological contexts. Childhood can be regarded as a time of apprenticeship to a culturally defined gendered norm. The cognitive world of the child is influenced by the gendered world in which s/he lives, that world being encapsulated in symbolic gendered meanings encoded within material culture. I do not wish to suggest that all individuals conceive of the world in the same way or that the models described above are universally applicable today or in the past. However, they do indicate that objects can play significant roles in the gender development of children. An examination of this development may go some way to accounting for the plurality of gender concepts and how they are passed on from generation to generation. It also emphasizes flexibility and age–related dimensions of gender, providing interesting avenues for the further examination of the negotiation of gender structures in archaeological contexts.

Notes

1. Developmental psychology is perhaps the one field with children (or more often 'the child') as its central focus. While it is recognized that research in this field is heavily biased towards North American and European values, it is felt that certain aspects may still be useful to the examination of children in antiquity.
2. The constancy of gender has recently been debated (Moore 1993). Kohlberg views gender in bipolar terms seeing it as intimately related to the biological sex of the individual.
3. Kohlberg's model has been corroborated by a number of researchers (e.g. Stagnor and Ruble 1987), although controversy exists regarding the age at which the stages occur and the meaning and importance of 'gender constancy' (Golombok and Fivush 1994).
4. As children learn more about gender, their knowledge about it becomes more organized (Golombok and Fivush 1994).

References

Bem, S. (1989) 'Genital knowledge and gender constancy in preschool children'. *Child Development* 60, 649–62.

Boddington, A. (1987) 'From bones to population: the problem of numbers' in A. Boddington, A.N. Garland and R.C. Janaway (eds) *Death, Decay and Reconstruction.* Manchester: Manchester University Press, pp.180–97.

Bonnichsen, R. (1973) 'Millie's camp: an experiment in archaeology'. *World Archaeology* 4, 277–91.

Burman, E. (1994) *Deconstructing Developmental Psychology.* London: Routledge.

Bussey, K. and Bandura, A. (1992) 'Self-regulatory mechanisms governing gender development'. *Child Development* 63, 5, 1236–50.

Claassen, C. (1992) 'Questioning gender: An Introduction' in C. Claassen (ed.) *Exploring Gender Through Archaeology. Selected papers from the 1991 Boone Conference.* Monographs in World Archaeology 11, Madison, WI: Prehistory Press, pp. 1–9.

Cole, M., Gay, J., Glick, J.A. and Sharp, D.W. (1971) *The Cultural Context of Learning and Thinking: An Exploration in Experimental Anthropology.* New York: Basic Books.

Collier, J. F. and Yanagisako, S.J. (eds) (1987) *Gender and Kinship: Essays Toward A Unified Analysis.* Stanford CA: Stanford University Press.

Conkey, M.W. and Gero, J.M. (1991) 'Tensions, pluralities and engendering archaeology: an introduction to women and prehistory' in J.M. Gero and M.W. Conkey (eds) *Engendering Archaeology: Women and Prehistory.* Oxford: Blackwell, pp. 3–30.

Conkey, M.W. and Spector, J.D. (1984) 'Archaeology and the Study of Gender' in M.B. Schiffer (ed.) *Advances in Archaeological Method and Theory* 7. New York: Academic Press, pp. 1–38.

Draper, P. (1975) '!Kung Women' in R.R. Reiter (ed.) *Toward an Anthropology of Women.* London: Monthly Review Press.

Fausto-Sterling, A. (1985) *Myths of Gender: Biological Theories About Women and Men.* New York: Basic Books.

Foucault, M. (1984) *History of Sexuality, An Introduction, Vol. 1.* London: Penguin.

Friedl, E. (1975) *Women and Men: An Anthropologist's View.* New York: Holt, Rinehart and Winston.

Gero, J.M. (1988) 'Gender bias in archaeology: then and now' in S.V. Rosser (ed.) *Feminism Within The Science And Health Care Professions: Overcoming Resistance.* Oxford: Pergamon Press.

Gero, J.M. (1991) 'Genderlithics: women's roles in stone tool production' in J.M. Gero and M.W. Conkey (eds) *Engendering Archaeology: Women and Prehistory.* Oxford: Blackwell.

Gibbs, L. (1987) 'Identifying gender representation in the archaeological record: a contextual study' in I. Hodder (ed.) *The Archaeology Of Contextual Meanings.* Cambridge: Cambridge University Press, pp. 79–89.

Golombok, S. and Fivush, R. (1994) *Gender Development.* Cambridge: Cambridge University Press.

Hammond, G. and Hammond, N. (1981) 'Child's play: a distorting factor in archaeological distribution'. *American Antiquity* 46, 634–6.

Harris, O. (1980) 'The power of signs: gender, culture and the wild in the Bolivian Andes' in C.P. MacCormack and M. Strathern (eds) *Nature, Culture and Gender.* Cambridge: Cambridge University Press, pp. 70–94.

Hess, B.B. and Ferree, M.M. (eds) (1987) *Analyzing Gender.* Newbury Park: Sage Publications.

Hodder, I. (1982) *Symbols In Action.* Cambridge: Cambridge University Press.

Hodder, I. (1987) 'The contextual analysis of symbolic meanings' in I. Hodder (ed.) *The Archaeology Of Contextual Meanings.* Cambridge: Cambridge University Press, pp. 1–10.

Hollimon, S. (1992) 'Health consequences of sexual division of labor among prehistoric Native Americans: the Chumash of California and the Arikara of the North Plains' in C. Claassen (ed.) *Exploring Gender Through Archaeology. Selected papers from the 1991 Boone Conference.* Monographs in World Archaeology 11, Madison, WI: Prehistory Press, pp. 81–8.

Howell, S. and Melhuus, M. (1993) 'The study of kinship; the study of person; a study of gender?' in T. del Valle (ed.) *Gendered Anthropology.* European Association of Social Anthropologists. London: Routledge, pp. 38–53.

Joyce, R. (1992) 'Images of gender and labor organization in classic Maya society' in C. Claassen (ed.) *Exploring Gender Through Archaeology. Selected papers from the 1991 Boone Conference.* Monographs in World Archaeology 11, Madison, WI: Prehistory Press.

Kohlberg, L. (1966) 'A cognitive-developmental analysis of children's sex-role concepts and attitudes' in E.E. Maccoby (ed.) *The Development of Sex Differences.* Stanford, CA: Stanford University Press.

Lorber, J. (1994) *Paradoxes of Gender.* New Haven: Yale University Press.

MacCormack, C.P. (1980a) 'Nature, culture and gender: a critique' in C.P. MacCormack and M. Strathern (eds) *Nature, Culture and Gender.* Cambridge: Cambridge University Press, pp. 1–24.

MacCormack, C.P. (1980b) 'Proto-social to adult: a Sherbro transformation' in C.P. MacCormack and M. Strathern (eds) *Nature, Culture and Gender.* Cambridge: Cambridge University Press, pp. 95–118.

MacCormack, C.P. and Strathern, M. (eds) (1980) *Nature, Culture and Gender.* Cambridge: Cambridge University Press.

McDonald, M. (1989) *We Are Not French! Language, Culture and Identity in Brittany.* London: Routledge.

Martin, C.L. (1993) 'New directions for assessing children's gender knowledge'. *Developmental Review* 13, 184–204.

Martin, C.L. and Halverson, C. (1981) 'A schematic processing model of sex typing and stereotyping in children'. *Child Development* 52, 1119–34.

Moogk, S. (1991) 'The construction of "woman" in the Nuu-chah-nulth Girls' Puberty Ceremony in 1910' in D. Walde and N.D. Willows (eds) *The Archaeology of Gender. Proceedings of the 22nd Annual Chacmool Conference.* Calgary: The University of Calgary.

Moore, H. (1986) *Space, Text and Gender.* Cambridge: Cambridge University Press.

Moore, H. (1988) *Feminism and Anthropology.* Cambridge: Polity Press.

Moore, H. (1993) 'The differences within and the differences between' in T. del Valle (ed.) *Gendered Anthropology.* London: Routledge.

Moore, J.A., Swedlund, A.C. and Armelagos, G.J. (1975) 'The use of life tables in palaeodemography'. *American Antiquity* 40, 57–70.

Nordbladh, J. and Yates, T. (1990) 'This perfect body, this virgin text: between sex and gender in archaeology' in I. Bapty and T. Yates (eds) *Archaeology After Structuralism.* London: Routledge.

Ortner, S.B. and Whitehead, H. (eds) (1981) *Sexual Meanings: The Cultural Construction of Gender and Sexuality*. Cambridge: Cambridge University Press.

Peacock, N.R. (1991) 'Rethinking the sexual division of labor: reproduction and women's work among the Efe' in M. di Leonardo (ed.) *Gender at the Crossroads of Knowledge: Feminist Anthropology in the Post-Modern Era*. Berkeley, CA: University of California Press, pp. 339–60.

Renfrew, C. (1994) 'Towards a cognitive archaeology' in C. Renfrew and E.B.W. Zubrow (eds) *The Ancient Mind: Elements of Cognitive Archaeology*. Cambridge: Cambridge University Press, pp. 3–12.

Scheffler, H.W. (1991) 'Sexism and naturalism in the study of kinship' in M. di Leonardo (ed.) *Gender at the Crossroads of Knowledge: Feminist Anthropology in the Postmodern Era*. Berkeley, CA: University of California Press, pp. 361–82.

Shanks, M. and Tilley, C. (1987a) *Re-constructing Archaeology*. Cambridge: Cambridge University Press.

Shanks, M. and Tilley, C. (1987b) *Social Theory and Archaeology*. Cambridge: Polity Press.

Shanks, M. and Tilley, C. (1989) 'Archaeology into the 1990s'. *Norwegian Archaeological Review* 22, 1, 1–54.

Siskind, J. (1978) 'Kinship and mode of production'. *American Anthropologist* 80, 860–71.

Sorensen, M.L.S. (1991) 'The construction of gender through appearance' in D. Walde and N.D. Willows (eds) *The Archaeology of Gender. Proceedings of the 22nd Annual Chacmool Conference*. Calgary: University of Calgary.

Spector, J.D. (1982) 'Male/female task differentiation among the Hidatza: toward the development of an archaeological approach to the study of gender' in P. Albers and B. Medicine (eds) *The Hidden Half: Studies of Native Plains Women*. Washington DC: University Press of America.

Spector, J.D. (1991) 'What this awl means: toward a feminist archaeology' in J.M. Gero and M.W. Conkey (eds) *Engendering Archaeology: Women and Prehistory*. Oxford: Blackwell.

Stagnor, C. and Ruble, D.N. (1987) 'Development of gender role knowledge and gender constancy' in L.S. Liben and M.L. Signorella (eds) *Children's Gender Schemata: New Directions for Child Development* 38. San Francisco: Jossey-Bass, pp. 5–22.

Vygotsky, L.S. (1962) *Language and Thought*. Cambridge, MA: MIT Press.

Vygotsky, L.S. (1978) *Mind in Society: The Development of Higher Psychological Processes*. Cambridge, MA: Harvard University Press.

Wylie, A. (1991) 'Feminist critiques and archaeological challenges' in D. Walde and D.E. Willows (eds) *The Archaeology of Gender. Proceedings of the 22nd Annual Chacmool Conference*. Calgary: The University of Calgary.

Yanagisako, S. J. and Collier, J.F. (1987) 'Toward a unified analysis of gender and kinship' in J. F. Collier and S.J. Yanagisako (eds) *Gender and Kinship: Essays Toward A Unified Analysis*. Stanford, CA: Stanford University Press.

15 Kid knapping: the missing children in lithic analysis

NYREE FINLAY

Despite the influence of feminist perspectives in archaeology drawing attention to the clear androcentricism in our discipline, there has been little examination of the adult bias in our constructions of the past. This chapter examines approaches to children in one specific area; lithic studies. Consideration will be given as to how concepts of time and temporality, in addition to gender, can inform lithic analysis at both a theoretical and methodological level.

My concern with children and stone tools arose during examination of one particular assemblage from the Mesolithic site of Coulererarch located on the West Coast of Islay in the Southern Hebrides, Scotland (Mithen and Finlay 1993). The presence of a number of poorly worked low quality flint pebbles, in combination with evidence for fine blade reduction, suggested the presence of knappers of varying abilities. At the time I was also engaged in my own personal quest to acquire the arcane knowledge of the knapper for part of my doctoral research on the social dimensions of Mesolithic lithic technology which involves a replication component. Many of the characteristics I identified in the archaeological material were comparable to my own tentative groping with stone. While the final analysis of the Coulererarch assemblage is not yet complete, a report appeared in the CBA newsletter that described the flaked pebbles as being the product of 'Mesolithic children playing with Daddy's toolkit' (Denison 1994: 2).

This chapter was prompted by the implicit assumptions contained in that phrase. Namely, that the sex and age of the knapper is always an adult male and by default knapping is a masculine activity. Such tacit assumptions perpetuate a masculine reality of access to stone tools and dominate the narratives we construct about their manufacture and use during prehistory. Secondly, in order to identify the child we make a number of assumptions about how children learn of lithic technology. This raises issues regarding lithic apprenticeship which have important implications for discussion of the child as a subject in lithic analysis.

This chapter is divided into four sections, in which I briefly examine gender constructs, definitions of the child, concepts of apprenticeship, and time and space.

Women and children first?

Joan Gero discussed the extent of androcentric bias in lithic analysis in her seminal paper, 'Genderlithics', such as the male monopoly in replication studies involving knapping (Gero 1991). More significant is the projection of these androcentric values onto the past. A high archaeological value is traditionally attributed to retouched artefacts. As a result of 'Man-the-Toolmaker' constructs, retouched artefacts are privileged in lithic analysis due to their archaeological visibility, morphological and manufacturing complexity. Such artefacts are implicitly gendered male, particularly when they can be rooted in traditional male activities such as hunting (Finlay n.d.). Ethnographic examples of women working stone and pressure flaking do exist (e.g. Holmes 1919; Man 1883). The Yamana have a legend about the prowess of a female knapper; a sister who made fine arrowheads for her lithically inept brothers (Gusinde 1961: 1126). However, such references tend generally to be overlooked. Women are more commonly associated with unretouched flake industries and low skill techniques such as bipolar knapping (Flenniken 1980: 171). While the issue of lower technological skill is implicitly read from such accounts, the context is rarely considered. Bipolar knapping is where the raw material is struck while resting on an anvil producing a large quantity of small sharp flakes and shatter. It is a technique commonly adopted for working poor quality raw materials such as quartz (Knight 1991). The ethnographic evidence for women undertaking bipolar knapping is in the context of large scale fish processing which demands a large number of sharp flakes; thus the task, as well as the material, dictates the technique. A dichotomy permeates the literature that links men with high skill and technological prowess and women with cruder more expedient techniques. This is at the expense of acknowledging the crucial role of function, as well as individual aptitude and personality, rather than simply gender alone, in lithic production. Privileging male claims are commonplace in the literature. An example of this can be seen in a paper by Kenneth Sassaman, where he discusses the time-space systematics of North American archaeology as being characterized by the continuity of change in the design of male artefacts (Sassaman 1992: 251). I am not entirely happy with such an approach which sees the gendering of artefacts and activities as given. For one, it privileges the masculine subject and narratives of the past, and secondly, it fails to acknowledge the contingency of activities and tool use. A rock has no gender, it is only through its use and association that it is imbued with social and symbolic meaning. Just as a rock has no gender, has it age? For where is the child to be located in the androcentric and adult-centred approaches that dominate archaeology.

The archaeological child

The concept of childhood and what constitutes a child is a social phenomenon that is culturally constructed. In Western society, the child is defined in opposition to adults, set apart in age and size. The child is also perceived as dependent, innocent and in need of socialization before it can participate fully in modern culture. Thus the child is marginalized in much the same manner as the aged

(Hockey and James 1993: 60). Consideration of the child as a social actor is a relatively new subject of analysis that raises a number of important issues, for example, what we consider as appropriate knowledge and behaviour in relation to age (James and Prout 1990).

Few archaeological studies have explicitly considered children. In 1989 Grete Lillehammer reviewed the state of archaeological approaches to the child's world and noted the lack of focus on children (Lillehammer 1989). Since then there have been few studies of children, despite the proliferation of feminist texts in archaeology (Claasen 1992; Walde and Willows 1991). Children present a problematic in terms of analysis for what is given priority: age or sex? (La Fontaine 1986). This issue of how to categorize children has implications for the fixed bipartite gender division of fe/male, drawing attention to the limitations of such constructs. Approaches to children involve both the actual identification of children in the archaeological record and to date, the more limited discussions of cultural transmission (Mithen and Finlay n.d.). Children have been identified from their physical remains and grave good associations as well as other artefactual evidence, for example the Roman child's leather sandal (Jones 1980) and the Mesolithic child's milk teeth impressions in resin (Bang-Andersen 1991). More problematic is the identification of children's activities due to the presence of toys, in particular the equation of the miniature item with the child. As Lillehammer (1989) states, miniature items are frequently identified as toys by virtue of their size alone. While such items may have more complex significance such as amulets or ritual representations, there is no simple equation that relates the size of the object to its educational or purely recreational use by a child, particularly when not directly associated with skeletal remains. Size has been used as a criterion to distinguish children in the lithic record. Knutsson attempted to correlate the size of bipolar cores with the thumb size of modern men, women and children in order to distinguish the activities of children in Swedish Mesolithic bipolar assemblages (Knutsson 1986).

This was based on the premise that a core, held between the thumb and forefinger would be worked until too small to hold. Children, with their smaller hands, would, therefore, produce smaller cores. Knutsson could find no correlation in his data and drew three conclusions; that the width of the thumb was not a decisive factor; that the thumb size of the modern population may be smaller than in the Mesolithic and finally, that children may not imitate adult hands in tool manufacture. This last point is important for we perceive that children will imitate adults to their own scale, producing small tools for small hands. Such a perspective is transformed if we consider the child as a producer, for then the child will make items to an adult or societal norm. A second factor to consider is equating the crude and poorly made with the child. This assumption lies at the heart of identifying children in the lithic record, by virtue of their being novice knappers. Acquiring the skills to knap stone is a complex process, which demands the interaction of different types of knowledge ranging from theoretical templates to practical ability in the execution of motor actions. Unlike other classes of material culture, lithics provide a rare opportunity to reconstruct through refitting the reduction sequence. While the raw material used in other craft production such as pottery and metalworking can be recycled, this is rarely the case with lithics. Thus the products of the learning sequence should be preserved and constitute a greater part of the lithic record than is generally given credit. The complexity of many lithic procedures, considered under the so-briquet of the *chaîne-opératoire* provide scope for the classification and differentiation of stages and corresponding requirements for skill (Karlin and Julien 1994).

Flint knapping is an esoteric activity for archaeologists and modern peoples in general. While Don Crabtree started experimenting from the age of seven onwards, the majority of knappers learn their craft as adults (Johnson 1978: 351). There have been no studies that have quantified lithic learning abilities in children, although there may be similarities with the manipulation of other physical objects, given childrens' intuitive understanding of physics (Spelke *et al.* 1992). Therefore, we have no measure of the time required to obtain lithic skills. It seems that few archaeologists are prepared to allow their children to experiment with stone. There has been little discussion of the process of learning mechanisms and changes in ability throughout the life course of the individual not just the child. An individual can lose as well as acquire skill, through trauma or fatigue on a short or long-term basis. Motor skills could deteriorate through injury or degenerative illness such as arthritis.

The ethnographic record provides a very limited data set about the contexts and nature of acquiring lithic skills. Most of the evidence is indirect and anecdotal in character. Binford noted the presence of children during his ethnoarchaeological study of Alyawara stone tool manufacture (Binford 1986). Here, children spread the news that tool replacement would take place and uninitiated young men came to watch the craftsmen work. Among the Yamana of Tierra del Fuego, the manufacture of slate and quartz arrowheads was learnt from the age of three onwards from the child's father in the context of manufacturing hunting equipment (Gusinde 1961: 563). This is similar to the Commanches, where historic accounts document a generational gap in education, again in the context of hunting equipment, from the age of five (Wallace and Hoebel 1952: 126).

Several replication studies have sought to quantify differences in the knapping styles of individual adults (Gunn 1977; Young and Bonnischen 1984). Phil Shelley (1990) has conducted a series of replication experiments over eleven years to document the learning abilities of students in biface and blade production. Shelley found the following correlates according to skill. Inexperienced knappers are more likely to make more frequent and consistent errors. These are likely to relate to the novices' limited appreciation of the necessary force required to detach flakes. As a result the cores produced exhibit step/hinge flake terminations leading to discard. On the other hand, more experienced knappers are likely to discard on completion or due to flaws in the raw material. However, the more experienced knapper is able to read the raw material, anticipate and correct errors, due to superior technological understanding and motor ability. Such patterning supports similar studies which have quantified lithic skill on the basis of observation (Ahler 1989). The old adage, practice makes perfect springs to mind, but it is questionable as to what extent one accepts a linear progression in the acquisition of lithic skills given the role of individual aptitude. While the above studies predict the range and character of errors that novices make, there is no explicit connection to age, for one does not necessarily have to be a child to be a novice.

The knappers apprentice

A series of archaeological studies have claimed to identify novices in the lithic record by the identification of items displaying a low level of knapping ability. This is facilitated by the ability to isolate the products of an individual knapper by detailed spatial analysis and refitting. This has been achieved at two Late Upper Palaeolithic Magdalenian sites in the Paris Basin. Nicole Pigeot has refitted 36 artefact clusters from one habitation unit, U5 at the site of Etoilles (Pigeot 1987; 1990). Of these clusters, 25 display an excellent mastery of knapping procedures, 11 are attributed to novice knappers. These lack platform preparation and maintenance of the core. Novice products are not circulated and transformed into tools and they are located in a peripheral location to the skilled clusters. Pigeot distinguishes three levels of competency reflected in the ability to manufacture long blades from very large nodules of flint. This tripartite division comprises best technicians, less talented technicians and apprentice-debutants. Ranging in skill from the ability to manufacture large quantities of well shaped blades to the less talented occasional knapper, and thirdly, to the novice where cores seem to have been worked for their own sake, the goal and gesture towards reduction being sufficient in itself (Pigeot 1990). Pigeot envisages learning by a combination of direct instruction and imitation. At Pincevent, Bodu *et al.* (1990) perceive the knapping to be more opportunistic, and conducted within the context of other activities, rather than the specialization inferred at Etoilles. In addition to the tripartite division in skills identified by Pigeot they add a third category – that of child. The 'child' is distinguished by the game-like and non-utilitarian character of poorly knapped pieces, displaying less skill than novices.

Another example of lithic education is the Late Glacial site of Trollesgave, Denmark (Fischer 1990). Here two concentrations of debitage focus around a large stone seat. These clusters, different in the degree of core preparation and quality of blades removed, are interpreted as the product of a highly skilled knapper and an untrained child: master and pupil.

A noticeable aspect of the above studies is the gendered nature of the interpretations. At Trollesgave the inexperienced flintknapper is a 'small boy training under the guidance of the skilled knapper, ... so pleased with the products of his labour that some of them had to be kept under his pillow' (Fischer 1990: 460–2). The reconstruction drawings shows the happy Late

Glacial nuclear family; dad knapping, mum scraping hides and the kids playing with spears. At Pincevent, Bodu *et al.* (1990) speculate on the name of the knappers identified: 'Will we eventually have to baptize them: Paul, Pierre, or Rahan, Noah, Greylag?' The generic use of the male subject is no coincidence, 'the possibility must be considered that flint-knapping was a dominant masculine activity, which excluded women as knappers. Possibly women only resharpened the tools they were using' (Bodu *et al.* 1990: 156).

These knapping narratives deny women access to lithic technology – along with the child they are not active producers of lithic material. While the (male) child has the capacity to transform via a period of apprenticeship, the woman is fixed in the role of the passive consumer. This is not to deny that genuine differences could and did exist between men and women in relation to lithic technology during prehistory, but any consideration of this has to acknowledge the contingency of lithic use. The association of men with technology is taken as given within Western society and such constructs resonate in the above narratives (see Wajcman 1991 for a discussion of engendered technologies). It is over a century since Worthington Smith illustrated his volume *Man the Primeval Savage* with images of women knapping (Smith 1894). Despite the more recent addition of a female knapper in the prehistory section of Huddersfield Museum, there is clearly scope for feminist revision in lithic studies and alternative narrative scenarios, for, at present, the lithic child is always a boy.

While the above studies are impressive and have contributed much to the methodological identification of different knapping abilities, there are a number of caveats. There is a danger that discussion of the identification of different skill levels and, therefore, the ability to identify children will be restricted to those rare occurrences where such refitting analysis is possible and where the individual can be distinguished on the basis of what is interpreted as non-rational behaviour. As Cross (1983) states such studies are time-consuming and expensive, although in the above examples the rewards have been considerable. There is also the question of identifying the individual *per se*, for Binford noted that among the Alyawara different knappers worked the same core (Binford 1986: 553). If knappers were of equal skill this would affect their archaeological visibility. Concepts of apprenticeship and specialization are integral to the above studies. The various teaching scenarios, for example, formal learning by instruction as opposed to imitation, and the use of terminology such as master and pupil, smacks of modern educational practice. The stress is on the acquisition of skills, rather than addressing learning as a medium for the transformation of the individual. It is in this respect that concepts such as situated learning and legitimate peripheral participation (LPP) have much potential as a conceptual framework (Lave and Wenger 1991). LPP places the emphasis not so much on skills but rather on increased participation in a community of practice, where both the relational character of knowledge and the negotiated nature of meaning can be appreciated. The application of this to archaeological material seems appropriate, given the inherent problems in quantifying the teaching mechanism and learning environment.

Time, space and stone tools

Approaches to the technological variation in lithic assemblages characteristically centres on issues of subsistence and settlement strategies (Binford 1979), raw material availability and concepts such as time budgeting (Torrence 1983). Variation arising from different knapping abilities are rarely considered, apart from the cases cited above, where it can be demonstrated via refitting and spatial patterning. Yet the processes identified by Pigeot and others must be occurring across time and space to some extent, for most basic lithic tasks demand some degree of knowledge and experience. It is this regard that a focus on the concept of time in relation to lithic skills can inform a discussion of the archaeological visibility of different skill levels. As discussed above, changes can occur throughout the life course of the individual. This does not necessarily equate to correspondences in aptitude with age. From the limited ethnographic evidence, there would appear to be a degree of age differentiation in the execution of tool manufacture and gender specific contexts for learning as with other skills for life. This suggests, in conjunction with concepts of LPP, that these would accord with what was considered appropriate knowledge for stages throughout the life course and may imply age-specific access to certain types of knowledge and practice. Such a process can be discerned in the Alyawara example discussed above, where the role of different age groups was dependent on their status. This finds parallels in the ritual proscriptions on access to lithic resources reported ethnographically (Taçon 1991).

This metaphor of time in relation to lithic knowledge can also be considered at a seasonal and regional level. Ingold (1993) has introduced the concept of the *taskscape* in order to explore the relationship between time and the action of agents in the landscape. Here we can begin to discuss, for want of a better term, the *knapscape*; how individuals interact with lithics throughout the life course. Lithic resources are rarely uniformly spread across a landscape (Gould and Saggers 1985). Thus we can anticipate differences in the scheduling of procurement of this material in a landscape context and in the organization of production. It appears probable that most of the practical hands-on experience of learning skills via experimentation would occur in those contexts where there was a plentiful supply of raw material such as at outcrops or quarry sites. A central tendency in skill levels is assumed and the crude character of assemblages attributed to expediency (Ericson 1984). Quarry sites are also the likely locales for specialization in manufacture, thus there is considerable potential for conflicting types of assemblages.

Such conflicting signatures are present in the Mesolithic material from Coulererarch. The inability to spatially separate components of the assemblage coupled with the lack of chronological resolution make skill one of several possible explanations. The presence of flaked pebbles with clear flaws demands explanation at a site no more than 500m from the source of flint pebbles on the beach. One scenario is that these small and flawed pebbles, rejected by more experienced knappers, were worked by those of little experience, probably very young children.

Paying the ransom: the future of children in lithics

This chapter has raised more questions than it has suggested solutions as to the identification and nature of the child in lithic studies. We know children are part of the archaeological record, whether or not we can necessarily identify them. Moreover, the ability to identify them is a clear problematic, grounded as it is on our perceived notions of child-like behaviour. At present we simply do not know enough about how children knap, or how long it takes to acquire lithic skills. One only has to consider the industrial productivity of the child in other parts of the world to appreciate the range and proficiency of skill in craft manufacture that questions the equation of age with technical prowess. This is not to deny child's play, rather it ought to make us more critically aware of the cultural baggage we take to the past. The addition of the child as a separate category of analysis is not going to change the implicit stereotypes that dominate archaeological discourse. 'Add children and stir' is not the solution, rather we need to transform how we discuss people and lithics. It is here that I have suggested that temporal frameworks offer much potential to create a different vocabulary for the discussion of lithics in relation to the individual. The methodological ramifications of identifying the child are as problematic as the identification of gender. The question of different levels of lithic skills requires value judgements about non-utilitarian production and consistency in manufacture. Likewise, the influence of child's play on the spatial patterning of artefacts demands more attention (Hammond and Hammond 1981).

Many factors are responsible for lithic assemblage variation and differences resulting from skill levels have to compete with a range of other variables that are traditionally privileged such as raw material constraints or economic rationales. The process of lithic studies with its almost unhealthy preoccupation with technological and typological analysis, frequently leaves little room for the discussion of people behind the stone. Consideration of the child may demand that the adolescence of the subject blossom into a more theoretical and people-centred maturity.

Acknowledgements

Thanks are due to Sherry and Conor MacCarthy for the title and Mark Lake for useful discussion and comments on an earlier draft.

References

Ahler, S.A. (1989) 'Experimental knapping with KRF and Midcontinent Cherts: overview and applications' in D.S. Amick and R.P. Mauldin (eds) *Experiments in Lithic Technology*. Oxford: British Archaeological Reports, International Series 528.

Bang-Andersen, S. (1991) 'Mesolithic adaptations in the southern Norwegian highlands' in C. Bonsall (ed.) *The Mesolithic in Europe*. Edinburgh: John Donald, pp. 338–50.

Binford, L.R. (1979) 'Organizational and formation processes: looking at curated assemblages'. *Journal of Anthropological Research* 35, 3, 255–73.

Binford, L.R. (1986) 'An Alyawara day and beyond'. *American Antiquity* 51, 547–65.

Bodu, P., Karlin, C. and Ploux, S. (1990) 'Who's who? The Magdalenian flintknappers of Pincevent, France' in E. Cziesla, S. Eickhoff, N. Arts and D. Winter (eds) *The Big Puzzle*. Bonn: Holos, pp.143–63.

Claassen, C. (ed.) (1992) *Exploring Gender Through Archaeology*. Madison, WI: Prehistory Press.

Cross, J.R. (1983) 'Twigs, branches, trees, and forests: problems of scale in lithic analysis' in J.A. Moore and A.S. Keene (eds) *Archaeological Hammers and Theories*. New York: Academic Press, pp.87–106.

Denison, S. (1994) 'Prehistoric children at work'. *British Archaeological News* 2, 2.

Ericson, J.E. (1984) 'Towards the analysis of lithic production systems' in J.E. Ericson and B.A. Purdy (eds) *Prehistoric Quarries and Lithic Production*. Cambridge: Cambridge University Press, pp. 1–10.

Finlay, N. (n.d.) 'Myths and Microliths: constructions of the Mesolithic'. Unpublished manuscript.

Fischer, A. (1990) 'On being a pupil of a flintknapper of 11,000 years ago' in E. Cziesla, S. Eickhoff, N. Arts and D. Winter (eds) *The Big Puzzle*. Bonn: Holos, pp. 447–64.

Flenniken, J.J. (1980) *Replicative Systems Analysis: A Model Applied to the Vein Quartz Artefacts from the Hoko River Site*. Unpublished PhD. Washington State University.

La Fontaine, J. (1986) 'An anthropological perspective on children in social worlds' in M. Richards and P. Light (eds) *Children of Social Worlds*. Cambridge: Polity Press, pp. 10–30.

Gero, J.M. (1991) 'Genderlithics: women's roles in stone tool production' in J.M. Gero and M.W. Conkey (eds) *Engendering Archaeology*. Oxford: Blackwell, pp. 163–93.

Gould, R.A. and Saggers, S. (1985) 'Lithic procurement in central Australia: a closer look at Binford's idea of embeddedness in archaeology'. *American Antiquity* 50, 1, 117–36.

Gunn, J. (1977) 'Idiosyncratic chipping style as a demographic indicator: a proposed application to the South Hills region of Idaho and Utah' in J.N. Hill and J. Gunn (eds) *The Individual in Prehistory: Studies of Variability in Style in Prehistoric Technologies*. London: Academic Press, pp. 167–204.

Gusinde, M. (1961) *The Yamana: The Life and Thought of the Water Nomads of Cape Horn*. New Haven: Human Relations Area Files 2.

Hammond, G. and Hammond, N. (1981) 'Child's play: a distorting factor in archaeological distribution'. *American Antiquity* 46, 634–36.

Hockey, J. and James, A. (1993) *Growing Up and Growing Old*. London: Sage Publications.

Holmes, W.H. (1919) *Handbook of Aboriginal Antiquities. Part I. The Lithic Industries*. Washington: Bureau of American Ethnology, Bulletin 60.

Ingold, T. (1993) 'The temporality of the landscape'. *World Archaeology* 25, 152–74.

James, A. and Prout, A. (1990) *Constructing and Reconstructing Childhood*. Basingstoke: The Falmer Press.

Johnson, L.L. (1978) 'A history of flint knapping experimentation, 1838–1976'. *Current Anthropology* 19, 337–72.

Jones, D.M. (1980) *Excavations at Billingsgate Buildings 'Triangle', Lower Thames Street, 1974*. Cornwall: Beric Tempest.

Karlin, C. and Julien, M. (1994) 'Prehistoric technology: a cognitive science?' in C. Renfrew and E.B. Zubrow (eds) *The Ancient Mind*. Cambridge: Cambridge University Press, pp. 152–64.

Knight, J. (1991) 'Technological analysis of the anvil (Bipolar) technique'. *Lithics* 12, 57–80.

Knutsson, K. (1986) 'Några ord om barn, stötkantkårnor och pieces esquilles'. *Fjölnir* 1, 29–39.

Lave, J. and Wenger, E. (1991) *Situated Learning: Legitimate Peripheral Participation.* Cambridge: Cambridge University Press.

Lillehammer, G. (1989) 'A child is born. The child's world in an archaeological perspective'. *Norwegian Archaeological Review* 22, 89–105.

Man, E.H. (1883) 'On the aboriginal inhabitants of the Andaman Islands (part 3)'. *Journal of the Anthropology Institute* XII, 327–81.

Mithen, S. and Finlay, N. (1993) 'Testpit survey and trial excavation at Coulererarch'. *The Southern Hebrides Mesolithic Project, 6th Interim Report.* Reading: Reading University.

Mithen, S. and Finlay, N. (n.d.) 'Child's play: cultural transmission and the interpretation of lithic assemblages'. Unpublished manuscript.

Pigeot, N. (1987) *Magdaleniens d'Etoilles: économie de débitage et organization sociale.* Paris: CRNS (suppl. 25 Gallia Préhistoire).

Pigeot, N. (1990) 'Technical and social actors: flintknapping specialists at Magdalenian Etoilles'. *Archaeological Review from Cambridge* 9, 1, 126–41.

Sassaman, K.E. (1992) 'Lithic technology and the hunter-gatherer sexual division of labour'. *North American Archaeology* 13, 3, 249–62.

Shelley, P. (1990) 'Variation in Lithic Assemblages: an experiment'. *Journal of Field Archaelogy* 17, 187–93.

Smith, W. (1894) *Man the Primeval Savage.* London: Edward Stanford.

Spelke, E.S., Breinlinger, K., Macomber, J and Jacobsen, K. (1992) 'Origins of knowledge'. *Psychological Review* 999, 605–32.

Taçon, P. (1991) 'The power of stone: symbolic aspects of stone use and tool development in western Arnhem Land, Australia'. *Antiquity* 65, 192–207.

Torrence, R. (1983) 'Time budgeting and hunter-gatherer technology' in G. Bailey (ed.) *Hunter-Gatherer Economy in Prehistory: A European Perspective.* Cambridge: Cambridge University Press, pp. 11–22.

Wajcman, J. (1991) *Feminism Confronts Technology.* Cambridge: Polity Press.

Walde, D. and Willows, N.D. (eds) (1991) *The Archaeology of Gender. Proceedings of the 22nd Annual Chacmool Conference.* Calgary: The University of Calgary.

Wallace, E. and Hoebel, E.A. (1952) *The Commanches: Lords of the High Plains.* Norman: University of Oklahoma Press.

Young, D. and Bonnischen, R. (1984) *Understanding Stone Tools.* Orono: University of Maine, Peopling of the American Process Series No 1.

16 Women and children in prehistory: resource sharing and social stratification at the Mesolithic-Neolithic transition in Ukraine

M. C. LILLIE

The following discussion considers patterns of dental pathologies as indicators of assumed differences in access to dietary resources in order to determine social stratification across the Early–Late Mesolithic and Early Neolithic periods in the Dnieper Rapids region of Ukraine. The identification of differentiation in access to resources may well provide insights into gender related issues such as restricted access to high protein resources, childhood stress due to inequalities in diet, and a general lowering of age at death for certain individuals. These factors are usually seen to be weighted in favour of males, to the obvious detriment of females, especially in hunter-gatherer societies.

The Dnieper Rapids region of Ukraine has a wealth of cemeteries relating to both the Mesolithic and Neolithic periods (Gokhman 1966; Konduktorova 1974; Telegin and Potekhina 1987). A number of these cemeteries are the subject of on-going investigation into the nature and frequency of pathological markers of dietary stress visible on the dentitions of the human populations of the region (Figure 16.1). The study of dental disease among prehistoric populations is an important area of palaeoepidemiological research (Schneider 1986). Numerous studies have utilized this evidence; which provides invaluable information relating to past dietary and subsistence patterns (Alexandersen 1988; Goodman et al. 1984; Littlejohn and Frohlich 1993; Lubell et al. 1994; Turner 1979; Y'Edynak 1978, 1989). It has been suggested that 'assessing the likelihood of agriculture through oral health is best done solely with the caries variable (dental decay), since it has the most direct and strongest relationship with amount, kind, texture, and adhesiveness of all possible foodstuffs' (Turner 1979: 631). This variable is utilized in the following study in order to assess the evidence for subsistence shifts across the Mesolithic-Neolithic transition in the Dnieper Rapids region.

Traditionally the Mesolithic-Neolithic transition in Europe was viewed as a shift from a hunter-gatherer to agricultural way of life via colonization from the Near East; with the hunter-gatherers being the passive recipients of what was perceived as a superior economic way of life (Zvelebil and Dolukhanov 1991).

The reconstruction of diet and subsistence is of particular importance when attempting to evaluate the relative health status of human populations during a period of assumed socio-economic change, such as that indicated by changes in

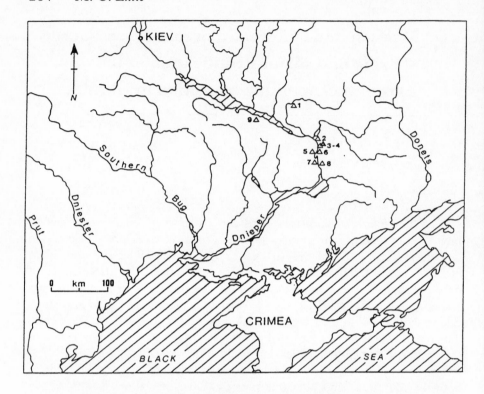

Figure 16.1 The Dnieper Rapids region, showing cemeteries discussed in text. 1. Osipovka; 2. Igren; 3. Vasilyevka V; 4. Vasilyevka III and II; 5. Nikolskoye; 6. Maryevka; 7. Vovnigi II; 8. Yasinovatka; 9. Derievka

activity patterns in the Dnieper-Donets Early Neolithic, around 5000 BC (Anthony 1994). In addition to the consideration of access to dietary resources a brief assessment of social differentiation based on analysis of burial contexts is attempted, with skeletal material and associated grave goods forming the core area of this research (Meiklejohn *et al.* in press). However, it is important to realize that the dead do not bury themselves, and as such certain decisions relating to grave goods and mortuary treatment will be reflections of societal articulations of active social constructs. In attempting to determine differentiation, we face the need to separate ritually determined activity from the individual identity (gender) and 'wealth' of the deceased.

Due to the fact that burial type is relatively uniform in the Neolithic period, consisting primarily of interment in the extended supine position (Telegin and Potekhina 1987), this element of the burial context is not evaluated in the consideration of gender determination of adults. The extension of this burial position to sub-adults may provide insights into the relative status of these individuals, and as such where the positioning of the deceased is determined it will be integrated with consideration of associated artefacts in order to assess the status of sub-adult burials.

Table 16.1 Chronological development of Ukrainian cemeteries

Cemetery	Radiocarbon age	Chronological stage
Vasilyevka III	10060 ± 105 BP	Mesolithic
	9980 ± 100 BP	
	10080 ± 100 BP	
Vasilyevka II	7920 ± 85 BP	Mesolithic
	7620 ± 80 BP	
	8020 ± 90 BP	
Marievka		Neolithic – Mariupol A1
Igren VIII		Neolithic
Vasilyevka V		Neolithic – Mariupol A1
Yasinovatka	5800 ± 300 BP	Neolithic – Mariupol A1–B1
Nikolskoye	5540 ± 400 BP	Neolithic – Mariupol A2–B2
Vovnigi II		Neolithic – Mariupol A2
Osipovka	6075 ± 400 BP	
	5940 ± 420 BP	Neolithic – Mariupol B1

Note: Radiocarbon dates for Vasilyevka II & III obtained from Hedges *et al.* 1995. 'Radiocarbon Dates from the Oxford AMS System: *Archaeometry* Datelist 19'. *Archaeometry* 37, 1, 195–214.

Dental pathologies: chronology, materials and methods

The sample considered in this study consists of Vasilyevka III and II for the Mesolithic period, and the cemeteries of Vovnigi II, Nikolskoye, Yasinovatka, Osipovka, Marievka, and a single interment from Igren VIII for the Neolithic period.

The entire periodization of the Ukrainian cemetery series has received some reconsideration in the light of a number of recently obtained accelerator radio-carbon determinations (Jacobs 1993 and discussion; Anthony 1994). These determinations have indicated that the dependence on assumed correlation between burial and artefact typologies (Telegin 1985) are insufficient criteria upon which to establish a chronological sequence. A revision of Telegin's proposed chronological outline (1968, 1987) has shown that the cemetery of Vasilyevka III must be considered as 'roughly contemporaneous with epi-Palaeolithic "cultural entities" of the Crimea and circum-Caucasus (Jacobs 1994: 4, and references therein), and the previously Neolithic cemetery of Vasilyevka II should now be viewed as Mesolithic in age (*cf.* Anthony 1994: 50–1).

The new radiocarbon determinations, obtained by the author[1] from human remains at the cemeteries of Nikolskoye, Yasinovatka, and Derievka have further highlighted the inadequacies of Telegin's proposed chronological sequence (Tables 16.1 and 16.2). These determinations, obtained from two individuals at Nikolskoye and Yasinovatka, and a single individual from Derievka, span the late sixth to early fifth millennia cal. BC (Housley pers. com.). The dates are inconsistent with conventional determinations, which place these cemeteries in the early to mid-fifth millennium BC (Anthony 1994: 51).

For the purpose of the current analysis the dental sample is analysed chronologically, in terms of Mesolithic versus Neolithic periods. Differential preservation, storage and cataloguing has led to a bias in favour of the cranial region

Table 16.2 Cemetery chronology according to the Oxford AMS System

Date	Cemetery	Radiocarbon age
OxA–5029	Nikolskoye	6300 ± 80 BP
OxA–5052	Nikolskoye	6145 ± 70 BP
OxA–5057	Yasinovatka	6260 ± 180 BP
OxA–5030	Yasinovatka	6330 ± 90 BP
OxA–5031	Derievka	6110 ± 120 BP

Table 16.3 Caries prevalence in the Ukrainian skeletal series

Cemetery	No. of individuals	No. of teeth	% Carious
Vasilyevka III	22	496	0.0
Vasilyevka II	14	324	0.0
Mesolithic Total	**36**	**820**	**0.0**
Marievka	11	98	0.0
Igren VIII	1	27	0.0
Vasilyevka V	14	146	0.0
Yasinovatka	31	444	0.0
Nikolskoye	18	244	0.0
Vovnigi II	26	488	0.0
Osipovka	4	17	0.0
Neolithic Total	**105**	**1464**	**0.0**

(skull) of the skeleton in eastern European institutions. As such, analysis of each skeletal sample entailed the application of the seriation method whereby a site-specific 'perfect male' and 'perfect female' were chosen as type specimens, and where possible assignment of biological sex was made by comparison with these 'type' specimens (Jacobs 1993, 1994). The sample consists of 820 teeth from 36 adult individuals of the Mesolithic period (Vasilyevka III and II), and 1464 teeth from 105 adult individuals from the Neolithic period (Table 16.3).

Age at death estimation of adult material is based primarily on observations of dental attrition rates following a combination of standards set by a number of investigators (Bouts and Pot 1989; Lovejoy 1985, 1991; Miles 1963; Smith 1984). Where possible these observations were supplemented by cranial suture closure (Meindl and Lovejoy 1985), and consideration of the pubic symphysis (Katz and Suchey 1989), and auricular surface (Lovejoy *et al.* 1985).

Dental Caries: The presence/absence of carious lesions (decay of dental enamel caused by acid attack) was recorded for all adult individuals in the skeletal series (Table 16.3). Caries' presence was determined by the author at the macroscopic level for each tooth, on all surfaces, with the lesions being defined as any 'necrotic pit in the enamel large enough to admit a dental probe' (Littleton and Frohlich 1993: 430).

Dental Calculus: Calculus deposition (calcified dental plaque) was recorded (Table 16.4) using the standard set by Hillson (1979: 155), with frequencies

Table 16.4 Calculus deposition frequencies

Cemetery	No. of individuals	Teeth	% Calculus
Vasilyevka III	22	496 (175)	35.28
Vasilyevka II	14	324 (124)	38.27
Mesolithic Total	36 (24*)	820 (299*)	36.46
Marievka	11	98 (62)	63.26
Igren VIII	1	27 (8)	29.62
Vasilyevka V	14	146 (101)	69.17
Yasinovatka	31	444 (285)	64.18
Nikolskoye	18	244 (213)	87.29
Vovnigi II	26	488 (233)	47.74
Osipovka	4	17 (13)	76.47
Neolithic Total	105 (91*)	1464 (915)	62.50

* Number of individuals with calculus deposition in evidence

Table 16.5 Enamel hypoplasia frequencies

Cemetery	Individuals	% Hypoplasias	Teeth	% Hypoplasias
Mesolithic				
Vasilyevka III	22 (5)	22.72	496	1.61
Vasilyevka II	14 (1)	07.14	324	0.30
Neolithic				
Marievka	11	0.0	98	0.0
Igren VIII	1	0.0	27	0.0
Vasilyevka V	14 (1)	07.14	146	3.42
Yasinovatka	31 (6)	19.35	444	2.47
Nikolskoye	18 (1)	05.55	244	0.81
Vovnigi II	26 (4)	15.38	488	2.04
Osipovka	4	0.0	17	0.0

Note: Figures in brackets are the number of individuals with hypoplasias in evidence.

reported as the percentage of individuals affected by calculus deposition at each cemetery.

Enamel Hypoplasias: These localized reductions in crown enamel thickness (disrupted tooth crown development) were recorded for all available dentitions from the Mesolithic and Neolithic periods (Table 16.5). Observations were made at the macroscopic level, with a dental probe being used to aid identification. The location of the hypoplastic event and its distance from the cemento-enamel junction was recorded using a thin-tipped caliper to 0.1 mm. Relative frequencies were recorded as a percentage of all teeth available for analysis by cemetery and period, with age of occurrence and severity of event being determined using the standards set by Goodman and co-workers (e.g. Goodman and Armelagos 1980; Goodman and Rose 1991).

Ante-mortem tooth loss: Incidence of pre-mortem tooth loss was determined in all cases where the alveolar bone was present.

Results

Dental Caries: Comparison for both periods (Table 16.3) shows that caries are universally absent in the entire skeletal series analysed to date. The absence of caries would be unusual in a fully Neolithic, i.e. farming community. However, in the current analysis this absence is indicative of a diet that is non-cariogenic in nature across the entire sample studied, and thus conforms to the general expression of this pathology within European hunter–gatherer populations.

Data reported by Turner (1979) have highlighted the variation in caries incidence in skeletal populations according to economy. In general, hunter–fisher–gatherer economies exhibit low caries frequencies (0.0–5.3%) while agriculturalists exhibit a range of between 2.3–26.5%. High caries incidence is associated with the frequent ingestion of fermentable carbohydrates. A major source of dietary carbohydrate is starch, this is a polymer of glucose and is found in a range of foodstuffs including cereals, roots, and seeds. As such high caries frequencies are generally associated with the exploitation of agricultural or horticultural economies. The absence of caries in the Mesolithic–Neolithic of Ukraine would support a hunter–fisher–gatherer lifeway with little or no emphasis placed upon the exploitation of cultigens.

While high attrition rates are thought to reduce the potential for certain types of caries (Lubell *et al.* 1994: 211), intensive wear was not a feature of the dentitions analysed, and where marked, this exhibited a positive correlation with old age. Dietary factors are clearly significant in the Ukrainian series, the available evidence suggesting an absence of high levels of dietary carbohydrate intake.

Calculus: Low levels of alveolar resorption occur throughout the dental series analysed, and a wide range of calculus deposition is also in evidence (Table 16.4). The number of individuals exhibiting calculus in each period are Mesolithic n = 24 (66.6% of sample), and Neolithic n = 91 (87.5%).

The presence of calculus has positive associations with the consumption of protein-based diets (Hillson 1979). Dietary intakes of protein are likely to have been obtained from a variety of sources within the Dnieper Rapids region. This is due to the fact that animal and plant-based protein alone could not contribute sufficient calorific intake in the hunter–forager diet, as there is a ceiling to the amount of protein that a forager can safely consume (generally between 20–30% on average). Also, differential access to meat resources has been shown to occur (Speth 1989, 1990; Speth and Spielmann 1983), as such total energy needs would have been supplemented by the exploitation of alternative resources. Among these alternative sources are animal fats, plant oils, roots and tubers, and carbohydrates.

Enamel Hypoplasias: Low levels of enamel hypoplasias are visible on the dentitions of individuals from both periods (Table 16.5). In the Mesolithic period 820 teeth are preserved, of these 12 (1.46%) exhibit hypoplasias, while in the Neolithic period 33 of the 1464 teeth preserved exhibit hypoplasias (2.25%). These are represented on the individual level by six individuals in the Mesolithic period (13.8%), and twelve individuals in the Neolithic period (11.5%).

The low number of preserved individuals exhibiting hypoplasias forces the following population-based generalizations to be extremely tentative in nature. It is perhaps significant that of the eighteen individuals with hypoplasias, fourteen are males between 20–45 years of age. This reflects a serious curation bias in favour of males throughout the skeletal series. Of the four females exhibiting hypoplasias, three are aged between 18–25 years, whilst one is between 35–45 years old. Although this distribution is clearly skewed, it appears to indicate that whereas childhood stress does not seem to have affected male longevity, females may well have suffered premature mortality resulting from a combination of decreased resistance to infection, coupled with the vagaries of childbearing in early adulthood. Clearly, the absence of a sufficient sample size precludes meaningful examination of the hypoplasia frequencies in evidence on the dentitions from the Ukrainian cemetery sequences analysed to date.

However, the distribution of hypoplasias between males and females indicates generalized systemic stress during childhood between the ages of two and six (Goodman and Rose 1991; Smith 1991), with 71.74% of occurrences between two and four years, and 28.26% between four and six years. The distribution conforms to that highlighted by Goodman and Armelagos (1985: 486–7) whereby, in general, weaning stress is thought to occur between one and four years of age, with variability being population specific in nature. Enamel hypoplasias are non-specific indicators of stress, and may be the result of a number of factors such as local trauma, hereditary conditions, nutritional deficiencies, infectious diseases and metabolic disruptions (Goodman and Armelagos 1985; Goodman *et al.* 1984; Huss-Ashmore *et al.* 1982; Moggi-Cecchi *et al.* 1994). However, 'of the several developmental dental defects that may be related to general and nutritional stress, macroscopic enamel hypolasia appears to be one of the more valid and reliable indicators' (Huss-Ashmore *et al.* 1982)

Ante-mortem tooth loss: This is restricted to a single incidence from each period. The low frequency of ante-mortem tooth loss indicates that this variable is not a significant factor in the absence of recorded caries incidence in the populations under consideration.

Social differentiation as evidenced by burial practices

Despite the apparent 'absence' of differentiation in terms of access to dietary resources, as indicated by the dental pathology, the earlier Neolithic of Ukraine has artefactual evidence for social change at around 5000 BC. These include a shift from point-based to flat-bottomed ceramic vessels, a decrease in the microlithic element in lithic assemblages, numerous changes in stone tool production (including increased production of polished axes), greater elaboration of ornamentation on ceramics and an increase in the number and 'value' of grave goods (Anthony 1994: 51).

Of particular interest in the context of these apparent changes are the cemeteries of Nikolskoye and Yasinovatka which are placed in stage 2 of the

Dnieper-Donets Neolithic sequence (Telegin and Potekhina 1987). The Ni-kolskoye cemetery was excavated by Telegin in 1959 and 1967, and Yasinovatka was excavated in 1978 by Telegin, Bodyansky, and Nuzhny (Telegin and Potekhina 1987). Both cemeteries exhibit similar depositional sequences in that the primary interments were placed in discrete pits of oval form, with both individual and multiple burials. The later phase Б² burials consist of interment in a large burial hollow, filled with ochre-coloured soil (Telegin and Potekhina 1987).

The Nikolskoye cemetery contained 137 burials when excavated, however part of the cemetery area had been destroyed prior to excavation. Of the 137 burials excavated, 80 adults, 13 adolescents, and 9 children were recovered. Thirty male and 21 female skeletons proved sufficiently complete for the determination of biological sex, the remainder are unsexed. According to the number of skulls found at Yasinovatka this cemetery contained 68 individuals, including 51 adults, 4 adolescents and 9 children. Among the adult burials, 36 skeletons were of males and 15 of females (I.D. Potekhina pers. com.).

It is clear that while sub-adult interments are represented in each of the above cemeteries, these, and the determination of female individuals, are somewhat under-represented, when compared to male determinations. Weiss (1972) has suggested that there exists a systematic bias in the sexing of adult skeletons, which is about 12% in favour of males, due to the nature of secondary sex characteristics in bone. The inaccurate sexing of adults clearly produces a bias in terms of demographic representation amongst males and females. A situation that is further compounded by the fact that age biases in preservation are much more important than sex biases (Walker et al. 1988).

In their analysis of two skeletal populations (Mission La Purisima and the prehistoric Californian cemetery Ca-Ven-110) Walker et al. (1988) have shown that the skeletal remains of young adults were better preserved than those of children or elderly adults. Under-representation of children is most likely the result of the comparatively rapid disintegration of their incompletely calcified bones, while aged individuals have decreased resistance to disintegration of the bones partly due to the accelerated loss of bone calcium in old age (Walker et al. 1988: 187). Both of these studies have also shown that the older the cemetery the higher proportional loss of sub-adults and aged individuals is to be expected.

To further compound the problems of determination of social differentiation, the grave goods incorporated into the burials in the cemeteries of the Dnieper Rapids region are often hunting–fishing derived items such as deer tooth pendants and Cyprinidae (Carp) teeth. Determining 'richness' on the basis of such associated grave goods is extremely problematic (Meiklejohn et al., in press).

Patterning in the mortuary rituals at both cemeteries indicates that while under-representation occurs, valid inferences are possible relating to the nature of the societies under analysis. In the Nikolsoye cemetery, stage A, three of the burial pits appear to have markers, in the form of stone cairns, placed over them. The main grave pit Б, was marked by a cairn, and had two paired burials in the upper layers, with the disarticulated remains of 15 individuals scattered through-out the basal layers of the pit. All of the paired individuals were in the extended supine position with heads to the west. The most abundant finds were associated with the lower paired burial (nos 25 and 26), only individual 26 has been sexed and aged, the deceased being a female aged 50–60 years. Associated finds, located at the feet of no. 25, include a fragment of flint spear point, two knife-like blades, a nearly intact boar tusk ornament, and three beads. At the entrance to this pit, about 1m away from this paired burial, fragments of a stone mace, copper pendants, and a gold pendant were discovered. The other paired burial from this context consisted of a female aged 35–45 (no. 22) and a male aged 40–45 (no. 23). A small copper bead was found on the skull of the male burial.

Further evidence for associated artefacts occurs in burial pit B, at the base of this feature two skeletons (nos 53 and 55) lay in good anatomical order. Individual no. 53, a female aged 20–25, had a string of agate beads (67 pieces) lying near the pelvis while individual no. 55, a male aged 35–45, had agate beads near the right shoulder and 50 Cyprinidae teeth and pendants of immature deer teeth near the left shoulder. Also buried in this pit were three individuals; evidenced by skulls, no. 52 was an adolescent, no. 54 was an adult and no. 56 was a child burial. It is possible to suggest that paired burials in this cemetery exhibit a male-female relationship.

The presence of child burials, not associated with adults, occurs under cairn III (nos. 70–72). Two children were represented by skulls, while a third (no.70) was evidenced by a well-preserved skeleton. This individual lay in the extended supine position, associated artefacts include a string of white annular beads found near the right shoulder, and a number of Cyprinidae teeth below the pelvic bones.

It is clear that this child was afforded burial in exactly the same style as the adults in the cemetery. Some indication of positioning of grave goods occurs in that, where discernible, artefacts are placed at the head, shoulders, pelvis, or feet of the individual, or a combination of these locations. The discovery of a sub-adult burial with grave goods, and in the case of no. 70, white annular beads which are not recovered in any other association, is significant given the rarity of child burials (not associated with an adult) that are accompanied by grave goods.

In the Yasinovatka cemetery sequence burials in the A pit graves include a group grave (A-4) in which a child aged 7–8 years (no. 40), a child aged 6–7 years (no. 41), and an aged female above 55 years (no. 42) were unearthed. All of these individuals were in the extended supine position, and near the feet of the child aged 7–8 years (no. 40) a deer tooth pendant was found. Of particular interest in the A-4 grave is the stratigraphically lowest burial of a male aged between 18–25 years. Associated artefacts include; near the mandible, on the left hand side lay a medium sized knife like blade, along the spinal column, starting from the thoracic vertebrae, lay 16 deer tooth pendants. In addition, two deer tooth pendants were found below the pelvic bones and on the left and right sides of the feet; at the same level within the limits of the grave, lay two Cyprinidae teeth. This positioning suggests that the individual in question was buried in a fully clothed state (Telegin and Potekhina 1987).

The grave pit A–2 contained six burials (55–58, 58a, and 59). Burial no. 55 was a male aged 25–30, no. 57 was an adult of indeterminate sex; no.58 was a male aged 20, and no. 59 was an aged male. Of particular interest in this context is the burial of a well preserved child in the extended supine position. On the humeral bones near the chest, and near the pelvis lay about 30 Cyprinidae teeth, and three deer tooth pendants were found near the feet. All of the burials in this grave were sprinkled with ochre. Paired burials are also in evidence, probably in an oval grave pit, a female aged 20–25 years (no. 19) and a mature adult male (no. 20) were unearthed, both were in the extended supine position.

In the later Б phase of interment at the cemetery of Yasinovatka the deceased are considerably disturbed by the constant re-cutting of graves. The disarticulated nature of the burials in this area has led to only one individual (no. 45) being unearthed with associated grave goods still in an undisturbed state. This individual, a male aged 20–25 years, had eleven ornaments in the form of plates made of boar tusk enamel, which were probably sewn onto the clothing, a small knife-like blade, and a fragment of a retouched blade in association.

The burials from the cemeteries of Nikolskoye and Yasinovatka consist of individual, paired, and group graves, with the deceased having either no grave goods in association (this is predominantly the case), few grave goods, or an apparent abundance of associated artefacts. It has been suggested that the presence of fish teeth, deer tooth pendants, beads and boar tusk plates found in association with burials of Mariupol type, such as those at Nikolskoye and Yasinovatka, were used either as applications on clothes and foot-wear or as components of necklaces (Telegin and Potekhina 1987: 114). It is significant that some value may be inferred for pendants of deer teeth, as in some cases they were simulated in bone (Telegin and Potekhina 1987). The animal derived artefacts of deer tooth, and Cyprinidae tooth pendants, do not appear to exhibit strong age and sex correlations, although deer tooth pendants do appear to be primarily associated with male burials. Child burials are often accompanied by a variety of these artefacts, thus suggesting that while recognized as significant social actors, specific gender determinations had not been achieved by the children prior to death. Of the artefacts that do appear to exhibit a strong sex association lithic forms such as knife-like blades and spear points, and boar tusk plates are most often found accompanying male burials (assuming that the paired burial at Nikolskoye, nos 25 and 26, are a male and a female).

While gender-related burial associations are indicated by the available evidence, the overall nature of socially embedded ritual deposition obscures realistic interpretation of differentiation based upon an analysis of grave goods. A similar situation occurs in the later Mesolithic of Denmark (Meiklejohn *et al.*, in press), where gender related burial associations are indicated, but a ritual burial pattern unconnected to the gender of the individual obscures an overall engendered explanation.

Discussion

The absence of dental caries in the Mesolithic–Neolithic of the Dnieper Rapids region of Ukraine suggests that the diet was not supplemented to a great extent by plants such as cereals, roots and seeds.

Hillson (1979), has argued that dental caries and dental calculus tend to be mutually exclusive because of the relationship with plaque pH. In general the frequent ingestion of fermentable carbohydrates (e.g. cereals, roots, and seeds) increases the degree of acidity to the point at which the enamel dissolves rapidly and eventually the pit-like lesions of dental caries occur (Meiklejohn *et al.* 1988). In contrast, protein (e.g. meat, fish, nuts) metabolism produces alkaline waste products which inhibit the enamel breakdown associated with high carbohydrate intakes. Prolonged alkalinity in the oral cavity results in the deposition of mineral material on the tooth surface in the form of dental calculus (Meiklejohn *et al.* 1988). As such the available evidence indicates that the emphasis was placed upon the consumption of a high protein based diet, i.e. *predominantly* meat, fish, and nuts.

In terms of frequencies of pathological indicators of stress on the dentitions from the Dnieper Rapids skeletal series, both males and females exhibit an absence of caries and presence of calculus with equivalent levels of hypoplasias and ante-mortem tooth loss. This suggests that, even accepting Speth's recent observations relating to the 'non-egalitarian' nature of food-sharing in hunter–gatherer societies (1990), there is no real evidence to indicate that differential access to resources caused a significant reduction in the quality of female dietary intakes (and subsequently sub-optimal health) in the Dnieper Rapids populations analysed to date.

Analysis of funerary contexts has indicated that some form of horizontal stratification may have occurred in the earlier Neolithic period within the Dnieper Rapids region. The nature of the rituals associated with interments confuses this issue in relation to ranking, and it is evident that children are often buried with goods that can be ascribed as status objects when associated with adult burials. The burial orientation of children, where discernible, is in the extended supine position, this is exactly the same as the majority of adult orientations occuring in cemeteries from the late Mesolithic site of Vasilyevka II through to the Neolithic period. As such, it appears that children may well have been considered significant social actors, the loss of whom warranted expression in the ritual context of the burial rites.

The early integration of children into the social context may reflect a number of factors relating to the societies considered. In general group mobility, economic stress, workloads, and the regulation of family size are cited among the reasons for the lack of consideration afforded to young children in a wide range of societies from prehistoric hunter–gatherers to the modern period (Mays 1995). Within the Dnieper Rapids region the exploitation of a rich resource spectrum (hunting–gathering–fishing) may have enabled younger children to play an active part in subsistence tasks from a relatively low age. The suggested dietary equivalence between males and females provides some support for this observation, as does the burial expression afforded to children. The continued exploitation of a predominantly hunter–gatherer–fisher economy, from the Mesolithic to Later Neolithic period (at least until the late-fifth millennium cal. BC where horse domestication is indicated at the settlement site of Derievka: Telegin 1986) despite close associations with neighbouring Tripolye culture farming groups to the west, is indicated.

The subsistence base was, therefore, sufficiently robust to support continued exploitation of wild resources over a period of at least a millennium; from initial contacts with the Tripolye culture in the late sixth millennium cal. BC, as indicated by recent radiocarbon determinations from the cemeteries of Ni-kolskoye, Yasinovatka, and Derievka. The suggested stability of the subsistence activities within the Dnieper region would have formed the basis for group stability (with the possibility of semi-permanent settlement), continuity and subsequent expansion. Presumably this combination would provide the eventual stimulus towards the integration of pastoralism and some agriculture into the subsistence base in the later Neolithic period due to increased residence permanence and group size.

Conclusions

The above discussion offers insights into both the nature and potential of the identification of resource sharing and social stratification during the Mesolithic and Neolithic periods in the Dnieper Rapids region of Ukraine. Analysis of patterning in burial contexts suggests that some form of horizontal stratification occurred. Limited engendering of grave goods is indicated by the presence of knife-like blades, spear points, and boar tusk plates, which are primarily found associated with male burials. Unfortunately the cemeteries analysed have not proved sufficiently robust to offer definitive conclusions relating to social stratification within the groups under consideration.

Despite the suggestion of some form of differentiation, at least in the ritual expression at death, children are afforded identical burial patterning to adults. This factor complicates any discussion relating to ranking in the Late Mesolithic to Early Neolithic societies analysed. This point has been determined for the Mesolithic period in the western Baltic region (Meiklejohn *et al.*, in press). This may well indicate that the determination of differentiation through an analysis of burial contexts is unrealistic when the societies investigated (primarily hunter–fisher–gatherer) are less 'complex' (i.e. structured) than later Neolithic (agriculturalist–pastoralist) societies.

Although Speth (1990) has shown that so called 'egalitarian' hunter–gatherer societies clearly practise inequalities in access to resources, and the above analysis of burial practices indicates some differentiation, there is little evidence to suggest that these 'inequalities' had a significant impact upon female and sub-adult health. In fact, there is no real evidence to indicate that differential access to resources caused a reduction in the quality of female dietary intakes (and subsequently sub-optimal health), in the Dnieper Rapids populations analysed to date.

The results of the analysis of pathological markers of dietary stress support the suggestion that the relative health status between males and females in the periods under consideration are broadly equivalent; this research indicates the exploitation of a resource procurement strategy based on hunting, fishing and gathering. The limited evidence available for children from the cemeteries analysed suggests that they are integrated into the social context from an early age, possibly due to their active role in the economic activities of the groups exploiting the Dnieper Rapids region. These individuals are buried with an identical ritual expression as that afforded to adults within the societies under consideration, thus supporting the growing notion that children were active participants within the prehistoric hunter–gatherer communities under consideration.

The palaeopathological indications of a mixed hunter–gatherer–fisher economy occuring between the late sixth to late fifth millennia cal. BC are in total accord with current theories that the economy of the Dnieper Rapids region of Ukraine remained relatively constant throughout the Mesolithic and Neolithic periods (Telegin 1968; Zvelebil and Dolukhanov 1991).

Acknowledgements

This research was funded by the Science and Engineering Research Council, Great Britain, between October 1991 and August 1993. Special thanks for access to materials housed in the Muzey antropologii i etnografii, St Petersburg and the Ukrainian Academy of Sciences, Kiev, and for invaluable discussion relating to the collections, are extended to Prof. Gokhman and Dr Kozinstev (Petersburg), and Prof. Telegin and Dr Potekhina (Kiev), and to Dr Rupert Housley and staff at the Radiocarbon Accelerator Unit, Research Laboratory for Archaeology and the History of Art, Oxford, for undertaking the dating of the skeletal materials.

Very special thanks are extended to Dr Vladimir Timofeev and family (Petersburg), and Dr Inna Potekhina and family (Kiev) for ensuring my study visits were both enjoyable and rewarding experiences. Also to Dr Marek Zvelebil and Dr Andrew Chamberlain, my supervisors at Sheffield University for their constant encouragement during my research and for comments on earlier drafts of this chapter, and Prof. Christopher Meiklejohn, University of Winnipeg, for advice and support during my research. Any errors and/or omissions are fully the responsibility of the author.

Notes

1. An on-going dating programme, aimed at dating individuals from separate/ distinct phases of interment within these cemetery sequences is currently being carried out jointly by the author and Prof. Dimitri Telegin and Dr Inna Potekhina of the Ukrainian Academy of Sciences, Kiev.
2. Cyrillic. The cemeteries used in this analysis were originally reported in Russian and Ukrainian literature. As such discrete pits and phases of interment

within the cemeteries were designated using the Cyrillic alphabet. Due to the fact that substitution of Cyrillic letters is not a straightforward task, the original designations are retained e.g. **А, Б, В**, which are the first three letters of the Cyrillic alphabet.

References

Alexandersen, V. (1988) 'Description of the human dentitions from the Late Mesolithic grave-fields at Skateholm, Southern Sweden' in L. Larsson (ed.) *The Skateholm Project: Man and Environment*. Sweden: Almqvist & Wiksell Int, pp.106–63

Anthony, D.W. (1994) 'On subsistence change at the Mesolithic-Neolithic Transition'. *Current Anthropology* 35, 1, 49–52.

Bouts, W. and Pot, T. (1989) 'Computerized recording and analysis of excavated human remains' in C.A. Roberts, F. Lee and J. Bintliff (eds) *Burial Archaeology: Current Research, Methods, and Developments*. Oxford: BAR Brit. Ser. 211, pp. 113–28.

Gokhman, I.I. (1966) *Naseleniye Ukraïny v epokhu mesolita i neolita (antropologecheskii ocherk)*. Moscow: Nauka.

Goodman, A.H. and Armelagos G.J. (1980) 'Enamel hypoplasias as indicators of stress in three prehistoric populations from Illinois'. *Human Biology* 52, 3, 515–28.

Goodman, A.H. and Armelagos G.J. (1985) 'Factors affecting the distribution of enamel hypoplasias within the permanent dentition'. *American Journal of Physical Anthropology* 68, 479–93.

Goodman, A.H., Armelagos, G.J. and Rose J.C. (1984) 'The chronological distribution of enamel hypoplasias from prehistoric Dickson Mounds populations'. *American Journal of Physical Anthropology* 65, 259–66.

Goodman, A.H. and Rose, J.C. (1991) 'Dental enamel hypoplasias as indicators of nutritional status' in M.A. Kelley and C.S. Larson (eds) *Advances in Dental Anthropology*. New York: Wiley Liss, pp. 279–93.

Hedges, R.E.M., Housley, R.A., Bronk Ramsey, C. and Van Klinken, G.J. (1995) 'Radiocarbon Dates from the Oxford AMS System: *Archaeometry* Datelist 19'. *Archaeometry* 37, 1, 195–214.

Hillson, S.W. 1979. 'Diet and dental disease'. *World Archaeology* 11, 2, 147–62.

Huss-Ashmore, R., Goodman, A.H. and Armelagos, G.J. (1982) 'Nutritional inference from palaeopathology' in M. Schiffer (ed.) *Advances in Archaeological Method and Theory* 5, 395–464.

Jacobs, K. (1993) 'Human postcranial variation in the Ukrainian Mesolithic-Neolithic'. *Current Anthropology* 34, 3, 311–24.

Jacobs, K. (1994) 'Human dento-gnathic metric variation in Mesolithic/Neolithic Ukraine: possible evidence of demic diffusion in the Dnieper Rapids region'. *American Journal of Physical Anthropology* 95, 1–26.

Katz, D. and Suchey, J.M. (1989) 'Age estimation of the male os pubis'. *American Journal of Physical Anthropology* 69, 427–35.

Konduktorova, T.S. (1974) 'The ancient population of the Ukraine (from the Mesolithic Age to the first centuries of our era)'. *Anthropologie* (Brno) 12 (1,2), 5–149.

Littleton, J. and Frohlich B. (1993) 'Fish-eaters and farmers: dental pathology in the Arabian Gulf'. *American Journal of Physical Anthropology* 92, 427–47.

Lovejoy, C.O. (1985) 'Dental wear in the Libben Population: its functional pattern and role in the determination of adult skeletal age at death'. *American Journal of Physical Anthropology* 69, 47–56.

Lovejoy, C.O., Meindl, R.S., Prybeck, T.R. and Mensforth, R.P. (1985) 'Chronological metamorphosis of the auricular surface of the Ilium: a new method for the determination of skeletal age at death'. *American Journal of Physical Anthropology* 68, 15–28.

Lubell, D., Jackes, M., Schwarcz, H., Knyf, M. and Meiklejohn, C. (1994) 'The Mesolithic-Neolithic transition in Portugal: isotopic and dental evidence of diet'. *Journal of Archaeological Science* 21, 201–16.

Mays, S., (1995) 'Killing the unwanted child'. *British Archaeology* 2, 8–9.

Meiklejohn, C., Baldwin, J.H. and Schentag, C.T. (1988) 'Caries as a probable dietary marker in the Western European Mesolithic' in B.V. Kennedy and G.M. LeMoine (eds) *Diet and Subsistence: Current Archaeological Perspectives. Proceedings of the 19th. Chacmool Conference.* Calgary: University Press, pp. 273–9.

Meiklejohn, C., Petersen, E.B. and Alexandersen, V. (in press) 'Anthropology and archaeology of Mesolithic gender in the western Baltic' in M. Donald and L. Hurcombe (eds) *Gender and Material Culture.* New York: Macmillan Publishing Co.

Meindl, R.S. and Lovejoy, C.O. (1985) 'Ectocranial suture closure ageing scheme'. *American Journal of Physical Anthropology* 68, 57–66.

Miles, A.E.W. (1963) 'The dentition in the assessment of individual age in skeletal material' in D.R. Brothwell (ed.) *Dental Anthropology.* Oxford: Pergammon Press, pp.191–209.

Moggi-Cecchi, J., Pacciani, E., and Pinto-Cisternas, J. (1994) 'Enamel hypoplasia and age at weaning in 19th Century Florence, Italy'. *American Journal of Physical Anthropology* 93, 229–306.

Schneider, K.N. (1986) 'Dental caries, enamel composition, and subsistence among prehistoric Amerindians of Ohio'. *American Journal of Physical Anthropology* 71, 95–102.

Smith, B.H. (1984) 'Patterns of molar wear in hunter-gatherers and agriculturalists'. *American Journal of Physical Anthropology* 63, 39–56.

Smith, B.H. (1991) 'Standards of human tooth formation and dental age assessment' in M.A. Kelley and J.C. Larson (eds) *Advances in Dental Anthropology.* New York: Wiley Liss, pp.143–68.

Speth, J.D. (1989) 'Early hominid hunting and scavenging: the role of meat as an energy source'. *Journal of Human Evolution* 18, 329–43.

Speth, J.D. (1990) 'Seasonality, resource stress, and food sharing in so-called "egalitarian" foraging societies'. *Journal of Anthropology and Archaeology* 9, 148–88.

Speth, J.D. and Spielmann, K.A. (1983) 'Energy source, protein metabolism, and hunter-gatherer subsistence strategies'. *Journal of Anthropology and Archaeology* 2, 1–31.

Telegin, D.Ya. (1968) *Dneipro-Donetska kultura.* Kiev: Naukova Dumka.

Telegin, D.Ya. (1985) *Pam'yatniki epokhi mezolita na territorii Ukrainskoy SSR.* Kiev: Naukova Dumka.

Telegin, D.Ya. (1986) *Derievka: a settlement and cemetery of Copper Age horse keepers on the Middle Dnieper.* Oxford: BAR Int. Ser. 287.

Telegin, D.Ya. (1987) 'Neolithic cultures of the Ukraine and adjacent areas and their chronology'. *Journal of World Prehistory* 1, 3, 307–31.

Telegin, D.Ya. and Potekhina, I.D. (1987) *Neolithic cemeteries and populations in the Dneiper Basin.* Oxford: BAR Int. Ser. 383.

Turner, C. G. II (1979) 'Dental anthropological indications of agriculture among the Jomon people of central Japan'. *American Journal of Physical Anthropology* 51, 619–36.

Walker, P.L., Johnson, J.R. and Lambert, P.M. (1988) 'Age and sex biases in the preservation of human skeletal remains'. *American Journal of Physical Anthropology* 76, 183–8.

Weiss, K.M. (1972) 'On the systematic bias in skeletal sexing'. *American Journal of Physical Anthropology* 37, 239–50.

Y'Edynak, G. (1978) 'Culture, diet, and dental reduction in Mesolithic forager-fishers of Yugoslavia'. *Current Anthropology* 19, 3, 616.

Y'Edynak, G. (1989) 'Yugoslav Mesolithic dental reduction'. *American Journal of Physical Anthropology* 78, 17–36.

Zvelebil, M. and Dolukhanov, P. (1991) 'The transition to farming in eastern and northern Europe'. *Journal of World Prehistory* 5, 3, 233–78.

17 Age, gender and biological reality in the Early Bronze Age cemetery at Mokrin

ELIZABETH REGA

This chapter is concerned with prehistoric social distinctions – how they are codified and represented in the material mortuary remains of a central European Bronze Age community and the manner in which these distinctions both shape and are shaped by more strictly biological concerns. I will make the argument that, in the cemetery at Mokrin, the primary axes of symbolic differentiation were sex, age and residence group. These elements of an individual's social persona were combined by the living in the material and formal attributes of the grave to represent and reaffirm the important organizing principles of Mokrin society. These depictions fully incorporate both women and children as social individuals in ways which have generally been – if not neglected – then perhaps undervalued in much archaeological literature.

Burials are only one aspect of mortuary ritual, but 'whether we look at graves with religious, economic, social or artistic questions in mind, the analysis of burials is the analysis of symbolic action' (Morris 1992). Despite the problematic connection between symbolic action and 'reality', archaeologists have long employed attributes of mortuary differentiation as hallmarks of societal structure. Interestingly, priority is most often accorded to explaining vertical status distinctions and their concommitant material correlates (Bradley 1984; R. Chapman 1990; Peebles and Kus 1977; Gilman 1981; S.E. Shennan 1982; S.J. Shennan 1993). Horizontal social distinctions – those of gender, age grade, kinship – while accorded some attention (Brown 1981; Morris 1992; Blanton *et al.* 1981), are also frequently considered confounding elements to be 'factored out' of the larger analysis (see O'Shea 1984; McKay 1988). Randsborg (1981: 43) in prioritizing the search for stratification, goes so far as to state: 'Obviously grave goods may vary between the sexes and along age lines. This variation can distort the pattern, making women seem of a higher or lower rank than they actually were.' The assumption that this variation represents a *distortion* rather than the pattern itself is logically troubling.

How to decide what rank 'women actually were' must be addressed outside the circular logic of grave good interpretation. In the absence of settlement data, the archaeological interpretation of the social information encoded in the Early Bronze Age cemetery at Mokrin, located in the Banat region of the former Yugoslavia (Figure 17.1), must be compared with independent biological data drawn from the occupants of the cemetery itself. The data consist of demo-

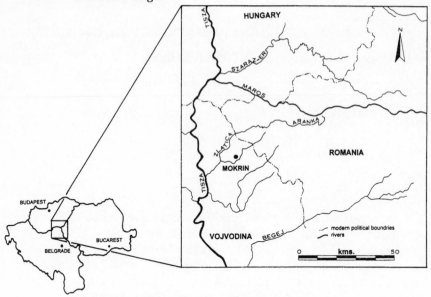

Figure 17.1 (Figure redrawn after Girić 1986)

graphic and dietary analysis obtained from macroscopic, microscopic and chemical assessment of the human skeletal remains. While this interdisciplinary approach has been advocated and employed by archaeologists and physical anthropologists (Bentley 1987; Blakely and Beck 1982; Buikstra 1981; R. Chapman *et al.* 1981; Goodman *et al.* 1984; Murray and Schoeninger 1985; Powell 1984, 1988; Rathbun and Scurry 1985) what is extolled in European archaeology is more often the potential of skeletal research than actual results (e.g. Cohen and Bennett 1993). Biological data here are an essential contribution to the core of the problem.

Mokrin and the Maros group

Much of eastern and central Hungary and a portion of northern Serbia and Romania were inhabited in the Early Bronze Age by the creators of the Perjamos (or Maros) culture (Bona 1963). The vast majority of sites were identified and excavated in the first third of this century (Childe 1957); the inhumation cemeteries of the Maros group in particular have received considerable archaeological attention as excavation of the settlements is rare, the cemeteries generally large and the grave goods rich (Coles and Harding 1979). Maros cemeteries are typically characterized by flexed primary single interments with variable quantities of grave goods. Ten major Maros cemeteries and a number of individual graves have been uncovered to date, but the paucity of provenance information and excavation documentation serve to compromise attempts at detailed funerary interpretation. The extremely limited quantity of skeletal material remaining from these excavations (Rega 1989, 1995) further impairs biological analysis by severely skewing the sample representation. Accurate demographic analysis of the existing skeletal remains is therefore exceedingly problematic, although for a few Maros group cemeteries, life table analysis based upon partial data has been attempted (O'Shea 1978).

The cemetery at Mokrin is unique. Excavated from 1958 to 1969, it is one of only two Maros group cemeteries to be excavated with strict attention to provenance and, importantly, where the majority of the human skeletal material was retained.[1] A total of 312 graves were uncovered, leaving one-third to half of the cemetery unexcavated (Girić 1971). Two hundred and sixty-eight of the skeletons from the 298 graves which actually contained human bones were examined by the author at the Narodni Muzeji in Kikinda, Yugoslavia in 1990. Macroscopic age and sex estimation were performed on site, and bone and tooth samples were collected for analysis. Details of the methodology can be found in Rega (1995).

Radiocarbon dates from Mokrin human bone fall between 2100–1500 cal. BC (Forenbacher 1993; O'Shea 1991; Rega 1995); however the utility of this data for determining exact use period of the cemetery is limited. None of the dates appear to support internal phasing of the cemetery, based upon either the ceramic types as tied to regional sequences (Girić pers. com.) or the spatial chronological division within the cemetery proposed by Soroceanu (1975). Approximately three-quarters of the graves are furnished with grave goods, most often one or two ceramic vessels, but also with jewellery and tools. The vessels in particular may form a base-line assemblage which is highly regular in its constitution, and which is frequently supplemented by the other symbolic goods (O'Shea 1978).[2] It is the apparent wealth of some graves compared to others with few or no goods which has been suggestive to some researchers of status differences (Girić 1971; Coles and Harding 1979; O'Shea 1978).

Gender, sex and grave orientation

Spatial orientation at Mokrin is very clearly an important structuring principle within the cemetery. Approximately two-thirds of the graves are clustered into lines running north-south; it is claimed that these represent family groups (Girić 1971). The orientation of the body within the grave corresponds with the sex of adult individuals (Farkas and Liptak 1971; Rega 1995). The females in the cemetery are generally oriented with their head to the south or southeast, on their right side facing east. The males are oriented with their head to the north or northwest on their left side, also facing east. Of the 146 adults where biological sex assignment was possible, 137 (94%) had a sex assignment which agreed with the grave orientation (Rega in press).

The opposition between biological sex as a reflection of reproductive potential and gender as a social construct is sufficiently essential to bear reiteration. Biological sex manifests itself in the possession of the organs of reproduction (Moore 1988) and can be determined from human skeletons with some variable degree of accuracy. Assignment of biological sex to people is indeed partly cultural (Weiss 1972) and the methodological difficulties with sexing skeletal material are acknowledged (Claassen 1992; Bumsted *et al.* 1990); however, methodological inadequacies do not really render the principle of biological sex

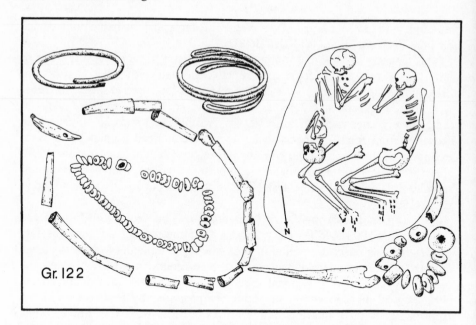

Figure 17.2 Burial on left oriented N-S is a child, aged approximately 5 years at death. Burials at right are adults. (Figure redrawn after Girić 1971)

itself ambiguous.[3] It is in relation to biological sex that gender is principally, though not exclusively defined. In the case of Mokrin, the high correspondence of biological sex to the symbolism of grave orientation suggests a highly gendered structure. Several individuals manifest a biological sex estimate which is at odds with the gender. Although the intriguing possibility of gender/sex discrepancy certainly exists, the 'misassignment' of the remainder is likely due to the inaccuracy inherent in the standard skeletal sexing techniques, as the results fall exactly into the expected range of sex estimation error (Steele and Bramblett 1989).[4] Interestingly, the same variation in grave orientation is extended to children as well, suggesting that they may be symbolically 'gendered' in a manner similar to that of the adults.

Checking the correspondence between biological sex and socially-assigned gender is very difficult for the skeletons of children, due to the immature state of the bony features used to identify sex (Chamberlain 1994; Holcomb and Konigsberg 1995). Indirect evidence comes from one of the rare multiple burials in grave 122, where a child is buried with an orientation opposing that of the accompanying adults. This suggests that the body orientation of children was also deliberate and culturally significant, even when somewhat inconvenient (Figure 17.2). In a more direct test, the only fully adult structures in children – the permanent teeth – were used to assess sex of the children where feasible. Three discriminant functions were developed in SPSS using measurements of the teeth of 'known sex' Mokrin adults; this was then applied to the children. These discriminant functions had an accuracy of sex assignment for the adults ranging from 69–79% (Rega in press). For the 17 children who could be assigned a sex estimate with a probability of p = 0.10 or higher, the agreement with grave orientation is 71% or 12 cases. The 71% agreement falls completely within the accuracy range of the dental discriminant function scoring of the 'known' sex individuals used to generate the discriminant functions and serves as one line of biological evidence linking sex of children to grave gender. Although by no means in itself conclusive, the best available evidence suggests that the sex of the children also corresponds to grave orientation.

Gendered grave goods

The archaeologically recoverable grave goods at Mokrin consist primarily of ceramic vessels, metal jewellery – bracelets, torques, beads, pendants, finger and hair rings – as well as non-metal jewellery, animal teeth and bone, shell, bone needles, polishing pebbles, stone and copper axes and copper knives. Over three-quarters of the graves at Mokrin contain some artefact. Ceramic bowls and beakers, often in pairs, constitute the most common grave good. The presence of the latter does not vary in frequency significantly either with regard to either age or sex (Rega 1995).

Some grave goods, including tools and jewellery, do appear to be strictly partitioned along the lines of gender. Based on the published age and sex data (Farkas and Liptak 1971) of a subsample of 232 Mokrin graves, O'Shea (1978), identified some grave goods as the exclusive provenance of a single sex, including beads, pierced animal teeth, bone pins, multiple coil bracelets, bronze 'spectacle' pendants, copper discs and plaques and arched pins as exclusively female and daggers and stone axes as male. Single coil bracelets, amphorae and cups were placed with sub-adults (O'Shea 1978). An analysis of artefactual associations on an expanded sample was combined in this study with updated sex and age data obtained by the author in 1990 and utilises multiple chi-square analyses run in the CROSSTABS module of SPSS. Fisher's exact test was run when samples violated the conditions for chi-square.

The results of the analysis are presented in Table 17.1. Several artefact associations are significantly associated with gender at the p = 0.05 level. Associations with females include clay, animal and mixed bead necklaces, copper arched pins, multiple spiral bracelets and bone needles. Of these artefacts, those found *exclusively* with females include multiple coil bracelets, bone needles and stone maces, although the latter is not statistically significant because of the small numbers. Bone needles are found individually or in pairs on or near the head or upper torso of both south-oriented children and adult females (Rega in press, *contra* O'Shea 1995) in frequencies averaging 20%. If needles represent a functional personal tool kit as well as symbolic presence, it may be that an apparently female-gendered activity – sewing – may have been performed by girls as well as women. However, it must be noted that half of the needles were not *fully* intact and functional, and in all likelihood the youngest age category would not have had sufficient strength, size and dexterity to use the needles as tools. The needle contributes to the redundancy of symbols employed

Table 17.1 Contingency table analysis of artefact by gender and age-at-death

Artefact type	Gender	Age	Association
clay beads	**.19669**	.00753	female
animal tooth beads	.10746*	-.00540	female
mixed beads	**.19027**	.02870	female
beakers	.05851	.12627	
loop amphora	.10972	-.13930	
pierced lug amphora	.08356	.08778	
lug amphora	.06074	.08346	
pedestal amphora	.01928	.04548	
cup	**.14878**	.05942	male
lid	.80342	.10857	
no handle bowl	.03231	-.09001	
asymmetric handle bowl	.04060	.06020	
multiple handle bowl	.75457	.10763	
incised	.09180	.02563	
grooved	.04556	-.04704	
rusticated	.03204	.04548	
copper dagger	**.18707**	.08592*	adult male
copper axe	.09906*	.04548	male
copper awl	.02736	-.012255	
stone axe	.07964*	.06456	adult male
stone mace	.09883*	.05580	adult female
bone needle	**.27070**	.01378	female
spiral spectacle pendants	.100071	**.17590**	adult
rolled plaques	.20855	**.19052**	adult
copper discs	.04399	.11363*	adult
large copper arched pin	**.16535**	.11363*	adult female
torque	.07865	.09136*	adult
gold lockring	.10081	-.04499	
multiple spiral bracelet	**.17075**	.02870	female
single spiral bracelet	.11128	-.08006	

* = not sig. but exclusive. All values are phi or Fisher's exact probability. Values in bold are significant.

Ages-at-death are pooled into two categories: sub-adult and adult. The post-pubertal juvenile age category is classed as adults – their sample size is, however, so small that assignment to one class or the other makes very little difference to the final result.

Gender was defined by grave orientation in this analysis, to allow gendering of the children and incorporation of the unexamined adults.

Artefacts were coded as binary presence/absence values. Any case where a grave may have been severely disturbed post-depositionally has been excluded from the analysis, as the recording of absent assumes that exclusion of an artefact from the grave assemblage is deliberate.

in gendering the cemetery and provides an additional line of evidence that female children were accorded a gendered identity overlapping with that of adults. In light of the fact that the highest percentage of graves with bone needles occurs in the 6 to 13 year old category, it may be equally justifiable to view these needles as girl-symbols carried to adulthood.

Combined gender and age-at-death association is also a factor at Mokrin.

Bracelets occur predominantly with female adults (83% of occurrence or 19 cases) – the multiple coil variants are contained exclusively in the south-oriented graves of female adults. In exclusive association with adult males are found copper daggers or knives. The seven intact knives are found only in adult male graves, yielding a mean frequency of 9%. Significantly, no knives are found in graves of males younger than eighteen, although a sub-adult female was found with a bracelet made from a knife blade. Whatever the exact circumstance of deposition, intact metal knives are the associative provenance of fully adult men. Copper axes, which occur in very small numbers, are primarily but not exclusively male in association – one old adult female (grave 208) has an impressive copper axe as part of her grave assemblage. Together with copper knives, intact stone axes are found with adult males (11 cases). Males of varying ages are also significantly associated with a one-handled form of cup.

Is everyone here?

It appears that biological sex, represented in the mortuary context by gendered cultural manifestations, was an important axis of social partitioning for the people of Mokrin. In further evaluating the extent to which biological sex affected the lives both adults and children, an examination of differential mortality is essential. It is first necessary in any mortuary analysis to ascertain whether the cemetery has a representative cross-section of the contributing population or only a selection of the community's dead (Buikstra 1981). Recognition of the ongoing debate over the defensibility of palaeodemography (Boquet-Appel and Masset 1982; Buikstra and Konigsberg 1985; Van Gerven and Armelagos 1983; Wood *et al.* 1992; Wood and Milner 1994) necessitates a 'tail-wagging-the-dog' approach to address the more cogent criticisms of the technique. Conventional demographic tools for comparison between population segments, such as life table analysis, are frequently violated by archaeologically-generated skeletal samples in that the assumptions necessary to generate meaningful figures (principally stable population and complete representation of population deaths) cannot be substantiated. This analysis turns the question on its head by examining the pattern of mortality and comparing it to the demographic dynamics in a variety of model populations in order to 'screen for' irregularities. This is accomplished via examination of the mortality profile and survivorship curve. In order to circumvent methodological inaccuracies inherent in the assessment of age-at-death, individuals have been assigned to broad age categories using standard physical anthropological techniques (Smith 1991; Saunders 1992; Katz and Suchey 1986; Walker *et al.* 1991), rather than make unreliable point estimates of age for each individual.

The mortality profile for age-at-death from Mokrin is presented in Figure 17.3. Individuals with age-at-death estimates crossing age categories were assigned proportionally to each category crossed, as is standard palaeodemographic practice (Chamberlain 1994). Immediately apparent is the total lack of individuals under one year of age. This is a category where risk of dying is typically high and one expects to see a large number of deaths, perhaps 15–30

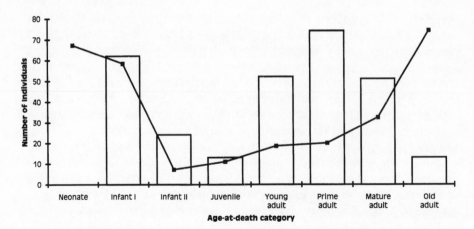

Figure 17.3 Mokrin mortality profile. For comparison, the line indicates expected mortality for an identical sample size with life expectancy at birth of 30 years. Different life expectancies change the values, but not the essential U-shape of the curve

per cent of the cemetery total. Moreover, skeletons in this age group are relatively easy to age accurately and thus they are unlikely to have been mis-assigned. Preservational factors alone do not account for the absence especially given the robust numbers in the next age category. As deaths in this age range must have occurred, their absence indicates that children under one year of age were disposed of elsewhere. Similar patterns of cemetery exclusion are probably characteristic of other Maros group cemeteries (Rega 1989). The only intact inhumation yet recovered from a Maros settlement is that of a perinatal infant burial accompanied by a two-handled amphora in a house floor at the Kiszom-bor Uj-Elet site in Hungary (Rega 1995; O'Shea 1995), and it may be that we should expect to recover further neonates from the, as yet, rarely excavated habitation contexts. Further analysis of the survivorship curve created from the mortality data reveals biologically realistic numbers for complete population representation between the ages of one and 20 years. Not coincidentally, these are the ages where skeletal assessment of age-at-death is most reliable. A marked surplus of deaths between the ages of 30 and 40 probably reflects systematic underaging of adults rather than increased risk of dying in this interval, although culturally-based systemic overrepresentation of this group in the cemetery cannot be excluded.

Sex-specific mortality

Inferences about the sexing of the sub-adults can be extended with a view toward evaluating sex-specific mortality. A mortality profile (Figure 17.4) for males and females was calculated for the range of ages incorporating the grave orientation evidence from every excavated grave. Apparent is the greater number of individuals sexed as 'female' in the infant and child categories. A chi-square 2 ×

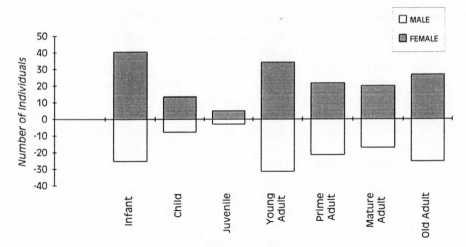

Figure 17.4 Mokrin sex-specific mortality

2 contingency table consisting of male and female infants differed significantly from the expected 1:1 sex ratio (p = 0.005). The null hypothesis that the differences in numbers of female and male infants in the Mokrin cemetery is due purely to chance must therefore be rejected.

The implications of this sex difference are intriguing. The relative proportion of the age classes after one year is realistic and the slope of the survivorship curves for both males and females is consistent with biological expectations for naturally-occurring non-catastrophic deaths. The age classes buried in the cemetery after one year are, therefore, experiencing similar mortality rates. Critical to remember is the entire class of people not interred in the cemetery – the children under one year of age. The statistically significant excess of female children between one and six years may be due to the fact that there are greater numbers of females actually alive in this age group and, therefore, the pool of those dying is larger. Assuming approximately equal number of males and females are born,[5] mortality, therefore, may be significantly greater for boys during the first year of life.

It has been suggested that male infant mortality is naturally slightly greater in human populations (Stuart-Macadam 1993; Stini 1969, 1985). There exists no *a priori* biological justification for this phenomenon, and modern demographic evidence in this regard is complex (Wiley 1994). In 'traditional' societies, sex ratios and natural mortality immediately post-partum are notoriously difficult to document due to the lack of hospitalization and medical records during this period. Evidence must frequently come from interviews, in which the very nature of the evidence will tend to obscure practices like infanticide. Maternal age and child-raising experience have been cultural factors implicated in sex ratio differences (Curtis *et al.* 1993). Non-culturally biased differences in infant mortality are most likely slight and do not alone account for the magnitude of difference observed in the Mokrin sample. The probable reason for a discrepancy of this magnitude is cultural – the increased male mortality may be caused by the intentional killing or neglect of male neonates. The neonatal period is 'prime time', as infanticide and neglect are less likely to be employed as a population manipulator once older ages are attained.

The practice of infanticide and neglect are viewed by the majority of non-clinical researchers as consciously-calculated adjustments in parental investment designed to achieve economic and cultural, as well as biological goals (Demeer *et al.* 1993; Hrdy 1992; Li 1991). The practice of sex-biased differential infanticide can profoundly skew the adult population sex ratios where immigration does not offset the imbalance (Lee *et al.* 1994). Although some archaeological instances of infanticide have been recognized (Mays 1993; Smith and Kahila 1992), none to date has been able to definitively identify sex-biased infanticide. In the clinical and ethnographic literature, differential infanticide is most commonly cited as disadvantaging female children (Kishor 1993; Hawkes 1981; Hughes 1981; Wilson 1988) and occurs in cultures where the social and economic contributions of males are more valued than those of females (Coale and Banister 1994; George *et al.* 1992; Judson 1994; Renteln 1992; Smith and Smith 1994).

A few instances of female-biased parental favouritism are documented. These occur in widely separated political and geographic contexts, such as Pakistan, New Guinea, the US, Britain, the West Indies and Kenya (Cronk 1989; Marks and Kumar 1993; Sargent and Harris 1992). In Jamaica, the favouritism shown toward female children has been ascribed to the greater role of women as economic providers and in maintenance of family stability in a matrilineal society; the consequent higher value of a daughter to the family in general and the mother in particular is apparent (Sargent and Harris 1992). The centrality of women in Jamaican ideology becomes manifest in prevalent childcare practices favouring girls. Among the Mukogodo of Kenya, the preferential treatment of girls in poor families is related to the real economic benefit accrued in a bride–wealth system. For the less-wealthy extended families, the very real difficulties in putting together sufficient capital for a male child to marry is complemented by the advantage of receipt of capital with the marriage of a girl (Cronk 1989, 1993). Interestingly, when these same Mukogodo were surveyed as to their opinion, most mothers claim to prefer sons over daughters. According to Cronk, 'this discrepancy makes sense only in the light of the pervasiveness of the Maasai-speaking culture, which is extremely male-biased' (1993: 279). Clearly, opinion and action can both contradict and co-exist.

Similar diets

Despite sex-biased differential mortality and/or cemetery access for sub-adults, other sex-based differences in biological quality of life among adult individuals are not apparent. Adult mortality is identical, as are the low rates of bony pathology, including trauma and degenerative disease. Given difficulties in interpretation of pathology (Wood *et al.* 1992; Wood and Milner 1994), it is most prudent to rely on chronic long-term biological indicators. Dental caries rates and dental attrition are indirect indicators of dietary carbohydrate consumption (Turner 1979) and very similar rates for males and females are found at Mokrin. Although factors other than food consumption can be involved in cariogenesis, the control in this context over age-at-death, spatial and temporal factors suggest that this correspondence is due to similar diets (Rega 1995).

More direct chemical methods of dietary investigation conducted on the bone samples collected from the Mokrin skeletons substantiate this conclusion.[6] Chemical palaeodietary analysis focuses on the relative consumption of meat versus plant foods or on the consumption of food items which leave particular elemental traces in the bone, such as maize, millet and marine foods. These methods are based upon the principle of fractionation, whereby the non-essential trace elements and heavier stable isotopes are actively discriminated against by animals, including humans, for incorporation into bone tissue. (Brown 1973; Murray and Schoeninger 1985; Schwartz and Schoeninger 1991; Sealy and Sillen 1988). In contrast, plant levels reflect the soil or atmospheric levels, some of which vary geographically (Gilbert 1975; Price *et al.* 1989). This fractionation continues up the food chain, with the result that consumption of a diet which consists principally of animal proteins and fats will result in sig-nificantly different levels than a diet heavily reliant on plant foods. Trace element and stable isotope analyses were performed on bone samples from adult in-dividuals; children were not assessed biochemically.

The results from the trace element analyses (n = 45) reveal no statistically significant differences between the sexes in either barium or strontium levels, the two most reliable elemental indicators of plant versus meat consumption (Rega 1995). Results from the analyses of the smaller sample of stable carbon isotopes (n = 12) reinforce the notion that similar proportions of meat and plant material are being consumed by the men and women of Mokrin (Figure 17.5).[7] Inter-pretation of similarities in trace element values is rendered problematic by the fact that enormous differences in meat/plant consumption need to exist before significant differences in trace elemental levels will be manifest (Burton and Wright 1995). Given this fact, however, several statistically significant differ-ences in the levels of both these elements *are* found between lines of burials within the cemetery – these may reflect intriguing differences in food consump-tion pattern between family and/or residence groups. These results are re-inforced by the dental caries data (Rega 1995), although results are inconclusive for blood-group and non-metric trait analyses (Lengyel 1972; Rega 1995). But where dietary differences occur at Mokrin, they are not apparently gendered.

Conclusion

It has been demonstrated demographically that access to the cemetery at Mokrin is partially dependent on age-at-death. Before the age of one year, a mortuary alternative to cemetery inhumation must have been in operation, as reflected in the absence of these individuals from the larger group cemetery. The transition to cemetery/community membership at around one year marks a significant alteration in perception of personhood, before which sex-biased population control measures such as infanticide and neglect may have been sanctioned.

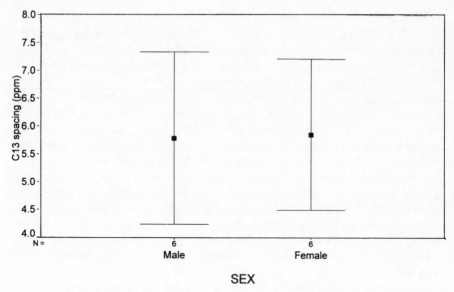

Figure 17.5 Sex comparison of spacing values between δC13 collagen and δC13 apatite. No significant difference is manifest between the sexes for spacing, δC13 collagen, δC13 apatite or δN15

This practice would explain the sex-biased representation in favour of females between the ages of one and six years, and would be consistent with ethnographic practice in societies where the material and/or social contribution of females is accorded vital importance. Obviously, an alternative explanation proposes that male children in this age group may be, for whatever reason, preferentially excluded from the cemetery; however, the latter hypothesis does not fully account for the results of demographic analysis which suggest an overall proportion of children to adults consistent with full community inclusion after one year of age.

Further symbolic differentiation on the basis of biological sex permiates the cemetery. Positioning of the corpse as well as types of grave goods delineate a highly gendered structure, which seemingly incorporates children in a manner at least in parallel to that of the adults. Any extrapolation, however, of the funerary differences to a gender hierarchy must be approached cautiously. Although the mortuary gendering of individuals is pervasive, these distinctions do not appear to extend to differential 'biological quality of life' as reflected in access to food resources, pathology or mortality.

On a strictly material level, the majority of grave goods and indeed the majority of the metal items (63%) is contained in the graves of females. One particularly notable grave contains the remains of an adult female wearing a gold-sheet crown or headpiece with perforated decoration, along with numerous bronze/copper items (Figure 17.6). An isomorphic interpretation along conventional lines might posit that Mokrin females had symbolic, if not actual, control of the metal trade axis considered vital to the development of social stratification

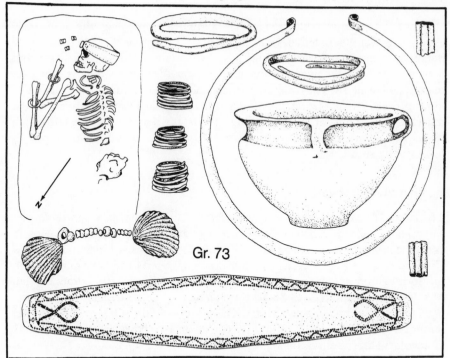

Figure 17.6 Grave of adult female. The lockrings are gold, the crown is pierced gold foil. The bracelets and fibulae are copper. (Redrawn from Girić 1971, artefacts not to scale)

in the Early Bronze Age. Such a formulation would indeed be consistent with interpretive frameworks routinely applied to male burials. However, a recent interpretation of strikingly similar findings from Slovakia (Shennan 1993), sees the larger quantity of metal grave goods in female graves primarily as a reflection of *male* wealth and prestige. This apparent double standard of judgement pronounces that rich male burials are rich, while rich females simply married well (see Renfrew 1986). 'In effect, archaeological convention peoples the past with men and robs women of their artefacts' (Kehoe 1992 citing Bird 1988: 28). While the metal wealth in female graves may indeed represent a male contribution, the mortuary data alone do not allow determination of 'ownership', whether symbolic or actual. Simple assertion of gendered arenas of power consistent with current virocentric assumptions is inadequate as an explanatory tool.

Similar to the practice in many other central European Early Bronze Age cemeteries (S.E. Shennan 1975, 1982; Chapman 1994), biological attributes at Mokrin figure significantly into cemetery spatial organization and the distribution of grave goods. At Mokrin, this is reflected in many levels of mortuary redundancy, where age and gender are critical differentiating factors. However, analysis of many central European cemeteries has suffered from not only a paucity of biological data, but also in some instances from a puzzling 'double-standard' of material evaluation which continues to privilege the adult male experience over that of females and children. Consideration is rarely given to the notion that 'rich' female graves may actually contain individuals of wealth and power, a peculiar fact given the vital importance of female productive labour in many small-scale societies. Although archaeologists continue to attribute enormous power in symbolizing, creating and maintaining social hierarchies to the movement and consumption of prestige goods, the real significance of the rich female graves and possible favouritism towards daughters in this context has yet to be widely addressed.

Acknowledgements

Thanks are due to Milorad Girić at the National Museum in Kikinda, former Yugoslavia, for his assistance in accessing and understanding the Mokrin skeletal collection, as well as maps and access to unpublished material. Andrew Chamberlain at the University of Sheffield contributed invaluable assistance in the formulation of the dental discriminant functions. Mark Edmunds, Ian Morris, John Chapman and Stuart Sumida offered helpful advice and suggestions on many drafts of this chapter. Colin Merrony drew Figure 17.1, Stuart Sumida redrew Figures 17.2 and 17.6. As always, however, the (hopefully momentary) lapses of reason are mine.

Grant funding for this research was provided by the International Research and Exchanges Board (IREX) and Sheffield University.

Notes

1. The skeletal remains from the ongoing excavation at Ostojicevo in the western Banat region, led by Milorad Girić at the National Museum in Kikinda, have also been systematically retained and are in very good condition. Unfortunately the ongoing civil war in Yugoslavia has prevented the examination of more than a small fraction of these skeletons.
2. Stylistic elements and assemblage characteristics of the ceramic vessels are in some cases significantly correlated with the burial lines, suggesting a horizontal, perhaps familial or residential association (Rega 1995).
3. There are biological intermediates who are truly inter-sexual, as a result of genetic, developmental or endocrine conditions, such as foetal androgenation, gonadal dysgenesis and testicular feminisation syndrome, amongst others (Moore 1988). These and other biological hermaphrodites are however *extremely* rare and although such individuals can be very important culturally, they do not constitute the major axis of sex identification in human societies.
4. These sex/gender discrepant individuals are currently undergoing further investigation by means of DNA analysis of sex indicator loci.
5. The actual ratio is nearer 105 boys : 100 girls for live births (Moore 1988).
6. Biochemical assessment of sub-adult diet was not attempted for the children of Mokrin, as many chemical values are erratically affected by diagenesis and other non-dietary factors (Price *et al.* 1989).

7. No differences between status groups as defined by quantity and quality of grave wealth were revealed in mortality, pathology or dietary analysis (Rega 1995). Systematic social inequalities indicative of an emerging elite are not supported by the biological evidence.

References

Bentley, G.R. (1987) 'The social structure of the Early Bronze Age IA Cemetery at Bab edh' dra, Jordon'. Unpublished PhD thesis. University of Chicago.

Bird, C. (1988)'Woman the Toolmaker'. Paper presented at the Stone Tool Conference, University of New England, Armidale, Australia.

Blakely, R. and Beck, L. (1982) 'Trace elements, nutritional status and social stratification at Etowah, Georgia'. *Annals of the New York Academy of Sciences* 376, 417–31.

Blanton, R.E., Kowalewski, S.A., Feinman, G. and Appel, J. (1981) *Ancient Mesoamerica.* Cambridge: Cambridge University Press.

Bona, I. (1963) *Die Mitlere Bronzezeit Ungarns und ihre Südostlichen Beziehungen.* Budapest: Akadémia Kiadó.

Boquet-Appel, J.P. and Masset, C. (1982) 'Farewell to palaeodemography'. *Journal of Human Evolution* 11, 321–33.

Bradley, R. (1984) *The Social Organization of Prehistoric Britain.* Cambridge: Cambridge University Press.

Brown, A. (1973) 'Bone strontium as a dietary indicator in human skeletal populations', PhD thesis. Ann Arbor: University of Michigan microfilms no. 74–15.

Brown, J.A. (1981) 'The search for rank in prehistoric burials' in R.W. Chapman and K. Randsborg (eds) *The Archaeology of Death.* Cambridge: Cambridge University Press.

Buikstra, J.E. (1981) 'Mortuary practices, palaeodemography and palaeopathology: a case study from the Koster site' in R.W. Chapman and K. Randsborg (eds) *The Archaeology of Death.* Cambridge: Cambridge University Press.

Buikstra J.E. and Konigsberg, L. (1985) 'Palaeodemography: critiques and controversies'. *American Anthropologist* 87, 316–33.

Bumsted, M.P. *et al.* (1990) 'Recognizing women in the archaeological record' in S.M. Nelson and A.B. Kehoe (eds) *Powers of Observation: Alternative Views in Archaeology.* Archaeological Papers of the American Anthropological Association no. 2.

Burton, J.H. and Wright L.E. (1995) 'Nonlinearity in the relationship between between bone Sr/Ca and diet: Palaeodietary implications. *American Journal of Physical Anthropology* 96, 273–82.

Chamberlain, A.T. (1994) *Human Remains.* Berkeley, CA: University of California Press.

Chapman, J.C. (1994) 'The living, the dead and the ancestors: time, life cycles and the mortuary domain in later European Prehistory' in J. Davies (ed.) *Ritual and Remembrance: Responses to Death in Human Societies.* Sheffield: Sheffield Academic Press, pp.40–85.

Chapman, R. and Randsborg, K. (1981) 'Introduction' in R.W. Chapman and K. Randsborg (eds) *The Archaeology of Death.* Cambridge: Cambridge University Press, pp. 71–82.

Chapman, R. (1990) *Emerging Complexity: The Later Prehistory of South-East Spain, Iberia and the West Mediterranean.* Cambridge: Cambridge University Press.

Childe, V.G. (1957) *The Dawn of European Civilization.* London: Book Club Associates.

Claassen, C.P. (1992) 'Questioning gender: an introduction' in C.P. Claassen (ed.) *Exploring Gender Through Archaeology*. Monographs in World Archaeology Series No. 11. Madison, 1–9.

Coale, A.J. and Banister, J. (1994) '5 decades of missing females in China'. *Demography* 31, 459–79.

Cohen, M.N. and Bennett S. (1993) 'Skeletal evidence for gender hierarchies in prehistory' in B.D. Miller (ed.) *Sex and Gender Hierarchies*. Cambridge: Cambridge University Press, pp. 273–96.

Coles J. and Harding, A. (1979) *The Bronze Age in Europe*. New York: Methuen.

Curtis, S., Diamond, I. and McDonald J. (1993) *Demography* 30, 33–43.

Cronk, L. (1989) 'Low socio-economic status and female-based parental investment: the Mukogodo example'. *American Anthropologist* 91, 414–29.

Cronk, L. (1993) 'Parental favoritism toward daughters'. *American Scientist* 81, 272–9.

Demeer, K., Berman, R. and Kusner, J.S. (1993) 'Socio-cultural determinants of child mortality in southern Peru, including some methodological considerations'. *Social Science and Medicine* 36, 317–31.

Farkas, G. and Liptak P. (1971) 'Physical anthropological examination of a cemetery in Mokrin from the early Bronze Age' in M. Girić (ed.) *Mokrin I: Nekropola ranog bronzanog doba*. Beograd: Archeolosko Drustvo Jugoslavije.

Forenbacher, S. (1993) 'Radiocarbon dates and absolute chronology of the central European Early Bronze Age' *Antiquity* 67, 218–20, 235–56.

George, S., Abel, R. and Miller, B.D. (1992) 'Female infanticide in rural south India'. *Economic and Political Weekly* 27, 1153–56.

Gilbert, R.I. (1975) 'Trace element analysis of three skeletal Amerindian populations at Dickson Mounds', PhD thesis. University of Massachusetts, microfilm no. 76–5854.

Gilman, A. (1981) 'The development of social stratification in Bronze Age Europe'. *Current Anthropology* 22, 1–23.

Girić, M. (ed.) (1971) *Mokrin I: Nekropola ranog bronzanog doba* (Mokrin I: The Early Bronze Age necropolis). Beograd: Archeolosko Drustvo Jugoslavije.

Girić M. (1972) *Mokrin II: Nekropola ranog bronzanog doba* (Mokrin II: The Early Bronze Age necropolis). Beograd: Archeolosko Drustvo Jugoslavije.

Girić M. (1986) 'Naselja Moriske Kulture' *Rada vojvodanskog muzeja* sv. 30 za 1986–1987, Novi Sad.

Goodman, A.H., Lallo, J., Armelagos, G.J. and Rose, J.C. (1984) 'Health changes at Dickson Mounds, Illinois (AD 950–1300)' in M. Cohen and G. Armelagos *Palaeopathology at the Origins of Agriculture*. New York: Academic Press, pp. 271–306.

Hawkes, K. (1981) 'A third explanation for female infanticide'. *Human Ecology* 9, 105–7.

Holcomb, S.M.C. and Konigsberg, L.W. (1995) 'Statistical study of sexual dimorphism in the human fetal sciatic notch'. *American Journal of Physical Anthropology* 97, 113–26.

Hrdy, S.B. (1992) 'Fitness tradeoffs in the history and evolution of delegated mothering with special reference to wet-nursing, abandoment and infanticide'. *Ethology and Sociobiology* 13, 409–42.

Hughes, A.L. (1981) 'Female infanticide: sex ratio manipulation in humans'. *Ethology and Sociobiology* 2, 109–11.

Judson, O.P. (1994) 'Killing the sex ratio'. *Nature* 372, 503–4.

Katz, D. and J.M. Suchey (1986) 'Age determination of the male *os pubis*'. *American Journal of Physical Anthropology* 69, 427–36.

Kehoe, A.P. (1992) 'The muted class: unshackling tradition' in C.P. Claassen (ed.)

Exploring Gender Through Archaeology. Monographs in World Archaeology Series no. 11. Madison, 23–32.

Kishor, S. (1993) 'May God give sons to all: gender and child-mortality in India'. *American Sociological Review* 58, 247–65.

Lee, J., Fend, W. and Campbell, C. (1994) 'Infant and child-mortality among the Quing nobility: implications for two types of positive check'. *Population Studies* 48, 395–411.

Lengyel, I. (1972) 'Laboratory analysis of the human bone finds from the Early Bronze Age cemetery at Mokrin' in M. Girić (ed.) *Mokrin II: Nekropola ranog bronzanog doba* (Mokrin II: The Early Bronze Age necropolis). Beograd: Archeolosko Drustvo Jugoslavije, pp. 75–90.

Li, L.M. (1991) 'Life and death in a Chinese famine: infanticide as a demographic consequence of the 1935 Yellow River flood'. *Comparative Studies in Society and History* 33, 466.

McKay, M. (1988) *The Origins of Hereditary Social Stratification*. Oxford: BAR International Series 3413.

Marks, M.N. and Kumar, R. (1993) 'Infanticide in England and Wales'. *Medicine Science and the Law* 33, 329–39.

Mays, S. (1993) 'Infanticide in Roman Britain'. *Antiquity* 67, 883–8.

Moore, K.L. (1988) *The Developing Human* (4th edition). Philadephia: W.B. Saunders.

Morris, I. (1992) *Death Ritual and Social Structure in Classical Antiquity*. Cambridge: Cambridge University Press.

Murray, M. and Schoeninger, M. (1988) 'Diet, status and social structure in Iron Age Europe' in D. Gibson and M. Geselowitz (eds) *Tribe and Polity in Late Prehistoric Europe*. New York: Plenum Press, pp. 155–79

O'Shea, J.M. (1978) 'Mortuary variability: an archaeological investigation with case studies from the nineteenth century central plains of north America and the early bronze age of southern Hungary'. Unpublished PhD dissertation. Cambridge University.

O'Shea, J.M. (1984) *Mortuary Variability*. Orlando: Academic Press

O'Shea, J.M. (1991) 'A radiocarbon-based chronology for the Maros Group of southeast Hungary'. *Antiquity* 65, 97–102.

O'Shea, J.M. (1995) 'Mortuary custom in the Bronze Age of southeastern Hungary: diachronic and synchronic perspectives' in L. Anderson Beck (ed.) *Regional Approaches to Mortuary Analysis*. New York: Plenum Press, pp. 125–46.

Peebles, C. and Kus, S. (1977) 'Some archaeological correlates of ranked society'. *American Antiquity* 42, 421–48.

Phenice, T.W. (1969) 'A newly developed visual method of sexing the *os pubis*'. *American Journal of Physical Anthropology* 30, 297–301.

Powell, M.L. (1984) 'Health, disease and social stratification in the complex Mississippian chiefdom at Moundville'. *American Journal of Physical Anthropology* 63, 205.

Powell, M.L. (1988) *Status and Health in Prehistory*. Washington DC: Smithsonian Institute.

Price, T.D., Armelagos, G. J., Buikstra, J., Bumsted, M. P., Chisholm, B.S., Ericson, J. E., Lambert, J. B., Van der Herwe, N. J., Schoeninger, M. J. and Sillen, A. (1989) 'The chemistry of prehistoric bone: recommendations and directions for future study' in T.D. Price (ed.) *The Chemistry of Prehistoric Human Bone*. Cambridge: Cambridge University Press, pp. 245–52.

Randsborg, K. (1981) 'Complexity, archaeological data, social equalities, and cultural diversity' in S.E. van der Leeuw (ed.) *Archaeological Approaches to the Study of Social Complexity.* pp. 39–53

Rathbun, T.A. and Scurry, J.D. (1985) 'Status and health in colonial South Carolina: Belleview Plantation 1738–1756' in D. Martin (ed.) *Skeletal Analysis of the Effects of Socioeconomic Status on Health* Research Report 25. Amherst: University of Massachusetts.

Rega, E.R. (1989) 'A bioarchaeological examination of the skeletal series from two Bronze Age mortuary sites in southeastern Hungary'. Unpublished MA thesis on file at the Department of Anthropology, University of Chicago.

Rega, E.R. (1995) 'Biological correlates of social structure in the Early Bronze Age Cemetery at Mokrin'. PhD thesis, University of Chicago.

Rega, E.R. (in press) 'The gendering of children in the Early Bronze Age cemetery at Mokrin' in L. Hurcombe and M. McDonald (eds) *Gender and Material Culture.* New York: Macmillan Publishing Company.

Renfrew, C. (1986) 'Varna and the emergence of wealth in prehistoric Europe' in A. Appadurai (ed.) *The Social Life of Things.* Cambridge: Cambridge University Press, pp. 1–18.

Renteln, A.D. (1992) 'Sex selection and reproductive freedom'. *Women's Studies International Forum* 15, 405–26.

Sargent, C. and Harris, M. (1992) 'Gender ideology, child rearing and child health in Jamaica'. *American Ethnologist* 19, 523–37.

Saunders, S.R. (1992) 'Subadult skeletons and growth related studies' in S.R. Saunders and M.A. Katzenberg (eds) *Skeletal Biology of Past Peoples.* New York: Wiley Liss, pp. 1–20.

Schwartz, H.P. and Schoeninger, M.J. (1991) 'Stable isotope analyses in human nutritional ecology'. *Yearbook of Physical Anthropology* 34, 283–321.

Sealy, J.C. and Sillen, A. (1988) 'Sr and Sr/Ca in marine and terrestrial foodwebs in the southwestern Cape, South Africa'. *Journal of Archaeological Science* 15, 425–38.

Shennan, S.E. (1975) 'The social organization at Branc'. *Antiquity* 49, 279–88.

Shennan, S.E. (1982) 'From minimal to moderate ranking' in C. Renfrew and S.E. Shennan (eds) *Ranking, Resource and Exchange.* Cambridge: Cambridge University Press, pp. 27–32.

Shennan, S.J. (1993) 'Settlement and social change in central Europe 3500–1500 BC'. *Journal of World Prehistory* 7, 121–61.

Smith, B.H. (1991) 'Standards of human tooth formation and dental age assessment', in M.A. Kelley and C.S. Larsen (eds) *Advances in Dental Anthropology.* New York: Wiley Liss, 143–168.

Smith, E.A. and Smith, S.A. (1994) 'Inuit sex-ratio variation: population control, ethnographic error or sex bias'. *Current Anthropology* 35, 595–624.

Smith, P. and Kahila, G. (1992) 'Identification of infanticide in archaeological sites: a case study from the Late Roman – Early Byzantine periods at Askalon, Israel'. *Journal of Archaeological Science* 19, 667–75.

Sorencceau, T. (1975) 'Die Bedeutung des Gräberfeldes von Mokrin für die relative Chronologie der frühen Bronzezeit im Banat'. *Praehistorisches Zeitschrift* 50, 161–79.

Steele, D.G. and Bramblett, C.A. (1988) *The Anatomy and Biology of the Human Skeleton.* College Station, Texas: A and M Press.

Stini, W.A. (1969) 'Nutritional stress and growth: sex differences in adaptive response'. *American Journal of Physical Anthropology* 31, 417–26.

Stini, W.A. (1985) 'Sex differences in environmental sensitivity during growth and development' in R.I. Gilbert and J.H. Mielke (eds) *The Analysis of Prehistoric Diets*. New York: Academic Press, pp. 191–226.

Stuart-Macadam, P. (1993) 'Biological vigor: exploring sexual differences in prehistory'. Abstract in *American Journal of Physical Anthropology* Supplement 16, 191.

Turner, C. (1979) 'Dental anthropological indicators of agriculture among the Jomon people of central Japan'. *American Journal of Physical Anthropology* 51, 619–35.

Van Gerven, D. and Armelagos, G.J. (1983) 'Farewell to palaeodemography? Rumors of its death have been greatly exaggerated'. *Journal of Human Evolution* 12, 353–60

Walker, P.L., Dean, G. and Shapiro, P. (1991) 'Estimating age from tooth wear in archaeological populations' in M.A. Kelley and C.S. Larsen (eds) *Advances in Dental Anthropology*. New York: Wiley Liss, pp. 169–78.

Weiss, K.M. (1972) 'On systematic bias in skeletal sexing'. *American Journal of Physical Anthropology* 37, 239–50.

Wiley, A. (1994) 'Neonatal size and infant mortality at high altitude in the western Himalaya'. *American Journal of Physical Anthropology* 94, 289–305.

Wilson, S. (1988) 'Infanticide, child abandonment and female honor in 19th century Corsica'. *Comparative Studies in Society and History* 30, 762–83.

Wood, J.W., Milner, G.R., Harpending, H. and Weiss, K. (1992) 'The osteological paradox: problems of inferring prehistoric health from skeletal samples'. *Current Anthropology* 33, 343–70.

Wood, J.W. and Milner, G.R. (1994) 'Reply to the osteological paradox reconsidered'. *Current Anthropology* 35, 629–37.

Commentary: Missing stages of life – towards the perception of children in archaeology

ANDREW T. CHAMBERLAIN

Much of archaeological practice is centred on the material and the monumental – archaeology is quintessentially the art of the visible. But vision is only one of several sensory modalities, the inputs of which are combined to form perception. Studies in the cognitive sciences have shown that perception is not an inductive process, reliant solely on data input. Instead we perceive by pattern recognition, that is the cognitive process of matching the evidence of the senses to our prior mental models and expectations of the world. As Arthur Conan Doyle illustrated, the fact that the dog did not bark becomes significant because it contradicts our prior expectations of what a dog should do.

In peopling the past we are engaged in a forensic study. The evidence before us, the archaeological record, is comprised of material cultural remains, perhaps combined with environmental evidence as well as the skeletal remains of the people themselves. Archaeologists and biological anthropologists, just like forensic scientists, are aware that this evidence is an incomplete and taphonomically selective sample of past people and their activities. Our task is to recognize meaningful patterning in the data, a task that is absolutely dependent on our prior expectations and models. It, therefore, behoves us to ensure that our models are unbiased representations of the past, otherwise we commit the fatal error of compounding any existing taphonomic bias with our own prejudicial and often unrecognized personal biases.

It is customary for academicians, who are invested with authority, status and peer recognition, to privilege certain classes of evidence and to render other types of evidence unimportant or even invisible. Such selectivity may be executed consciously at the level of individual decision-making, but frequently the root cause of this selectivity is to be found deeply embedded in the cognitive and social structures that are prevalent in our own culture. Mary Baker (Chapter 13) argues forcefully and persuasively that both our primary gender distinction, male/female, and our major age categories, adult/child, are not symmetrical dichotomies. What is defined and invested with meaning is adultness and maleness. Their complement, femaleness and the state of childhood, describe categories that lack the defining attributes of adult maleness, or are imperfect and incomplete reflections of the adult male. Mary Baker uses the striking metaphor of the brick wall, whose meaning is solid and immutable, off which other and alternative meanings can only rebound. Thus femaleness and childhood become relative terms, perpetually in semiotic thrall to their adult male masters.

Another central idea articulated by Mary Baker is the structural homology that links the male/female and the adult/child dichotomies. This idea is at once illuminating and restrictive. It illuminates because it starkly re-emphasizes the dialectic that underpins adult male hegemony, but it is restrictive in confining and relegating our discourse of the 'child problem' in much the same way as socialists have subordinated the political issues of race and gender to the more 'important' issue of class. As several of the contributors to this volume demonstrate, the interplay of gender and age categories is much more complex than this simple model of their structural analogy allows, and furthermore it is possible to approach the 'child problem' independently of, and without reference to, gender.

In seeking to clarify the debate about children in archaeology Joanna Sofaer Derevenski (Chapter 14) emphasizes a theme that runs through the work of all of the authors participating in this section, that children contribute to the archaeological record *whether or not we are competent to recognize them*. There should be no surprise at this notion. Uniformitarianism lies at the heart of archaeology, and we should be secure in our suppositions that, for example, past societies possessed language, engaged in trade and/or warfare, constructed spatially distinct living areas, and raised children, *regardless* of whether we possess any material evidence for these activities. It is undeniable, however, that the meaning of the term childhood is culturally dependent, and even Lillehammer's broad definition of childhood as the period between infancy and puberty depends on ethnoculturally variable boundaries. So it is instructive to turn to the disciplines of biological anthropology and demography to provide a more secure foundation for examining the nature of children in past societies.

Studies in demography have revealed the extent to which different human populations, both past and present, exhibit extraordinary regularities in population structure, such that the single parameter of childhood mortality predicts much of the global variation in population structure. There is now considerable evidence that most prehistoric populations had childhood mortality of at least 50%, and for a stable or slowly growing population this implies that at least half of the living individuals in any given community were children (defined here as people under the age of 18 years). The children were most certainly there in the past, *and* there were lots of them. We also know that every living population in the world, and by reasonable inference in the past as well, possesses a proportion of individuals living to at least 80 years of age, regardless of crude population mortality rates. Palaeodemography has, unfortunately, shown a certain measure of irresponsibility in concealing the fact that standard methods for estimating adult age at death from the skeleton have been shown to be inaccurate, and that the widespread theory that people in the past were all dead by the age of 50 is based on wholly false premises. Grandparents should also be numbered among the casts of past societies.

Using these regularities in demography, biological anthropologists now have a very secure basis for determining who is (and who is not) entering the burial record. This allows us to correct for biases in past funerary behaviour so that we can determine, for instance, whether child burials are normative or an exceptional practice. Elizabeth Rega (Chapter 17) and Malcolm Lillie (Chapter 16) describe case studies of prehistoric mortuary ritual in which individuals appear to be treated as adults at a precociously early stage of childhood. At Elizabeth Rega's site of Mokrin there is clearly strong gendering of children's burials and there appears to be little distinction between the nature and extent of gender marking in the childhood and adult age categories. In Malcolm Lillie's sample the child burials are not gendered, yet their style and richness is comparable with that of the adults. Both authors advance the hypothesis that these practices reflect the early integration of children into the social and economic activities of their respective groups. In each case their interpretations are buttressed by bio-anthropological evidence. In both the Late Mesolithic/Early Neolithic Dnieper Rapids cemeteries and in the Bronze Age Maros Group burials the anthropological data (which include dental caries rates, the incidence of enamel hypoplasia, trace element levels and stable isotope ratios) show little evidence for differential access to dietary resources, either between the genders or between age classes. These careful studies reinstate children as social beings in their own right, and go some way to dispelling the still prevalent and reactionary notion that rich female and child burials reflect nothing more than male wealth and prestige.

There is still a long way to go before children become fully visible in archaeology. Nyree Finlay (Chapter 15) observes it is Scandinavia, with its strong social emphasis on child care, that has generated much of the original research on children in archaeology. Joanna Sofaer Derevenski points out that in contrast to traditional societies, in developed western cultures children are deemed to be more dependent on adults and are denied a political and social role. These entrenched values are difficult to change: for example in Britain the legal profession is currently grappling with novel and controversial proposals such as the lowering of the age at which a child is held to have responsibility for its actions, the admission of children as witnesses in major trials, and allowing children a voice in their own custody proceedings.

Meanwhile, within archaeology it is imperative that we avoid the issue of children being ghettoized, a situation which unfortunately still characterizes the attitude of many traditional archaeologists towards gendered archaeology. Even the most cursory reference to publications in the social and cognitive sciences shows how central and crucial is the consideration of children and their development. In sociology and developmental psychology, studies of children provide the key to understanding how the individual develops within society, and how societies reproduce their cultural repertoires. Archaeologists would be ill-advised to ignore the presence of children, who, after all, are numerically the predominant group of individuals in most past societies. The contributors to this volume have shown, in different ways, how the archaeological record can be approached with an open mind, one that is receptive to the presence of children.

Conclusion: The visibility of the invisible

JENNY MOORE

> We argue that the archaeological 'invisibility' of females is more the result of a false notion of objectivity and of the gender paradigms archaeologists employ than of an inherent invisibility of such data.
>
> Conkey and Spector (1984: 6)

Reading through the bibliographies of the contributors to this volume, there is apparent a commonality in the foundation material drawn upon: Conkey and Spector (1984), Walde and Willows (1991) and Gero and Conkey (1991). From the inception of an ideology of gender in archaeology in the 1970s, this begs two questions: how have gender studies in archaeology progressed; and why is it only now that there is a volume, this one, directly writing gender and childhood into European archaeology?

Clearly, there has been a paucity of mainstream publications in the intervening time. What is happening to gender studies in archaeology? Have gender studies become so enmeshed in the concerns of feminist archaeology they no longer have an identity of their own? This may come as a surprise to those who fail to appreciate there is any difference between the two fields – one of the contributors was informed his chapter was appearing in a radical feminist publication. Whilst not denying the debt that gender studies in archaeology owe to the feminist movement, I have tried to separate the fields by simple definitions which appear in the glossary. There are undoubtedly better definitions, and more complex, but the simplicity of terminology emphasizes, to me, the divergence of gender and feminist studies. The necessity for divergence is discussed in Boyd and Lesick, where the inherent distortions resulting from conflation of the two fields are summarized.

To my mind, a purely feminist approach can lead us into the same trap as androcentrism. Scott (this volume) refers to a scepticism about the possibility of any objective historical truth which is not the vehicle of some particular interest group. I see this as exemplified by the romanticized image of the 'mother goddess' (see Chapman and Bevan for discussions). The imagery available to archaeologists in their interpretation of women in the past is subverted. In order for women to become, in twentieth century terms, 'valuable', they are interpreted as 'mother goddess' – all-powerful women, representing an era when men were suppressed, merely useful for reproductive purposes. This approach results in the subtle dynamics between members of a society being overlooked, as confounding as androcentrism. The analyses of imagery undertaken by Hitchcock, and Kokkinidou and Nikolaidou, show the potential such images have for revealing gender relations and changes in the power dynamics of a society over time. These images are distinctly a specific sex, which had an entirely unambiguous meaning for the society. Their style and context of discovery will equally have been dictated by their gender. The relationship of the figurines to social practice is a dynamic which has failed to be acknowledged, and, therefore, the significance of gender dynamics in structuring a society is unseen. Histories have already been written for us many times over, with biases reinforced or subverted depending on the predilection of the author. We must not write women as dominant because that is what we want to see. We devalue gendering the past by surrendering to our own illusions, and become no better than those with an androcentric bias. Gender must be written as a factor in societal relationships, and as a dynamic, an interactive process between participants in organized groups. Only by evaluating gender relationships within a society can that society become fully understood.

The defence of those challenged on their androcentrism is that women – and, even more so, children – are inaccessible through the archaeological record. A perhaps unfortunate statement from Alison Wylie that women and their activities must be reconstructed from 'highly enigmatic data' (Wylie 1991: 31) reinforces those who choose to ignore the necessity of peopling the past. In this volume, there is enough direct evidence of women and children in the past to satisfy the strongest empiricist, and indeed some of the contributors consider themselves to be 'empiricist' (see Baker). It is interpretation of the data which continues to be imbalanced, the biases in the mindset of the analyst. We are still in an era of gender-exclusive rather than gender-inclusive interpretation, and assumed artefactual sex linkages. We cannot engender archaeology simply by digging down to the big stone penis or vulva (Lesick, this volume). As Bevan (Chapter 7) points out, we are constantly faced with the opposition of material culture and death and the dismissal of women's daily lives, the structuring of which is discussed by Picazo (Chapter 5).

There are subtleties of invisibility which are not apparent in the quotation at the beginning of this discussion. Gero and Conkey (1991) refer to the passivity of vocabulary where changes in material culture are related to women. Women cannot be active instigators of economic change, but passive adopters. Presumably, if children had been studied to any extent in archaeology, this would apply to them as well. Gero and Conkey (1991: 18) refer to Hawkes *et al.*'s (1988) discussion of 'hardworking Hadza grandmothers' as being a western interpretation of how societies use an otherwise 'useless', in reproductive terms, members of that society. I take a stronger view, that this is direct devaluation of elderly women. Chamberlain and Bender (this volume) refer to the elderly as being a class of gender which needs evaluation in archaeology, and Lesick (Chapter 3) discusses old age as a stage in life of gender ambiguity. However, statements such as that of Hawkes *et al.* (1988) show how it is necessary to find a use for a woman whose only value to the society can have been through childbearing. Western males appear unable to interpret the onset of menopause in other societies as a positive rite of passage, where women are freed from the constrictions of fertility and sexuality, moving into a new sphere of life and increased status within the society. Such societies may not have had such an option for 'post menopausal' men, whose status could potentially decrease with failure to undertake that for which they had been valued.

Hurcombe succinctly deals with how our perception of people in the past is coloured visually and in writing, and the strength of the biases therein. As Hurcombe points out, the images reach a far wider audience than academia, and unless we put our own house in order, how can we expect this to filter through to popular literature. We have the 'Ice Man', but what of the rich female burial from Siberia (Polosmak 1994) which is now referred to as the 'Ice Maiden'? This epithet is demeaning, suggesting a virgin, sweet and demure, awaiting her knight in shining armour. Yet, the grave goods indicate she was a very powerful woman in her own right, possibly holding controlling status in her society. Even within the bounds of popular terminology, she should have the descriptive of 'Snow Queen', although one feels that this could potentially lead to an excavation to find her consort, the 'Snow King'. Leading on from here, Scott's reference (this volume) to the *faux pas* committed by feminist and sociological writers, in inferring women's lives and gender relationships in the past from dubious sources, deserves comment. Rather than be critical, we should see this as an encapsulation of the entire problem – where are these authors to go for their material? Women and other gender categories have not been written into the past. Their invisibility is absolute when not subverted through such distorted images as the 'mother goddess'. In such a reference source as *The Times Atlas of World History*, women should be accessible in an accurate and effective manner, similar to any other information acquired from a typical encyclopaedic volume. But they are not, because archaeology has so effectively failed to *write* women and other gender categories. The failure is entirely that of the discipline of archaeology. Those outside find it impossible to understand that a field of research ostensibly 'peopling the past' can so comprehensively have failed to study a substantial part of the population composing any society. At the start of a short course on the archaeology of women at Manchester University's Department of Continuing Education, the participants were asked to write down everything they could think of relating to the archaeology of women and women in archaeology. The majority, with no background in archaeology or history, had a very clear and accurate idea of how women could be accessed in the archaeological record, as active participants in a society. From Baker's work (this volume), the same applies to children, they can write themselves into prehistory without a masculist agenda.

Chronology becomes unimportant in gender studies in archaeology, because of the continuity of gender bias. Until there is a stronger framework for gender studies in archaeology, it is necessary to explore how gender may be understood as a whole. Gender relationships have/create their own time spans and are not necessarily exemplified by technological changes, often denoted as male achievements (see Picazo). The indirect contribution of women, and children or a change in their activity which materially affects the economics of a society fails to receive accreditation. We know women and children were present in the past, but the tacit assumption is simply that they were 'there', rather than active and dynamic participants structuring their society. Harlow (Chapter 12), in examining asceticism and gender, strongly identifies a form of social construction of gender, but feels it necessary to justify the combination of text and archaeology. Scott and Gilchrist (this volume) speak of their hopes for historical archaeology being rewritten so it is speaking to all ages, classes, creeds and genders. Yet the American historical archaeology experience does not show this trend. While theory and historical archaeology in America have been companions for only 30 years, two schools of thought prevail: the historically descriptive and the cultural materialists. There are those who write in multiple voices and perspectives, but the prevailing ideology is dominated by the two schools of thought, whose contest for domination has more to do with white male power than seeking an objective truth (Mary Beaudry pers. com.). We must not be complacent and believe that archaeology will automatically incorporate gendered themes and theoretical debates into dialogues of the past. The discipline is notorious for the selective application of structuring theories and the pervading influence of those who choose cannot be regarded as diminishing. It is they who must be convinced of gender as a structuring force in a society.

Scott (this volume) sets out the 'tricks' by which invisibility is maintained: exclusion, pseudo inclusion and alienation, with which I would combine devaluation. This process is beautifully encapsulated in Parker-Pearson (1993: 134), quoted at the beginning of Bevan's chapter. Women are mentioned, but they are tied to the compound, relegated to preparing and serving food to the male controllers of dynasties. They are both peripheral and subservient. I would include in the realm of 'tricks' used to maintain invisibility, what I would term 'interpretative gymnastics'. Desperate contortions are performed and fiery hoops leapt through, in order for data to be interpreted so that women are devalued and remain subservient to men. Gilchrist (Chapter 4) sets out the stereotypical terminology of Steane (1985) and refers to Stalsberg (1991) proposing the apparently radical term: 'tradeswomen'. Prior to this, interpretation had varied from merchants' wives, to women who happened to die while covering for an absent husband, to incorrectly sexed skeletons. It was impossible to allow the simple explanation of the burial goods associated with these women as indicating they were tradeswomen. Sadly, these are not isolated case studies from the Dark Ages of pre-gender consciousness. Bevan (Chapter 7) refers to a cemetery in Bronze Age Italy, where women's roles are described as: 'less numerous and socially less important than male ones, although their funerary artefacts are usually richer, both in fine decorated pottery and personal ornaments ... ' (Bietti Sestieri 1994: 255). At the stroke of a pen the role these women may have had in their society is relegated to being inferior to men. Rega (Chapter 17) refers to Shennan (1993) writing about the larger quantity of metal grave goods in female graves in Slovakia which are interpreted as primarily a reflection of *male* (her emphasis) wealth and prestige. Interpretation is always open to the idiosyncrasies of the analyst, but failure to propose alternative hypotheses, or justification of the weighting of the interpretation in a particular gendered direction, is inexcusable. As Rega states, the double standard continues, the invisibility continues. In the context of cemeteries and grave goods, the contributions of Chapman and Lucy (this volume) show that once stereotypes and biases are removed, a gender-based interpretation can clarify societal relations.

Several contributors approach the dilemma of biological sex and gender (Lesick, Lucy and Rega), and this is eloquently addressed by Hodder in his commentary. There are those who would see sex and gender as having precisely the same meaning, and those who would argue that sex has become purely biological and separated from gender. Quotes in a review article in *Current Anthropology* (vol. 36, no. 4) indicate the confusion reigning. Herdt (1994) believes there is an overemphasis on gender and underdevelopment of sexuality as a subject in anthropology. Trumbach (in Herdt 1994) takes *sex* to mean man and woman and *gender* to mean female and male. The former is taken to identify biology (genetic, socially constructed and scientifically 'read') and the latter a more wholly sociocultural construction of behavioural characteristics loosely applied to the attributed biological sex. Roscoe (Herdt 1994: 341) defines gender as 'a multidimensional category of personhood encompassing a distinct pattern of social and cultural differences.' I think we are in danger of reinforcing binary oppositions in attempting to clarify definitions and several contributors (Boyd, Gilchrist and Lesick) call for an acceptance of fluidity of gender, which broadens the sphere for understanding of interaction within a society.

In archaeology, the contribution children have made to past societies has largely been ignored. At the Neolithic Studies Group meeting 'Women and Children in the Neolithic', David Coombs succinctly summarized current understanding of children in the past – dogs have been more studied than children in the archaeological record. The defence for this failing is the usual old chestnut, the lack of surviving remains. Children appear not always to be buried in cemeteries, and when buried there is a poor survival rate of the remains. As Chamberlain points out in his commentary, if there is a mortality rate of 50% in children, there still must have been a substantial proportion of the population under 18 years of age. Yet, rather than assess what this would mean in terms of presence and requirements, the archaeological literature has become fixated with infanticide, invariably in terms of female infanticide. Neatly, the female and the child are linked (see Baker for discussion), and immediately disposed of. Scott forcefully points out that this is another example of western constructs effectively eliminating a non-male adult category from the archaeological record. Rega, on the other hand, firmly places gendered children within the society she has studied, *and* proposes male infanticide.

The contributions from Rega and Lillie have unquestionable empirical strength in the data, and, I would suggest, are not isolated examples in the archaeological record. The evidence is already available, when the minds of analysts are not clouded by western perceptions of children in society and concepts of lifecycles. If someone less enlightened than Lillie (Chapter 16) had assessed the data from the cemeteries, the significance of children being accorded status in burials across a wide age range and the lack of gender differentiation to food resources may not have been evaluated. These children were 'individuals', active participants in a hunter/gatherer society.

Sofaer Derevenski and Finlay both consider children and material culture, in differing contexts. Sofaer Derevenski (Chapter 14) examines children's understanding of gender, and how children engender objects. The active involvement of children in a society can be reconstructed through gendered objects as much as 'exchange systems' can be. Finlay (Chapter 15) approaches material culture and gender in relation to children from the perspective of acquisition of skills by an apprentice flint knapper. A small object has often been classified as a 'toy' (see also Bevan and Hitchcock), but in the production of material culture, size will depend on whether the item is being produced in imitation, or in production, in which case the item will be normal size. As Finlay states, her chapter raises more questions than it answers, but both she and Sofaer Derevenski show the potential there is for constructing a gendered childhood through material culture.

Gender is not invisible in the archaeological record, as the contributors clearly show, so how is it that gender studies have failed to reach the mainstream of archaeological consciousness? Are we 'stammering' when we write gender? This analogy is paraphrased from Richard Bradley's paper, *Archaeology: the loss of nerve* (Bradley 1993). The thesis of the paper is that archaeologists may have ceased to believe they can talk about the past. Have we, who write gender, ceased to believe in what we are doing? I do not think so, but it may be we have not been 'talking loudly' enough, and only to each other. This omission resulted in an eminent archaeologist standing up at the end of the 'Women and Children in the Neolithic' day school and asking what relevance the day's proceedings had for archaeology. We have to write people and processes in letters large. There is no point in reinforcing our beliefs with internal dialogue.

Just as there was society, so were there gender relationships which formed that society's interaction paths. The data is there, but as Bender (this volume) points out, we are still in an era of gender-blindness and gender-biased views of the past. Equally, whilest androcentrism can be exposed, we should not fall into the trap of writing a 'wished for' perspective on gender relations in the past. As Hodder states in his commentary, biases are inbuilt in interpretations, and gender studies cannot be regarded as immune to this.

If we, as archaeologists, are to reconstruct past societies in their fullest sense, every gender and the constructing processes must be evaluated. It is not enough to expose androcentrism, gender needs to be at the forefront of archaeological consciousness. Scott (this volume) emphasizes that this is not a problem of feminism, but a problem of scholarship and calls for more publications on the archaeology of gender. There is currently a shortage of mainstream publications on archaeology of gender, which in some way this volume redresses, but this is only a step along the way. In evaluating a past society, gender must become integral to archaeological interpretation, not peripheral.

In strengthening the theoretical conceptualization of gender called for by Bender, there needs to be a radical evaluation of engendering processes, of lifecycles and societal interactions. The contributions to this volume show not only what is possible, but how much more there is to be done. It lies with us to

unroll the canvas and make the picture of people in the past, and their interactions, visible.

References

Bradley, R. (1993) 'Archaeology: the loss of nerve' in N. Yoffee and A. Sherratt (eds)
Archaeological Theory: Who Sets the Agenda? Cambridge: Cambridge University Press,
pp. 131–3.

Conkey, M.W. and Spector, J.D. (1984) 'Archaeology and the study of gender' in M.B.
Schiffer (ed.) *Advances in Archaeological Method and Theory* 7. New York: Academic
Press, pp. 3–30.

Conway-Long, D. (1995) '(Trans) gendering history and anthropology' a review of
Third Sex, Third Gender: Beyond Sexual Dimorphism in Culture and History by G. Herdt
(ed.). *Current Anthropology* 36, 4, 709–11.

Gero, J. and Conkey, M.W. (eds) (1991) *Engendering Archaeology: Women and Prehistory.*
Oxford: Blackwell.

Herdt, G. (ed.) (1994) *Third Sex, Third Gender: Beyond Sexual Dimorphism in Culture
and History.* New York: Zone Books.

Parker, G. (ed.) *The Times Altas of World History.* 4th edn. Times Books ed. G.
Barraclough. London: HarperCollins.

Polosmak, N. (1994) 'A mummy unearthed from the pastures of heaven'. *National
Geographic* 186, no. 4.

Shennan, S. J. (1993) 'Settlement and social change in central Europe, 3500–1500 BC'.
Journal of World Prehistory 7, 121–61.

Walde, D. and Willows, N. (1990) *The Archaeology of Gender: Proceedings of the 22nd
Annual Chacmool Conference.* Calgary: University of Calgary.

Wylie, A. (1991) 'Gender theory and the archaeological record: why is there no
archaeology of gender?' in J. Gero and M.W. Conkey (eds) *Engendering Archaeology:
Women and Prehistory.* Oxford: Blackwell, pp. 31–54.

Glossary

Note: this glossary is intended to aid the reading of the chapters in this particular book. Where the same terms are used in other contexts in other works, additional clarification and definition may be required.

Agency
The potential for individual social actors to engage in active social practice.
Agrios
A complex term, introduced by Ian Hodder in *The Domestication of Europe* (1990) to characterize the wild, nature, the opposite of *domus*, within the network of symbolic oppositions defining the Eurasian Neolithic worldview.
Alveolar bone (resorption)
The alveolar bone makes up the alveolar processes which surround and support the teeth. In health, the alveolar crest is smooth and forms convex to flat surfaces faciolingually, whereas in disease the cortex is resorbed and the surface bones become roughened. Perhaps the most important aspect of periodontal disease is loss of the alveolar bone and the subsequent loss of teeth.
Ameloblastic matrix
The tooth crown enamel matrix is formed by secretory ameloblasts. If these ameloblasts are disrupted to a degree that they lose their functional ability less matrix will be formed and the result will be reduced enamel thickness (enamel hypoplasia).
Androcentric
Male-centred; theorizing about or interpreting archaeological evidence from a male point of view.
Androgeny
Possessing both male and female physical characteristics.
Annular
Ring-like.
Ascetic
A person who practises severe self-discipline and abstains from all forms of pleasure, especially for religious or spiritual reasons.
Berdache
A Native North American term referring to young male or female transvestites who chose to assume the role and identity of their biological opposites.

Bipolar technique
A *knapping* technique where the *core* is rested on an anvil stone and struck from above. The force detaches pieces from both ends simultaneously producing many flakes and splintered pieces.

Blades
A *knapping* term, meaning flakes with a length:breadth ratio of > 2:1.

Cemento-enamel junction
The junction between the cement layer that coats the root of the tooth and the enamel crown of the tooth.

Context
There are two kinds. One refers to the findspot of the object and the network of spatial associations and relationships between the object and its surroundings. Understanding the impact of these relationships and determining the limit of these contextual associations becomes a problem of interpretation. The other type of context is the social and institutional context of the archaeologist and how these relationships in the present affect the archaeologist's interpretation of the object and its context in the past.

Core
A piece of lithic raw material worked systematically during *knapping* to produce flakes or *blades*.

Domus
The obverse of *agrios*. Domus means the home, the house, fertility, nurture, security and domesticity.

Epi-Palaeolithic
Period immediately following the Palaeolithic era (old/earlier stone age) after which a continuation in both human adaptation and stone tool technology is apparent. The transition between Palaeolithic and Mesolithic (middle stone age) periods is generally placed at 10,000 years ago. The term epi-Palaeolithic is often used in areas, such as southern Europe, where the transition from Palaeolithic to Mesolithic periods is not a clear cut distinction due to the apparent continuities of culture traits.

Epistemology
The theory of knowledge, especially with regards to its methods and validation.

Feminism
There are many definitions of feminism. One such definition is that feminism is the political philosophy that women, by virtue of their being human beings, are deserving of social, economic and spiritual equality with men. Other definitions incorporate the idea of a 'struggle' or 'battle' in order to achieve such equality (see below: **feminist studies**).

Feminist studies
Feminist studies challenge male dominion in all spheres of relationships, often in a direct confrontation of female versus male.

Gender
There are many possible definitions of gender, and its meaning is much debated. A common definition is that gender is the cultural construction of sexuality. See **sex**.

Gender studies
Gender studies evaluate the interaction between people in cultural – social, economic and symbolic – contexts. Such studies evaluate the cultural constructions of masculinity and femininity as well as examining other 'alternative' genders.

Hermaphrodism
A state combining male and female elements. From the Greek Hermaphroditos, the mythological son of Hermes and Aphrodite who joined bodies with the nymph Salmacis.

Hermeneutic
Originally, concerning interpretation, especially Scripture and literary texts. In archaeology, the term could be understood simply as the framework(s) of interpretation employed by the archaeologist in the present who is trying to understand the remains of the past through a process of 'dialogue' with the object in an ongoing circle or spiral of interpretive practice.

Humour
A term relating to the Classical and medieval medical theory that was linked with Galen (born AD 129). It was proposed that the human body was made up of four basic elements, which also made up the universe: fire, water, earth and air. The dominance of a particular element in an individual's complexion created the corresponding humours, choleric, phlegmatic, melancholy and sanguine.

Idoloplastic
The art of figurine-making. The term is also used collectively for the end-products, the figurines.

Ithyphallic
Describing a figure with erect phallus.

Knapping
The process of working stone by the application of force to the surface for the production of stone tools.

Kourotrophos
An ancient Greek word for a woman nurturing or nursing a child. It is used sometimes to describe female figurines holding a child.

Metaphysics
Abstract general reasoning. The theoretical philosophy of being or knowing.

Ontology
The branch of *metaphysics* dealing with the nature of being.

Palaeoepidemological
Study of the occurrence of disease prevalence in ancient populations at a specific time in their development.

Paradigm
A framework for organizing research agreed by a particular community of researchers or, rarely, the whole field of researchers, within a discipline.

Patrilocality
The tradition by which, following marriage, women move to their husbands' place of origin.

Polygyny
The practice for a man to have more than one wife simultaneously.

Primogeniture
A situation in which the right of inheritance belongs to the eldest son.

Post-processualism
Post-processual archaeologists are fairly united in their criticism of *processualism*. There is an interest in material culture as not just reflecting but also actively affecting social relations, as well as a renewed interest in culture, especially the social, symbolic and ideological. There is more emphasis on the individual, which includes a desire to make women, children and gender relations more visible. The individual is seen as an active agent rather than a passive victim of great external forces beyond their control – this is essentially the debate about the relationship between *agency* and *structure*.

Processualism
Usually equated with the 'New Archaeology' of the late 1960s onwards. Processualism introduced 'scientific' *paradigms* into archaeology which emphasized objective hypothesis-testing approaches, which have been criticized for being largely positivist, functionalist, determinist and reductionist models of the past. Favoured topics of study were production, technological developments, social hierarchies and the importance of ranking and exchange in state formation, frequently amidst the search for general archaeological 'laws' of human behaviour.

Serological analysis
The physical anthropological analysis of the blood groups of skeletal material, usually carried out to determine the genetic relations between individual population members.

Sex
A natural, biological classification which is used primarily to distinguish male from female, man from woman. However, 'the male sex' and 'the female sex' are to some degree socially constructed categories – what is deemed to be 'natural' is in fact a cultural decision. See **gender.**

Steatopygous
This term describes a body with a high concentration of fat deposits in the area of the buttocks. The term is used to describe female Neolithic figurines with an emphasized lower body.

Structuralism
The doctrine that *structure* rather than function is important. In archaeology, structuralism is particularly concerned with finding the symbolic 'rules' – often in the form of binary opposites – which hold a culture in place, such as Hodder's division of certain European Neolithic settlements into *agrios* and *domus*.

Structure
The underlying and interconnecting parts of a complex whole; the unwritten 'rules' governing cultures.

Teleology
A philosophical term, generally meaning the explanation of phenomena by the purpose they serve rather than by postulated causes.

Tell
An artificial mound composed of settlement debris, indicating repeated and/or continuous occupation of the same site and the successive flattening of clay building remains before new construction.

Index